D0878941

CONSTITUTIONAL ANALYSIS

IN A NUTSHELL®

THIRD EDITION

THOMAS E. BAKER
Member of the Founding Faculty
The College of Law at Florida
International University

Nutshell Series, In a Nutshell and the Nutshell Logo are trademarks registered in the U.S. Patent and Trademark Office.

Printed in the United States of America

ISBN: 978-1-64020-208-5

In all governments there is a perpetual intestine struggle, open or secret, between AUTHORITY and LIBERTY; and neither of them can ever absolutely prevail in the contest. A great sacrifice of liberty must necessarily be made in every government; yet even the authority, which confines liberty, can never, and perhaps ought never, in any constitution, to become quite entire and uncontroulable. * * * In this sense, it must be owned, that liberty is the perfection of civil society; but still authority must be acknowledged essential to its very existence * * *.

— DAVID HUME

It may be a reflection on human nature that such devices should be necessary to control the abuses of government. But what is government itself but the greatest of all reflections on human nature? If men were angels, no government would be necessary. If angels were to govern men, neither external nor internal controls on government would be necessary. In framing a government which is to be administered by men over men, the great difficulty lies in this: you must first enable the government to control the governed; and in the next place oblige it to control itself.

— JAMES MADISON

To
Jane Marie

FOREWORD TO THE
THIRD EDITION

This book is written for the intelligent novice. Again with this new edition, my goal is to help law students and lawyers better understand constitutional law. But I hope this book also will be read by the curious general reader, *i.e.*, anyone who wants to better understand the U.S. Constitution and the role and function of the Supreme Court of the United States. I will describe in careful detail how our rights and liberties are protected by the Constitution and how the Constitution reconciles those fundamental rights with fundamental government powers. Indeed, the technique of this book is to "draw a picture"—literally and figuratively—of our constitutional system. Chapter 3 introduces and explains this constitutional diagram.

Nobel laureate physicist Richard Feynman once remarked about quantum mechanics—after studying the subject his entire lifetime: "No one understands it. You just get used to it * * *." The same might be said for constitutional law. I have been thinking and writing about the subject for more than four decades. I have guided and mentored thousands of beginning students studying constitutional law at five different universities. And, like Feynman, I have become used to it. I want to help my reader become used to it too and even get you to begin to understand it, at least as through a glass darkly. If you stick with me, if you work through this book and understand my drawings, you will make progress mastering our subject. That mastery is important for the final examination, for the bar exam, and for being a good lawyer-citizen in this great republic of ours.

The emphasis throughout this book will be on the primary and most important function of the Constitution, *i.e.*, to define and protect individual liberty against government power. Chapter 1 provides a summary of the foundational principles of American constitutionalism. Chapter 2 explains the importance and function of the American invention of judicial review. Chapter 3 introduces and explains the constitutional diagram that is the central feature of this book. Chapter 4 chronicles civil rights and civil liberties protected by the Constitution. Appendix A (Leading Case Outline of Constitutional Liberty) provides granular detail of those civil rights and liberties in a leading case outline of Supreme Court precedents. The holdings and doctrines highlighted there give content and meaning to individual liberty in our constitutional diagram. Those four chapters along with Appendix A roughly correspond to the topics in the typical "Constitutional Law II" law school course.

As will be further elaborated in Chapter 4, the Constitution performs three other necessary functions, besides defining and preserving individual liberty: to establish the national government; to control the relationship between the national government and the states; and to enable the government to perpetuate itself. The leading Supreme Court decisions about establishing the national government and controlling the relationship between the national government and the states are discussed in considerable detail and depth in Chapter 5 (Government Powers) and Chapter 6 (Structure of the Constitution). The perpetuation-of-government function is the subject of Chapter 1, § 11 (Amendments). Those discussions roughly correspond to the typical "Constitutional Law I" law school course. (Students enrolled in a stand-alone "Constitutional Law" course or some advanced elective course are obliged to match topics covered in their particular course with the relevant chapters in the Outline of Contents.)

Chapter 7 is a long term contribution to your liberal education, in addition to being a study aid for your constitutional law course in the immediate short term. It takes a theory to beat a theory and if everyone else has their own theory of the Constitution, then you should too. Your con law prof has his or her own theory and this chapter will help you figure out what it is. If you want to wander deeper into this intellectual rabbit hole, check out: MICHAEL J. GERHARDT, STEPHEN M. GRIFFIN, THOMAS D. ROW, JR. & LAWRENCE B. SOLUM, CONSTITUTIONAL THEORY: ARGUMENTS AND PERSPECTIVES (4th ed. 2013). My own exploration can be found in this aptly-named article: Thomas E. Baker, *Constitutional Theory in a Nutshell*, 13 WM. & MARY B. RTS. J. 57 (2004).

The text of the Constitution of the United States is not relegated to last place in the book to take away from its importance—which I suspect is the reason it appears last in some casebooks. Rather, placing it there makes it easier to thumb through it at frequent and regular references as the reader goes through the book. Indeed, I always tell my students to "begin with the text" and now dear reader you are one of my students.

The pictures I draw to explain constitutional law are derived from the first edition work of the late Jerre S. Williams, scholar and jurist. His "Williams diagram" will be referred to simply as our "constitutional diagram" in this Third Edition but my debt to his concept is acknowledged—along with named others—in the Foreword to the Second Edition which follows. For this Third Edition, special thanks goes to friends and colleagues who looked over portions of this Third Edition with a mind to save me from howlers: Lawrence Alexander, Warren Distinguished Professor of Law, University of San Diego School of Law; Erwin Chemerinsky, Dean, University of California Berkeley School of Law; and Ronald D. Rotunda, Doy and Dee Henley Chair and Distinguished Professor of Jurisprudence, Chapman University School of Law (*Requiescat in Pace*). I also want to give a shout out to Dean Antony Page of the College of Law at Florida International University. I am grateful to Maria Larrazabal for her staff assistance and to my student research assistants who participated in this Third Edition: Andrew Balthazor (who took the lead), Sarah E. Morgado, Cecilia B. Torres-Toledo, and George Zeckler. Associate Dean Angelique Ortega Fridman provided an extra pair of eyes on the manuscript. The editorial staff at West Academic Publishing were patient and helpful, especially Laura Holle, Emma Kaiser, Greg Olson, and Austin "Mac" Soto. Michelle Bassett did the exceptional artwork on the constitutional diagrams.

Finally, a personal note is in order. I dedicate this Third Edition to my bride Jane Marie. She is the love of my life. For two score and four years, she has rendered my life a love sonnet but she was the one, not me, who made it rhyme. She is my inspiration in all that I do. She deserves credit for all that I am.

THOMAS E. BAKER
thomas.baker@fiu.edu
MIAMI, FLORIDA

This 17th Day of September in the Year of our Lord 2018 and the Two-hundred and forty-second Year of Independence of the United States of America

FOREWORD TO THE
SECOND EDITION

This book is written for the intelligent novice. In addition to being helpful to law students and lawyers, my hope is that this book will be read by the curious layperson—anyone who wants to better understand the Constitution and the role of the Supreme Court of the United States. Set out here is a basic framework and the background required for understanding the fundamental nature of our system of government: how our rights and liberties are protected by the Constitution and reconciled with governmental power.

English legal historian Frederic W. Maitland's famous characterization of the common law applies in kind to our subject: constitutional law is "tough law." It is tough to master—tough to teach and tough to learn. This little book will help in our common undertaking to achieve a mastery of constitutional law.

I have been teaching this subject for more than twenty years at three different law schools. The First Edition of this book helped me as a beginning teacher. A generation of law students relied on it. I undertook this Second Edition to preserve and extend its promise for the next generation. It provides a simple but elegant framework for understanding constitutional analysis.

Jerre S. Williams (1916–1993) had a distinguished career in the law. He was a respected professor of law at the University of Texas for 46 years and served as president of the Association of American Law Schools. He served with distinction on the United States Court of Appeals for the Fifth Circuit for 13 years, alongside four of his former students. He was the first Chair of the Administrative Conference of the United States; later, Presidents would appoint him to help settle several major national labor strikes. But most of all he was a teacher's teacher. He published the First Edition in 1979.

I did not know him well, but he and his First Edition have always been an important part of my constitutional law course. As long as I have been teaching, I have been recommending this book to my students and each Spring Semester I stand at a blackboard and draw what might be called "Williams diagrams"—the constitutional law equivalents of those Venn diagrams we all remember from mathematics classes of overlapping circles depicting number sets relationally. The Williams diagrams always seem to help me explain to my students and always seem to help them to understand the deep structure and subtle nuances of constitutional law.

The Appendix presents a "Leading Case Outline of Constitutional Liberty." This is not designed as a general text or a detailed exposition on the subject. But in order to develop an analytical framework and a deeper understanding, a basic outline of the case law is a needed and useful reference.

The text of the Constitution of the United States is not relegated to last place in the book to take away from its importance. Rather, placing it there makes it easier to locate for frequent and regular reference as the reader goes through the book. I always tell my students to "begin with the text."

In this Second Edition, therefore, I have done my best to preserve the best features of the First Edition. Enough of Jerre S. Williams is in this Second Edition that he is my coauthor in a proper sense. I have done my part, however, to update and to improve this book, which is an extension of my teaching. My teaching and this book are inspired by all my students—past, present, and future.

I want to acknowledge the influence and support of two special colleagues, each one a constitutionalist of the first order. Much of my understanding of constitutional law is derived from the path-breaking work of Ronald D. Rotunda, the George Mason University Foundation Professor of Law, and he has greatly influenced my teaching of the subject. *See* Thomas E. Baker, *Mastering Modern Constitutional Law*, 21 SEATTLE U. L. REV. 927 (1998). My dear kind friend Erwin Chemerinsky, the Sydney M. Irmas Professor of Public Interest Law, Legal Ethics and Political Science, University of Southern California, encouraged me and supported me by reviewing drafts of this book and I am very grateful.

Without further attribution, I acknowledge the intellectual debt of borrowing heavily from three text books for the organization, the themes, and some of the content of Chapter 7 (Constitutional Theory):

JOHN H. GARVEY & T. ALEXANDER ALEINIKOFF, MODERN CONSTITUTIONAL THEORY: A READER (4th ed. 1999); MICHAEL J. GERHARDT, THOMAS D. ROWE, JR., REBECCA L. BROWN & GIRARDEAU A. SPANN, CONSTITUTIONAL THEORY: ARGUMENTS AND PERSPECTIVES (2d ed. 2000); WALTER F. MURPHY, JAMES E. FLEMING & SOTIRIOS A. BARBER, AMERICAN CONSTITUTIONAL INTERPRETATION (2d ed. 1995). Most of the articles referenced in the Chapter are excerpted in the first two readers. These three texts are widely-used and I have used them in my own teaching of the basic course and elective courses. If my reader wants to pursue the subject further, these three books will take you a long way toward understanding constitutional theory and philosophy and they also contain extensive reading lists. Michael J. Gerhardt, Arthur B. Hanson Professor of Constitutional Law, Marshall-Wythe School of Law, College of William & Mary, and Thomas D. Rowe, Jr., Elvin R. Latty Professor, Duke University School of Law, reviewed this Chapter and I thank them.

I want to express appreciation for the support and encouragement of Dean Leonard P. Strickman of the College of Law at Florida International University. This also is the place to acknowledge that my work on this book began while I held the James Madison Chair in Constitutional Law and served as the Director of the Constitutional Law Center at Drake University Law School (1998–2002). Thanks to several of my students from the Honors Section who served as readers: Todd E. Chelf; Michael Hirschkowitz; William J. Miller; Lindsey A. Moore; Nicholas J. Podsiadly; Curtis W. Stamp; Mary

Trachian-Bradley, and Amanda G. Wachuta. I add a word of special thanks to my colleagues Tanya B. Bartholomew, Angelique Ortega Fridman, and Charles P. Bubany, who looked over my prose. The editorial staff at West Group were patient and always helpful, especially Louis Higgins, Timothy L. Payne, and Pamela Siege.

Finally, a personal note is in order. I formally dedicate this book to my bride Jane Marie. After three decades together, however, to do so seems somehow insufficient and almost unnecessary because I myself am dedicated to her in the most profound way imaginable. I am always, always, grateful for her love and support.

THOMAS E. BAKER
thomas.baker@fiu.edu

Miami, Florida
25 February 2003

OUTLINE

TABLE OF CASES

References are to Pages

TABLE OF AUTHORITIES

References are to Pages

CONSTITUTIONAL ANALYSIS

IN A NUTSHELL®

THIRD EDITION

CHAPTER 1
AMERICAN CONSTITUTIONALISM

1. CONSTITUTIONAL BLUEPRINT

This Chapter provides some background on the Constitution and the foundational principles of American constitutionalism. Read it for the "big picture." Constitutional analysis ought to and does begin with the text. Every student and every interpreter of the Constitution is a documentarian. The complete Constitution appears in the back of this book. *See* Appendix B. Always start with the text. But our study of constitutional law requires some appreciation for the historical and philosophical context of the Constitution.

American constitutionalism re-imagined the relationship between the government and the individual and codified the new social compact in a written document that is higher law. James Madison, known as the "Father of the Constitution," identified the central dilemma: how to empower the government sufficiently for its tasks and, at the same time, how to prevent it from overreaching the individual. All of constitutional law—and all the rest of this book—is about how we attempt to resolve that dilemma. Madison described it most elegantly in *Federalist Paper No. 51*:

> It may be a reflection on human nature that such devices should be necessary to control the abuses of government. But what is government itself but the greatest of all reflections on human

nature? If men were angels, no government would be necessary. If angels were to govern men, neither external nor internal controls on government would be necessary. In framing a government which is to be administered by men over men, the great difficulty lies in this: you must first enable the government to control the governed; and in the next place oblige it to control itself.

In 1776, the *Declaration of Independence* proclaimed, "Prudence, indeed, will dictate that governments long established should not be changed for light and transient causes." In the *Articles of Confederation*, the original thirteen colonies had allied themselves in what they called a "perpetual union," ratified in 1781 to form a national government that was a loose confederation of member states. But, before long, prominent American leaders became convinced that the nation desperately needed a new charter. Their sense was that the national government simply was not equal to the tasks of nationhood, and there was a fear that the state legislatures were going out of control. Americans were beset with grave worries that their hard-fought revolution would be for naught, that their country would come apart from within or be conquered from without. After a meeting in Annapolis in September 1786, reformers recommended a national convention and the states agreed. The Continental Congress responded in February 1787 by calling on the states to send delegates the following summer to a convention to be "held at Philadelphia for the sole and express purpose of revising the *Articles of Confederation*."

The delegates to the Constitutional Convention of 1787 quickly resolved to draft an entirely new constitution. Their "more perfect union"—as they described it in the Preamble—was designed to solve Madison's dilemma of self-government. They relied on structural mechanisms, a wonderful clockwork design of checks and balances, for protecting individual liberty while at the same time energizing the national government. They, at once, understood and mistrusted both human nature and power. They feared tyranny, especially the tyranny of the majority. They did not need to read George Orwell to appreciate that government power was the antithesis of individual liberty. They had lived under George III.

The constitutional blueprint of these political architects called for a foundation built upon the rule of law and republican theory. They would build a new national government to political specifications of limited government. They laid out a governmental structure arranged horizontally in separation of powers and vertically in federalism. It was on this elaborate structure that they depended for the protection of the individual against the seemingly historically inevitable corruption of all forms of government into despotism. They intended their government to be just and lasting, an example to the world. They believed that it was up to their generation and their posterity to answer the historical question, as Alexander Hamilton put it in

Federalist Paper No. 1, "whether societies of men are really capable or not of establishing good government from reflection and choice, or whether they are forever destined to depend for their political constitutions on accident and force."

2. RULE OF LAW

"It is the proud boast of our democracy that we have 'a government of laws and not of men.'" *Morrison v. Olson*, 487 U.S. 654, 697 (1988) (Scalia, J., dissenting). The rule of law is the fundamental principle that both the governed and the government are bound to follow and obey the law of the land. Belief in the rule of law is a way of imagining the relationship between the state and the individual.

This principle can be traced back to Aristotle and the writings of Cicero and followed through in *Magna Carta*. The Framers of the Constitution, classical scholars that they were, deemed this an essential tenet. In their writings leading up to the *Declaration of Independence*, revolutionists like Thomas Paine and John Adams insisted the rule of law was the *sine qua non* of self-government.

The Framers believed the rule of law was essential to a system of ordered liberty to guarantee social order and individual rights. If our relationships with each other and with the government are subject to a set of rules, rather than the mere whim of the individual, we are more likely to be free individuals and less likely to suffer authoritarian tyranny or despotism from government. The rule of law thus obliges both the individual and the government to submit to the supremacy of the law.

The rule of law often finds expression in the power of judicial review (discussed in the next Chapter), *i.e.*, the idea that the will of the people—expressed in the Constitution—is superior to the will of the people's representatives in Congress or in the state legislatures—expressed in mere statutes. The Constitution is law and all three branches of the national government as well as all three branches of each state's government must adhere to the rule of law in the Constitution. *See* U.S. Const. art. VI (Supremacy Clause).

This principle also animates various constitutional provisions that disapprove of laws that are not of general applicability or laws that are not prospective, for example: the Due Process Clauses in the Fifth and Fourteenth Amendments; the Equal Protection Clause in the Fourteenth Amendment; and the prohibitions on bills of attainders and *ex post facto* laws and impairments of contracts in Article I, Section 10.

Just as the *Declaration of Independence* insisted that the King should be held accountable, so too the Constitution insists that Congress and the President are accountable to the rule of law:

> The essence of free Government is "leave to live by no man's leave, underneath the law"—to be governed by those impersonal forces which we call law. Our Government is fashioned to fulfill this concept so far as humanly possible. * * *

> With all its defects, delays and inconveniences, men have discovered no technique for long preserving free government except that the Executive be under the law, and that the law be made by parliamentary deliberations.

Youngstown Sheet & Tube Co. v. Sawyer, 343 U.S. 579, 654–55 (1952) (Jackson, J., concurring).

3.   REPUBLICAN FORM OF GOVERNMENT

The story is told that at the end of the Constitutional Convention an onlooker asked 81 year-old patriarch Benjamin Franklin, "Well, Doctor, what have we got, a republic or a monarchy?" "A republic," he replied, "if you can keep it." The foundational political philosophy of our Constitution is republicanism. In their *Declaration of Independence*, the Framers resolutely had previously rejected monarchy with its grandiose claims of the divine right of kings to rule over men. In a republic such as ours, popular sovereignty is the order of the day. Sovereignty—the ultimate measure of legitimacy in governmental power—resides in "We the People," *i.e.*, in the consent of the self-governed.

The Framers patented the convention as the proper mechanism for constitution-making. They drafted the Constitution in the Constitutional Convention of 1787 and held conventions in each of the states to ratify it in order to legitimatize the Constitution with popular sovereignty.

However, ours is not a pure democracy, like the democracies in ancient Athens or in a New England town meeting, where every person has a say and a vote on every decision, even down to such details as whether to build a road. In a republic, our laws are made by our representatives, hence the term "representative democracy." Popularly elected officials serve for specified limited terms and must stand for regularly scheduled elections. The history of the franchise in the United States has been to broaden participation, more accurately, to undo historical discriminations based on class, wealth, race, and gender. There is a decided emphasis on majority rule, but the majority rules within proscribed limits that respect political minorities and protect individual rights.

That is the kind of national government the Framers carefully designed in the Constitution. They went on to guarantee a republican form of government in the states as well. U.S. Const. art. IV, § 4.

The ideals of civic republicanism contemplate an informed, active, and involved citizenry—individuals possessed of the qualities of integrity, political good faith, and civic virtue—always striving with high-minded purpose to pursue the common good. These ideals emphasize the centrality of individual First Amendment rights in the process of self-government and on the importance of accessibility and equality in participatory politics. Good government is not just a means to an end, but it is also an end in and of itself. In his famous concurring opinion in *Whitney v. California*, 274 U.S. 357, 375 (1927), Justice Louis D. Brandeis eloquently explained:

Those who won our independence believed that the final end of the State was to make men free to develop their faculties, and that, in its government, the deliberative forces should prevail over the arbitrary. They valued liberty both as an end, and as a means. They believed liberty to be the secret of happiness, and courage to be the secret of liberty. They believed that freedom to think as you will and to speak as you think are means indispensable to the discovery and spread of political truth; that, without free speech and assembly, discussion would be futile; that, with them, discussion affords ordinarily adequate protection against the dissemination of noxious doctrine; that the greatest menace to freedom is an inert people; that public discussion is a political duty, and that this should be a fundamental principle of the American government.

4. LIMITED GOVERNMENT AND ENUMERATED POWERS

In our form of limited national government, the appropriate governmental goals or objectives are specifically enumerated. For example, Article I, Section 8 lists the powers of the Congress in some detail, adding at the end the Necessary and Proper Clause, sometimes called the Sweeping Clause or the Elastic Clause, "To make all laws necessary and proper for carrying into Execution the foregoing Powers * * *." *See* Chapter 5, § 3 (Implied Federal Powers). How the government may decide what goals to pursue and how it will pursue them is thus prescribed in advance. Each of the first three Articles of the Constitution outlines procedures for the three branches of government, the legislative, the executive, and the judicial, respectively. Finally, the manner in which the government may pursue those objectives is limited by guarantees of individual liberty to be found in various places in the text, especially in the Bill of Rights.

Consider a pair of examples which appear in your casebook. When the Patient Protection and Affordable Care Act came before the Supreme Court, a majority of the Justices concluded that a key provision of the statute—the individual mandate, which required persons to purchase health insurance—was not a valid exercise of the Commerce Clause plus the Necessary and Proper Clause. However, a different majority of the Justices concluded that that individual mandate was a valid exercise of the Taxing and Spending Clause plus the Necessary and Proper Clause. Therefore, Chief Justice Roberts wrote an opinion which in effect upheld the constitutionality of the individual mandate. That the statutory provision failed under one power clause did not matter so long as it passed under the other power clause. *NFIB v. Sebelius*, 567 U.S. 519 (2012). In a famous earlier case, the Supreme Court upheld a federal regulation of the amount of wheat a farmer could grow on his farm as a valid exercise of the Commerce Cause plus the Necessary and Proper Clause and simultaneously and impliedly rejected the farmer's claim of an individual Fifth Amendment Due Process Clause right to grow as much wheat as he wanted to grow.

The regulation was a valid exercise of the power clause which did not otherwise violate the protection of the individual right clause. *Wickard v. Filburn*, 317 U.S. 111 (1942). *See* Chapter 5, § 4 (Federal Commerce Power). The negative pregnant of this holding is that a statute that violates any individual constitutional right is unconstitutional and invalid. *Cf.* U.S. Const. art. VI ("This Constitution, *and the laws of the United States which shall be made in pursuance thereof* * * * shall be the supreme law of the land * * *.") (emphasis added).

It is not a digression, however, to emphasize that individual rights are not "granted" by the Constitution. Read the First Amendment, for example. Congress is expressly forbidden from abridging "the freedom of speech," a freedom that is assumed to preexist the Constitution and to be inviolate. The constitutional understanding, carried forward from the *Declaration of Independence*, is that freedom and liberty are the inalienable birthrights of all humankind.

The Framers' ultimate goal was to energize the national government to allow the United States to take its rightful place among the nations of the world and, at the same time, to preserve and protect individual civil rights and civil liberties.

5. SEPARATION OF POWERS

The separation of powers depends on the insight from history that a people who depend on governmental self-restraint to protect their liberty will come to regret their political naiveté. In

Federalist Paper No. 48, Madison lauded the way the Constitution would "guard against those encroachments which lead to a tyrannical concentration of all the powers of government in the same hands." He invoked the "oracle" of separated powers, 18th-century French political philosopher Baron Montesquieu, to justify and defend the system of having three separate branches of government "connected and blended" to ensure that each has some "constitutional control over the others." Bicameralism, dividing the legislature into two houses, was added to ensure greater deliberation and to protect against the mischiefs of popular government.

But your seventh-grade civics class description— "the Legislative Branch makes laws, the Executive Branch enforces the laws, and the Judicial Branch interprets the laws"—is neither complete nor fully accurate. Our separation of powers is much more complicated and sophisticated. *See* Chapter 6 (Structure of the Constitution). Functions are shared. Powers are blended. Consider two examples. Congress may pass a bill and then the President may veto it, but then Congress may override the veto by a two-thirds vote. A law duly passed by Congress and signed into law by the President may be declared unconstitutional by the Supreme Court, but then Congress and the states may override the High Court with an amendment to the Constitution. The branches of government were arranged in an elaborate kind of orrery of powers—like one of those mechanical planetarium models of the solar system in which a planet moves only and always in relation to the other planets.

6. FEDERALISM

Like separation of powers, the principle of federalism is not found in so many words in the text but nonetheless is a basic feature of the constitutional structure. *See* Chapter 6 (Structure of the Constitution). Even though today we take it for granted, we should be reminded that the concept that two sovereign governments could somehow occupy the same territory and govern the same people at the same time was an invention of our 18th-century political philosophers. Back then it was a novel experiment, a way of organizing government that many critics at that time believed could not work in theory and would not work in practice. "The Framers split the atom of sovereignty. It was the genius of their idea that our citizens would have two political capacities, one state and one federal, each protected from incursion by the other." *U.S. Term Limits, Inc. v. Thornton*, 514 U.S. 779, 838 (1995) (Kennedy, J., concurring).

The great powers of nationhood—waging war and making peace, taxing and spending for the general welfare—were assigned to the national government. But many important powers and everyday governmental responsibilities were left to the states. Although the Framers disagreed among themselves and many were uncertain about this division between the national and the state governments, they all fully expected that there would be conflicts over sovereignty and power. Disputes over federalism have figured in critical episodes of our constitutional history, beginning at the Constitutional Convention and continuing to the present day. Indeed, a profound disagreement over federalism principles contributed greatly to the worst cataclysm in our constitutional history, the Civil War. The Supreme Court's epithet for that crisis was penned three years after the peace of the Appomattox courthouse by Chief Justice Chase: "The Constitution, in all its provisions, looks to an indestructible Union, composed of indestructible States." *Texas v. White*, 74 U.S. (1 Wall.) 700, 725 (1868).

Today, federalism rhetoric often is used like red, white and blue bunting to hide baser political motives. Federalism philosophy, as originally understood by the founding generation, contemplated two distinct spheres of exclusive powers, one national and the other state. Each respective government would operate without interference from the other and each would respect the other's sovereignty. History trumps philosophy, however, and federalism today has come to be understood as encompassing the myriad of interrelationships and cooperations between the national and state governments. Choosing between state or federal responsibility often has a lot to do with arguments about greater efficiency and better political participation. Ever since President Franklin D. Roosevelt and his Congress and his Supreme Court reconfigured the constitutional landscape during the 1930s, however, governmental power has flowed from the state capitals to Washington, D.C., as a river flows to the sea.

Though some national politicians, obese with power, today sing the end of federalism, the constitutional opera is not over so long as the states continue to play their role on the constitutional stage. The science of government is the science of experimentation. In his day, Justice Louis D. Brandeis was fond of observing, "It is one of the happy incidents of the federal system that a single courageous State may, if its citizens choose, serve as a laboratory; and try novel social and economic experiments without risk to the rest of the country." *New State Ice Co. v. Liebmann*, 285 U.S. 262, 311 (1932) (Brandeis, J., dissenting). In many areas of public policy, this is still true today. Debates in Congress in the present day still reverberate with arguments that the states can do some things better than Washington. The Justices continue to wage a war of words over questions of federalism, in closely divided rulings and turgidly reasoned opinions.

7. LEGISLATIVE POWER

On the 150th anniversary of the first Congress, Chief Justice Charles Evans Hughes began his address to the assembly by saying, "Here in this body we find the living exponents of the principle of representative government—not government by direct mass action but by representation which means leadership as well as responsiveness and accountability." Congress is a constitutional creation designed to be responsive to the people, but like the other branches, Congress cannot go beyond the Constitution, even in the name of the people. The legislative Article starts off by saying as much: "All legislative Powers herein granted [read in the words: 'and no other powers'] shall be vested in a Congress of the United States which shall consist of a Senate and a House of Representatives." U.S. Const. art. I, § 1. *See* Chapter 6, § 9 (Separation of Powers—Legislative).

The very idea of "legislative power" is a relatively modern concept in human history. The medieval notion was that all authority was attributable to God, nature, or custom and that human institutions merely discovered and enforced the preexisting divine will. Part of the Enlightenment rethinking of mankind's place in the universe was that laws were made, not found, and their meaning was derived from the will of the lawmakers.

During the founding period, however, this very concept of sovereignty was redefined and relocated. Under the British constitution, familiar to the Framers, sovereignty was defined as the will of the Parliament in assembly. This notion was carried over in the early experiences of the states, whose legislatures took it upon themselves to write and ratify state constitutions upon becoming independent of the mother country. The Federalists, who favored adoption of the proposed Constitution, were obliged to rethink these assumptions in order to legitimatize a truly national government possessed of its own sovereign powers, independent from and supreme over state sovereignty. They came to believe that the ultimate sovereignty in a republic flowed directly from the people. The people surrendered portions of their ultimate sovereignty directly to the United States in bundled powers and to the state governments in an omnibus sovereign police power, respectively. What remained beyond the people's delegations to their governments defined the inalienable freedoms and liberties of the individual. *See* U.S. Const. amend. X.

Thus, the legitimacy of the Constitution and the national government it created did not, in any way, depend on the states or the state legislatures. Once ratified, the Constitution became "the supreme Law of the Land," U.S. Const. art. VI, § 2, and the powers of the national government, within their proper spheres, were superior to the powers of the states. This explains the full import and significance of the Preamble's beginning invocation of "We the People." It also explains the hue and cry raised about that wording by the Antifederalists, who placed their loyalty to their own state first and foremost and who therefore opposed the proposed Constitution.

These foundational principles of popular sovereignty were nowhere more obvious or more important than in Article I. Early in the Constitutional Convention, James Wilson, a delegate who would later serve as a Supreme Court Justice, described the basic dichotomy that "there are only two kinds of bad governments—the one which does too much and is therefore oppressive, and the other which does too little and is therefore too weak."

The *Articles of Confederation* generally were considered to be the weak variety of bad government, and the delegates believed it imperative that the new national government would be equal to the necessary tasks of government, something they were convinced was not possible without a radical restructuring. This was the period historians have labeled "the critical period in American history." Many of the Framers, Federalists and Antifederalists alike, believed that their generation faced a turning point in history, that in a world of monarchy their political trial was the last best hope for republican self-government.

At the same time, there was a great anxiety abroad in the land, especially among those who served in the national government, that the state legislatures were devolving into bad governments of the other kind Wilson mentioned, governments that did too much and thus were oppressive and guilty of democratic excesses. Many modern historians believe that the Framers of the Constitution were primarily motivated to empower the national government in order to restrain the states from doing too much. These "small-r" republicans—like James Madison who had served in the Virginia legislature—were appalled at what we might call today the interest-group politics and self-dealings practiced in the state houses, for example, debt-forgiveness statutes enacted at the behest of debtors against creditors. In their minds, legislators were supposed to be statesmen who should resist factional politics and rule with civic virtue for the common good.

The more-nationalistic Federalists believed that a natural elite would rise to positions of national leadership, especially in the Congress of the United States, so that was where the greatest political powers ought to be located. At least, it would be more difficult, if not impossible, for any single faction to capture the national legislature because there would be so many factions as to cancel each other out in the competition for influence. Madison concluded *Federalist Paper No. 10*, his treatise on the inevitability of political factions and the vagaries of human nature, with a warranty that "the influence of factious leaders may kindle a flame within their particular states but will be unable to spread a general conflagration * * *." The real power to govern would be placed beyond the reach of the less worthy, those of a parochial rather than a continental vision.

The legislative Article establishes the structure and the general manner of proceedings of the Congress. The accepted principle of bicameralism afforded one more check on government power; under the terms of the so-called "Great Compromise" between the large and small states, the two houses would have different characters. Seats in the House of Representatives were apportioned among the states on the basis of population and filled by popular elections every two years by voters qualified under state election rules. Each state legislature would choose two Senators for staggered six year terms; in 1913, the Seventeenth Amendment would make them popularly-elected. Other proscribed procedures include: eligibility requirements for members; meeting requirements; quorum requirements;

provision of an oath; authority to supervise the behavior of members; requirement of an official journal; designations for presiding officers; and establishment of general lawmaking procedures, including how to override an executive veto.

The great traditional powers of government, consistent with the separation of executive powers, are to be found in Article I, Section 8: to lay and collect taxes; to spend for the general welfare; to borrow money; to regulate commerce; to regulate immigration and naturalization; to regulate bankruptcy; to coin money; to fix standards of weights and measures; to regulate the mail; to regulate patents and copyrights; to establish federal courts; to define crimes; to declare war; to raise and support military forces; to regulate the militia; and to perform several other particular powers. To be sure, there are other clauses in the first Article, dealing with subjects like *habeas corpus*, *ex post facto* laws, and bills of attainder, that restrain the Congress. But it was intended that the Congress would wield the great powers of government as the United States began to take its place among the nations of the world.

Perhaps the most expansive power the Constitution vests in Congress—or in any other branch for that matter—is the power "To make all Laws which shall be necessary and proper for carrying into Execution the foregoing Powers, and all other Powers vested by this Constitution in the Government of the United States." U.S. Const. art. I, § 8, cl. 18. There are similar provisions in the

Thirteenth, Fourteenth, Fifteenth, Nineteenth, Twenty-Fourth, and Twenty-Sixth Amendments.

Nevertheless, a written constitution, by its very nature, is a limited constitution. Article VI specifically obliges Senators and Representatives to be "bound by Oath or Affirmation, to support this Constitution." This is why President Franklin D. Roosevelt was constitutionally misguided, in an infamous 1935 incident, to lobby members of Congress to support a bill by urging:

> Manifestly, no one is in a position to give assurance that the proposed act will withstand constitutional tests. But the situation is so urgent and the benefits of the legislation so evident that all doubts should be resolved in favor of the bill, leaving to the courts, in an orderly fashion, the ultimate question of constitutionality.

The President was acting improperly to ask the members of Congress to ignore the oath he and they had sworn. Under our Constitution, political ends do not justify unconstitutional means.

On the other hand, some constitutionalists have expressed concern that the pendulum of judicial review has at times swung too far toward distrust of legislative judgments, because legislatures may be becoming accustomed to judicial supervision and more and more readily inclined to ignore their sworn responsibility to follow the Constitution in the pursuit of politically expedient policies. Equally problematic, in terms of the first principle of limited and enumerated powers, is the legislative hubris that Congress can do whatever it likes, so long as the Constitution does not expressly forbid something. In our federalism, the states, not the Congress, are possessed with a sovereign police power to legislate for the general welfare. Its members always need to be mindful that the Constitution speaks directly to Congress.

To recognize that Congress is obliged to make judgments about the meaning of the Constitution, however, is not to suggest a congressional supremacy in the interpretative function. In our history, there have been episodic claims of legislative supremacy. Early on, the Jeffersonians brooded over the idea. During the Reconstruction Congress, Radical Republicans moved in the direction of asserting hegemony over the other branches by impeaching President Johnson and by restricting the jurisdiction of the Supreme Court. But it is a basic tenet of constitutionalism that legislatures simply cannot have the final word. Alexander Hamilton explained in *Federalist Paper No. 78*, "It is not otherwise to be supposed that the Constitution could intend the representatives of the people to substitute their *will* to that of their constituents." Nonetheless, the Congress necessarily shares the responsibility to maintain our constitutional order. Political scientists refer to this theory and practical reality as "coordinate construction." We will leave it to the historians to decide whether the Congress or the Supreme Court has had the better record of being true to the Constitution.

8.   EXECUTIVE POWER

The delegates to the Constitutional Convention were deeply persuaded of the importance of crafting a strong Executive. Drawing on lessons from the classical education they all shared, Alexander Hamilton articulated this principle of American constitutionalism in *Federalist Paper No. 70*:

> Energy in the executive is a leading character in the definition of good government. It is essential to the protection of the community from foreign attacks; it is not less essential to the steady administration of the laws; to the protection of property against those irregular and high-handed combinations which sometimes interrupt the ordinary course of justice; to the security of liberty against the enterprises and assaults of ambition, of faction, and of anarchy. Every man the least conversant in Roman history knows how often that republic was obliged to take refuge in the absolute power of a single man, under the formidable title of dictator, as well against the intrigues of ambitious individuals who aspired to the tyranny, and the seditions of whole classes of the community whose conduct threatened the existence of all government, as against the invasion of external enemies who menaced the conquest and destruction of Rome.

George Washington, like Cincinnatus in ancient Rome, was expected to come to the rescue of the Republic and then could be trusted to surrender power and return to his plow. Indeed, Washington's character and performance in office did more than the Constitution itself to establish the office of President as the republican opposite of a Caesar. For all subsequent generations, however, the constant constitutional anxiety has been how to avoid the potential evils that two eminent contemporary scholars identified in the titles to their book-length critiques of presidential behavior: CLINTON ROSSITER, CONSTITUTIONAL DICTATORSHIP (1948) and ARTHUR SCHESINGER, THE IMPERIAL PRESIDENCY (1973).

The delegates debated the executive Article more than any other topic, and that debate has yet to be concluded. They rejected a plural arrangement of ministers in favor of a unitary chief executive. They compromised on the manner of selection by creating the electoral college, which may deserve the prize for their most Byzantine invention. They settled on four-year terms and an open-ended tenure, though George Washington's tradition of two terms stood until Franklin D. Roosevelt broke it, only to be restored formally with the Twenty-Second Amendment (1951). They situated the Presidency within the system of checks and balances with interactive provisions such as the power of the veto, the treaty making power, the power of appointments, and the power of commander-in-chief.

The Framers sought to ensure energy in the national government through its chief executor of the laws. Indeed, the office was a central feature of their nationalism project. They sought to empower the President against the Congress, which they feared was the most dangerous branch given its patent of powers. At the same time, they sought to make the chief executive accountable to the people. In the process, they rejected, once and for all, the form of executive that was predominant in their time, hereditary monarchy. The office they created in place of a king completely captured the imagination of succeeding generations here and abroad. Republics around the world have adopted the office of president for their executive branch at least in part because of the constitutional experience of the United States. At the same time, it has not been uncommon for notorious dictators to misappropriate the title President in an attempt to legitimate themselves, much like the German and Russian monarchs called themselves "Kaiser" and "Czar" to appropriate the image of "Caesar."

Fast forward 200 years and consider what the modern American Presidency has become in the Twenty-first century. Some contemporary constitutionalists have concluded that the Constitution has become an anachronism, that politics and power have overtaken the 18th-century republican design. They insist that presidential powers have become enormous and amorphous while the checks and balances have become gossamer and evanescent.

Even if one is not persuaded with this verdict of history, there is no arguing with the premises that the President wields great, yet still largely undefined, powers and that the other two branches, especially the Supreme Court, have contributed to the aggrandizement of powers in the modern Executive. Supreme Court Justice Robert H. Jackson once chillingly quoted Napoleon's maxim as if to shrug this off as being inevitable, "The tools belong to the man who can use them."

Historically and philosophically, there have been two competing approaches to understanding the import of Article II. The fundamental point of disagreement between the two competing views of the Presidency is how to understand the first sentence of Article II, which reads simply: "The Executive Power shall be vested in a President of the United States of America." *See* Chapter 6, § 10 (Separation of Powers—Executive).

Is this first sentence simply a designation of the office as the locus which is assigned the powers listed in Article II, but only those powers specifically enumerated and no others? Or is everything that follows in the Executive Article surplusage because the first sentence itself is a grant of all imaginable plenary powers of an omnipotent executive, so that the clauses that follow are merely illustrative examples, not an exhaustive list, of presidential powers? What does the Constitution ultimately contemplate: a President with powers that are limited and enumerated, like the Congress's, or a President with open-ended powers that are equal to unforeseen threats, foreign and domestic, more akin to the powers acceded to the Roman dictators? Among the Framers, James Madison took the narrow view and Alexander Hamilton took the broad view of the Executive's power.

This is one time when a close reading of the text cannot resolve the debate. Indeed, adherents of both views of presidential powers invoke the text. Those who take the broad view point out that the first sentence in Article II does not contain the limiting reference to "the powers herein granted," unlike the first sentence in the legislative article, Article I. Those who take the narrow view point out that Article II does not contain an expansive "necessary and proper" clause, like the one found in the list of legislative powers in Article I, Section 8, clause 18.

Presidents themselves have debated this issue in terms of their own incumbency. Theodore Roosevelt took the view that the Executive power was limited only by specific restrictions and prohibitions appearing in the Constitution or congressionally enacted statutes. His successor, William Howard Taft, who served as President and Chief Justice, took the opposite view that a President can exercise no power unless it is fairly and reasonably based on a specific grant of power in Article II. Taft's narrow understanding may have been the original understanding of the 18th-century Framers themselves, but Roosevelt's broad understanding is more accurate and necessarily realistic for today's Presidents.

It can be observed without fear of contradiction that the Presidency has evolved along with historical changes in the dominant role of the United States in world affairs and in the pervasive role of the national government in domestic matters. Both roles were far simpler and much more modest back in 1789, as was the institution of the Presidency, when George Washington took the first oath of office.

9.   JUDICIAL POWER

In the United States, we take federal courts for granted. But other modern countries with federal systems do not have two complete sets of federal and state courts coexisting alongside one another, as we do. Instead, other countries typically have trial courts that are all state courts and the only federal courts they have are appellate courts. It is a little-remembered fact that the United States came close to adopting this model.

The debate at the Constitutional Convention of 1787 over the judiciary was protracted and intense. The arguments went back and forth, without much prospect for compromise. Things got so heated that at one point the delegates voted to strike a provision they had tentatively agreed upon, and instead they voted to eliminate any and all mention of a national Judicial Branch in the new Constitution. The argument was that the existing courts in the states were equal to the judicial tasks of the nation and, therefore, all that was needed was to provide for appeals from the state courts to a supreme national court. After a great deal more parliamentary wrangling, another version of compromise was reached, however, that yielded what we know as Article III. There would be one Supreme Court. Congress was authorized—but not required—to "ordain and establish" a separate and independent system of federal courts, separate from the state courts and independent from the other two branches of the federal government. U.S. Const. art. III, § 1. *See* Chapter 6, § 11 (Separation of Powers—Judicial).

The delegates' hard-fought compromise continued to be the subject of high and full controversy in the subsequent ratification debates in the states. Five entire issues of *The Federalist Papers, Nos. 78–82*, were devoted to defending the idea of a separate and independent federal judiciary, with considerable political passion, against the sustained attacks of the Antifederalists. Federalists insisted that the lack of a federal judiciary was a serious deficiency in the *Articles of Confederation* and they portrayed the proposed federal courts as guardians of civil liberties.

For their part, Antifederalists mistrusted all three heads of the federal Leviathan. They felt especially threatened by the congressional power to create a new federal judiciary because they believed federal courts would aggrandize power toward the central government and away from the state sovereigns, all to the eventual detriment of individual rights. At the same time, they argued that the lack of a written bill of rights was reason enough to oppose the proposed Constitution.

In the end, the Federalists prevailed. The Constitution was ratified, though barely and by close margins in several key states: Massachusetts 187–168; Virginia 89–79; and New York 30–27. Thus, from the beginning, the Article III judiciary and civil liberties have been linked together fundamentally and inextricably in high political controversy.

One of the transcendent achievements of the first Congress assembled under the newly ratified Constitution was to enact the Judiciary Act of 1789, a statute that has come to be considered a great law because, once and for all, it established the tradition of a separate and independent system of federal courts. Act of Sept. 24, 1789, 1 Stat. 73. But the role those courts would play within the separation of powers and in our federalism was left to be determined by constitutional experience. History and tradition have elaborated on the Delphic generality of Article III. The federal courts themselves, especially the Supreme Court, have done a great deal to shape this history and tradition by annotating the sparse language of Article III with an extensive body of case law and elaborate opinions.

The Supreme Court of the United States, of course, has been from the beginning, and remains, the most important as well as the most controversial federal court. Justice Oliver Wendell Holmes, Jr. aptly remarked, "We are very quiet there but it is the quiet of a storm centre, as we all know."

The Supreme Court is the only court created directly by the Constitution. It has supervisory and appellate jurisdiction over the lower federal courts and reviews cases involving federal issues from the highest courts of the states. It is composed of nine Justices—although the number of Justices has been changed no fewer than seven times by congressional statutes and has varied between five and ten members—who are appointed by the President, with the advice and consent of the Senate. U.S. Const. art. II, § 2, cl. 2.

Members of the Supreme Court are as independent as the lot of humanity will allow. Justices serve "during good behaviour"—effectively until they retire or die—and they are protected against having their salaries diminished while they serve. U.S. Const. art. III, § 1. The House of Representatives can impeach and the Senate can remove a Justice upon conviction of "Treason, Bribery, or other high Crimes and Misdemeanors." U.S. Const. art. I, §§ 2 & 3, art. II, § 4. Early in our history, however, impeachment became what Thomas Jefferson called "a mere scarecrow." It would be unthinkable today for Congress to impeach and remove a Justice based on some ruling or a judicial opinion.

The Framers' expectation was to create a federal judiciary that was independent, but neither too much nor too long at odds with popular sovereignty. Predicting what specific issues will come before the Court has been impossible, except in the short term, and then only in the most general terms. Furthermore, predicting how any individual jurist will interpret the Constitution over the course of lifetime tenure is highly problematic. Nevertheless, Presidents and Senates engage in such political-branch forecasting each time a vacancy occurs so the nomination and confirmation process is the primary external restraint on the Supreme Court, although it has had virtually negligible lasting effect.

Confirmation battles between a President of one party and a Senate majority of the other party, too recent to be called history, have shed more heat than light on what is at stake for the Constitution. There are no constitutional rules beyond James Madison's mechanism of "ambition checking ambition." *Federalist Paper No. 51*. These political confrontations have been more about game theory than the Constitution.

A President can nominate a person for the Supreme Court for good reason or for bad reason or for no reason at all. The Constitution is completely silent on qualifications. Merit is almost always the announced criterion, of course, although other reasons that have been invoked over the years have included political and personal patronage, geography, race, religion, and gender. For periods in its history, particular chairs have been temporarily designated, such as "the Jewish (or Catholic) seat" or "the African-American (or Woman's) seat," but these appellations are by and large newspaper constructions. For the most part, a President wants a Justice who will be faithful to the President's views about the Constitution on the issues the President deems politically important. And, for the most part, Presidential sponsors have been pleased by their judicial protégées.

The Senators can confirm or reject a nominee for any of the same reasons that a President chooses a nominee. In 2016, the Senate succeeded at thwarting a presidential nomination until the next presidential election was determined. President Trump's nominee, Neil Gorsuch, replaced President Obama's nominee, Merrick Garland, as the successor to

Justice Antonin Scalia. In a controversial nomination battle between the President and the upper chamber, the Senators usually end up bowing to the will of their constituencies, more so now that the proceedings are televised. This is high stakes politics, but politics nonetheless. In the constitutional long run, nomination and confirmation shape the Supreme Court as an institution in the image and likeness, not of the 18th-century Framers, but of "ourselves and our posterity."

From the beginning down to modern times, Americans have singled out particularly controversial decisions—on such divisive issues as racial remedies, the death penalty, abortion, and the contested Presidential election of 2000—but for the most part, Americans consistently have maintained their confidence in the Supreme Court as an institution of government. Over the 200-plus-year history of the Constitution, "We the People" seem to have been arguing about its meaning the entire time. The Supreme Court, like a republican schoolmaster, has presided over that debate.

The role of the Supreme Court in our constitutional regime is at once profound and subtle, and as difficult to understand as it is impossible to overstate. In the 1830s, French sociologist and political theorist Alexis De Tocqueville already recognized this:

> The peace, prosperity, and the very existence of the Union rest continually in the hands of these [nine] judges. Without them the Constitution would be dead letter; it is to them that the executive appeals to resist the encroachments of

the legislative body, the legislature to defend itself against the assaults of the executive, the Union to make the states obey it, the States to rebuff the exaggerated pretensions of the Union, public interest against private interest, the spirit of conservation against democratic instability. Their power is immense, but it is power springing from opinion. They are all-powerful so long as the people continue to obey the law; they can do nothing when they scorn it. Now, of all powers, that of opinion is the hardest to use, for it is impossible to say exactly where its limits come. Often it is as dangerous to lag behind as to outstrip it.

ALEXIS DE TOCQUEVILLE, DEMOCRACY IN AMERICA 150 (J.P. Mayer, ed. 1969).

10. INDIVIDUAL RIGHTS

The Constitution of the United States has been described as one of the greatest achievements of political philosophy. The underlying philosophy of American constitutionalism is the philosophy of individual rights. *See* Chapter 4 (Constitutional Liberty).

The subject of individual rights takes us back to the Madisonian dilemma, which was introduced earlier in this Chapter. There is, at bottom, a fundamental contradiction in liberal political theory. "Liberal," of course, refers to the political traditions of western democracies and includes Federalists and Antifederalists, Democrats and Republicans, liberals and conservatives. The fundamental contradiction is that the justification of the state, ultimately, is to provide the legal force necessary to protect all individual rights, including basic rights in property as well as political and civil rights. Thus, liberal political theory calls the state into existence, and the citizen needs the state to protect individual rights. The state, at the same time, represents the greatest threat to the realization and enjoyment of our rights.

How is it possible to make government more powerful without making those subject to its authority less free? This is the fundamental paradox at the bottom of all constitutional analysis—the irreducible question of American constitutionalism. This paradox explains, in large part, how and why constitutional law issues are so open-ended, forever being reconsidered and reargued, never being fully and finally settled. The relationship between individual liberty and government power, by theoretical and practical necessity, is subtle and complex and is constantly evolving. Internalizing this paradox will go a long way towards mastering constitutional analysis. *See* Chapter 3, § 2 (Individual Liberty Versus Government Power).

Liberalism, with its primary emphasis on the individual, is the ideology of rights, of capitalism, and of the limited state. It is at the opposite end of the ideological spectrum from communitarianism, which is the ideology of relatedness, of social solidarity, of an activist state with an emphasis on the collective. The United States always has been a country of rights. Lockean or liberal constitutionalism posits a sphere of individual liberty, guaranteed by property rights writ large, with a fixed government constituted by majority consent. A liberal constitutional government is representative, responsible, and limited, and its great powers are separated among coordinate branches. It is maintained by a perpetual threat of popular revolution, at least in theory. *See Declaration of Independence*. In practice, the consent of the governed is expressed in regular elections participated in by an enfranchised citizenry. "Here the people rule," remarked Gerald Ford, upon taking the oath of office as President.

Indeed, the idea of rights was part of the United States even before there was a Constitution. In the beginning, there was the dramatic invocation of unalienable rights in the *Declaration of Independence*, based on the belief that the governed could withdraw or withhold their consent from government: "We hold these Truths to be self-evident, that all Men are created equal, that they are endowed by their Creator with certain unalienable Rights, that among these are Life, Liberty, and the Pursuit of Happiness." Though this familiar declaration is now more than two centuries old, it was a quite radical departure in its day. The English constitution, by comparison, had been limited only by the rule of law and by established procedures as were to be found in *Magna Carta*. English constitutional history, the legal history of the colonists, could not imagine any limits in principle on the purposes of government. No one in the 18th century could even imagine a British version of the First Amendment—"Parliament shall make no law * * *." Americans

would be different. We would have a written
Constitution and then a written Bill of Rights. With
those formative documents our liberal American
constitutionalism became forever rights-centered.

We need only compare the nearly
contemporaneous revolution in France to understand
the uniqueness of this development in its time. The
French people followed Rousseau toward more
equality and fraternity than liberty; these values
were expressed in the general will of the community;
but there were no individual "rights" against the
general will. The people in the French republic, as in
England, enjoyed rights only by laws, by legislative
grace, because only the Parliament spoke for the
general will. Our *Declaration* insisted otherwise. Our
political creed was based on the fundamental tenet
that certain rights were inherent in human nature,
that individual human dignity did not depend on
government authority and was superior to it. While
Magna Carta granted rights, our Constitution grants
no rights, not because we do not value individual
rights, but because our understanding is that liberty
is not a matter of governmental grace.

The Framers' first line of defense of individual
rights was to be found in the structure of their
government. Government power always and
everywhere was to be mistrusted; it had to be divided
to be limited. Federalism principles divided power
vertically between the states and the national
government. Separation of powers divided power
horizontally within the national government. The
most powerful branch, the Legislative Branch, was

further subdivided by bicameralism. Their system of checks and balances was designed with all the complexity of the inner workings of a clock. Their purpose was to prevent government power from becoming concentrated in one institution that would then lord over individual liberty.

The new national government would be limited to enumerated powers and necessary and proper powers, no less nor no more. The Framers sought to empower the government sufficiently for its essential tasks and, at the same time to prevent it from overreaching the individual. Thus, the Constitution, as originally intended and understood, was arranged in its entirety to protect the individual. This is why the delegates did not take long to consider and reject a proposal to add a bill of rights—suggested almost as an afterthought towards the end of the Constitutional Convention—by a unanimous 10–0 state vote. It was not that the delegates were opposed to a bill of rights. Rather they deemed one basically unnecessary. For Federalists like Alexander Hamilton, "the Constitution is itself, in every rational sense, and to every useful purpose, a bill of rights." *The Federalist Paper No. 84.* He concluded, "For why declare that things shall not be done which there is no power to do?" There was no need to elaborate further and state what the national government could *not* do, in the first place because it could only do what it was expressly empowered to do, and in the second place because of the peril that any list of rights might be incomplete and overlook some freedom or fail to anticipate some essential liberty.

Federalists' protestations notwithstanding, it soon became apparent that the lack of a bill of rights, like the ones to be found in the contemporary state constitutions, was a serious flaw in the proposed Constitution. Virginia's George Mason refused to sign the Constitution for this reason. Thomas Jefferson chastised his friend James Madison for leaving out a bill of rights. In the ratifying conventions in state after state, Antifederalists raised the alarm for individual liberties. For a time, it looked like the Federalists had made a serious political miscalculation. Antifederalist opponents of the proposed Constitution were prominent and influential and their attacks on the Constitution gained momentum. It was only after Federalist leaders, Madison included, pledged to add a bill of rights immediately upon ratification that the proposed Constitution garnered the necessary support and then only by slim margins in several key state conventions.

One of James Madison's claims to fame as a statesman of the highest integrity is that he kept his campaign promise to sponsor a national bill of rights. After defeating the Antifederalist candidate James Monroe, one of the first things Madison did as a member of the House of Representatives was to sponsor a set of constitutional amendments. In a speech on June 8, 1789, he pledged: "I shall proceed to bring the amendments before you and advocate them until they shall be finally adopted or rejected." He continued, "this House is bound by every motive of prudence, not to let the first session pass over without proposing to the State legislatures some things to be incorporated into the Constitution, that will render it acceptable to the whole people of the United States." He explained his belief that most of those who had opposed the Constitution "disliked it because it did not contain effectual provisions against encroachments on particular rights." The newly-elected President, George Washington, who had presided at the Convention and then lent his critical support to the proposed Constitution, had himself made note of the fact of the widespread demand for a bill of rights in his first official message to Congress. Now, Madison insisted, it was up to the Congress under Article V "to provide those securities for liberty and expressly declare the great rights of mankind secured under this constitution." Madison deserves credit for being the prime mover behind the proposed bill of rights. He framed it and he shepherded it through the Congress. Madison's influence also was felt when his own Virginia was the necessary eleventh state to ratify on December 15, 1791, making the Bill of Rights part of the Constitution.

In the grand scheme of American constitutionalism, the Bill of Rights has amounted to much more than a mere parchment barrier to the majority will—in large part owing to an ever-vigilant and independent federal judiciary. Each guarantee represents a hard-fought victory for human dignity and individual integrity in the centuries-old struggle between the individual and government. More than any other part of the Constitution, the Bill of Rights is deeply ingrained in our people's collective consciousness, as a cherished part of our political heritage. More than any other branch, the Article III

Judicial Branch has performed as the guardian of our civil rights and civil liberties.

However, there was one not-so-small constitutional difficulty that had to be overcome to realize the full potential of the Bill of Rights. This was a consequence of federalism. The Constitution of the United States, after all, is a national document that, for the most part, establishes the terms of the social compact between citizens and the national government. Consequently, there was no room for disagreement or dispute when Chief Justice Marshall and a unanimous Supreme Court ruled in *Barron v. Baltimore*, 32 U.S. (7 Pet.) 243 (1833), that the provisions in the Bill of Rights were effective only against the national government and not the states. This was the original understanding, demonstrated by the text itself, as for example the First Amendment prohibition that "Congress shall make no law * * *." The national government was expressly bound by the Bill of Rights, but the states could have their way with individual liberties, subject only to state laws and state constitutions.

Historic later amendments and the Supreme Court's power of interpretation changed all this. The Fourteenth Amendment was ratified in 1868, in the aftermath of the constitutional paroxysm of the Civil War. Along with the Thirteenth Amendment, which abolished slavery and forever banished that witch of the 1787 christening, and the Fifteenth Amendment, which guaranteed the freedmen the franchise, the Fourteenth Amendment was addressed directly to the states. For the longest time, however, its constitutional potential went unrealized because the earliest Supreme Court interpretations of the Fourteenth Amendment were begrudgingly narrow. Tentatively at first, later more insistently during the Warren Court years (1953–69), in case after case the Supreme Court "interpreted" the guarantee of "liberty" in the Fourteenth Amendment Due Process Clause to include almost all of the particulars of the Bill of Rights. This development is known in constitutional circles as the "incorporation doctrine," because the formal conception is that the 1868 Due Process Clause incorporated the particular 1791 Bill of Right protection and made it applicable to the states. The national and state governments today are both obliged to respect the same Bill of Rights guarantees, with few exceptions. That this process of incorporation is virtually complete and now almost taken for granted is demonstrated when Supreme Court Justices themselves lapse into the *lingua franca* and refer to a state having violated the First Amendment freedom of speech, for example, even though, technically speaking, the amendment being violated is the Fourteenth Amendment. *See* Chapter 3, § 4 (History of Constitutional Liberty).

Nothing is rooted more deeply in our constitutional culture and political tradition than the American creed of individual civil liberties and civil rights. The vocabulary of rights is the dominant dialectic of modern constitutional law. This has been true from the beginning. From the *Declaration of Independence*, through the Bill of Rights and the Reconstruction Amendments, the debate has never been whether or not individuals hold rights against their government. That truth has been self-evident. The debate has been over the scope and content of rights, how the balance ought to be struck in particular situations, *i.e.*, determining where in a particular case the Constitution draws the line between government power and individual liberty.

In all this "rights talk," the Supreme Court must always be mindful of the Madisonian dilemma. Our Constitution demonstrates a profound bias against claims of absoluteness from either side, the individual or the government. It is the genius of American constitutionalism that neither government powers nor individual rights should ever be allowed to reach their logical extreme. Rights and powers coexist in balance and, properly understood, are always in tension. Thus, the constitutional relationship between the individual and the government can be described as a zero-sum game. That is the *leitmotif* of this book. That is this NUTSHELL in a nutshell.

11. AMENDMENTS

Article V of the Constitution represents the Framers' best effort to reconcile the need for change with the desire for stability in government structures. In the words of James Madison, the amending procedures are designed to "guard equally against that extreme facility, which would render the Constitution too mutable; and that extreme difficulty, which might perpetuate its discovered faults." *Federalist Paper No. 43.*

There are two procedural steps to amend the Constitution and two alternatives for each step, arranged in what Madison described as a process that is "partly federal, partly national." *Federalist Paper No. 39.* First, amendments may be proposed either by a two-thirds majority in both houses of Congress or by a special convention called at the request of two-thirds of the state legislatures. Second, amendments are ratified by three-fourths of the states, either by the existing state legislatures or by special state conventions, depending on which forum Congress designates. U.S. Const. art. V.

The amendment procedure was a deliberate compromise between those who feared that Congress would seek to increase its powers at the expense of the states and those who feared that the states would seek to truncate the powers of the federal government. Like so many other compromises at the Convention, the delegates resolved to align those competing jealousies in direct opposition in order to check and balance each other.

Thus, amending the Constitution was made difficult, but not impossible, in significant contrast to the predecessor constitution, the *Articles of Confederation*, which had required the unanimous consent of all the states for amendments. The Framers did not anticipate frequent or detailed amendments, however. Rather, regular lawmaking in the form of statutes would respond to economic, political, cultural, and moral developments in American society. They understood the Constitution to be a permanent and higher law intended to last for the ages.

Amending the Constitution is very much an exercise in representative democracy, another important responsibility of republican self-government. The whole responsibility for amendments is given over to the elected representatives of the people: the Congress in conjunction with the state legislatures. And it is a super-majoritarian arrangement. Thus, 34 Senators, or 146 Representatives, or any combination of 13 state legislative chambers are sufficient opposition to keep a proposed amendment from becoming part of the Constitution. It is no surprise that only 27 amendments have made it through this political gauntlet.

There is no explicit role for the Executive provided in the text of Article V; a President need not sign and cannot veto a congressional proposal. Of course, there is nothing to prevent the President from initiating or participating in the formation of public opinion supporting or opposing a proposal to amend the Constitution.

In numerous decisions, the Supreme Court has consistently ruled that Article V places the primary responsibility for amending the Constitution within the province of the Congress. The High Court has refused to play any role in the process of considering amendments, either substantively or procedurally. Such questions are left to the political branches. *See Coleman v. Miller*, 307 U.S. 433 (1939) (questions of the efficacy of state ratifications are for Congress).

The judicial role only begins once an amendment is ratified and becomes part of the law of the Constitution, which is the province and responsibility of the judiciary to interpret. There have been six amendments ratified to reverse various Supreme Court case holdings: Eleventh Amendment (1795); Thirteenth Amendment (1865): Fourteenth Amendment (1868); Fifteenth Amendment (1870); Sixteenth Amendment (1913); and Twenty-Sixth Amendment (1971).

By some estimates there have been more than 10,000 bills introduced in Congress to amend the Constitution. Of these, only 33 garnered the necessary two-thirds vote in both houses and proceeded to the states, and only 27 have received the necessary ratifications of three-fourths of the states. Thus, the American Constitution is one of the most difficult constitutions to amend—more difficult than the state constitutions and more difficult than the constitutions of other countries. This political reality has necessary implications for the role of the Supreme Court as its interpreter.

There has never been a convention for proposing amendments. All 27 amendments have been proposed by Congress, although in the 1980s as many as 32 states had at one time or another issued a variety of calls for a constitutional convention to consider an amendment to require a balanced budget for the federal government. All but one of the amendments have been ratified by the state legislatures. Only the Twenty-First Amendment, which repealed the Eighteenth Amendment's failed social experiment with Prohibition, was ratified by state conventions upon the stipulation of Congress.

It is significant that, ever since the initial historic precedent of the Bill of Rights in 1791, amendments have been added at the end of the document, rather than incorporated directly into the existing text that is being amended. This long-standing practice symbolizes the fact that an amendment is a separate and contemporaneous exercise in constitution-making and serves to remind us that it is *a constitution* we are amending. *See McCulloch v. Maryland*, 17 U.S. (4 Wheat.) 316, 407 (1819) (Marshal, C.J.) ("[W]e must never forget, that it is *a constitution* we are expounding.").

Looking back at the history of American constitutionalism, we can see that amendments have been ratified in constellations shaped by the political issues and national priorities of four distinct eras in American history. Between 1789 and 1804, the "Anti-federalist" or "Jeffersonian" amendments were adopted. The first ten amendments, popularly known as the Bill of Rights (1791), secure the fundamental rights of the individual against the national government. The Eleventh Amendment (1795) prevents federal courts from entertaining lawsuits against the states. The Twelfth Amendment (1804) sought to solve the problems that occurred in the 1800 election between Thomas Jefferson and Aaron Burr.

The "Civil War Amendments," the Thirteenth, Fourteenth, and Fifteenth Amendments, were ratified during the Reconstruction era, in the years

1865, 1868, and 1870, respectively. Ratified in the aftermath of a cataclysm that shook the constitutional structure to its foundations, those majestic provisions ended slavery, enforced due process and equal protection against the states, and guaranteed the recently freedmen the right to vote.

The populist and progressive movements at the beginning of the 20th century yielded four ratifications: the federal income tax in the Sixteenth Amendment (1913); the direct election of Senators in the Seventeenth Amendment (1913); the national Prohibition in the Eighteenth Amendment (1919); and women's suffrage in the Nineteenth Amendment (1920).

The most recent spate of amendment ratifications revolved around federal election reforms: the Twenty-Second Amendment (1951) limited the President to two terms in office; the Twenty-Third Amendment (1961) awarded the District of Columbia three electoral votes in presidential elections; the Twenty-Fourth Amendment (1964) abolished the poll tax; the Twenty-Fifth Amendment (1967) established rules for presidential succession and disability; and the Twenty-Sixth Amendment (1971) lowered the voting age to eighteen.

Admittedly, this patterning is not perfect and a few amendments cannot be drawn into these four groupings: the Twentieth Amendment (1933) limited the lame duck session of Congress and the Twenty-First Amendment (1933) repealed Prohibition. The Twenty-Seventh Amendment (1992) requires that any pay increase for members of Congress can go into effect only after an election. It was proposed by the first Congress as part of the original Bill of Rights and was all but forgotten for more than 200 years before it was dusted off and ratified in 1992 by the requisite number of states—something that is not likely to happen again because the modern practice is for Congress to include a time limit, usually seven years, in proposed amendments.

Congress has voted to propose six amendments that have failed to be ratified by the requisite three-fourths of the states. An amendment proposed along with the Bill of Rights would have set a population limit for congressional districts which, given today's population, would have required more than 6,500 members in the House of Representatives. In the early 19th century, an amendment was proposed that would have automatically expatriated anyone who accepted a title or honor from any foreign government without the consent of Congress, a measure that would have played havoc with Nobel Prize winners and knighted former Presidents. There was a desperate and futile effort on the eve of the Civil War to appease the Southern states by proposing to prohibit any future amendment that would eliminate slavery. As part of the progressive movement in the 1930s, a proposed amendment would have authorized Congress to regulate child labor in the face of an unwilling Supreme Court, but the Justices eventually came around to finding the power in the Commerce Clause. In the 1970s, a Democrat-majority in Congress proposed to grant congressional representation to the District of Columbia, but the political reality that the measure would result in the election of at least three more Democrats to Congress was enough for Republicans to stall the measure in the statehouses.

The most important recent showdown over a proposed amendment was the ten-plus years of debate whether to add an amendment for sex or gender equality, the Equal Rights Amendment (E.R.A.). Congress proposed the E.R.A. in 1972 with the usual seven-year deadline for ratifications, then extended the period for three more years. After some early momentum, however, in the end only thirty-five states ratified the measure—three short of the number needed—and some states that had ratified the proposal went back to try to rescind their earlier ratifications.

Opponents of the controversial measure warned that it would lead to co-ed bathrooms, women in combat, and the elimination of marital alimony in favor of no-fault divorce laws. It is interesting that many of their cultural predictions have come true despite the failure of the proposed amendment. In the years since, more than two dozen states have added equal rights amendments to their state constitutions and every state has enacted legislation against categorical invidious discrimination. And Supreme Court interpretations of the Equal Protection Clause in the Fourteenth Amendment have gone a long way toward achieving the constitutional change that was intended by the drafters of the E.R.A.. *See United States v. Virginia*, 518 U.S. 515 (1996) (excluding women from a state military college did not satisfy the requirement of an exceedingly persuasive

justification under the Equal Protection Clause).
Still, women's rights organizations continue to press
Congress to resubmit the E.R.A. to the states to
preserve political gains and to serve as an important
symbol to the nation. In 2017, Nevada ratified the
E.R.A. and, in 2018, Illinois did the same. Those two
states did so on the express assumption that
Congress could waive its own expired ratification
deadline. Diehard proponents argue that Congress
should do so once the count of ratifying states reaches
38 states without counting the past state rescissions.
If Congress declares the amendment to be ratified,
that declaration almost certainly would be a political
question and nonjusticiable. *See* Chapter 2, § 6
(Nonjusticiable Political Questions). Comparatively,
modern constitutions around the world have
entrenched explicit protections for women (and other
identifiable groups) against discrimination. *See, e.g.*,
German Basic Law, Art. 3; South African
Constitution, Ch. 2, § 9. International law likewise
has recognized an international norm against gender
discrimination. *E.g.*, *U.N. Convention on the
Elimination of All Forms of Discrimination Against
Women* (1979). In recent years, a proposed LGBT
Rights Amendment has been introduced in Congress
which would protect against discrimination based on
sexual orientation and gender identity.

The amendments being debated at any given time
usually include the most divisive political issues of
the day. One side or the other, sometimes both sides
of a contentious issue, often seeks to ratchet its point
of view up to the next level of politics with the hope
of constitutionalizing its policy preference once and

for all. Often, proponents of constitutional amendments have been disappointed in the regular lawmaking process in Congress. They also regularly try to use Article V in attempts to trump controversial Supreme Court decisions with which they disagree.

Some critics complain that Congress seems to be suffering from a bad case of "amendmentitis"—an inappropriate willingness to attempt to rewrite the Constitution. A sampling of the amendments recently considered by Congress include proposals to: authorize Congress to prohibit and punish flag burning; authorize the President to exercise a line-item veto; require that federal judges be re-confirmed every ten years; abolish the electoral college to provide for the direct election of the President; establish term limits for members of Congress; abolish the income tax; and guarantee rights to victims of crimes. As with all things political, different people assign different value and importance to these various proposals to change the nation's fundamental law. Thus, the perceived wisdom—or the perceived folly—of a particular proposal to amend the Constitution often is in the eye of the beholder. The formal amendment rules are available to those with good motives and those with ill motives, as well.

Some amendments go out of fashion while they are still under consideration, disappearing from popular concern. For example, the balanced budget amendment was in the headlines and looked close to passing Congress in the 1980s, partly as a consequence of pressure felt from the calls of thirty-two states for a constitutional convention to consider it. But when the burgeoning economy began to yield federal surpluses, the political pressure for passage lessened and the measure disappeared from view, at least temporarily. And by now the bills introduced annually over the last so many years to propose amendments to permit prayer in public schools or to outlaw school busing or to ban abortions have become more symbolic rituals than realistic efforts to change the Constitution. They amount to rallying cries for organizations on their side of the issue for purposes of direct-mail fundraising and membership recruitment, but they are no longer perceived by the other side as a genuine political threat.

The experience with amending the Constitution illustrates an important feature of American constitutionalism. Ultimately, it is the Constitution that unites us as "We the People," thus only matters of a lasting national consensus fully deserve our constitutional allegiance. Everything else, from the mundane to the important, is merely politics. Just as all politics is said to be "local," all politics is temporary and always in play—always debatable and always subject to another vote. Most things Congress and the state legislatures do can be undone by the next election. That is to say that the people always can "vote the rascals out" and replace them with new legislators who can repeal the unwise or unwanted laws. Not so with constitutional amendments which must be repealed by the arduous procedure of ratifying another amendment. Only one amendment has ever been repealed: Prohibition was ratified in 1919 and eventually repealed in 1933. *See* U.S. Const. amend. XVIII & XXI.

The reason that there have been only 27 amendments over more than 200 years is that constitutional amendments must have the sustained and one-sided support of great majorities in the Congress and across the fifty states. Very few political issues ever garner that level of priority and support. Consider, for example, that by one account the political campaign to guarantee women the franchise took 72 years and included 56 state referenda campaigns, 480 state legislative campaigns, 47 state constitutional conventions, 277 state party conventions, 30 national party conventions, and 19 campaigns in successive Congresses before finally succeeding in 1920 with the ratification of the Nineteenth Amendment.

Most issues of public policy are too evanescent or too controversial or too closely contested to achieve and sustain the necessary super-majorities at the national and state levels. Such issues neither merit nor permit constitutional amendment. In American constitutionalism, this is how most issues in our democratic republic properly are left to ordinary politics—to simple and temporary majorities in the legislature—to determine and to change through the regular legislative process. The Constitution is a higher order of politics and properly understood so too is constitution amending. A measure that successfully runs the Article V gauntlet rightly belongs in the Constitution. Our experience with amending the Constitution demonstrates beyond peradventure that such measures are few and far between.

12. CONCLUSION

In the very first reported case decided by the Supreme Court upon the express authority of the Constitution, Justice James Wilson concluded, "Whoever considers, in a combined and comprehensive view, the general texture of the Constitution, will be satisfied, that the people of the United States intended to form themselves into a nation for national purposes." *Chisholm v. Georgia*, 2 U.S. (2 Dall.) 419, 465 (1793) (Wilson, J., concurring). Thus was born the modern American notion of nationhood.

American constitutionalism has been characterized, from the beginning, by republicanism, the separation of powers, federalism, the rule of law, and by majority rule along with minority rights. These are the foundational principles—the deep structure—of our system of government.

In his greatest decision, the great Chief Justice John Marshall proclaimed, "A written constitution" was for its time "the greatest improvement on political institutions." *Marbury v. Madison*, 5 U.S. (1 Cranch) 137, 178 (1803). By the law of the Constitution, Americans ordained and established, organized and coordinated, empowered and limited their government for themselves and their posterity. Every republic founded in the succeeding two centuries—the whole world over—has borrowed from their political principles, the fundamental principles that constitute a regime that Abraham Lincoln described as a "government of the people, by the people, and for the people."

CHAPTER 2
JUDICIAL REVIEW

1.   ORIGINS OF JUDICIAL REVIEW

The Supreme Court of the United States (its official and formal name) is the most powerful judicial body in the world. The manifestation of this power is the doctrine of "judicial review." The phrase "judicial review" is but a shorthand expression for the role the Court plays as the final authority on most, although not all, issues of the constitutionality of governmental actions. It "reviews" these actions to see that they conform to the Constitution. The Court engages not only in judicial review of the constitutionality of legislation, both state and federal, but also of the actions of chief executives, state and federal, as well as decisions of other courts, both state and federal. The Court exercises its constitutional authority when it validates as well as when it invalidates what some governmental actor has done.

The institution of judicial review is so deeply engrained in the American system that it is difficult for us to conceive of our legal system without it. *See* Chapter 7, § 2 (Who Interprets the Constitution?). Our federal and state governmental powers are limited by the Constitution for the purpose of preserving individual liberty, and federal powers are further limited to preserve the powers of state governments. The Supreme Court exercises the ultimate authority in enforcing these limitations. Yet the concept of judicial review was a unique American invention. It is fair to say we developed the principle of judicial review out of the common law of England. Although England has a similar history, governmental philosophy, and governmental institutions, it never has developed an American-style judicial review. The United Kingdom still adheres to the doctrine of parliamentary sovereignty but it did create a Supreme Court in 2009. That court cannot overturn primary legislation but it can declare a law to be incompatible with the European Convention on Human Rights—something like judicial review lite. Indeed, other western parliamentary democracies still do not have the full-blown American-style judicial review, although there is a modern trend abroad toward greater judicial authority and independence along the lines of the UK's 21st century Supreme Court. Contemporary constitution writers do seem to be enamored with American-style judicial review, at least as a means to guarantee individual constitutional rights.

The Constitution does not provide explicitly for the exercise of judicial review by the Supreme Court of the United States. Whether or not the power is implied by the language of the Constitution is in some academic dispute among constitutional historians. But the doctrine did not spring suddenly and spontaneously from the forehead of John Marshall, like Pallas Athena sprang from the forehead of Zeus. Judicial review has a respectable intellectual lineage.

The concept of judicial review coalesced from three themes found in the common law in England and the formative law of the United States. The first theme is the concept of "divine law," which later became "natural law" to those who did not demand divinity in the law. This concept of law—that there is divinely ordained law higher than man-made law—was and is familiar enough. It is manifested in the Ten Commandments and other basic rules of human conduct found in religions and ethical systems in all times and in all societies, what C.S. Lewis called the "Tao." The Framers believed that there was a body of ethical imperatives that were inherent in human nature and discoverable by human reason. These fundamental tenets, whether "divine" or "natural," have been viewed in our history as "higher law," *i.e.*, higher than the temporal or secular law that governs everyday life. There are some eternal truths, self-evident and discoverable by the application of right reason, some propositions that are valid for all persons for all time, Truths with a capital "T."

The second fundamental theme is the principle of "due process of law," which has its beginnings in *Magna Carta* in 1215. The majestic generality "due process of law," widely used in modern constitutional law as a shorthand description for various procedural and substantive aspects of liberty, developed from the phrase "law of the land," found in Section 39 of *Magna Carta*. The phrase in *Magna Carta* expressed the then-radical principle that even the king was bound by the "law of the land." To the present day, we continue to boast that ours is "a government of laws, not of men." *See* Chapter 1, § 2 (Rule of Law).

The third coalescing theme was the 18th-century insistence that the fundamental law, which controls the organization of government, should be in writing. The British Parliament, in 1689, enacted the British "Bill of Rights." At the same time, Thomas Hobbes and John Locke were advancing the philosophical concept of the social compact. In their theories the natural law was converted to the concept of natural rights. Men and women existed in a state of nature and then they organized governments only for the purpose of protecting their rights and property. Thus, government was limited, and it was limited by the social compact, the agreement between the citizens and their government. While the social compact was not originally envisioned as necessarily having to be in writing, the idea that basic liberties must be formally stated for purposes of solemnity and protection became self-evident. In the new world, covenant theology thus gave way to covenant politics beginning with the Mayflower Compact.

A more explicit fruition of this third theme was occurring simultaneously in the separate colonies. The acceptance of the need for a written constitution was a natural development from the colonial charters. The charters were the organic written principles of government of the charter colonies. They were detailed, and they were readily viewed as statements of the fundamental law controlling the operation of the colonies. These charters of government evolved into state constitutions between the *Declaration of Independence* (1776) and the drafting and ratification of the *Constitution of the United States* (1787). Some of these state constitutions notably contained specific provisions for judicial review of the acts of state legislative bodies.

These three themes were invoked as the basis for the creation of our nation by Thomas Jefferson in the immortal words of the *Declaration of Independence*:

> We hold these truths to be self-evident, that all men are created equal, that they are endowed by their Creator with certain unalienable Rights, that among these are Life, Liberty and the pursuit of Happiness—That to secure these rights, Governments are instituted among Men, deriving their just powers from the consent of the governed * * *."

However, there remained the issue: who in our governmental structure would define and enforce our fundamental rights? During the Constitutional Convention, the concept of judicial review was discussed, but the Constitution itself contains no words which could be taken as stating clearly and unequivocally that this power to declare laws unconstitutional would exist in the newly created Supreme Court of the United States. *See* U.S. Const. art. III, § 1.

Yet there was one important formative constitutional document that did clearly recognize the power of judicial review before the principle was established by the Supreme Court. This was *Federalist Paper No. 78*, written by Alexander Hamilton as part of the series of newspaper articles urging the ratification of the newly drafted

Constitution. Hamilton set forth the principle of judicial review in determined and measured terms. In his discussion, he even presented some of the reasoning which Chief Justice John Marshall would borrow to write the Supreme Court opinion that would claim the power of judicial review for the Supreme Court in the name of the Constitution.

All of these developments came together in the great case of *Marbury v. Madison*, 5 U.S. (1 Cranch) 137 (1803). This is the most important case in all of constitutional law because it established the doctrine of judicial review as a fundamental principle of American constitutionalism. The Supreme Court, in the famous opinion by Chief Justice Marshall, held unconstitutional a provision of the Judiciary Act of 1789 on the ground that the statute attempted to give original jurisdiction to the United States Supreme Court in a case in which the Constitution limited the Supreme Court's power to appellate jurisdiction only. The remarkable irony of this decision was that the Court established its great power of judicial review by holding unconstitutional a statute of Congress that attempted to give the Court more power—power to hear certain kinds of cases and to grant certain kinds of relief that the Court held the Constitution would not allow.

Actually, there was nothing controversial about the Judiciary Act. It had been written by Senator Oliver Ellsworth of Connecticut, a distinguished constitutional lawyer who was Marshall's immediate predecessor as Chief Justice. The statute's wording was somewhat ambiguous, but if the same issue were presented today, we would confidently expect the Court to interpret the statutory words to avoid a conflict with the Constitution. Chief Justice Marshall's organization and logic thus were strained and convoluted.

But the argumentation in his opinion was meticulous and detailed and even brilliant. He found the authority for the concept of judicial review lodged largely in two constitutional provisions. Article III sets up the judicial structure of the federal government, and the second clause of Article VI establishes the principle of the supremacy of the United States Constitution. The key words relied upon by the Court were the words of Article III, Section 2: "The judicial Power shall extend to all Cases, in Law and Equity, arising under this Constitution, * * *." The case of *Marbury v. Madison* was a "Case * * * arising under the Constitution," and the Constitution provides that "*all*" such cases are within the judicial power of the federal government.

The Constitution is law and "it is emphatically the province and duty of the judicial department to say what the law is." The "very essence of the judicial duty" is to follow the higher law of the Constitution—the written law ratified by the sovereign people—over a mere statute—enacted by the people's representatives in Congress. The Constitution is the law for the government. The Constitution trumps a statute, therefore, judges must prefer and enforce the Constitution over a statute. William Marbury lost his case and did not get to be a justice of the peace, but

John Marshall went down in history as the greatest Chief Justice. The judicial branch was the real winner.

Shortly after this landmark decision, other decisions served to complete the dominance of the Supreme Court in constitutional interpretation. Acts of state legislatures were declared unconstitutional, *Fletcher v. Peck*, 10 U.S. (6 Cranch) 87 (1810); state criminal proceedings were made subject to Supreme Court review, *Cohens v. Virginia*, 19 U.S. (6 Wheat.) 264 (1821); and final decisions of the highest courts of the states were deemed reviewable in the Supreme Court under the Constitution, *Martin v. Hunter's Lessee*, 14 U.S. (1 Wheat.) 304 (1816).

It also is important to remember that the law of the Constitution applies to judges on lower federal courts and on state courts. Consequently judges on those courts wield the power of judicial review to strike down acts of government as being unconstitutional, although their decision-making is subject to the hierarchy of appellate review and the limitations of *stare decisis*.

The 20th century experience of the Court in dealing with the determined defiance and wholesale evasion by state officials of court orders concerning racial desegregation in the public schools proved to be the occasion for one of the most heroic invocations of the power of judicial review, in the critical case of *Cooper v. Aaron*, 358 U.S. 1 (1958). The decision grew out of the lawless defiance by the Governor of Arkansas of the federal court order to desegregate the public schools in Little Rock. In a symbolic gesture without precedent, the unanimous opinion of the Supreme Court was signed by each of the nine Justices by name, and emphatically reaffirmed the historic decision in *Brown v. Bd. of Educ.*, 347 U.S. 483 (1954) declaring "separate but equal" schools to be a *per se* denial of the Equal Protection Clause. The *per curiam* opinion formally invoked Chief Justice Marshall's great opinion to say: "This decision declared the basic principle that the federal judiciary is supreme in the exposition of the law of the Constitution, and that principle has ever since been respected by this Court and the Country as a permanent and indispensable feature of our constitutional system." 358 U.S. at 18.

But the doctrine of judicial review and the Supreme Court as an institution both have their share of critics and defenders. They disagree whether the Justices do exercise judicial self-restraint or whether judicial review has devolved into a kind of judicial supremacy that Chief Justice Marshall could not have imagined. Conservative constitutional scholars on the political right and liberal constitutional scholars on the political left have tried to make the case that the country would be better off without judicial review, given the boundless hubris of the Supreme Court, although they cite different lines of cases as examples of the Court's villainy. These commentators go so far as to advocate that the Constitution be amended to relocate the ultimate final authority to interpret the Constitution in the Congress. There is no question that particular exercises of judicial review in particular decisions have been and will continue to be highly controversial, even historically so, but even those decisions have their supporters. Perhaps there is no better exemplar of the potential for controversy than the decision that proved to be the *denouement* of the presidential election of 2000, *Bush v. Gore*, 531 U.S. 98 (2000). Thus, the debate over the proper exercise of the awesome power of judicial review continues. Indeed, the academic debate over judicial review and the interpretation of the Constitution continues to rage in the law reviews without any sign of lessening. *See* Chapter 7 (Constitutional Theory).

2.   CASE OR CONTROVERSY REQUIREMENT

This brief historical account of the development of the doctrine of judicial review leads us to consideration of the circumstances under which constitutional questions can be brought to the Supreme Court of the United States and decided there. *See also* Chapter 6, § 11 (Separation of Powers—Judicial).

The first and critical requirement is that there must be a *"case"* or *"controversy"* in the vernacular of Article III. The case must be one that is appropriate for judicial determination. The Court does not decide academic questions of constitutionality in abstract or hypothetical situations. The dispute must be genuine and real between the parties. It must involve someone who will be actually harmed by the law or by some other governmental action that is being challenged as being unconstitutional.

The Court has generally defined a justiciable case or controversy to be a court proceeding that is a *bona fide* adversarial dispute in which important legal rights are being threatened by the governmental action in issue, the threatened harm will be directly caused by the governmental action, and the Court has the authority and power to redress the threatened harm and thus resolve the dispute. Feigned cases or friendly and collusive lawsuits are not the appropriate occasion for exercising judicial review. The parties must be genuinely adversarial; this provides the deciding court with the necessary perspective for decision. Someone must suffer some real, genuine harm from the governmental action being challenged, not some generalized grievance or fanciful complaint. It is by this means that the constitutional issues are developed and presented in a form appropriate for judicial review.

This requirement that there actually be a flesh-and-blood controversy involving real people caught in a real, live dispute is critical to understanding the function the Court is being called upon to perform. In so many words, Chief Justice Marshall's original justification for claiming the power of judicial review was based upon the constitutional responsibility to decide cases or controversies. It is not so much the Court's power in the abstract as it is the Court's proper role to provide a judicial remedy for individual harms from constitutional violations: "The very essence of civil liberty certainly consists in the right of every individual to claim the protection of the laws, whenever he receives an injury." *Marbury v. Madison*, 5 U.S. (1 Cranch) 137, 163 (1803). Judicial review is bottomed on the protection of the rights of the individual against the government.

Constitutional decisions necessarily depend upon the specific facts and circumstances presented in the particular case or controversy. Consider some straightforward examples of the need for actual cases to allow the Court to perform its judicial review function. In determining the scope of power of the national government to control matters in interstate commerce, the Court has held that the federal power extends to all of those matters that "substantially affect" interstate commerce. A determination whether something affects interstate commerce necessarily depends upon the actual factual situation and relevant market facts.

Similarly, actual cases are necessary to the effective constitutional evaluation of statutes controlling subversive speech. It would be totally unrealistic to try to decide the constitutionality of a statute in the abstract without having before the Court the actual words uttered by the person accused of subversive speech or without knowing the context and setting. The Court must determine whether the words were prohibited by the statute and whether they were of such a clear and present danger to our governmental system that the government has the power to prohibit them in spite of the protection of free speech in the First Amendment.

A third example might involve the matter of controlling meetings in a public park through the issuance of permits. Such events, of course, involve issues of free speech and assembly. Suppose that the public authorities refuse to issue a permit for a particular event. What is the nature of the event? Are other similar organizations allowed to hold similar events in the park? Is there any substantial danger that the event will erupt into violence? Are there serious problems for noise or traffic control or littering or damage to public property in the park? All of these questions and more are critical to the determination of the constitutionality of denying the right to hold a particular meeting in a public park. Such issues cannot be resolved in the abstract.

The Justices perform as judges deciding cases or controversies, not as lawyers giving legal advice. The Supreme Court is not competent to deliver advisory opinions and to do so would violate the separation of powers. The Supreme Court, like all federal courts, is a court of limited jurisdiction. The judicial power of the United States is limited by the Constitution to decide only cases or controversies. U.S. Const. art. III, § 1.

The power to declare a law unconstitutional arises only when the act of Congress conflicts with the higher, fundamental law of the Constitution. In a case refusing to issue an advisory opinion, despite the express invitation of Congress, the Supreme Court explained:

> The exercise of this, the most important and delicate duty of this court, is not given to it as a body with revisory power over the action of Congress, but because the rights of the litigants in justiciable controversies require the court to choose between the fundamental law and a law

purporting to be enacted within constitutional authority, but in fact beyond the power delegated to the legislative branch of the government.

Muskrat v. United States, 219 U.S. 346, 361 (1911).

The requirement, then, is that to challenge the constitutionality of some governmental policy you must become involved in a lawsuit. You must sue someone or you must be the subject of someone else's lawsuit. The lawsuit can originate either in a state or federal court and can be either a criminal case or a civil suit between private parties. One of the common and best known ways to challenge the constitutionality of regulatory legislation is to violate it for the purpose of creating a constitutional test. The fact that it is a test case does not in any sense lessen its genuineness, however. The individual making the challenge will suffer the consequences if his or her challenge is unsuccessful. In these more modern days of efficient civil procedures, constitutionality is often challenged by a suit for declaratory and injunctive relief to halt enforcement of a regulatory statute.

3. STANDING, RIPENESS, AND MOOTNESS

The Supreme Court has undertaken to insure that the cases that it decides involve real parties and actual cases or controversies by developing the doctrines of "standing," "ripeness," and "mootness." Standing is the most important conceptually and practically.

The doctrine of standing in the party raising the constitutional issue basically requires that the party have an actual stake in the outcome of the case. *Duke Power Co. v. Carolina Envtl. Study Grp., Inc.*, 438 U.S. 59 (1978). Return again to the simple situation of a requirement in a municipal ordinance that a permit must be obtained to hold a meeting in a public park. Suppose we have a well-meaning citizen who believes that meetings should be allowed in public parks without restriction. But this citizen is not planning a meeting in the public park, has never attended a meeting in the public park, and indeed never has used or intends to use that public park for any purpose whatsoever. This citizen is simply someone who believes that the ordinance is unconstitutional in the abstract. The citizen has no "standing" to raise the constitutional issue concerning the granting of permits for meetings in that public park. The citizen has shown no reason why he or she should be allowed to raise this question. It is simply an abstract question to this particular person, a kind of generalized grievance shared by everyone; by comparison, the issue would not be an abstraction to someone who had been denied a permit for a meeting and was seeking a remedy in court.

The essence of standing is the determination that the person making the constitutional argument is the right person to present the issue to the court. First, the person must have sustained some injury in fact, not merely a fanciful, abstract, generalized, or hypothetical worry or concern that everyone has in common. Second, the injury must be fairly traceable to what the other party to the lawsuit did or did not do, *i.e.*, the other party has caused the injury. Third, the injury must be one that the court can remedy, *i.e.*, the injury is judicially redressable. The underlying constitutional principle is that the federal courts are reserved for resolving real live disputes that matter to someone, and the Judicial Branch should not invade the policy-making province of coordinate branches. In the garden-variety tort lawsuit, the plaintiff sues the defendant who ran into the plaintiff's car asking for money damages; the injury, causation, and redressability are apparent and there is no guesswork about who should bring suit. In so-called public law cases that allege constitutional injuries arising from governmental policies and programs, standing can become rather metaphysical.

A troublesome question involving the right of the individual to raise constitutional issues is whether a taxpayer has the right to challenge how tax money is spent by the government. Does the fact that the taxpayer contributed to the Treasury from which the money for the spending emanates give standing to challenge the spending?

In *Massachusetts v. Mellon*, 262 U.S. 447 (1923), the Supreme Court held that generally a taxpayer may not challenge spending from the U.S. Treasury. The interest of a single taxpayer is too small and too generalized to give standing to challenge federal expenditures. If this decision had gone the other way, theoretically every taxpayer would have been entitled to raise the constitutional issue of every instance of federal spending because every cent that the federal government spends must have constitutional authorization. Otherwise, the Judicial Branch—ultimately the Supreme Court—would have to sign-off on every expenditure of every federal program. That would prove too much, for the Court and for the Constitution.

But this holding did raise the specter of widespread, unconstitutional governmental spending that could never be stopped because no one could be found who would have standing to raise the constitutional issues in court. The Supreme Court made a distinction to allow taxpayer standing if the federal program being challenged is an exercise of the congressional spending power and if the federal action allegedly exceeds a specific constitutional limit on that power. So it was that when the federal Elementary and Secondary Education Act of 1965 provided for some federal financial aid to private religious schools, a taxpayer was afforded standing to challenge the measure as being a violation of the First Amendment prohibition of the establishment of religion. *Flast v. Cohen*, 392 U.S. 83 (1968).

This is an important but a narrow exception to the general rule against taxpayer standing. A later Court distinguished *Flast* to hold that an organization dedicated to the separation of church and state could not bring suit to challenge the decision of a federal agency (not Congress) to give away federal land (not the spending of federal tax money) to a religious education institution. *Valley Forge Christian Coll. v. Americans United for Separation of Church & State, Inc.*, 454 U.S. 464 (1982). The law of standing is characterized by such fine-spun distinctions. *See, e.g., Ariz. Christian Sch. Tuition Org. v. Winn*, 563 U.S. 125 (2011) (*Flast* rule did not apply to state tax credits); *Hein v. Freedom From Religion Found., Inc.*, 551 U.S. 587 (2007) (*Flast* rule did not apply to federal Executive Branch actions and expenditures).

A state cannot sue the United States as *parens patria* of its own citizens, because the United States government represents all its citizens. *Massachusetts v. Melon*, 262 U.S. 447 (1923). A state might sue the United States in its own right, however. *Missouri v. Holland*, 252 U.S. 416 (1920). And one state may sue another state. *Wyoming v. Oklahoma*, 502 U.S. 437 (1992). Members of Congress who vote against a measure that is enacted over their opposition do not have standing to go into court and ask for a do-over. *Raines v. Byrd*, 521 U.S. 811 (1997). Finally, the fact that no one may have standing to sue is not reason alone to afford someone standing who does not otherwise qualify. However, some individual who meets the requisite injury, causation, and redressability prongs can usually be found to bring suit. *See Clinton v. City of New York*, 524 U.S. 417 (1998).

There are some other non-constitutional, merely prudential, court-created rules on standing that have more play in the joints and provide judges with some discretion to allow the case to go forward. Generally, a third party cannot bring a lawsuit to vindicate the constitutional rights of another person, unless the third party is in a special relationship with the other person and there is some good reason that the other person cannot practically bring suit. For example, a physician will be allowed to challenge a state law that allegedly burdens female patients' right to seek an abortion. *Singleton v. Wulff*, 428 U.S. 106 (1976). In free speech cases, the substantial overbreadth doctrine allows a court to strike down a statute that might be constitutional as applied to the party before the court if the court believes that the statute on its face will chill substantial free speech of others. *See Broadrick v. Oklahoma*, 413 U.S. 601 (1973). An association or organization can have standing to sue in its own right or can have standing to represent its members who would themselves have standing, so long as the nature of the claim and the relief sought do not require the individual members to participate. *Warth v. Seldin*, 422 U.S. 490 (1975). For example, a union might have associational standing to represent the rights of its members. *Int'l Union, United Auto., Aerospace, & Agric. Implement Workers of Am. v. Brock*, 477 U.S. 274 (1986).

In addition to the requirement that there be standing to raise the constitutional issue, the Court insists that the issue be "ripe" for judicial decision. Ripeness, as the metaphor suggests, is a matter of timing. The doctrine serves to avoid premature adjudication and the entanglement of the courts in abstract disagreements that may or may not mature into a genuine case or controversy. It further defines a posture of judicial deference vis-à-vis the other branches and other agencies of government. Potentially important constitutional cases usually present nettlesome legal issues that are best decided in the context of a fully developed factual record without having to speculate what might happen and without having to fill in gaps with judicial guesswork. The Court will wait and see what happens and then decide the issue with the benefit of hindsight. *Int'l Longshoremen's & Warehousemen's Union, Local 37 v. Boyd*, 347 U.S. 222 (1954).

A good example of how the doctrine of ripeness works is *United Public Workers v. Mitchell*, 330 U.S. 75 (1947). The case involved a constitutional challenge against the Hatch Act ban on partisan political activities by federal employees. The Court held that federal employees who claimed only that they planned to engage in various types of political activity sometime in the future did not present an issue that was ripe for constitutional decision. They had not yet undertaken to do these things but were simply thinking about doing them, so they had not yet been injured by the statute.

The political employees involved were the ones who ultimately were going to be harmed by the statute, and they were planning the kind of activities that would bring them into direct violation of the statute. It can be said, therefore, that they were proper persons to have standing because their legal rights were threatened. But they had not gone far enough in their planning or activities to make the issue one that should be decided now. So the constitutional issues had not matured; the issues were not yet ripe.

Fortunately for the purpose of resolving the issues involved in the constitutionality of the Hatch Act, one of the government employees bringing the suit had in fact actually engaged in some of the kind of conduct that violated the statute. So as to that particular employee, the case clearly was ripe, and the Supreme Court did reach and decide the constitutional merits of the statute as it applied to this government employee. The Court has adhered to the notion that the delay in the judicial resolution of an uncertain legal issue does not amount to the kind of immediate harm that renders a case ripe for judicial review. *Nat'l Park Hosp. Ass'n v. Dept. of the Interior*, 538 U.S. 803 (2003).

If the ripeness doctrine is about a lawsuit brought too early, the mootness doctrine is about a lawsuit brought too late. The case or controversy limitation on federal courts permits them to decide only on-going disputes between parties with a live personal stake in the outcome. If events subsequent to the filing of a lawsuit in effect resolve the dispute, the case must be dismissed as moot, whether at the trial level or on appeal, and even in the Supreme Court itself. Various subsequent events might moot a case. If the parties settle the matter, the controversy is no longer alive. If the challenged statute or regulation expires or is repealed, the controversy is over. Any change in circumstances that has the practical effect of ending the dispute is grounds for declaring the lawsuit moot.

DeFunis v. Odegaard, 416 U.S. 312 (1974) was a dramatic example. The case presented the important issue whether affirmative action policies in state university admissions programs violated the Fourteenth Amendment. By the time the case was fully briefed and orally argued in the Supreme Court, however, the plaintiff bringing the challenge was enrolled in his last quarter of law school and the university represented to the Court that he would not be prevented from completing his degree program. The Supreme Court dismissed the case as moot and did not reach the merits of this important issue, an issue that roiled in the lower courts for three decades before percolating up again for decision.

Contrast that case with *Super Tire Engineering Co. v. McCorkle*, 416 U.S. 115 (1974), decided the same day. The labor strike the plaintiffs had held was over by the time their case challenging restrictive state regulations finally reached the Supreme Court. The Court had no trouble reaching and deciding the merits, however, because those same plaintiffs might go out on strike again and so the issue of the constitutionality of the state regulations was deemed "capable of repetition but evading review" and therefore not moot. In the famous privacy right case, for example, the Supreme Court recognized that human gestation takes only nine months compared to the considerably longer time required to try a case, take an appeal, and petition for Supreme Court review. Besides, an individual woman might become pregnant again in the future. *Roe v. Wade*, 410 U.S. 113 (1973).

A helpful mnemonic for the requirements of standing and ripeness/mootness is found in the words of Justice Stone in the case of *Nashville, Chattanooga & St. Louis Railway v. Wallace*, 288 U.S. 249, 262 (1933). In that opinion, he referred to "valuable legal rights" that were being "threatened with imminent invasion." The valuable legal rights constitute the standing and the threat of imminent invasion constitutes the ripeness/mootness.

The various doctrines originating in the case or controversy requirement have the effect of opening or closing the door to the federal courthouse for litigants and their constitutional questions. How an individual Justice applies these doctrines has a lot to do with the particular Justice's vision of the proper role of the Third Branch. *See* Chapter 6, § 11 (Separation of Powers—Judicial).

4.   JURISDICTION AND PROCEDURES

Great constitutional cases often begin in humble circumstances, in the every-day life of regular people who demonstrate the courage of their convictions. For example, one of the greatest cases in the history of the Supreme Court involved the decision by an eleven-year-old African-American school girl named Linda Brown in Topeka, Kansas, who, with her parents, brought suit challenging the legal requirement that she had to attend a separate public school for blacks. This, of course, was the famous case of *Brown v. Bd. of Educ.*, 347 U.S. 483 (1954) & 349 U.S. 294 (1955), which struck down *de jure* segregation in the public schools and eventually led to the dismantling of the racial apartheid in the South known euphemistically as "Jim Crow." Only a year later, Rosa Parks refused to sit in the "colored section" of a city bus on her way home from work and her civil disobedience led to the historic Montgomery

Boycott under the leadership of Martin Luther King, Jr., and Ralph Abernathy, among others. Thus, politics in the streets mirrored Thurgood Marshall's NAACP litigation strategy.

Constitutional issues arise in the interrelations between the government and the individual. A police officer breaks up a demonstration. A city official refuses a parade permit. A public school teacher is fired. A fire fighter is passed over for a promotion. A prisoner challenges the procedures that were followed at the criminal trial. A zoning board orders a property owner to stop using the property for some purpose or in some way the property owner desires. Such are the beginnings of constitutional cases or controversies. *See* Chapter 3, § 2 (Individual Liberty Versus Government Power).

Like all the other federal courts, the Supreme Court is a court of limited subject matter jurisdiction. A case must fall within "the judicial Power of the United States," as defined in Article III of the Constitution. Congress has enacted jurisdictional statutes for the Supreme Court. Under the Constitution and these statutes, the Supreme Court has original jurisdiction and appellate jurisdiction.

Cases can be filed directly in the Supreme Court's original jurisdiction only in the most limited circumstances. In theory the original jurisdiction of the Supreme Court is self-executing and needs no statutory implementation, but because there has always been a statute on the subject that theory has never been tested. U.S. Const. art. III, § 2, cl. 2; 28 U.S.C. § 1251. The most common type of case filed in the Supreme Court's original jurisdiction involves a dispute between two states, for example, a boundary dispute or a suit over water rights involving an interstate river. *Virginia v. Maryland*, 540 U.S. 56 (2003). Here the Court's jurisdiction is original and exclusive. The Court itself does not hold a trial, instead the matter usually is referred to a special master who conducts a hearing and then makes recommendations how to resolve the dispute. In some other classes of cases, the Court's jurisdiction is original and not exclusive so that the Court can—and normally will—stand by and allow for the matter to be resolved in the first instance in a lower federal court. *California v. Nevada*, 447 U.S. 125 (1980). Consequently, the original jurisdiction cases do not amount to a large or an important part of the Court's docket today.

Under Article III, Section 2, Clause 2, Congress has the power to make exceptions to the appellate jurisdiction of the Supreme Court, unlike the original jurisdiction. The Supreme Court understands this power to mean that a statute that grants specified appellate jurisdiction necessarily implies an exception of any and all jurisdiction not specified in the statute. By providing for certain types of appeals, the Congress impliedly negates all other types of appeals not provided in the statute. Congress can go so far as to repeal an appellate jurisdiction after a case has been briefed and argued but before it has been decided, and the Court can only dismiss the case for want of subject matter jurisdiction. *Ex parte McCardle*, 74 U.S. (7 Wall.) 506 (1869). Congress's power does not go so far, however, as to reopen and redetermine cases that have been fully and finally resolved by the courts. *Plaut v. Spendthrift Farm, Inc.*, 514 U.S. 211 (1995).

Constitutional issues arise in cases in federal and state trial courts throughout the country. Once a case involving a constitutional issue begins, it follows the established procedures of that court system for all cases. Typically, there is trial and a final judgment followed by one appeal as of right, with written briefs and an oral argument about the law before a panel of judges sitting on an intermediate court of appeals. There is no guarantee, however, that the constitutional issue will be decided by the Supreme Court of the United States. Our highest Court has a limited jurisdiction and in most instances the discretion whether to hear and decide a case.

Cases arrive at the United States Supreme Court from either a lower federal court or the highest court of a state, usually called a supreme court, but occasionally called a court of appeal. If under state procedures the case is not within the jurisdiction of the highest state court but contains a constitutional issue, it can go directly to the Supreme Court from the lower state court that has the final authority to rule on the issue. *See* 28 U.S.C. § 1257(a); *Brown v. Texas*, 443 U.S. 47 (1979). Most federal cases come up from the United States courts of appeals, the federal intermediate courts, but some cases come up from the United States district courts, the federal trial courts. 28 U.S.C. §§ 1253 & 1254. There are three procedures under which a case may move from a lower federal court or a state's highest court to the Supreme Court of the United States.

The first of these three procedures is "certification"—a technically possible though highly improbable procedure under which the United States Court of Appeals, one of the regional courts which hear appeals as-of-right in the federal system, can write an opinion merely stating a particular legal issue and asking the Supreme Court for a binding decision on the issue. The Supreme Court can then either answer the stated question or call the entire case up for review. Although this procedure is still "on the books" it is almost never used and so rarely used as to be mentioned here merely for the sake of completeness. *See* 28 U.S.C. § 1254(2); *Wisniewski v. United States*, 353 U.S. 901 (1957). The same statute does provide, however, for the extraordinary procedure of the Supreme Court taking a case up for review before the United States Court of Appeals has ruled, a procedure the Supreme Court occasionally does follow in compelling and historic cases when an expeditious and final decision is a matter of imperative public importance and an intermediate appeal would serve no judicial purpose. *See* 28 U.S.C. § 1254 (1); Sup. Ct. R. 11. The Supreme Court bypassed the Court of Appeals to bring up *United States v. Nixon*, 418 U.S. 683 (1974), and then ruled that President Nixon had to obey a district court subpoena of tape recordings of his White House conversations, a dramatic ruling that directly led to his resignation under threat of impeachment by the House of Representatives.

Earlier jurisdictional statutes elaborately distinguished between the two other procedures for achieving Supreme Court review. First, some cases were heard by "appeal"—using the word in a narrow technical sense to mean a statutory right to have the merits decided. Second, some cases were heard by the Court "granting a writ of *certiorari*"—by which the losing litigant asks and the Court exercises its discretion to grant review. Some of the older cases in your casebook will sometimes make this distinction. One other distinction under the former statutory scheme was that every affirmance and reversal of an appeal was a decision on the merits and carried some precedential effect. Even so, the Justices managed to avoid deciding a considerable proportion of appeals on jurisdictional grounds, such as dismissals for want of a substantial federal question.

In 1988, responding to this evolved reality and to the Justices' entreaties for more formal control over their docket, Congress all but did away with Supreme Court appeals. *See* Act of June 27, 1988, Pub. L. No. 100–352, 102 Stat. 662. Appeals are still technically a matter of right only in cases decided by a three-judge district court, which is nearly an extinct creature of the federal court system now limited by statute to trying challenges to the constitutionality of the apportionment of congressional districts and statewide legislative districts. 28 U.S.C. § 2284(a). Consequently, appeals arise in few cases and now show up on the Supreme Court's docket on the ten-year census-and-redistricting cycle. *Easley v. Cromartie*, 532 U.S. 234 (2001). Congress rarely, but occasionally, will include a particular designated grant of jurisdiction in a controversial piece of legislation that is sure to be challenged on constitutional grounds, such as the 1989 federal anti-flag burning statute, to provide for an automatic appeal from the federal trial court directly to the Supreme Court, bypassing the intermediate appellate court. *United States v. Eichman*, 496 U.S. 310 (1990).

Today, most all of the cases the Supreme Court hears and decides, whether from lower federal courts or the highest court of the state, are there only because the Court in its discretion has granted a petition for a writ of *certiorari*. 28 U.S.C. §§ 1254 & 1257. The Justices' discretion over their docket is virtually complete and they have delegated considerable responsibility to their law clerks, the best and the brightest of recent law school graduates who serve a one-year apprenticeship usually after having spent a year in the chambers of a federal appeals court judge. Each Justice typically has four law clerks. The petition and a response are filed with the Court and a law clerk in the "cert pool" of law clerks writes a short memorandum to recommend whether or not the case is "certworthy." Any individual Justice can place a petition on the "discuss list" for a vote at their Conference but most cases do not even make it to the discuss list. Grants and denial are published on the orders list. (The "Conference" also is what the Justices call themselves when they act corporately to deal with administrative matters, like when they promulgate the Supreme Court's procedural rules.) Under the Court's rules, only compelling cases that present an important issue of federal law or a conflict in the way lower courts have ruled have a viable claim on the Justices' discretion. Sup. Ct. R. 10. But 99 out of 100 cases are denied review inside the Skinnerian black-box called the writ of *certiorari*.

Two other procedures have grown up around these jurisdictions. The Court will "dismiss as improvidently granted" ("DIG") a case after full briefing and sometimes oral argument when the Justices change their minds and conclude that the petition should not have been granted in the first place. *Nike, Inc. v. Kasky*, 539 U.S. 654 (2003). And in some cases, the Court will dispose of a case after reviewing only the petition for *certiorari* and the brief in opposition and without full briefing or oral argument; sometimes the Court simply will decide to grant review, summarily vacate the judgment, and remand ("GVR") a case without an opinion for further consideration in light of an intervening Supreme Court decision; sometimes the Court will issue a brief *per curiam* opinion reversing (or rarely affirming) the result below, frequently over a dissent complaining about the truncated appellate procedure. *Terrell v. Morris*, 493 U.S. 1 (1989).

Thus, the clichéd threat, "I will take this case all the way to the Supreme Court!" may be literally possible, but the odds are greatly against obtaining a Supreme Court ruling on the merits of any case. In the vast majority of cases brought before them, the only thing the Justices officially conclude and formally announce is that they will not hear or decide the issues. "The petition for a writ of *certiorari* to the court below is denied" is the lawyers' parlance. "*Certiorari*" was the name the common law gave a writ from a higher court to a lower court ordering that the record in a case be sent up for review. This is why newspapers can be very misleading when they report that the Supreme Court "approved" of some ruling by some lower court, when all that the Justices have done is deny review of the case. By tradition, it takes four Justices to agree to hear a case. Thus, a minority sets the agenda.

The Supreme Court only sits *en banc*, that is, all the Justices participate and decide every case. Its annual Term begins the first Monday in October and continues usually through the end of June. The Term is divided between two-week "sittings," when the Justices hear arguments and deliver opinions, and alternating "recesses," when they review petitions and work at writing their opinions. Its annual docket consists of more than 8,000 cases. Each October Term, the Court hears oral arguments (usually 30 minutes per side) and reads briefs (something of a misnomer for book-length written arguments filed by lawyers) in fewer than 100 cases—in recent Terms right around 80 cases. For these argued cases, the Justices write detailed, scholarly opinions, like the ones excerpted in your casebook but much longer. More often than not, some of the Justices will write concurring opinions, explaining why they agree with the outcome but for different reasons, and others will file dissenting opinions, explaining why they think the majority is wholly mistaken. The Chief Justice— or the most senior Justice in the majority when the Chief Justice is in the minority—assigns the responsibility of preparing a draft opinion for the Court. Individual Justices, however, are free to write separate opinions, and frequently do so, expressing their own views in a case. In *Marks v. United States*, 430 U.S. 188, 193 (1977) the Court provided the reader with this rule when there is no majority opinion: "When a fragmented Court decides a case and no single rationale explaining the result enjoys the assent of five Justices, the holding of the Court may be viewed as that position taken by those Members who concurred in the judgments on the narrowest grounds." However, that rule sometimes is very difficult for lawyers and lower court judges to apply. A full set of opinions in a major decision can run well over a hundred turgid densely written pages. So you should be grateful for the sorting and sifting of these opinions performed by the editor-author of your casebook.

All documents and briefs are matters of public record. Oral arguments are conducted in public. The decisions are announced in open court and then published. The only secret procedures are the Justices' conference—when the nine meet without any others present to discuss and vote on cases—and their confidential individual work in chambers. The Justices are aided by their law clerks in the arduous task of preparing opinions: researching the law, checking the lower court record, studying briefs and legal authorities, and exchanging memoranda with each other to argue points of law and to suggest changes in drafts. Not infrequently, this secret back-and-forth can result in one or more of the Justices rethinking an earlier vote thus shifting the ultimate outcome 180 degrees in a closely decided case. This can happen even in a high-profile case. *E.g.*, *Lee v. Weisman*, 505 U.S. 577 (1992) (Justice Kennedy changed his vote and changed the outcome to end up forbidding prayers at public school graduations).

In October Term 2017, the Court resolved 72 cases fully on the merits—only about 1% of the total petitions—and reversed or vacated 52 (72.2%) of them. The nine Justices wrote 71 majority opinions, 45 concurring opinions, and 49 dissenting opinions. There were 28 (39.4%) unanimous decisions. There were 19 (26.7%) decisions by a five to four vote. Volumes 568 to 570 of UNITED STATES REPORTS, the official reporter for the Supreme Court, contain 2,131 pages of opinions of the merits decisions for October Term 2017. Thus, each year more and more ponderous Talmudic volumes are added to the shelves of published interpretations of our great charter.

One thing is certain, whether the Court denies review or grants review and decides the merits: there is no further appeal. Justice Robert H. Jackson once aptly described the High Court's place atop the judicial hierarchy: "We are not final because we are infallible, but we are infallible only because we are final." *Brown v. Allen*, 344 U.S. 443, 540 (1953) (Jackson, J., concurring).

5.   AVOIDING THE MERITS

The Supreme Court has frequently admitted an institutional   reluctance   to   pass   on   the constitutionality of a duly-enacted statute even when the case technically falls within the counter-majoritarian doctrine of judicial review. Neither the convenience of the parties nor the importance to the public nor the policy preferences of the Justices are controlling. In his famous concurring opinion in *Ashwander v. Tennessee Valley Authority*, 297 U.S. 288, 341 (1936), Justice Brandeis codified a series of prudential rules under which the Supreme Court has avoided having to make an unnecessary or inappropriate constitutional ruling. He identified several categories of avoidance: a friendly or collusive suit, advisory opinions, issues not yet ripe for decision, the party bringing suit lacks standing from some injury in fact suffered resulting from the unconstitutional law which will be redressed by a judgment, an interlocutory appeal without a full and final judgment, and moot cases. These categories are familiar from the discussion earlier in this Chapter. Three other rules of judicial self-restraint deserve further amplification here.

First, there is an appellate procedural requirement that the Supreme Court has in common with all other appellate courts which applies to constitutional issues as well as to other issues on appeal, namely, the contemporaneous objection rule of procedure. *Cf.* FED. R. CRIM. P. 51. Constitutional law issues must be formally preserved as error to be appealable. A timely and proper objection must be made at trial to afford the trial court an immediate opportunity to avoid the alleged error and to signal the importance the party attaches to the question. Likewise, the issue must be presented on the first appeal as of right, again to offer that court the opportunity to remedy the error. This practice systematically reduces the need and demand for constitutional decisions by the Supreme Court and is a matter of deference towards the lower courts in the judicial hierarchy, as well. The writ of *certiorari* allows the Supreme Court complete control to select which of the issues presented in the petition will be granted review even so far as when the Court actually redrafts and restates the issue or issues to be briefed and argued by the parties.

Second, the Court will not consider a constitutional issue if the case has been disposed of in the lower court on some other non-constitutional ground that is sufficient to justify the final decision. The non-constitutional ground can be procedural or substantive. The non-constitutional ground must be independent and adequate. It must be independent of the federal constitutional ground and not be entwined with it either explicitly or implicitly. It must be adequate in the sense of being *bona fide* and broad enough to sustain the judgment and dispose of the case, *i.e.*, of sufficient legal significance to decide the case and to justify the Supreme Court's declination to reach the federal constitutional issue.

In cases from the highest court of a state, the independent and adequate state ground doctrine demonstrates due respect for the state court and avoids the risk of rendering unnecessary or advisory opinions in matters of federal constitutional law. Consequently, in *Michigan v. Long*, 463 U.S. 1032 (1983), the Supreme Court announced the prudential rule that a state supreme court must clearly state in its opinion that it is deciding the case on the independent and adequate state law ground and then the United States Supreme Court will not hear or decide the case. Otherwise, without the plain statement, the federal constitutional issue will be deemed still in play and subject to judicial review by the Supreme Court. In close and difficult cases, the Supreme Court still may remand the case to the state supreme court for a clarification of the basis of its decision.

The independent and adequate state ground doctrine highlights the importance of the Supremacy Clause and the structure of federalism. The interpretations of the United States Constitution by the United States Supreme Court establish the floor below which the state courts cannot go in protecting individual rights; state supreme courts can raise the ceiling and afford greater protections by interpreting state rights under the state constitution. For example, once the United States Supreme Court determined that commercial speech was protected by the First Amendment, a state supreme court could not reinterpret the First Amendment or some provision of the state constitution to say it somehow was not protected. That is the floor. However, once the United States Supreme Court ruled that obscene material was not protected by the First Amendment, a state supreme court could still interpret its state constitutional rights of conscience to protect obscene material. That would be raising the ceiling.

Third, one of the most significant of the prudential rules of self-restraint in the exercise of judicial review obliges the Supreme Court, in effect, to interpret the congressional statute being challenged in a way that makes it constitutional and valid. Faced with a statute that is ambiguous, as is often the case, the deciding court must choose between a broader interpretation that would make it unconstitutional and invalid versus a narrower interpretation that would render it constitutional and valid. It is obviously better for the administration of justice to choose the narrower interpretation when it is reasonable and appropriate. The Court should not go out of its way to declare statutes unconstitutional. It should not assume that the Congress intended to pass a statute that would be unconstitutional rather than one that would pass constitutional muster. Indeed, the assumption is just the opposite: whenever an otherwise acceptable construction of a statute would raise serious constitutional problems, the Supreme Court will interpret the statute and give it a reading that avoids such problems unless that reading is contrary to the plain intent of Congress. *Solid Waste Agency v. U.S. Army Corps of Eng'rs*, 531 U.S. 159, 173 (2001). This mechanism of interpreting statutes in a constitutional manner is a matter of deference to the Legislative Branch that is commonly used by the federal courts with regard to federal statutes and by the high courts of the states concerning their own state statutes.

There is, however, one quite important limitation on this judicial technique: the inexorable principle that the Supreme Court of the United States may use this technique only with respect to *federal* statutes.

It cannot interpret state and local statutes to render them constitutional. Rather, the Supreme Court must accept the state statute as it has been duly interpreted by the state court. The Supreme Court has no authority to narrow a state statute to make it constitutional. This limitation necessarily results in some decisions by the Supreme Court declaring state statutes and city ordinances unconstitutional in situations in which, if the statute were federal, the laws would not be declared unconstitutional but would simply be given a narrower interpretation.

This may be part of the reason that in the 200-plus years the Supreme Court has been reviewing statutes it has struck down an order of magnitude more local and state laws (approximately 1000) than federal statutes (approximately 150) as being unconstitutional. Recall that Justice Holmes once observed that he did not believe the United States would come to an end if the Supreme Court lost its power to strike down acts of Congress but he did believe that the Union would be imperiled if the Supreme Court did not take seriously its responsibility to strike down unconstitutional state laws.

Federalism and the concept of state sovereignty oblige this approach to state and local laws on the part of federal courts. The state court is the final authority on the meaning of its own state laws. No provision in the Constitution authorizes any part of the federal government to determine for a state what its law is. So too the Supreme Court of the United States has no authority whatsoever to change the definitive interpretation of state law by a state high court. It may and must, however, evaluate its constitutionality based on how the state law has been interpreted by the state court.

This is in some ways a peculiar and radical doctrine—the highest court of the state is *the final authority* on the interpretation and application of state laws. One important manifestation of this principle may be found in the so-called *Erie* Doctrine, which is often the bane of first-year Civil Procedure students. *See Erie R.R. Co. v. Tompkins*, 304 U.S. 64 (1938). As a matter of constitutional law, state law— not general federal common law—is the rule for decision in a diversity suit in federal district court between parties from different states. *See* 28 U.S.C. § 1332. A federal court must follow the lead of the state's highest court and must go so far as to follow the lead of lower state courts when there is no decisional law from the state's highest court; the federal judge must imagine how a state court would rule even if no state court has ever actually ruled on the question of state law at issue. However, the rule of state law that the federal court discerns, even if the federal court is the Supreme Court, is not at all binding precedent on the state courts in subsequent cases. Our federalism is a complicated system of government. *See* Chapter 6, § 1 (Federalism and Separation of Powers Illustrated).

6. NONJUSTICIABLE POLITICAL QUESTIONS

The power of judicial review is the power to interpret the Constitution in deciding cases and controversies. There is a category of cases, however, in which the Supreme Court interprets the Constitution to conclude that the issues presented are not proper issues for a court to decide in a case or controversy. Rather, political questions are to be resolved fully and finally by the coordinate political branches, the elected branches of the federal government, namely, the Congress and the President. This is an aspect of separation of powers in the federal government, particularly regarding the relationship and role of the Judicial Branch vis-à-vis the other two branches. *See* Chapter 6, § 11 (Separation of Powers—Judicial).

The Judicial Branch is constitutionally compromised from dealing with certain themes of government, for example, the procedures for amending the Constitution in Article V, the clause that guarantees to each state a republican form of government in Article IV, and the whole field of foreign relations, which is not addressed in so many words in the Constitution but which is understood to be an inherent aspect of external sovereignty under the primary control and responsibility of the President. *See Coleman v. Miller*, 307 U.S. 433 (1939); *United States v. Curtiss-Wright Exp. Corp.*, 299 U.S. 304 (1936); *Luther v. Borden*, 48 U.S. (7 How.) 1 (1849).

The "political question" doctrine—which the Justices also refer to as the "nonjusticiability doctrine"—does not place off-limits all issues or all cases that are somehow related to politics. Quite the contrary is the case. *See Bush v. Gore*, 531 U.S. 98 (2000) (dramatically ending the Florida recount in the Presidential election). The modern case that redefined the doctrine held that an Equal Protection challenge to the malapportionment of a state legislature was justiciable. *Baker v. Carr*, 369 U.S. 186 (1962). The holding was predictable once it was understood that the separation of powers was not in play. The case was about the Fourteenth Amendment and the state legislature and had nothing to do with the Congress or the President. There are several formulations of the political question doctrine, each one being a reason for the court to dismiss the case: (1) a constitutional commitment of the issue to a coordinate branch; (2) a lack of judicially manageable standards; (3) an initial policy determination calling for nonjudicial discretion; (4) the impossibility of deciding the case without disrespecting the other branches; (5) an unusual need to adhere to the political decision already made; and (6) the potential for embarrassment from multiple conflicting pronouncements by the different branches. These factors are rather abstract and the modern Supreme Court seems quite reluctant to apply them to conclude that an issue is a political question and nonjusticiable.

The judicial corollary to the political question doctrine, which preserves the power of judicial review, is that whether one of these formulations applies to commit the issue to a coordinate branch and the scope of that commitment are matters for the courts to hear and decide. The Supreme Court thus remains the ultimate interpreter of the Constitution. *Powell v. McCormack*, 395 U.S. 486 (1969).

If the Supreme Court determines that a case presents a nonjusticiable political question, that determination has the ultimate effect of leaving in place the decision of the coordinate political branch and that branch's underlying interpretation of its own constitutional powers. For example, the Supreme Court held that the procedures the Senate had followed in an impeachment trial of a federal judge, including a Senate rule by which a committee heard evidence and reported to the full Senate, were within the constitutional commitment of Article I, Section 3, Clause 6 that "The Senate shall have the sole Power to try all Impeachments." Thus, the Supreme Court's refusal to decide the merits allowed the Senate to determine its own procedures without being subject to judicial review. *See Nixon v. United States*, 506 U.S. 224 (1993).

7. CONCLUSION

It is a solemn moment, full of drama and importance, when the Marshall of the Supreme Court intones:

> *Oyez, oyez, oyez!* All persons having business before the Honorable, the Supreme Court of the United States, are admonished to draw near and give their attention, for the Court is now sitting.

God save the United States and this Honorable Court.

But each and every case has followed a prescribed jurisdictional and procedural path to that moment. Each and every case tells a story about real flesh-and-blood people, a genuine case or controversy over the wrongs they have suffered and the rights they seek to remedy. What the Supreme Court decides will determine the rule in their particular case and settle the general rule of law that is the Constitution for the entire nation. In the next Chapter we will turn our attention to the framework of constitutional analysis that provides the context for resolving these constitutional issues.

Finally, a legal practice tip: should you ever be struck by Supreme Court lightning and obtain a grant of a petition for a writ of *certiorari*, you should immediately repair to the Bible of Supreme Court practice: STEPHEN M. SHAPIRO, KENNETH S. GELLER, TIMOTHY S. BISHOP, EDWARD A. HARTNETT & DAN HIMMELFARB, SUPREME COURT PRACTICE (10th ed. 2013). *Oyez*!

CHAPTER 3
CONSTITUTIONAL ANALYSIS

This Chapter provides a theoretical and analytical justification for the overall approach of this book. It introduces the basic "constitutional diagram" that visually depicts all constitutional analysis to be the relative balance between individual freedom and liberty versus government power. This constitutional diagram will be the *leitmotif* throughout the rest of this book.

1. FUNCTIONS OF THE CONSTITUTION

The Preamble to the Constitution—the only part of the document most Americans know by heart because they memorized it in elementary school or because they sang along on Saturday morning on *Schoolhouse Rock!*—is merely an introductory filigree that was added at the conclusion of the Constitutional Convention by the Committee on Style. "Although that preamble indicates the general purposes for which the people ordained and established the Constitution," the Supreme Court has explained, "it has never been regarded as the source of any substantive power conferred on the government of the United States, or any of its departments." *Jacobson v. Massachusetts*, 197 U.S. 11, 14 (1905). The Constitution is not merely another text to be read or just another law to be interpreted, however. It is what Justice Holmes called "a constituent act" that calls into being a government and gives it a form and defines its organic nature.

Missouri v. Holland, 252 U.S. 416, 433 (1920). This generative document must be read as a whole to understand its purposes and functions.

If one reads the document functionally to appreciate its essential purposes, the Constitution performs four fundamental governmental functions:

(1) To establish a national government: Articles I, II, III, VI, and VII and Amendments 12, 16, 17, 20, 22, 23, 25, and 27.

(2) To control the relationship between the national government and the governments of the states: Article I, §§ 8 & 10, Article III, § 2, Article IV, and Amendments 10, 11, 18, and 21.

(3) To define and preserve personal liberty: Article I, § 9, and Amendments 1–10 (Bill of Rights), 13, 14, 15, 19, 24, and 26.

(4) To enable the government to perpetuate itself: Article V.

This rather general analysis can be made more useful by a closer examination of these four functions. The last-mentioned function, the power to amend the Constitution, is a unique and specific power in Article V that is essential to the Constitution to be sure, but it is of little direct concern to the substantive provisions of the Constitution that form the core of what we know as the study of "constitutional law." *See* Chapter 1, § 11 (Amendments).

Further, the first function, setting up a national government, and the second function, ordering the relationship between that national government and the governments of the states, may be treated together as constituting one of the two major relational aspects of constitutional analysis. *See* Chapter 5 (Government Powers); Chapter 6 (Structure of the Constitution). This leaves the remaining of the four functions as the other major relational aspect of constitutional analysis, namely the protection of individual liberty by limiting and restraining government power. *See* Chapter 4 (Constitutional Liberty); Appendix A (Leading Case Outline of Constitutional Liberty).

Therefore, constitutional analysis can be divided into two fundamental inquiries. One of these inquiries examines the relationship between governments, state and national, their respective organization and function, and their mutual authority. The other inquiry examines the protection of the civil rights and civil liberties of citizens against the exercise of government power, state and national, that would burden or deny individual freedom.

The various teaching materials used to teach the subject of constitutional law almost invariably are organized to first consider the constitutional provisions concerning the establishment of the national government and the relationship between the national government and state governments. Then, the materials typically go on to consider second the protections of individual liberty. While this analysis may be historically acceptable, arguably it is not analytically sound.

The earliest important Supreme Court cases interpreting the Constitution did involve issues about the organization and powers of the newly-established national government and how the exercise of those powers related to the powers of the state governments. But that was because back then the Constitution left the protection of individual liberty largely to the states. Subsequent amendments and consequential Supreme Court interpretations have changed all that, however. Therefore, while the historical approach to the subject might place the examination of government powers first and save individual liberty for last, the dynamic of modern constitutional law is all about individual rights.

Therefore, it is not analytically sound to consider the organization of the federal government and its relationship to the state governments before considering the constitutional aspects of individual liberty. This is because fundamental constitutional questions concerning the protection of individual liberty arise in all constitutional cases, including those allocating government power respectively to the national government or the state governments. So any analysis of the cases involving the distribution of powers between the state and federal governments merely postpones the more fundamental inquiry necessarily presented in each and every constitutional case or controversy: whether either government has the power to engage in the regulatory activity involved or whether neither government can impose the regulation because such regulation would interfere with constitutionally protected individual liberty.

The entire design of the written Constitution has as its primary purpose the protection of individual freedom and liberty. The Framers divided the government and set it against itself in an elaborate system of checks and balances, arranged vertically between the national and the state governments and horizontally among the three federal branches. The most powerful branch of the federal government was further subdivided into two houses, which together wield legislative powers that were limited and enumerated powers. This system of majority rule includes important safeguards against the possibility of a tyranny by the majority. A Bill of Rights (1791) was ratified almost immediately. The advent of the counter-majoritarian power of judicial review soon followed in 1803. The American constitutional regime thus is intended to minimize the likelihood of governmental tyranny and to maximize individual freedom and liberty. The underlying assumption is that government power and individual liberty exist in the oppositional tension of a zero-sum ratio: more government power results in less individual liberty and more individual liberty results in less government power. This is the perpetual dilemma of our constitutionalism: how to empower the government sufficiently to perform its essential tasks, and, at the same time, how to limit it from overreaching the individual. *See* Chapter 1 (American Constitutionalism); Front Materials page iii (quoting David Hume & James Madison). Our system is a system of ordered liberty, a system of law and order—not one without the other. The essence of the Constitution is that it is the law that the government must obey.

2. INDIVIDUAL LIBERTY VERSUS GOVERNMENT POWER

To aid in understanding the nature of the fundamental distinction between individual liberty and the exercise of government power and to provide us with a foundation for the rest of constitutional analysis, let us develop a simple imaginary concept that will be used throughout this book—the constitutional diagram.

Imagine, if you will, that we took all of the powers that a government might possibly wield—any government, anywhere, and any time in history, including the most autocratic and despotic governments imaginable—and we placed them all in a huge oblong box. Imagine the fictional dystopias from George Orwell's NINETEEN EIGHTY-FOUR or Aldous Huxley's BRAVE NEW WORLD. The box would contain the traditional and generally acceptable government powers, like the power to tax and spend for the general welfare, the power to regulate commerce, and the power to declare war and make peace. But also found in our box would be the tyrannical powers of the most fascist and totalitarian regimes throughout history and down to the present day. The box would contain the power for government troops to break into a person's home at night and drag the person out into the street and then shoot the person without charges or a trial. So also would be included the power to throw a person in prison for criticizing the government or the power to take away a person's home and other property without any excuse or reason and without any compensation. Other despotic powers would include using secret police to torture, imprison, or kill political dissenters and even turning the military on the citizenry to bomb and gas them in order to stay in power. So assume, if you will, that the box contains all imaginable government powers, including the most despicable and the ugliest examples of power practiced by evil governments like Nazi Germany and the former Soviet Union and modern-day Syria. Think of a *coup d'état* militaristic regime that depended on force and fear rather than elections and votes and constitutional processes. Think of a Star-Chamber-style government characterized by secrecy and acting irresponsibly and arbitrarily and oppressively. There are no individual rights and liberties. Government is all powerful. There are places like that in the world today where people live dehumanized and fearful existences. If this seems far-fetched to you, a 1L student living in the United States today, consider this social science factoid: in the Twentieth Century it is estimated that governments killed 262 million of their own people. That rate of "democide" was six times the number of people who were killed in combat in all the foreign and civil wars of the last century. *Google it!* That is the awful power of awful governments. In such an apocalyptic political system, only absolute government powers exist without limit—there are no individual rights:

Government Power

In the United States, under our Constitution, we divide this long oblong box into two parts. We will represent this here by drawing a vertical line through the box as shown:

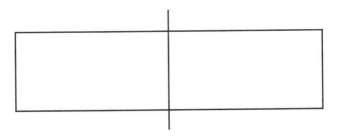

The reason for dividing the box in two parts is to take away from the government those powers that we do not allow our government to exercise. We deny the arbitrary and excessive powers of the despot and the tyrant in many particulars. We protect the individual citizen's rights of conscience against intrusions upon the freedom of speech and the free exercise of religion. We protect private property against arbitrary governmental interference. We provide procedural protections to those accused of a crime and we require full and fair court procedures before anyone can be punished by fine or imprisonment. So we set aside a considerably large part of this box of potential government powers. We declare that our government cannot have powers that would infringe upon our liberty. We guarantee rights to the individual in so many words in the Constitution.

After we have separated these excessive and undesirable government powers out of our total of all imaginable powers, we set them aside and place them totally off-limits to the government. We call governmental attempts to do these awful things in these constitutionally protected areas of personal autonomy either denials of "freedom" or violations of "individual liberty." Or, as we will see later, we sometimes simply invoke the shorthand expression "due process of law" to order that the government to cease and desist its improper conduct. We accomplish this withdrawal of awful government powers by writing into the Constitution a Bill of Rights and other protections of individual liberty. And we expect courts to enforce these constitutional limitations when the government does not respect its own limits, for the Constitution is the law for the government. *See* Chapter 1, § 2 (Rule of Law).

So now our imaginary box of government powers looks like this:

Freedom or Individual Liberty	Government Power

This is the basic constitutional diagram, although there will be further refinements and variations in the rest of this book. On the left side, within the dotted lines, we have that part of the original box of government powers where power has been taken away from our government under our constitutional system. Government is denied the power to do those things *to* us. We call that area: freedom or individual liberty. On the right side are the remaining government powers. Those are the legitimate powers that are not taken away by our constitutional guarantees of liberty. Government is given the power to do those things we want the government to do *for* us. It is the Constitution that divides our box by drawing the line that protects our liberties from government powers. American constitutionalism depends for its legitimacy on the consent of the governed; sovereignty, the source of all government power, is located in the people. *See* Chapter 1, § 3 (Republican Form of Government).

A word of caution: although our schematic line is drawn down the middle of our constitutional diagram, it was carefully stated above that the box was divided into two parts, not precisely divided in half. There is no attempt by the placement of the line to show how much government power has been taken out of the total potential of absolute, corrupt, despotic, and tyrannical powers. At the moment, we are not interested in the quantity of power granted or denied to the government. We are interested only in the nature of the qualities of the powers involved and their zero-sum relationship with individual freedom and liberty. Understand this and you understand what is at stake in Constitutional Law.

To understand the application of this imagined configuration of rights and powers, which from now on will be referred to as simply the constitutional diagram, consider a simple, although profoundly important, constitutional issue. Suppose a person makes a speech endorsing and advocating the revolutionary overthrow of the government. As many readers probably already know, under the Constitution, this revolutionary advocacy is not automatically subject to criminal prosecution and punishment by our government, as it might be under the regimes of some other countries. If this endorsement of revolution merely amounts to advocacy of an abstract and philosophical nature, that there is a theoretical right to revolution, or even if the advocacy goes farther to claim that the resort to violence is morally and politically proper, nonetheless, it is protected under the First Amendment freedom of speech. According to well-established Supreme Court precedents, the government may act to forbid or proscribe such advocacy if and only if it is "directed to inciting or producing imminent lawless action" and the advocacy also is "likely to incite or produce such action." *Brandenburg v. Ohio*, 395 U.S. 444 (1969).

In terms of our constitutional diagram, the issue in such a case is simply whether the case falls on the left side of the dividing line, in the area of individual freedom, *i.e.*, the government may not prohibit the speech [1], or whether the case falls on the right side in the area of government power, *i.e.*, the government does have the power to control the speech [2]:

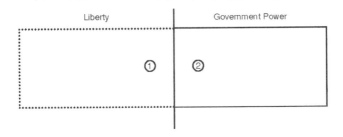

To make this analysis even clearer, consider another example also illustrated in the above Figure. Suppose a book is alleged to be obscene. Is it protected free speech, or is it a book that is not protected free speech and, therefore, it is a book that can be censored and banned from circulation by the government? The issue in terms of our constitutional diagram is whether the result of the case falls in the area of individual liberty of the author, the publisher, and the reader, on the left side [1], or whether the case falls in the area of government power on the right side of the line [2]. Again, the vertical line that divides our constitutional diagram is the dividing line between protected individual liberty on one side and legitimate government power to control the activities and conduct of persons on the other side.

Virtually all constitutional issues involving individual liberty are subject to this simple and elegant representation, although the actual decision in many cases is a difficult and complex one that is not easily predicted by the constitutional diagram. The purpose of this simplified analysis is not to suggest that constitutional decision-making is simple and easy. Rather, the purpose of the constitutional diagram is to better understand the essential nature of constitutional decision-making, *i.e.*, what constitutional interests are being balanced and how the balancing affects those interests.

Implicit in the description of the nature of individual liberty set out above is a fundamental principle of constitutional analysis. Constitutional individual liberty in our system of government, with a few qualifications yet to be described, is almost always an issue of individual freedom against *government power*. It consists of the protection of the individual from overreaching or undue intrusion *by the government*. Liberty, in constitutional definition, usually does not consist of individual freedom from intrusions by other private individuals. Society protects an individual from intrusion by other private individuals with the law of torts and through the enforcement of the criminal law. Those civil law remedies and criminal law protections, which are the creation of the common law and legislative enactments, protect the property and the personal security of the individual against being harmed by other individuals. Such governmental policies and protections must always satisfy the Constitution. Thus, when the government intervenes on the side of the victim to punish the wrongdoer, the government is exercising its constitutional power and the wrongdoer's individual liberty is being truncated to the benefit of the particular victim and to the general benefit of society in terms of law and order.

This point is fundamental. It can be demonstrated with a simple example. Suppose Cain, a private citizen, mugs Abel, another private citizen, and robs him at gunpoint of his wallet containing $200, his cellphone, and his expensive designer wristwatch. Has the Constitution been violated? Clearly not. Yet certainly citizen Abel, in the words of the Constitution, has been "deprived of his property without due process of law." But it is not unconstitutional for private citizen Cain to rob private citizen Abel because the Constitution prohibits only the *government,* state or federal, from depriving a person of property without due process of law. The protection of the individual person's right not to have his personal property taken from him by another private person is contained in the criminal law enacted by the state government. Abel might also bring a civil lawsuit sounding in torts against Cain. Criminal law and tort law are legal protections created by the government, not protections contained in the Constitution. Only if the *government* takes the property of a person does the Constitution come into play to require due process and just compensation. U.S. Const. amends. V & XIV.

This principle, which is absolutely basic to the understanding of constitutional rights, explains why it is important to emphasize that it is the limitations and prohibitions upon *government* power that are represented on the left side of the constitutional diagram. The constitutional liberty depicted on that left side of the constitutional diagram involves the protection of the individual from governmental intrusion, not the protection of the individual from harms or offenses committed by wrongdoers who are other private persons. The Constitution—and in turn the Supreme Court interpreting the Constitution— are concerned only with the relationship between the individual person and the government.

This principle is called the "state action doctrine," although that term is something of a misnomer because the Constitution applies in the relationship of the individual citizen with both the states and the federal government. Furthermore, every governmental actor in each of the three branches must follow and obey the Constitution when acting under color of law. The dichotomy is that state action is subject to the Constitution and private action is not. *Civil Rights Cases*, 109 U.S. 3 (1883). The Supreme Court's state action doctrine is elaborated with considerable detail in the Appendix. *See* Appendix A, § 3 (State Action).

For present purposes, however, there is one important exception to the state action requirement, as well as some relevant qualifications of the doctrine. The Thirteenth Amendment is the textual exception. The wording of that Amendment is peculiar when compared to the wording of the other Amendments. The First Amendment uses the noun of direct address: "Congress shall make no law * * *." The Fourteenth Amendment reads, in part: "No State shall * * *." However, the Thirteenth Amendment is written differently: it abolishes the institution of slavery so far as the government *and* individuals are concerned. Thus, in theory and in practice (though the cases are rare today), a private person can violate the Thirteenth Amendment by holding another person in slavery or involuntary servitude. If Cain held Abel in slavery, Cain would be violating the Thirteenth Amendment.

The state action doctrine is not much of a doctrine in that the Supreme Court has eschewed any formal test in favor of a totality of the circumstances approach "sifting facts and weighing circumstances" on an *ad hoc* or case-by-case basis. *Burton v. Wilmington Parking Auth.*, 365 U.S. 715, 722 (1961). In most cases, however, whether or not there is state action is so obvious that the requirement is not even discussed. When a state legislature passes a law, when a Governor enforces a statute, or when a state court issues an order, those are obvious examples of state action and the constitutional analysis moves straight away to the merits and the constitutional diagram to balance individual liberty against government power. *Shelley v. Kraemer*, 334 U.S. 1 (1948).

The qualifications of the doctrine are found in wavering and often overlapping lines of Supreme Court precedents. When the government has become entangled with private conduct by authorizing, encouraging, or facilitating the private conduct, the private actor must comply with the Constitution. *Lugar v. Edmondson Oil Co.*, 457 U.S. 922 (1982). To apply the Constitution to a private party, however, the court must be satisfied that the claimed constitutional deprivation resulted from the exercise of some right or privilege having its source in state authority and that the private party being charged with the deprivation can be fairly described as a state actor. *Edmonson v. Leesville Concrete Co.*, 500 U.S. 614 (1991).

The other wrinkle in the state action doctrine involves a statute enacted by Congress pursuant to its powers to enforce the Fourteenth Amendment by appropriate legislation. U.S. Const. amend. XIV, § 5. In these cases, the court must decide first if the private party comes under the statute and second if the statute is within the legislative powers of Congress. *See* Chapter 4, § 7 (Congressional Enforcement).

To emphasize by repetition, in the run of constitutional cases, the state action requirement is plainly satisfied and the federal court will move on to the constitutional analysis of the merits. There is no denying, however, that in difficult and close cases the application of the state action doctrine can be divisive and frustrating even to the Justices, as well as to students of the Supreme Court. When the majority in

DeShaney v. Winnebago Cty. Dept. of Soc. Servs., 489 U.S. 189 (1989), held that a state agency's failure to protect a young boy from his father's repeated violence did not violate due process, the dissent accused the majority of "retreating into a sterile formalism which prevents it from recognizing either the facts of the case before it or the legal norms that should apply to those facts." *Id.* at 212 (Blackmun, J., dissenting). In the aftermath of such a constitutional holding—that the Constitution does not apply to the alleged wrongdoing—the parties are left with non-constitutional remedies sounding in state tort law and criminal law. *See also Castle Rock v. Gonzales*, 545 U.S. 748 (2005) (the failure of the police to enforce a restraining order did not violate the Due Process Clause even though the consequence of their failure resulted in murder); Chapter 4, § 8 (Liberty from Private Violations).

For present purposes and subject only to the peculiar exception and qualifications mentioned above, it should be clearly understood that when we refer to individual liberty, civil rights and civil liberties, constitutional freedoms, or due process of law, we are referring to protections of the individual from actions of the government that might infringe upon those freedoms and liberties. In the terms of the constitutional diagram we are developing, the constitutional analysis adjusts the tension between individual liberty on the one side and government power on the other. Again, our constitutional system is a system of ordered liberty.

3.   LIBERTY AND FEDERALISM

The balance between individual liberty and governmental power is the first of the two major and fundamental constitutional issues identified earlier in this Chapter. The other fundamental issue can best be demonstrated by returning to our constitutional diagram. Only after it has been decided that the constitutional question does not fall in the area of freedom or individual liberty does this second constitutional question arise. It does not arise at all in most nations; it does not arise in the United Kingdom, for example. But it does arise in the United States because ours is a federal system. The Framers were the first to invent the theory that two sovereign governments could govern the same territory and the same people at the same time. *See* Chapter 1, § 6 (Federalism).

All constitutional government power is either a federal power or a state power or a shared federal and state power. The principle of the limited and enumerated congressional powers merely is a mirror of the principle of reserved state police powers to legislate for the health, safety, morals, and general welfare. If a power has been expressly delegated to the national government, then the Tenth Amendment expressly disclaims any reservation of that same power to the states. Likewise, if a power is an attribute of state sovereignty that has been reserved to the states by the Tenth Amendment, then it is necessarily not a power that has been conferred on the national government. *New York v. United States*, 505 U.S. 144 (1992).

Under our Constitution, therefore, we take the government powers remaining after the initial denial of power, which constitutes the fundamental reservation of our individual liberty, and then we divide those remaining legitimate powers again, into two sets of government powers, one state and the other federal. This is how it appears in simplified form on our constitutional diagram:

Liberty	Government Power
	Federal
	State

Again, there must be a word of caution about the constitutional diagram. The depiction above is not an attempt to indicate the quantitative distribution of power between the state and federal governments. This new line is only a stylized representation of the fact that in a federal system we subdivide our government powers into federal powers and state powers. This version of the constitutional diagram is admittedly highly unrefined.

Later in this Chapter and in later Chapters, we will contemplate more nuanced questions about the distribution of power between state and federal governments and we will refine the constitutional diagram to illustrate the intricate and complex nature of the allocation of federal and state power over constitutional history. *See* Chapter 5 (Government Powers); Chapter 6 (Structure of the Constitution). We will study later, in some detail, how a particular subject of public policy might be concurrently regulated by both the states and the federal government. *See* Chapter 5, § 8 (Dormant or Negative Commerce Clause). Theoretically, it is more complete and more accurate to think of three different and distinct categories of government powers: exclusively federal; exclusively state; or shared by the states with the federal government. So in the previous constitutional diagram with the federal/state dividing line, an exercise of government power might be above the line and exclusively federal or below the line and exclusively state or simultaneously above and below the line to be shared by both the states and the federal government.

For now, this diagram is adequate to focus us on the second of the two fundamental constitutional issues: Which government, state or federal, has the power to engage in this kind of regulation? Or, as just mentioned, can both levels of government do so? As was explained above, however, this second issue need be considered only after it has been decided first that the case falls on the government power side of the diagram, *i.e.*, only after it is has been decided that the particular governmental action being challenged does not fall on the side of freedom and individual liberty protected by the Constitution.

This constitutional diagram illustrates the typology of rights and powers memorialized in the

Tenth Amendment, which was ratified in 1791 as part of the original Bill of Rights, and which reads: "The powers not delegated to the United States by the Constitution, nor prohibited by it to the States, are reserved to the States respectively, or to the people." Sovereignty—governmental power and legitimacy—has its source in the people. The people delegated limited and enumerated powers to the national government in the Constitution, like the power to regulate commerce among the states in Article I, Section 8, Clause 3. The people prohibited the States from performing some powers, like the prohibition against states making treaties in Article I, Section 10, Clause 1. Other powers are reserved to the states so far as the states exercised those powers before the Constitution. All other residual powers are reserved to the people. *See U.S. Term Limits, Inc. v. Thornton*, 514 U.S. 779 (1995). That is the Tenth Amendment tautology.

Sometimes it is helpful to posit a hypothetical situation that is improbable and even far-fetched to better understand the constitutional analysis and to make it more memorable. Let us assume such an imaginary situation to see how constitutional issues may arise with respect to both fundamental constitutional questions: (1) the balance of individual liberty versus government power and (2) the distribution of power between the state and federal governments. Suppose that a *state* passed a law requiring that all U.S. coins containing silver and copper be turned in to the state government in exchange for new aluminum alloy coins of the state's making of the same face value. The state's obvious motive would be to recover the silver and copper from the coins and sell the more valuable metals as a means of increasing the state treasury.

A numismatist citizen challenges the state's new policy claiming that it interferes with his individual freedom. He asserts the state may not take the silver and copper coins, which are part of his prized coin collection, and compel the exchange for new alloy coins of the same denomination that are intrinsically not as valuable and not as attractive to numismatists. The coin collector asserts that he is being deprived of property without due process of law.

But the lawyer who represents the coin collector, if she knows her constitutional analysis, will also assert an additional argument in the alternative: even if it is decided that the government may force citizens to give up their coin collections and take in exchange other coins of the same face value, the *state* government has no power to do this because under our constitutional system only the *federal* government has this power. The argument is that the federal government's power over coins and currency is an exclusive power and is forbidden to the states.

Our citizen thus has two chances to prevail. He may win on the individual liberty claim, which is that neither government, state nor federal, can force him to give up his silver and copper coins for ones of the same face value but of less intrinsic value. But even losing on that point, he may nonetheless prevail on his claim that state governments in our system have no power to coin money—that only the federal government has the power to do so.

On the basis of cases that arose as the result of the United States government going off the gold standard and requiring citizens to turn in gold coins in the middle 1930s, we can be more certain in this hypothetical than we can on most constitutional issues about how this case would come out. The Supreme Court would be expected to hold that the citizen may be compelled, as against the claim of individual liberty, to turn in the "coin of the realm" and be compensated only for the face value through new coins of the same denomination. *Gold Clause Cases*, 294 U.S. 240 (1935). The citizen would lose on the individual liberty versus government power constitutional issue.

Nonetheless, our citizen in this hypothetical case will prevail against the state policy. The constitutional decisions clearly indicate that the coinage of money and the establishment of money as legal tender are matters exclusively for the federal government and the states have no control or power over our monetary system. Indeed, the text of the Constitution is abundantly clear: Congress is delegated the power to coin money in Article I, Section 8, Clause 5, and the states are expressly prohibited the same power in Article I, Section 10, Clause 1. *See also* U.S. Const. art. I, § 8, cl. 18 (Necessary and Proper Clause) & art. VI (Supremacy Clause).

The first constitutional issue in our hypothetical case was whether the policy fell on the side of individual liberty or on the side of government power and the decision was to locate it on the side of government power. But then by showing affirmatively that the governmental power to engage in this activity is lodged wholly and exclusively in the federal government, our citizen wins his challenge to the state law. Let us mark this sequence of constitutional analysis on the constitutional diagram:

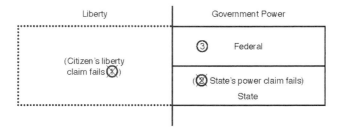

The result in this case is that the claimed power is found in the federal portion of the government power representation [3]. The citizen fails in the first claim of liberty [1]. But the citizen prevails because, by showing that the power to regulate is solely in federal hands [3], the state's assertion of power to regulate must be rejected [2]. Only if the Court had somehow found that power lay in the state, could the state win this case.

This hypothetical demonstrates how a case nearly always involves both basic constitutional issues but the second issue of distribution of power between state and federal governments is pertinent only if the first issue is decided in favor of government power as against individual liberty. *Cf. Wickard v. Filburn*, 317 U.S. 111 (1942) (individual wheat farmer did not have a due process right to grow as much wheat as he desired and the federal government had the power to limit how much wheat he could grow under the Commerce Clause plus the Necessary and Proper Clause). These two questions follow in logical sequence. This is why we always begin our constitutional analysis by first balancing constitutional freedom or individual liberty against government power. The constitutional diagram illustrates this analytical sequence.

4. HISTORY OF CONSTITUTIONAL LIBERTY

As we learned in Chapter 1, § 10 (Individual Rights), the underlying philosophy of American constitutionalism is the philosophy of individual rights. Modern constitutional law is dominated by rights and rights talk. Our constitutional analysis visually depicted in the constitutional diagram follows suit. We have been preoccupied and will continue to be preoccupied with the balance between individual liberty versus government power.

Therefore, the next important question is to ask: Where in the text does the Constitution provide for the protection of these fundamental civil rights and civil liberties? The modern answer to that question is to refer to the Bill of Rights. For historical reasons, however, that answer requires further elaboration and a brief digression.

The delegates to the Constitutional Convention of 1787 depended on structural limitations to protect individual liberty: the national powers were limited and enumerated; the national powers were separated among the three branches; the national legislative power was subdivided between two houses; and the three branches of the national government were set against each other in a system of checks and balances. This structure was designed to protect individual liberty and at the same time to empower government sufficient unto its necessary and proper tasks. As far as federalism was concerned, the state governments were expected to be the guardians of individual liberty guaranteed in their state constitutions. The original Constitution did not contain a federal bill of rights. *See also* Chapter 6 (Structure of the Constitution).

The intense debate over ratification of the Constitution revised this fundamental expectation. The powerful opposition of the Antifederalists persuaded even the Constitution's Federalist proponents that a bill of rights was needed to complete their work. The widely perceived threat to individual liberty then was the newly created national government. A set of amendments were quickly proposed by the first Congress and duly ratified by the states in 1791. The purpose of the Bill of Rights, therefore, was to protect individual citizens against the federal government—specifically and only the federal government. This was their intended meaning and their obvious effect. While the First Amendment is quite explicit in this regard ("Congress shall make no law * * *."), this was the understanding of all the other amendments, as well. This understanding was confirmed relatively early in our constitutional history by a unanimous Supreme Court decision authored by Chief Justice John Marshall. *Barron v. Baltimore*, 32 U.S. (7 Pet.) 243 (1833).

Consider the implications of this early principle and early decision for constitutional analysis at the time. There was no protection for the right of free speech or the free exercise of religion in the Constitution of the United States if it was a state law that was restricting the speech or interfering with the religious exercise of an individual citizen. Ditto for all the other provisions in the Bill of Rights that today we take for granted to be fundamental and fully protected. Back then, the prevailing constitutional faith was that the state legislatures and state courts, bound by their state bills of rights in their state constitutions, would protect citizens from intrusion upon personal liberties by the states. The Bill of Rights in the Constitution of the United States was only addressed to the national government. In effect, this amounted to something of a constitutional double-standard: the national government was bound to observe the Bill of Rights but the state governments were not.

The constitutional paroxysm of the Civil War brought about a complete reorientation with respect to individual liberty and government power. Until the Civil War, those who were concerned about personal liberty feared a strong federal government and expected the protection of the state governments.

After the Civil War, the states were no longer trusted to protect and preserve liberty. Again, the shift in political understanding resulted in a set of important amendments, the Civil War Amendments, sometimes called the Reconstruction Amendments. Eventually, these amendments and their Supreme Court interpretations would put an end to the constitutional double-standard.

The Thirteenth Amendment (1865) abolished slavery. The Fifteenth Amendment (1870) undertook to preserve the right to vote regardless of race, color, or previous condition of servitude. But the Fourteenth Amendment (1868) eventually would become the great engine of individual civil rights and civil liberties. Indeed, the greatest part of modern constitutional law originates in one sentence in the Fourteenth Amendment, really from only two clauses: the Due Process Clause and the Equal Protection Clause. Four words—"due process" and "equal protection"—generate the largest portion of pages in your casebook.

More than a century later, there is still a somewhat unresolved historical debate about the scope of the Fourteenth Amendment. Was the first section designed to overrule *Barron v. Baltimore* and make all the protections of the Bill of Rights applicable to the states? If so, the federal government and the federal courts would become responsible for insuring that the states did not interfere with the freedom of speech, the free exercise of religion, the various criminal procedure protections, and the other rights listed in the first eight amendments.

The Supreme Court is a court of law, not a court of history, and the Justices are trained in law, not history. Over the years, various historians have assigned passing or failing grades to the different opinions of the Justices on this subject. But whatever side Clio, the Muse of history, might have taken, we will endeavor to faithfully rehearse their debates for our own understanding of what is at stake for constitutional analysis.

Though the holding of the case has been overruled, *Adamson v. California*, 332 U.S. 46 (1947), is notable for the classic debate between Justice Hugo Black and Justice Felix Frankfurter. In dissent, Justice Black took what is called the "total incorporation" view to argue that the Fourteenth Amendment totally incorporated all the provisions in the Bill of Rights and made them all applicable to the states in the same way they applied to the federal government. In his separate concurring opinion, Justice Frankfurter rejected Justice Black's approach in favor of a "selective incorporation" approach that defined due process of law to include only those rights that are deemed necessary to assure the fundamental fairness of a scheme of ordered liberty. Each side of the debate scored points by using the text, the history, and the logic of the Constitution.

This historical dispute went on unabated in the pages of U.S. REPORTS for a generation. *See Moore v. City of East Cleveland*, 431 U.S. 494 (1977) (White, J., dissenting) (summarizing the Supreme Court debate over the issue). It would be accurate to say that the "selective incorporation" approach has resulted in a nearly-but-not-quite-total incorporation of the provisions in the Bill of Rights. The modern test of incorporation is whether the right is "fundamental to the American scheme of justice * * *." *Duncan v. Louisiana*, 391 U.S. 145, 149 (1968). Most but not all provisions have been incorporated. Furthermore, once a provision in the Bill of Rights is deemed incorporated into the Fourteenth Amendment and applied to the states, it has the same content and imposes the same limitations on the states as it imposes on the federal government. *Malloy v. Hogan*, 378 U.S. 1 (1964). From time to time, however, some individual Justices have taken the view that an incorporated right ought to be applied less strictly against the states. *E.g., Apodaca v. Oregon*, 406 U.S. 404 (1972) (Powell, J., concurring); *Roth v. United States*, 354 U.S. 476 (1957) (Harlan, J., concurring and dissenting). And a pair of recent Justices seem to have hinted that some clauses, particularly the Establishment Clause, could and should somehow be un-incorporated. *See Zelman v. Simmons-Harris*, 536 U.S. 639, 676 (2002) (Thomas, J., concurring); *Lee v. Weisman*, 505 U.S. 577, 641 (1992) (Scalia, J., dissenting).

The history of the Supreme Court's approach towards interpreting the Fourteenth Amendment to subject state intrusions against individual liberty to the prohibitions and limitations in the Bill of Rights is an instructive episode in how constitutional law changes and develops.

The key decision came early, only five years after the adoption of the Fourteenth Amendment in 1868.

In the *Slaughter-House Cases*, 83 U.S. (16 Wall.) 36 (1873), the Court turned firmly away from interpreting the Privileges or Immunities Clause of the amendment to incorporate the Bill of Rights and make them applicable against the states. The plaintiff challenged a state-created business monopoly in slaughterhouses asserting that his right to engage in the slaughterhouse business, prohibited by the government-created monopoly, was a "privilege or immunity" of a United States citizen under the Fourteenth Amendment. The Court denied that he had a federal right to engage in the slaughterhouse business. The impact of the decision was that the citizen was not entitled to claim liberties against state intrusion in the United States Constitution; he could look only to the laws of his state as a source of his rights on the matter.

For all intents and purposes, this decision and others that followed it read the Privileges or Immunities Clause out of the Fourteenth Amendment. Since 1873, only one case applied this clause to strike down a state law, *Colgate v. Harvey*, 296 U.S. 404 (1935), and even that case was overruled five years later, *Madden v. Kentucky*, 309 U.S. 83 (1940). That was what the clause meant— zip-zero-nothing-*nada*—until the 1999 decision in *Saenz v. Roe*, 526 U.S. 489. That decision surprised constitutionalists when the Supreme Court struck down a state welfare law that burdened the "right to travel"—the right to move from one state to another—that the Court deemed was protected by the Privilege or Immunities Clause. Whether this decision will ever lead to a judicial revitalizing of the clause still remains to be seen. In a concurring opinion, Justice Clarence Thomas did suggest that the Court's interpretation of the clause in the *Slaughter-House Cases* "contributed in no small part to the current disarray of our Fourteenth Amendment jurisprudence * * *." *Id.* at 527–28. In *McDonald v. City of Chicago*, 561 U.S. 742 (2010), however, a majority expressly declined the petitioner's new invitation to reconsider the 1873 interpretation of the Privilege or Immunities Clause. But that is getting ahead of the story of the Court's interpretation of the Fourteenth Amendment and how the "current disarray" developed.

At first haltingly and with considerable uncertainty in *dicta*, then in holdings which eventually developed the momentum of *stare decisis*, the Supreme Court began to give content to the Due Process Clause. The earliest cases were more about protecting property rights, but they were followed by cases involving liberty that coincided with the development of what is called substantive due process. *Lochner v. New York*, 198 U.S. 45 (1905). But again, we are getting ahead of the story.

After the *Slaughter-House Cases* and other similar cases that adhered to that narrow interpretation of the Fourteenth Amendment, and before the Supreme Court began to develop any momentum to protect individual liberty as against state governments, our basic constitutional diagram of constitutional analysis looked like this:

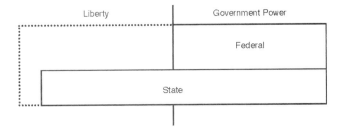

Now we are for the first time engaging in a *quantitative* evaluation as we examine this constitutional diagram. As far as the Constitution of the United States was concerned, there was little protection of liberty against state government powers. The protection against the federal government, of course, was broad because the Bill of Rights applied there. We draw our line indicating the sweep of state power as against the liberty claim still leaving some protection of liberty against the states, but not very much. There are a few provisions to be found in the original text of the Constitution in Article I, Sections 9 and 10, which protect individual liberty and limit state government power, like the prohibitions on bills of attainder, e*x post facto* laws, and laws impairing the obligation of contracts, as well as the prohibition of suspending the privilege of the writ of *habeas corpus*. But this was all there was for a long time.

For the first 150 years of our Constitution, until the Great Depression and World War II called into being the modern federal Leviathan we take for granted today, the federal government was a relatively modest entity of government, at least domestically. Consequently, there were few occasions for the Supreme Court to interpret and apply the Bill of Rights even to the federal government. Some First Amendment cases percolated up around World War I. The failed constitutional experiment with Prohibition (Eighteenth Amendment (1919) repealed by the Twenty-First Amendment (1933)), generated some issues concerning criminal procedures. But by and large our federalism was balanced in favor of the states. Our constitutional diagram is a diagram depicting the balance of individual liberty versus government power under the Constitution of the United States only; it does not reveal anything about the state constitutions. Thus, the previous constitutional diagram shows the narrow scope of the authority of federal constitutional control over state power when the states were accused of violating the federal rights of citizens of the United States.

Late in the 19th century and early in the 20th century, however, the Supreme Court began a gradual process of deciding that particular provisions in the Bill of Rights—understood by their own terms to apply only to the federal government—did apply to the states as well through the Due Process Clause in the Fourteenth Amendment.

The phrase "nor shall any State deprive any person of life, liberty, or property, without due process of law" could well have been taken as guaranteeing procedural rights and procedural rights only. The Supreme Court so interpreted it early on and individual members of the Court persisted in that interpretation for some time. Exercising the power of judicial review, the Supreme Court repeatedly was called on to give meaning and content to the concepts of "due process" and "liberty." The Justices developed a dichotomy that only a legally trained mind could conceive when they began to distinguish between a logical redundancy and a logical contradiction: between "procedural due process" (process-process?) and "substantive due process" (substantive process?). Thus began the so-called "Incorporation Doctrine" debate that was described earlier.

The Fourteenth Amendment was ratified in 1868. One of the earliest decisions to incorporate a provision from the Bill of Rights and to apply it to the states was an 1897 case, *Chicago, Burlington, & Quincy R.R. Co. v. City of Chicago*, 166 U.S. 226 (1897), that held it was a denial of "due process of law" under the Fourteenth Amendment when a state deprived a citizen of property without just compensation within the meaning of the so-called "eminent domain" provisions found in the Fifth Amendment. Eminent domain is the governmental power to condemn private property—to take title and possession of it—for public use by paying just compensation. *See* Appendix A, § 7 (Takings).

In the full sweep of American constitutional history, it is surprising to realize that it was not until 1925 in the case of *Gitlow v. New York*, 268 U.S. 652, that the Supreme Court for the first time incorporated the First Amendment protection of the freedom of speech into the Fourteenth Amendment and applied it to the states. So it was not until 135 years after the adoption of the Constitution that the Supreme Court recognized and established its power to protect an individual citizen's free speech liberty against an oppressive state law. And it was not until 1940, in the case of *Cantwell v. Connecticut*, 310 U.S. 296, that the First Amendment protection of the free exercise of religion was made applicable to the states by reading it into the "due process of law" clause of the Fourteenth Amendment. Today, we take for granted these protections of the freedom of conscience.

The incorporation doctrine has just about run its course. Over the last century, gradually and in fits and spurts, most of the provisions in the Bill of Rights have been incorporated into the Due Process Clause of the Fourteenth Amendment and applied to the states. Most recently, a majority incorporated and applied the Second Amendment right to bear arms to the states through the Due Process Clause. *McDonald v. City of Chicago*, 561 U.S. 742 (2010). In our constitutional diagram, the effect of these decisions has been to shrink the area of permissible state intrusion into the field of individual liberty protected by the Constitution as indicated with the dotted lines and the arrow:

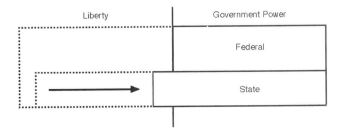

This process of incorporation accelerated during the Warren Court era (1953–69), especially in the area of constitutional criminal procedure. Indeed, earlier editions of the casebooks and courses in constitutional law a generation ago actually included chapters on criminal procedure until those annotations became so numerous and the law so detailed and complex that the subject developed into multiple "spin-off" courses in the law school curriculum that emphasize the Fourth, Fifth, Sixth and Eighth Amendments. This follows the emphasis of the authors of the Bill of Rights: 12 of the 23 separate rights in the first eight amendments relate to criminal procedure. In early English history and in the contemporary world, government regimes are prone to make expedient use of the criminal law.

Today, most of the provisions in the Bill of Rights have been made applicable to the states by interpreting them into the expansive "due process of law" clause of the Fourteenth Amendment. The ones that have not been incorporated make for a shorter list, as one reads down the first eight amendments. The Third Amendment prohibition on quartering troops has not been the subject of Supreme Court holdings to make it applicable to the states. The clause in the Fifth Amendment requiring an indictment by a grand jury is the only clause in that amendment that has not been incorporated. The Seventh Amendment right to jury trials in civil suits over $20 has not been incorporated. The Ninth Amendment and the Tenth Amendment do not apply to the states at all and for that reason some constitutionalists do not even consider them to be part of the Bill of Rights strictly speaking, although they were proposed and ratified together with the other amendments. These last remaining provisions that have not been incorporated are not likely ever to be incorporated. Therefore, the lines in our constitutional diagram above that demarcate federal power and state power under the Constitution still do not lineup exactly.

This process of incorporation has become so complete and so ingrained that sometimes constitutionalists and even some Justices commit a mental lapse and refer to "the freedom of speech" issue or "the First Amendment issue" in a case bringing a challenge to a state statute. *See Texas v. Johnson*, 491 U.S. 397, 399 (1989) (Brennan, J., majority opinion). The careful constitutional analyst, however, would correctly invoke and cite to "the Due Process Clause of the Fourteenth Amendment as it incorporates the Free Speech Clause of the First Amendment and applies it to the states." *Caveat lector*!

Certainly, this history is important to know because the earlier cases refer to a concept of "selectively incorporating" only portions of the Bill of Rights into the Fourteenth Amendment and those precedents continue to be cited and quoted. Knowing that there was a gradual process of incorporation is the only way to make sense of these references. More importantly for our purposes, this background allows for a fuller understanding of the constitutional analysis of individual liberty versus government power and Supreme Court interpretations of the Bill of Rights and the Fourteenth Amendment.

There is a "reverse incorporation" doctrine that deserves mention here. The conceptual move the Supreme Court makes is to take some constitutional right that exists against the states that does not apply in so many words to the federal government and incorporate it into the Fifth Amendment Due Process Clause in a case challenging some policy of the national government.

Compare the Fifth Amendment, ratified in 1791, with the Fourteenth Amendment, ratified in 1868. Notice that the Fourteenth Amendment introduces the textual norm of equality into the Constitution, but the Fifth Amendment does not contain an Equal Protection Clause. In the 1954 school desegregation decision, the Supreme Court held that "separate but equal" public schools were a *per se* violation of the Equal Protection Clause. *Brown v. Bd. of Educ.*, 347 U.S. 483 (1954). One of the companion cases involved a similar challenge to the public schools in the District of Columbia, over which the Congress has a delegated power to legislate. U.S. Const. art. I, § 8, cl. 17. Writing for a unanimous Court, Chief Justice Warren concluded that it simply would be "unthinkable" that the same Constitution would impose a different or lesser duty on the Congress. He reasoned that the "liberty" guaranteed by the Due Process Clause in the Fifth Amendment was violated by racially segregated public schools in the nation's capital. *Bolling v. Sharpe*, 347 U.S. 497 (1954).

It would be difficult to overstate the importance of this interpretation of the Fifth Amendment. The equal protection component of the Fifth Amendment Due Process Clause mirrors the clause in the Fourteenth Amendment. What is unconstitutional for the states to do under the Equal Protection Clause in the Fourteenth Amendment is likewise unconstitutional for the Congress to do under the Fifth Amendment Due Process Clause. All racial classifications, whether imposed by federal or state government, must satisfy a strict scrutiny level of judicial review to be narrowly tailored to serve a compelling governmental interest. *Adarand Constructors, Inc. v. Pena*, 515 U.S. 200 (1995). Few classifications satisfy this high standard of judicial review, which might be described as being strict in theory but nearly always fatal in fact, *i.e.*, the classifying law is almost always struck down. Furthermore, the Equal Protection Clause covers not just racial classifications but all government classifications that discriminate based on gender, religion, national origin, *et cetera*. And the concept of equality applies as well to prevent the government from burdening the exercise of our most fundamental rights that are found in the text and beyond the text of the Constitution. *See* Appendix A (Leading Case Outline of Constitutional Liberty, § 9 (Equal Protection)).

Without the concept of reverse incorporation, we would suffer the constitutional anomaly that Congress could invidiously discriminate against individuals based on their race and get away with it. The process of reverse incorporation may be illustrated in our constitutional diagram:

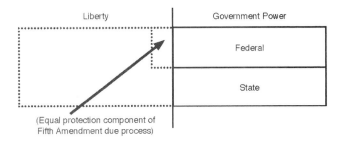

This constitutional diagram nicely illustrates a consistency and congruence in the constitutional analysis of the balance between individual liberty and government power. With the most minor, almost insignificant variations, today we can say that the scope of freedom and individual liberty is virtually the same whether the alleged violation arises in the exercise of federal governmental power or state governmental power. The minor variations on the state side include the few provisions of the Bill of Rights that have not been incorporated into the Fourteenth Amendment and applied to the states, discussed above. The minor variations on the federal side are the few clauses in the text of the Constitution, like the Contracts Clause in Article I, Section 10, that only apply to the states and for which the Fifth Amendment Due Process Clause might be applied less searchingly. *See Pension Benefit Guar. Corp. v. R.A. Gray & Co.,* 467 U.S. 717 (1984).

5. WHAT CONSTITUTIONAL ANALYSIS IS NOT

To better understand what American constitutional analysis *is*, we might briefly describe what it *is not*. *See generally* Chapter 7 (Constitutional Theory). Here a brief discursion into comparative constitutional law will be instructive. American constitutional analysis is not the kind of extreme balancing analysis performed by courts outside the United States. Human rights adjudication in Europe, Canada, India, South Africa, and elsewhere employs the principle of proportionality. *See generally* Stavros Tsakyrakis, *Proportionality: An Assault on Human Rights?*, 7 INT'L J. CONST. L. 468 (2009).

To determine the constitutional validity of a new law or statute that interferes with a claimed individual right, a proportionality-minded foreign court must determine: (1) whether the statute is suitable for achieving its legislative purpose; (2) whether the statute is necessary for that purpose; and (3) whether the statute burdens the individual right excessively compared with the benefits the statute is intended to secure. The foreign judges themselves weigh the diminution of individual liberty caused by the measure—the lost liberty—against the importance of the public benefit sought to be gained by the measure—the alleged public good. Proportionality review pretends to be capable of quantifying intensity and degree of both these interests, the individual liberty interest and the government's public policy purpose.

The closest idea in American constitutional law is so-called "balancing." But that metaphor properly understood is only a metaphor. No American judge will ever write an opinion along these lines: "I have determined that the government's interest is more important than the individual's right, so the government wins" or "I have determined that the individual's right is more important than the government's interest, so the individual wins." Why not? First, proportionality review of this kind would allow the legislature (or Parliament) to define individual rights through ordinary legislation (which is a central characteristic of the parliamentary systems in other countries). That is not the system of government in the United States. Second, proportionality judicial review would empower courts to become super-legislatures with a judicial veto power over the legislative branch. In the process, the foreign constitutional court basically acts like a council of revision for the constitution of that other country. But students of American history will recall that such a "council of revision" was proposed and decidedly rejected at the Constitutional Convention of 1787. The American concept of a written

Constitution and the related principle of the rule of law would be futile under a rule of proportionality.

No less an historic figure than the great Chief Justice John Marshall explicitly rejected this role for the U.S. Supreme Court in the landmark case of *Marbury v. Madison* (1803). *See* Chapter 2, § 1 (Origins of Judicial Review). He concluded, "the framers of the constitution contemplated that instrument as a rule for the government of courts, as well as of the legislature." Here he was paraphrasing Alexander Hamilton who had famously predicted:

A constitution is, in fact, and must be regarded by the judges, as a fundamental law. It therefore belongs to them to ascertain its meaning, as well as the meaning of any particular act proceeding from the legislative body. If there should happen to be an irreconcilable variance between the two, that which has the superior obligation and validity ought, of course, to be preferred; or, in other words, the Constitution ought to be preferred to the statute, the intention of the people to the intention of their agents * * *.

Federalist Paper No. 78. Otherwise, constitutional law would be unstable and unknowable unless and until a court decided a case and then only until the next decision by that same court. The un-American nature and the political unattractiveness of such an undemocratic "juristocracy" should be obvious.

Finally, the balancing metaphor never actually comports with its famous origins—the blindfolded female figure of Justice holding a pair of scales and a sword. It masks a conclusion, as revealingly stated above, that the judge merely has a subjective personal preference for one side or the other of "the government-versus-the-individual-lawsuit." For balancing to be objective, rational, and empirically authentic it would have to be scientifically quantifiable in a wholly impossible way. For example, the judge would have to explain the metrics by writing an opinion that said: "The value of the legislature's policy in this case is 10 constitutional *utils* and the value of the individual's right is only 6 constitutional *utils*, so the government must prevail" or alternatively "The value of the individual right in this case is 10 constitutional *utils* but the value of the government's policy is only 6 *utils*, so the individual must prevail." Obviously, there is no such thing as a "constitutional *util*," an objective unit of measure of the constitutional value of a statute or the constitutional harm done to an individual right. That may well be the metaphorical constitutional analysis in other countries, but it is not the actual constitutional analysis in the United States as best described in this NUTSHELL.

Do not be deceived by the metaphor of balancing. Go back to the constitutional analysis diagram introduced in this Chapter. The U.S. Constitution draws the line between government power and individual liberty or freedom. The Constitution delegates government powers. The Constitution protects individual rights. The Supreme Court makes a constitutional value judgment whether the government's policy being challenged is on the government power side of the line—and therefore valid—or whether the government's policy is on the individual liberty and freedom side of the line—and therefore invalid. *See* Chapter 7, § 4 (How to Interpret the Constitution?). The constitutional analysis is a zero-sum game: a statute is either constitutional or unconstitutional. A statute cannot be just a little bit unconstitutional any more than a woman can be just a little bit pregnant.

6.   CONCLUSION

We began this Chapter to imagine a box in which all imaginable government power—legitimate powers of good governments and illegitimate powers of bad governments—had been placed. We removed a great bulk of potential government power, those arbitrary and excessive government powers that cannot be allowed under our constitutional system that guarantees and protects the civil rights and civil liberties of the individual. The Constitution is the law that the government must obey.

The diagrams in this book are intended to aid the reader's understanding of constitutional law. By way of an assurance or disclaimer, some readers might not find them as helpful. No matter. The text and content of the book stand on their own as an aid to learning our subject.

We next turn our attention to some examples of how the Constitution guarantees individual liberty and the role of the Supreme Court to exercise its power of judicial review. Our constitutional analysis will also suggest how, at least in some instances, the Court's judicial opinions have mistakenly overlooked the fundamental relationship of constitutional liberty versus government power.

CHAPTER 4
CONSTITUTIONAL LIBERTY

The subject of this Chapter is constitutional liberty. The emphasis of this Chapter is on the left side of the constitutional diagram introduced in Chapter 3. The next chapter will examine government powers on the right side of the constitutional diagram.

The Constitution preserves and protects individual liberty. In the exercise of its power of judicial review, the Supreme Court is the guardian of the Constitution. This Chapter provides an overview of how the Supreme Court performs that role, how its legal doctrines define the scope of our civil rights and civil liberties, how it draws the constitutional boundary between individual liberty and government power that is visually depicted in our constitutional diagram. The Supreme Court reviews issues of constitutional law presented in a case or controversy. The Court determines which constitutional facts are controlling. The Court sometimes resolves conflicts between competing constitutional rights. The Congress plays a respectful legislative role to protect individual rights, as well, under the Court's watchful constitutional eye.

Along these lines, it is helpful to distinguish between *interpretation*—the judicial activity of determining the linguistic meaning of a provision in the Constitution—and *construction*—the judicial activity of translating that meaning into a legal test or doctrine or rule for decision. *See* Chapter 7

(Constitutional Theory). The Court interprets the meaning of the clauses in the Constitution and then develops doctrines of constitutional law to implement that meaning; the Court derives these specific rules of decision to decide cases from the general provisions of "Due Process" or "Equal Protection" or "Freedom of Speech" and the like. For example, the Court interprets the words "due process of law" in the Fifth and Fourteenth Amendments to entrench a requirement of fairness on the part of the government when dealing with an individual's property or liberty. Then the Court spins that norm into a doctrine such as the test whether the government's procedures are reasonable under the circumstances to afford the individual reasonable notice and an meaningful opportunity to be heard before being deprived of property or liberty. The Court examines three factors to make this assessment: (1) the private interest being affected; (2) the risk of error in the procedures that were followed and the probable value of additional or substitute procedures; and (3) the government's interest. This is the cycle of interpretation and construction. "Due process of law" is interpreted to require fair dealing by the government. Doctrine is constructed when fair dealing is measured by a test of reasonableness applying these three factors. That is how constitutional interpretation and doctrinal construction work.

This Chapter sketches these themes of the protection of liberty. A more detailed and elaborate depiction of constitutional law doctrine is on full display in Appendix A (Leading Case Outline of

Constitutional Liberty). This Chapter and that Appendix go together. To master our subject, you are obliged to learn the constitutional doctrines that define and protect individual liberty and how to apply them properly.

1. CONSTITUTIONAL ANALYSIS *REDUX*

The Constitution seeks to "establish Justice" and "secure the Blessings of Liberty" by providing for "the judicial Power of the United States." U.S. Const. preamble & art. III, § 1, cl. 1. Congress and the President have important but secondary roles. The Supreme Court's power of judicial review is the primary protection of individual liberty and freedom against government power. It is the power of the courts to interpret the law of the Constitution. The Constitution is the law the government must obey.

The most basic question of constitutional law is whether the challenged governmental action deprives the individual of constitutional liberty and thus lies beyond the constitutional powers of government. *See* Chapter 3 (Constitutional Analysis). Does the challenged action fall on the liberty side [1] or on the government power side [2] of the constitutional line? The constitutional analysis of this irreducible question is depicted in our basic constitutional diagram:

It is the Supreme Court, of course, that has the ultimate responsibility for interpreting the Constitution. But its power is derived from the Constitution and its decisions must be reasoned interpretations. Alexander Hamilton explained in *Federalist Paper No. 78* that the judiciary "has no influence over either the sword or the purse" and that the Supreme Court "may truly be said to have neither FORCE nor WILL but merely judgment."

There is a certain family resemblance between what the Supreme Court of the United States does and what a state supreme court does. Both courts decide cases. Both courts provide reasoned opinions and justifications for their decisions.

But when a state supreme court decides a tort case to discard the rule of contributory negligence and adopt the rule of comparative negligence or decides a contract case by declaring that the parol evidence rule provides that a writing intended by the parties to be the final embodiment of their agreement may not be contradicted by other kinds of evidence, the state supreme court is doing something different in kind. Besides deciding the case *sub judice*, the state judges are declaring the common law for the state. They are policy makers making policy for the state. They are expected to reason towards what they themselves believe is the best public policy, the best rule of law, for the state. The common law method is a law making method by state courts on par with the state legislature's law making method to enact statutes. *See Cruzan v. Dir., Mo. Dept. of Health*, 497 U.S. 261, 277 (1990) ("State courts have available to them for decision a number of sources—state constitutions, statutes, and common law—which are not available to us.").

Justices on the Supreme Court of the United States do not have that kind of power or authority. They are interpreters of the Constitution. They are not its authors. Their power of judicial review derives from the legitimacy and the supremacy of the Constitution and not from their personal and subjective policy preferences. They cannot strike down an otherwise valid statute merely because they do not personally approve of the public policy. They cannot impose a requirement on the Legislative Branch or the Executive Branch solely because they themselves think it would be a good idea. Otherwise, constitutional law would amount to the "rule of five"—at any given time whatever five Justices liked would be constitutional and whatever five Justices did not like would be unconstitutional. That is not the theory or philosophy of American constitutionalism. *See* Chapter 1 (American Constitutionalism).

What Karl Von Clausewitz said about war might be said about constitutional law: "It is a continuation of politics by other means." Presidents nominate and the Senate confirms the members of the Supreme Court, but once on the Supreme Court the Justices are not supposed to behave like the elected officials in the political branches behave. They are supposed to behave like judges. From the original decision establishing the power of judicial review, *Marbury v. Madison*, 5 U.S. (1 Cranch) 137, 178 (1803), to the present day, the fundamental premise is that the law of the Constitution is something different from politics. It would be illegitimate for a Justice or a majority of the Justices to write an opinion that says, "The Constitution does not require or in any way justify our decision today in this case, but we think we have reached the right result and we are satisfied that this ruling is a good idea." That political law making activity belongs across First Street, Northeast, to the occupants of the Capitol.

Anyone who can read can tell you what the Constitution *says*; but we need the Supreme Court to interpret what the Constitution ultimately *means*. To be sure, the answer is not always easy or obvious, even to the Justices themselves, as is demonstrated by the plethora of concurring and dissenting opinions in controversial cases as well as by the relative frequency of overrulings of prior precedents. Their ongoing duty to interpret the Constitution cannot be avoided.

2. CONSTITUTIONAL LAW DOCTRINES

The boundary between individual liberty and government power in the constitutional diagram is drawn in particular cases or controversies and articulated in judicial opinions as constitutional law doctrine. There is law—a body of legal rules—to learn in constitutional law, just as there are rules to learn in your other 1L basic courses like torts and contracts and property. Most Supreme Court opinions—and most constitutional law final examination questions by the way—follow the traditional law school "IRAC" sequence to (1) identify the *issue*; (2) state the *rule* of law; (3) *analyze* the facts and the law; and (4) reach some *conclusion*. When you read Supreme Court opinions, be on the lookout for the rule of decision, the "R" in the "IRAC" sequence. That is the important take away.

Supreme Court opinions are full of balancing tests, multiple-part tests, levels of scrutiny, tiered-analyses, *et cetera*, that provide rules for decisions. Interpreting the meaning of the Constitution produces these legal constructions. The text of the Constitution is constant, but constitutional doctrines accumulate and develop and evolve over time. *Cf.* JOHN HENRY CARDINAL NEWMAN, AN ESSAY ON THE DEVELOPMENT OF CHRISTIAN DOCTRINE (1878). Most of these doctrines are identified and summarized at the end of this book in Appendix A (Leading Case Outline of Constitutional Liberty). That Appendix augments this Chapter to describe the variety of legal doctrines and to summarize the legal analysis that performs the primary function of guaranteeing civil rights and civil liberties under the Constitution. The richness and variety of constitutional law doctrine is on full display in Appendix A. Only a few familiar examples need be mentioned here to illustrate the basic constitutional analysis for individual civil rights and civil liberties. Otherwise, the reader is encouraged to study Appendix A. Constitutional liberty is elaborated there at much greater length.

The guarantee of procedural due process in the Fifth and Fourteenth Amendments requires that the government provide adequate notice and a meaningful opportunity to be heard when the government deprives a person of life, liberty, or property. To determine if the government must provide a pre-termination hearing and what procedures must be afforded, the Court's balancing test considers: (1) the private interest being affected; (2) the risk of error in the procedures that were followed and the probable value of additional or substitute procedures; and (3) the government's interest. Ultimately, "the straightforward test of reasonableness under the circumstances" is all that is required by the guarantee of procedural due process. *Dusenbery v. United States*, 534 U.S. 161 (2002) (held the government need not provide actual notice; it must only attempt to provide actual notice). Consider two leading cases. In *Goldberg v. Kelly*, 397 U.S. 254 (1970), the Court held that a state had to hold a pre-termination hearing and provide a quasi-judicial evidentiary hearing before cutting off public assistance payments to a welfare recipient. In *Mathews v. Eldridge*, 424 U.S. 319 (1976), the Court held that a less formal hearing was adequate procedure for the termination of Social Security disability benefits because the nature of the determination was essentially a medical decision that was based on written evidence and medical reports. In the constitutional diagram, the *Goldberg v. Kelly* holding was situated on the individual liberty side [1] and the *Mathews v. Eldridge* holding was situated on the government power side [2].

Substantive due process analysis is characterized by two different tiers of analysis that can be traced to a famous footnote in an otherwise not-so-famous case: footnote 4 in *United States v. Carolene Products Co.*, 304 U.S. 144, 152 n.4 (1938). There the Supreme Court announced a weak form of judicial review of economic regulations to defer to the legislature and to uphold statutes that have a rational basis, going so far as to assume facts that would make the regulation appear reasonable. At the same time, however, the Supreme Court announced a strong form of judicial review that would presume certain laws to be unconstitutional and shift the burden of justifying the regulations onto the government to show that the regulation was a justifiably narrow and necessary means of achieving a particularly compelling governmental purpose. Three justifications triggered this strict scrutiny judicial review: to protect fundamental rights guaranteed by the Constitution; to guard against legislation that effectively restricts or limits participation in the political process; and to act as the champion of discrete and insular minorities who are disadvantaged in the traditional majoritarian process. Most statutes analyzed on the rational review tier will be upheld to be on the right side or the government power side of the constitutional diagram [2]. Most statutes analyzed on the strict scrutiny tier will be struck down for violating

protected individual liberty on the left side of the
constitutional diagram [1].

There are three different tiers of equal protection
analysis that are applied to different types of
governmental classifications. At the minimal level of
judicial scrutiny, the means chosen, the
classification, must merely be rationally related to a
purpose that is within the legitimate exercise of the
state police power to regulate for the health, safety,
morals, and general welfare of society. *Ry. Express
Agency, Inc. v. N.Y.*, 336 U.S. 106 (1949). Most
challenged laws meet this low threshold and are
validated as legitimate constitutional government
powers falling on the right side of the constitutional
diagram [2]. Indeed, rational review is a formula for
upholding legislation.

At the other end of the spectrum, racial
classifications are deemed invidious and suspect and
subjected to the strictest scrutiny, *i.e.*, the
government must justify any racial classification as
being narrowly tailored to achieve a compelling
governmental interest. *Brown v. Bd. of Educ.*, 347
U.S. 483 (1954). Most challenged classifications fail
strict scrutiny to fall on the left side or the individual
liberty side of the constitutional diagram [1]. In
Adarand Constructors, Inc. v. Pena, 515 U.S. 200
(1995), however, the Court ruled that so-called
benign racial classifications could pass constitutional
muster under strict judicial scrutiny, *i.e.*, strict
scrutiny is strict in theory and not always fatal in
fact. It is therefore possible for an affirmative action
program to fall on the government power side [2] of

the constitutional diagram if it is narrowly designed to remedy past discrimination and is not based on illegitimate racial prejudices or stereotypes. Some affirmative action admissions procedures in higher education pass strict scrutiny and some do not. *Compare Gratz v. Bollinger*, 539 U.S. 244 (2003) (University of Michigan procedures invalidated) *with Grutter v. Bollinger*, 539 U.S. 306 (2003) (University of Michigan Law School procedures upheld). But while race may be taken into account to remedially desegregate *de jure* segregated public schools, race may not be used to achieve an idealized racial balance to integrate public schools. *Parents Involved in Cmty. Schs. v. Seattle Sch. Dist. No. 1*, 551 U.S. 701 (2007).

Between rational level review and strict scrutiny review, there is an intermediate level of Equal Protection review that requires that the government's purpose be "important"—something in between "compelling" and "legitimate"—and requires that the classification be "substantially related" to the asserted governmental interest—a relatedness somewhat less than "necessary" and somewhat more than "reasonable." Consequently, the outcomes in cases applying intermediate scrutiny to classifications concerning gender, illegitimacy, and alienage are much less predictable, sometimes falling on the government power side [2] and sometimes falling on the individual liberty side [1] of the constitutional diagram. *E.g.*, *United States v. Virginia*, 518 U.S. 515 (1996) (holding the state could not withhold from women the unique educational program of a prestigious state military academy);

Michael M. v. Superior Court, 450 U.S. 464 (1981) (upholding definition of "statutory rape" applicable only to males).

The First Amendment doctrines protecting the incorporated freedom of speech likewise neatly fit the constitutional diagram. Making a speech endorsing and advocating the revolutionary overthrow of the government is protected individual liberty [1], so long as the speaker's endorsement of revolution merely amounts to advocacy of an abstract and philosophical nature, that there is a theoretical right to revolution, or even if the advocacy goes farther to claim that the resort to violence is morally and politically proper. According to well-established Supreme Court precedents, the government may act to forbid or proscribe such advocacy if and only if it is directed to inciting or producing imminent lawless action and the advocacy is also likely to incite or produce lawlessness. *Brandenburg v. Ohio*, 395 U.S. 444 (1969). Thus, there is a government power [2] to punish speech only if the speech creates a "clear and present danger," such as a person *falsely* shouting "Fire!" in a crowded theater and causing a panic. *Schenck v. United States*, 249 U.S. 47, 52 (1919).

Under the incorporated Free Exercise Clause, a city ordinance prohibiting specified practices of animal slaughter was struck down because it was purposely designed to suppress a particular religious sect. *Church of the Lakumi Babalu Aye, Inc. v. City of Hialeah*, 508 U.S. 520 (1993). A state statute that was applied to deny unemployment compensation to drug counselors who were fired for using peyote in a

Native American religious ceremony was upheld as a neutral and generally applicable law. *Emp'l Div. v. Smith*, 494 U.S. 872 (1993). The Supreme Court deemed the city ordinance to invade individual liberty [1], but the state statute fell within the government power [2].

These selected examples can be replicated over and over again for the basic constitutional diagram. The point is that the Supreme Court draws the boundary between individual liberty and government power by interpreting the Constitution to decide particular cases or controversies and by articulating constitutional law doctrine in its judicial opinions. Interpretation and construction are generative judicial activities. To be sure, there are a whole host of different interpretative methodologies available to the Justices. *See* Chapter 7 (Constitutional Theory). But the basic task those various methodologies perform is to give meaning to the majestic generalities of the Constitution; the Supreme Court derives legal doctrines for deciding cases from its great clauses, like the Due Process Clause or the Equal Protection Clause or the Free Speech Clause. To the extent that this doctrinal approach to constitutional analysis seems indeterminate or uncertain, constitutional law is indeterminate and uncertain. *See generally* Appendix A (Leading Case Outline of Constitutional Liberty). The challenge to the beginning student is to begin to get used to this quality of Constitutional Law.

3. ROLE OF THE SUPREME COURT

Controversy not infrequently swirls around particular exercises of the power of judicial review. This has been so in the past and it will continue to be so in the future. Thomas Jefferson was highly critical of Chief Justice John Marshall's reasoning in *Marbury v. Madison*, 5 U.S. (1 Cranch) 137 (1803), calling the decision an "impropriety" and "gratuitous" and a "perversion of the law." In the aftermath of *Brown v. Bd. of Educ.*, 347 U.S. 483 (1954), more than 100 members of Congress from 11 states signed a tract declaring the decision to be "a clear abuse of judicial power" and commending the states to "resist enforced integration by any means." Controversial decisions afford us a better understanding of what is at stake in constitutional analysis as well as some insight into the *realpolitik* of judicial review.

Certainly one of the most controversial constitutional decisions is *Roe v. Wade*, 410 U.S. 113 (1973), in which the Supreme Court declared state laws criminalizing abortion to violate the constitutional right of privacy. In constitutional analysis, this means that the pregnant woman's individual right to choose to have an abortion is a liberty protected by the Due Process Clauses in the Fifth and Fourteenth Amendments, which explicitly protect against governmental intrusions upon life, liberty, or property without due process of law. The government has no power to prohibit abortions or to criminalize the procedure, although some regulations are allowed.

Try to set aside your personal feelings about this controversial issue for a moment and concentrate on the constitutional analysis. Before this case was decided, the practical conclusion had to have been that the regulation of abortion by the government was a constitutionally accepted power. Abortion had been the legislative subject of a criminal offense both for the pregnant woman and the person who performed it, including physicians, since the early history of the country, at the time of the ratification of the Fourteenth Amendment, and down to the day the Supreme Court announced its decision. Then, suddenly and dramatically, because of a 7–2 decision and an opinion by the Supreme Court of the United States, abortion became a fundamental right protected by the Constitution.

In terms of our constitutional analysis, this means that the dividing line between individual liberty and government power has been moved to encompass this new right within the area of individual liberty. In the zero-sum approach of the Constitution, government power has been reduced by a constitutional decision of the Supreme Court that enlarged the area of individual liberty. In the constitutional diagram, we represent the decision in *Roe v. Wade*, or the right to an abortion, with asterisks—one asterisk under state power and one under federal power. While *Roe v. Wade* involved a state statute, its principles obviously were applicable also to the federal government, which had laws against abortion in the territories and the District of Columbia and which could regulate nationally under the Commerce Clause power. *See* Appendix A, § 9 (Equal

Protection—Privacy and Personal Autonomy). We find the situation *before* the decision of *Roe v. Wade* represented by the dotted vertical line dividing liberty from government power and the situation *after Roe v. Wade* by the solid line dividing individual liberty from government power in a new ratio. The Supreme Court, by the exercise of its power of judicial review, has essentially and effectively enlarged constitutional liberty and reduced government power:

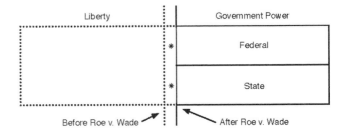

There followed a myriad of Supreme Court decisions reviewing various state legislative efforts to regulate abortion, decisions that often were decided by the narrowest margin and usually engendered elaborate concurring and dissenting opinions. Then in 1992, a plurality opinion, jointly authored by Justices O'Connor, Kennedy, and Souter, reaffirmed the basic holding in *Roe v. Wade* but also substantially revised the doctrine. *Planned Parenthood of Se. Pa. v. Casey*, 505 U.S. 833 (1992). The state may not by purpose or effect impose an undue burden on a woman's constitutionally-protected decision to terminate her pregnancy. Ordinary state medical regulations are appropriate so long as they serve the state's interest to protect the health and safety of the woman. The state may likewise promote its interest in the potential life of the fetus with appropriate regulations so long as they serve the state's interest in the life or health of the woman. But if the physical or mental health of the patient medically indicates that an abortion is appropriate and the woman makes that decision, the state cannot interfere in any significant way. That the operative and controlling constitutional value is the woman's autonomous decision-making is further illustrated by the Supreme Court's nuanced decisions applying the undue burden test. The Court struck down a state ban on so-called partial birth abortions that did not have an exception for the health of the pregnant woman, *Stenberg v. Carhart*, 530 U.S. 914 (2000), but upheld a federal prohibition of a specific abortion procedure (intact dilation & evacuation) apparently as an exercise of the Commerce Clause power, *Gonzales v. Carhart*, 550 U.S. 124 (2007).

For decades, the controversy over abortion has roiled in the state legislatures, in Congress, in the courts, and in the streets. The protests and demonstrations continue down to the present day. The political and academic debate shows no sign of abating. Some constitutionalists deem the right to privacy self-evident and fundamental; other constitutionalists maintain that the right to privacy is not so much bad constitutional law but not constitutional law at all. Presidents and Senators on both sides use the issue as a litmus test for Supreme

Court nominees. Confirmation battles are waged over the issue. Interest groups on both sides use the issue for fundraising and to motivate their members to vote. While in its joint opinion in *Planned Parenthood* "the Court's interpretation of the Constitution call[ed] the contending sides of a national controversy to end their national division by accepting a common mandate rooted in the Constitution," 505 U.S. at 924, thus far the contending sides have not accepted the Court's invitation.

On the merits of the particular case of *Roe v. Wade*, should liberty be defined to include this right of a pregnant woman to choose whether to terminate her pregnancy or continue to the end of her term? This is a difficult question about personal autonomy about which reasonable persons can differ as a matter of morals and philosophy, and members of the Supreme Court have differed as a matter of constitutional law. But ultimately this legal question is no different from asking the same question about a holding of the Supreme Court in any difficult constitutional decision. Did the Court reach the right result for the right reasons? In the difficult cases, each person answers, sometimes "yes," and sometimes "no." No one agrees with all of the constitutional decisions of the Supreme Court, not even the Justices themselves, especially not the Justices, who often divide five-to-four in the difficult constitutional cases. Indeed, a cynic might observe that this is the reason there are an odd number of Justices on the High Court. As Justice Holmes observed:

Great cases like hard cases make bad law. For great cases are called great, not by reason of their real importance in shaping the law of the future, but because of some accident of immediate and overwhelming interest which appeals to the feelings and distorts the judgment. These immediate interests exercise a kind of hydraulic pressure which makes what previously was clear seem doubtful, and before which even well settled principles of law will bend.

N. Sec. Co. v. United States, 193 U.S. 197, 400–01 (1904) (Holmes, J., dissenting).

4.   CONSTITUTIONAL LAW AND CONSTITUTIONAL FACTS

The Supreme Court is often called upon to survey the boundary between individual liberty and government power in cases "at the margin," so to speak. Three related concepts come into play in these cases: vagueness, overbreadth, and the least restrictive means test. Usually, a challenge to a state statute is "as applied," meaning that the person bringing the challenge is objecting to the statute as it is being applied in the particular case to the particular person. A successful "as applied" challenge leaves the law on the books. The statute can be enforced in other cases against other persons. But constitutional analysis also permits challenges to a statute "on its face" to argue that the statute itself is vague or overbroad and that there is no limiting interpretation that would save the law. If so, then the statute cannot be enforced in any other case against any other person.

An unconstitutionally vague statute fails to give adequate notice to the average person of reasonable understanding just what conduct the statute prohibits and what conduct the statute permits. The lack of clear guidelines for individual behavior is exacerbated by the lack of guidance for those with responsibility to enforce the law, police and prosecutors, and for triers of fact, judges and jurors, who must apply the law to the particular circumstances. Vague laws are deemed unfair and unjust because they violate Due Process—the constitutional norm that the government must treat its citizens with basic fairness. The Court struck down an ordinance that required gang members to disperse if ordered to do so by the police because the law did not adequately define either the behavior that was prohibited (loitering) or the behavior that would avoid being charged (dispersing). *City of Chicago v. Morales*, 527 U.S. 41 (1999). Vague laws that regulate speech are even more likely to be struck down because of the concern that otherwise protected speech would be chilled, *i.e.*, that people will censor themselves rather than risk being sanctioned. The Supreme Court struck down a state statutory prohibition of attorney solicitation of clients that had been applied to the NAACP for informing persons of their rights and referring them to lawyers. *NAACP v. Button*, 371 U.S. 415 (1963).

The substantial overbreadth doctrine measures the precision of a law. A statute will be struck down even if it is designed to punish activities that are not constitutionally protected if its prohibition reaches substantial activities that are constitutionally protected. The statute is written too broadly or more broadly than is necessary. The Court struck down a city ordinance prohibiting solicitations by any charitable organization that did not use at least 75% of its receipts for charitable purposes. *Vill. of Schaumburg v. Citizens for Better Env't*, 444 U.S. 620 (1980).

Even if the legislative purpose is legitimate and substantial, the government cannot pursue its purpose through means that unnecessarily burden fundamental liberty when the same purpose can be achieved by less restrictive means. For example, a city ordinance that prohibited all door-to-door solicitation had a valid purpose to protect night-shift workers who slept during the day, but their interests could be protected by the less restrictive policy to simply prohibit soliciting of any household that posted a "no solicitation" sign. *Martin v. City of Struthers*, 319 U.S. 141 (1943). The Court struck down an ordinance that required door-to-door solicitors to obtain a permit: the individual and societal interests in traditional religious proselytization, anonymous canvassing, and grassroots political activity far outweighed the government interests in the prevention of fraud and crime and the protection of residential privacy, which could be achieved with more narrowly tailored regulations. *Watchtower Bible and Tract Soc. of N.Y. v. Vill. of Stratton*, 536 U.S. 150 (2002).

What these three concepts of vagueness, overbreadth, and the least restrictive means all have in common is how the Supreme Court will strictly enforce the boundary between individual liberty and government power. This is especially true in cases that involve the preferred freedoms guaranteed by the First Amendment. When the Legislative Branch pushes the envelope to exceed its constitutional limits, even at the margin, even slightly, the Supreme Court is there to strike down laws that violate the autonomous space of individual liberty and freedom. The concept of constitutionality is an all or nothing proposition, even "slightly unconstitutional" laws are invalid. What is being preserved here is a marginal increment of individual liberty against a marginally excessive exercise of government power:

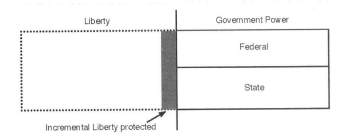

Properly understood, issues of constitutional law are questions of law for the court to decide, not questions of fact for the jury to decide. This becomes immediately apparent when one realizes that the Constitution and its interpreters are supposed to be separate and independent from majoritarian sentiment. Jurors resemble legislators as being representatives. With lifetime tenure and a salary guarantee, the Article III judiciary is set apart. Judicial review gets its authority from the supremacy of the Constitution over ordinary laws. We must distinguish between the proper roles of the judge and the jury, respectively, under the Constitution.

An important internal debate on this point took place in *Dennis v. United States*, 341 U.S. 494 (1951), which upheld the Smith Act that made it a federal crime to willfully and knowingly conspire to advocate the duty and the necessity of overthrowing the government of the United States by force and violence. This precedent invoked the "clear and present danger" doctrine under the First Amendment, later refined to draw the distinction between the protected advocacy of abstract belief in the violent overthrow of the government and the unprotected advocacy of taking actual concrete action—the constitutional difference is between asking someone to merely *believe* something and asking someone to actually *do* something. *Yates v. United States*, 354 U.S. 298 (1957).

The "clear and present danger" test is used in deciding cases involving subversive or radical advocacy. We tolerate such advocacy as part of the freedom of speech in our constitutional system unless and until the advocacy creates a "clear and present danger" that it will bring about serious social disruption and harm. In other words, it is not within the power of our federal or state governments to outlaw in all instances even advocacy of the overthrow of the government by force and violence. But the government does have a constitutional power to forbid or even to proscribe "advocacy of the use of force or of law violation" if and only if the speech "is directed to inciting or producing imminent lawless action and is likely to incite or produce" such lawlessness. *Brandenburg v. Ohio*, 395 U.S. 444, 447 (1969).

In analyzing these cases in terms of our constitutional diagram, the line between individual liberty and government power is drawn on the basis of the "clear and present danger" doctrine. Whether the case falls in the area of individual liberty or in the area of government power depends upon whether a constitutional "clear and present danger" exists that the advocacy will bring about these serious evils that the state has the right of self-protection to prevent. If no "clear and present danger" is found, then our case involving subversive advocacy falls on the side of liberty [1] and the speech is protected. If there is a "clear and present danger," then our case falls on the side of government power [2] and the government may exercise its right of self-protection. Because the control of subversive speech is almost entirely in the hands of the national government, the opposition between liberty and government power when the subject matter is subversive advocacy is shown in our diagram at the federal level:

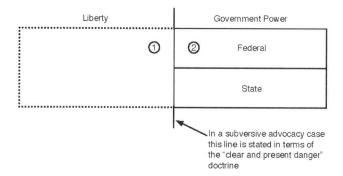

In the case of *Dennis v. United States*, the trial court judge made the decision that the advocacy constituted a "clear and present danger." In other words, the determination was made by the court as a "question of law." Justice Douglas, dissenting in that case, said: "I had assumed that the question of the clear and present danger, being so critical an issue in the case, would be a matter for submission to the jury. * * * The Court, I think, errs when it treats the question as one of law." *Dennis v. United States*, 341 U.S. 494, 587 (1951) (Douglas, J., dissenting).

Was the majority correct on this point in the *Dennis* case or was Justice Douglas correct? Look at our constitutional diagram. Who decides constitutional issues? Do we submit constitutional questions to a jury or are our constitutional liberties a question of law for decision by the courts? Stated in another way, should a jury have the power to establish the line dividing liberty and government power? In deciding this issue, it should be remembered that if the jury were to have the power to establish the line, it presumably would have the power to move the line in either direction. This would mean that the jury could find that there was a "clear and present danger," even though a court did not think so, as well as find there was not a "clear and present danger," even though a court did think so.

In other words, if we were to allow this question to be decided by the jury, we could have a case in which the jury might move the line to the left to encompass free speech that otherwise would be in the area of liberty and relocate it within the area of government power, as this constitutional diagram indicates:

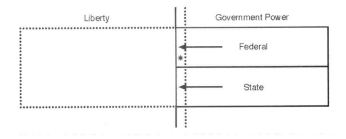

The only way to avoid this dangerous power in the jury would be to say that the jury somehow has the power only to increase the scope of liberty but not to decrease it. Logic and constitutional analysis, however, do not justify any such one-way ratcheted jury power.

With a proper understanding of our constitutional analysis illustrated by our constitutional diagram, we must conclude that the majority was correct and that Justice Douglas was wrong in his dissent. We cannot allow a jury—unskilled in the law, unlearned in the meaning of the Constitution, and unsophisticated in the important and delicate responsibility of protecting civil rights and civil liberties—to make this basic and fundamental constitutional distinction between individual liberty and government power in constitutional cases. As the example illustrates, if we were to submit the issue of "clear and present danger" to the jury, that is exactly what we would be doing because it is the "clear and present danger" doctrine that defines the boundary between constitutionally protected liberty and constitutionally legitimate government power. That is not our system of American constitutionalism. The jury in a courtroom performs from a majoritarian perspective, not unlike a legislature. Judicial review is the counter-majoritarian ballast.

Thus, we do not submit the constitutionality of subversive speech to a jury; we submit only the factual issue of "what happened" to the jury—what was said under what circumstances and with what consequences. The most critical of all constitutional decisions is to draw the line between individual liberty and government power. And, as was described earlier in this Chapter, the Supreme Court performs this constitutional analysis, first by articulating the doctrines and then by applying them to the facts. This much the Supreme Court has recognized in cases applying the "clear and present danger" doctrine, at least by implication, when the Justices themselves have reexamined the facts case-by-case to set aside factual findings and judgments of conviction in order to protect the freedom of speech. *Hess v. Indiana*, 414 U.S. 105 (1973).

The constitutional law shorthand for this practice is the "doctrine of constitutional facts." That doctrine posits the power and authority of a reviewing court, including the Supreme Court of the United States, to conduct an independent *de novo* reexamination of the facts in a First Amendment case, rather than to defer to the findings of fact by an administrative agency or a lower court. The normal rule of appellate review— that the appellate court is bound by the lower court's findings of fact unless they are clearly erroneous— goes by the boards. This doctrine is well-established. The cases are legion. *See, e.g., Hurley v. Irish-American Gay, Lesbian & Bisexual Grp. of Bos.*, 515 U.S. 557 (1995); *Bose Corp. v. Consumers Union*, 466 U.S. 485 (1984).

This discussion of constitutional law and constitutional facts leads to the further conclusion that the Supreme Court was mistaken to assign this responsibility for constitutional analysis to the jury in cases involving obscenity. That it was mistaken is suggested, in fact, by the Supreme Court's own subsequent case law, as we shall see. Consider the following instructive digression.

The Supreme Court's approach to obscenity can be traced back to *Roth v. United States*, 354 U.S. 476 (1957), which held that obscenity is utterance outside the area of protected speech and press. Conveniently for the Court, there was no issue raised or litigated in that seminal case whether the particular material involved was or was not obscene; the obscenity *vel non* of the material in question was stipulated, which may have given the Court something of a false confidence that it could define the difference between protected erotic speech and unprotected obscenity. After a long period of going back and forth indecisively over many decisions, a Supreme Court majority eventually revised the definition of obscenity in *Miller v. California*, 413 U.S. 15, 24 (1973), in a manner resembling how a legislature might draft a statute:

> (a) whether "the average person, applying community standards" would find the work, taken as a whole, to appeal to prurient interest; (b) whether the work depicts or describes, in a patently offensive way, sexual conduct specifically defined by the applicable state law; and (c) whether the work, taken as a whole, lacks serious literary, artistic, political, or scientific value.

The second factor includes "hard-core" sexual material including ultimate sexual acts, whether normal or perverted, actual and simulated, masturbation, excretory functions, and lewd exhibitionist presentations of genitalia as defined in the applicable law as written or construed. The third factor calls for a reasonable person test and a national standard. *Pope v. Illinois*, 481 U.S. 497 (1987). But consider the first factor: it rejects a national standard in favor of a community standard. The majority confounded the constitutional analysis to conclude: "In resolving the inevitably sensitive questions of fact and law, we must continue to rely on the jury system, accompanied by the safeguards that judges, rules of evidence, presumption of innocence, and other protective features provide * * *." *Miller v. California,* 413 U.S. 15, 26 (1973).

That the majority itself might have been confounded is suggested by the internal inconsistency of this opinion that proclaims that "[u]nder a National Constitution, fundamental First Amendment limitations do not vary from community to community * * *", *id.* at 30, but then goes on to add the *non sequitur* proposition that "[t]he mere fact juries might reach different conclusions as to the same material does not mean that constitutional rights are abridged," *id.* at 26 n.9. There is no disputing the first statement. However, when the same material is deemed protected free speech by Jury A and deemed unprotected obscenity by Jury B, the majority's second statement can be correct as a matter of constitutional analysis only under one circumstance. If the material itself is in fact and in law obscene, then Jury A got it wrong, but there is no constitutional harm done since no protected speech was punished in that case. On the other hand, if the material is not obscene and is in fact and law protected free speech, then Jury B got it wrong, and the defendant's freedom of speech has been violated in that case. That logical and realistic possibility renders the majority's approach a problematic and troublesome development for constitutional analysis. The Supreme Court only made matters worse by holding that the same standard applied to federal prosecutions without identifying or defining what measure of community is supposed to be reflected in the "community standards." *Hamling v. United States*, 418 U.S. 87 (1974).

There is some institutional sympathy for this "community standard" approach. The Supreme Court was attempting to rid itself of the responsibility for being the national censorship board for the entire United States under a national standard for determining obscenity. Admittedly, the Court cannot function to decide as a question of law whether every challenged publication is obscene or protected speech. But the unanswered institutional question is to ask the majority the rhetorical question: how this would be any different than any other area of constitutional law that generates an overwhelming number of cases, so many that it is impossible for the Court to grant review in a significant or even a representative sample of the cases—the Fourth Amendment protection against "unreasonable searches and seizures," for example? It would seem that the jurisdictional rules and *certiorari* procedures described in Chapter 2 (Judicial Review) are sufficient protection of the unique function of the Court against the burden of caseload.

But more importantly, leaving the interpretation of the First Amendment to local juries is simply unsound constitutional analysis and practically problematic. The same majority that decided *Miller v. California* soon admitted as much by necessary implication. When a state court jury found the 1971 movie *Carnal Knowledge* obscene—a movie directed by Mike Nichols and starring Jack Nicholson and Ann-Margaret, who garnered an Oscar nomination for her performance—the jury's act of censorship proved too much even for the reluctant movie-goers on the Supreme Court. The Justices unanimously reversed the case outright. *Jenkins v. Georgia*, 418 U.S. 153 (1974). Conceding that the obscenity standard involved questions of fact that were supposed to be left to the jury, the majority insisted that the jury could not have "unbridled discretion" to find something obscene and beyond the protection of the First Amendment. Trial judges and appellate courts were still responsible for performing an "independent review" of the First Amendment issue. Indeed, by admitting that "[o]ur own view of the film satisfies us that 'Carnal Knowledge' could not be found [obscene] * * *," the Justices in effect backed off the extreme position they had taken in *Miller v. California* to completely turn over obscenity cases to the jury under the "community standards" doctrine. In an earlier case setting aside a jury's conviction, Justice Stewart succinctly stated the constitutional necessity for an independent judicial evaluation in his oft-quoted line, "But I know it when I see it * * *." *Jacobellis v. Ohio*, 378 U.S. 184, 197 (1964) (Stewart, J., concurring). The doctrine of constitutional fact thus came to the rescue of the First Amendment.

Let us draw the analysis of the current constitutional law on obscenity on our constitutional diagram. Remember that this version of the diagram applies only to the obscenity issue because only in this area of constitutional law does the Supreme Court purport to allow the jury to make even a preliminary constitutional decision. The two solid lines would mark the Supreme Court's outer limits on the leeway it would allow a jury in drawing the line between protected and unprotected speech. If the case under analysis is represented either as [1] or [3] below, this would mean that the Court was concluding for itself either that the material was in the area of individual liberty and protected [1] or that the material was in the area of the government power and unprotected [3]. But presumably, if the Court were to decide that the material in the case fell in between, in the "twilight zone" between the two clearly marked areas [2], then the Supreme Court would leave it to the jury to decide whether the case involved constitutionally protected individual liberty under the First Amendment or an acceptable exercise of government power to control:

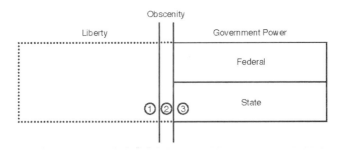

Arguably, there is some justification for allowing such a question to go to the jury in the first place. We recognize that we regularly submit to the jury certain "mixed questions of law and fact" that allow the jury within narrow limits to draw legal conclusions based upon the facts. The concept of "negligence" in tort law suits is one such concept. For example, the jury is allowed to decide not only what actually happened in an accident but also determines whether the defendant was "negligent" or not. Procedurally, we restrict this jury power within defined limits by reserving to the trial court the power to set aside a verdict and by providing for an appeal as of right to allow an appellate court to review the decision and reverse when the judges decide that the jury's conclusion on the mixed question of law and fact is erroneous "as a matter of law." This, in effect, is what the Supreme Court itself did in the case involving the motion picture *Carnal Knowledge*.

Nonetheless, our constitutional analysis demonstrates that in actuality what the Supreme Court's obscenity doctrine does in the first place is to authorize the jury to balance individual liberty against government power to reach an initial verdict in the case. This is no more a traditional jury function in our constitutional system than is the determination of whether there is a "clear and present danger," or whether the free exercise of religion includes the right of polygamous marriages. The role of the jury is to find the facts—to determine what happened and how it happened—not to find whether something is constitutionally protected or subject to government power. That responsibility partakes of the power of judicial review—the power to interpret the Constitution—and that power belongs to courts and judges. The doctrine of constitutional facts resets this balance and reasserts the essential constitutional role of the courts.

But the current state of the law on obscenity is particularly troublesome and, indeed, inconsistent with our constitutional analysis for still another related reason. The problematic practical consequence of the Supreme Court's current obscenity doctrine is that a particular publication might be categorized by one jury in one community as being obscene and not protected, yet, in other communities where the same material was published, it is not just lawful but it is constitutionally privileged under the Free Speech Clause and the Free Press Clause in the First Amendment. Thus, the author's and publisher's and the reader's First Amendment rights are not only at the mercy of one jury in one community but their federal constitutional rights are at the mercy of every jury in every community in the country. The logical problem of allowing a jury, in effect, to interpret the Constitution in practice is exacerbated by a dubious judicial doctrine that allows for different juries to give different interpretations of the Constitution for the same material and the same author and publisher. There is only one Constitution and only one First Amendment. The Constitution creates only "one supreme Court" in order to achieve a uniformity and a consistency in constitutional law. U.S. Const. art. III, § 1. The Constitution does not have time zones or zip codes.

There are some vague hints of a waning judicial enthusiasm for this problematic approach. The "community standard" provision written into a federal statute designed to protect children from pornography on the World Wide Web received the full endorsement of only three Justices and several Justices indicated their preference for a national standard. Although they did recognize the significance of the issue—or perhaps because they fully appreciated the difficulty of the issue—the Justices were not able to reach any consensus on how to define the "community standard" for materials distributed on the World Wide Web. So this remains an open question. *See Ashcroft v. ACLU*, 535 U.S. 564 (2002). This is a good example of how the technology of the internet and the World Wide Web present new issues for old doctrines. *See* Appendix A, § 10 (Freedom of Speech and Press—Obscenity).

Finally, from the perspective of this NUTSHELL, the analytical fallacy in the *Miller v. California* definition of obscenity is antecedent and fundamental. The Supreme Court's obscenity standard puts the questions in reverse. The Supreme Court majority first assumes that the category of obscene speech is unprotected speech and then the majority attempts to define what is obscene under a juror-determined community standard. But labeling a publication "obscene" is a conclusion, not constitutional analysis. The Supreme Court seems to be trying to avoid the reality that every incident of regulating obscenity raises a constitutional issue under the First Amendment freedoms of speech and the press. The constitutionality of the regulation must be faced in those terms. The constitutional analysis cannot be avoided. Labeling something "obscene" can be justified only as the statement of the result after that essential constitutional analysis has been undertaken and performed. Under the I-R-A-C approach of Issue-Rule-Analysis-Conclusion, merely declaring that a publication is obscene and unprotected is all "C" and no "A." That is a kind of 1L beginner's mistake. We should expect more from the Justices. In our constitutional diagram, the unavoidable issue of constitutional law is whether the regulation of the publication in the case falls in the area of protected individual liberty or in the area of regulable government power. The only way to decide that issue is to articulate and balance the considerations for individual liberty and freedom [1] against the countervailing considerations for government power [2].

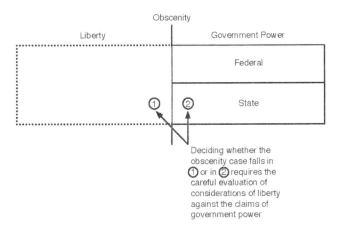

One might posit the idea of federalism as a counterpoint to this critique of the Supreme Court's obscenity jurisprudence. Different communities have different laws on a whole series of public policy issues such as the sale of liquor, Sunday closing laws, wagering and gambling, and the like. We do not have nation-wide standards on most matters. As you go from one community to another, you must be careful to obey the laws of that particular community concerning those matters.

This valid local diversity must be carefully and completely distinguished from local diversity with regard to constitutional matters that should be suspect in theory and practice. As the Supreme Court itself understands and as our constitutional analysis has demonstrated, the First Amendment freedoms of speech and the press apply to the publications in these obscenity cases. In the other areas of public policy mentioned, there is no serious issue of individual liberty under the Constitution. For example, there is no constitutional right to gamble; the state has the police power to regulate gambling. It is for the state legislature to decide whether to allow gambling or to outlaw gambling and even whether to differentiate among different types of gambling from private casinos to state lotteries to charitable bingo games.

There is a well-recognized governmental power to make these sorts of legislative choices state-by-state. So these issues fall squarely within the right-hand side of our constitutional diagram, the government power side, and they do not pose any serious constitutional issues of individual liberty. These controls of individual conduct are simply comparable in constitutional analysis to general traffic laws and reasonable zoning regulations. In theory, the hypothetical failure of a state to pass criminal laws prohibiting murder, robbery, rape, and other serious crimes might well be a constitutional violation of the liberty of its citizens as a result of the state's unwillingness to protect against those serious crimes to the person. (That is why it was such an important question and such a significant holding in *Roe v. Wade*, 410 U.S. 113 (1973), that a fetus is not a person for purposes of the Fourteenth Amendment.) But the great mass of general governmental regulation under the sovereign police power does not fall under that fantastical theory.

For the most part, the state legislature can regulate for the safety, health, morals, and general welfare of society subject only to the lowest level judicial review of rational review under the Due Process and Equal Protection Clauses. The everyday liberty of the citizen is subject to garden variety regulations imposed by the legislature that are consistent with the Constitution. As Justice Scalia once had occasion to observe: "there is no basis for thinking that our society has ever shared that Thoreuavian 'you-may-do-what-you-like-so-long-as-it-does-not-injure-someone-else' beau ideal—much less for thinking it was written into the Constitution." *Barnes v. Glen Theatre, Inc.*, 501 U.S. 560, 574–75 (1991) (Scalia, J., concurring).

The more difficult question of constitutional analysis for these general police power regulations is the federalism inquiry—whether the particular exercise of power falls within the area of national power or the area of state power. *See Murphy v. NCAA*, 138 S. Ct. 1461 (2018) (invalidating federal statute that prohibited states from allowing sports gambling). This will be the subject of detailed consideration with the use of the constitutional diagram in Chapter 5 (Government Powers) and Chapter 6 (Structure of the Constitution).

5. COMPETING CONSTITUTIONAL LIBERTIES

We continue our constitutional analysis of constitutional liberty by considering the not uncommon situation when two different persons claim constitutional liberties that compete with each other. How this tension is adjusted provides further insight into the concept of liberty itself, as well as the occasion to explore the relationship between the Legislative Branch and the Judicial Branch in the performance of their respective duties to protect individual liberty.

This particular exercise in constitutional analysis will focus on the right of association and its permutations. As we will see, the constitutional right of association is a variation on the theme of discrimination, *i.e.*, an individual classifies others and treats them differently, either to associate with them or to disassociate from them in various situations and for various reasons. We understand the basic notion, however, that the Constitution orders the public relationship between the government and individuals and that it does not apply, for the most part, to the private relationship between two individuals. Private ordering between individuals is regulated by the state, if at all, by the criminal law and by the civil law that includes the law of torts, contract law, and property law. Therefore, when we consider competing constitutional liberties we necessarily must be contemplating a third party—the state—getting involved and regulating the associational practices between or among two or more rights-bearing individuals.

Neither the First Amendment nor the Fourteenth Amendment mentions the "right of association" in so many words, but the Supreme Court has interpolated the right of association with other individuals as being a necessary corollary of the rights that are mentioned in the First Amendment and applied to the states through the Fourteenth Amendment. This makes sense if one thinks about it. Freedom of speech requires a speaker and a listener; freedom of the press requires a publisher and a reader; petitioning government is a group activity of gathering signatures or making a public protest and the like; free exercise of religion traditionally takes place within a worship community; and the right of assembly would not make much sense as an individual activity without the participation of others. The Supreme Court thus could not help but conclude that "freedom to engage in association for the advancement of beliefs and ideas is an inseparable aspect of the 'liberty' assured by the Due Process Clause of the Fourteenth Amendment * * *." *NAACP v. Alabama ex. rel. Patterson*, 357 U.S. 449, 460 (1958).

The right of association necessarily has a positive and a negative dimension: individuals have a freedom to choose with whom to associate and a freedom to choose with whom not to associate. Membership organizations afford groups of individuals the collective and individual right to formally associate with fellow members on any variety of common interests and, at the same time, to formally disassociate themselves from nonmembers. The constitutional protection of the right to associate and the right not to associate depends on the nature of the organization and its purposes and activities. The purpose of any social club is to include some people of likeminded interests and to exclude other people, *i.e.*, to define what sociologists label the "in-group" and the "out-group."

The Supreme Court has differentiated among different types of associations along a continuum of greater to lesser constitutional protection from intimate associations to expressive associations to economic associations. The nature of the organization is determinative, taking into account its size, purpose, policies, programs, selectivity, congeniality, and significant characteristics.

At one end of the spectrum, the highest protection is afforded intimate or familial associations that fall within the fundamental right of privacy. The state could not make it a crime for a man and a woman to marry someone of a different race. *Loving v. Virginia*, 388 U.S. 1 (1967). Nor could a state interfere with a family's living arrangement that went beyond the nuclear family to include close relatives. *Moore v.*

City of East Cleveland, 431 U.S. 494 (1977). Such highly personal relationships enjoy a general immunity from state interference. The right to associate or not is defined by the individual and the government has no power to interfere.

Farther along the spectrum, expressive associations engage in the very type of activities explicitly protected in the First Amendment: speech, assembly, petition for redress of grievances, and the free exercise of religion. Expressive associations, like political parties, are as protected against state regulation as are the underlying fundamental rights they exercise. *Eu v. S.F. Cty. Democratic Cent. Comm.*, 489 U.S. 214 (1989). The government can regulate an expressive association if and only if the regulation serves a compelling state interest unrelated to the suppression of ideas that cannot be achieved by less restrictive means. Expressive associations can discriminate in ways that would be unconstitutional for the government and that the government does not have the power to prohibit: the NAACP can refuse to admit a member of the KKK and *vice versa*.

Economic associations are at the other end of the spectrum. Commercial organizations like a labor union or a trade association are exercising the basic liberty that is protected by the Due Process Clauses against irrational or arbitrary regulation. The government can exercise its sovereign powers to regulate their membership and organizational activities subject only to the lowest level or rational level of judicial review, at least when there is no effect from the regulation on protected activities like free speech. *Am. Commc'ns Ass'n v. Douds*, 339 U.S. 382 (1950).

Applications of state laws that prohibit discrimination in public accommodations have been the occasions for the Justices to draw sometimes fine distinctions among different types of organizations and the attendant associational rights of members and would-be members. In the leading case, *Roberts v. United States Jaycees*, 468 U.S. 609 (1984), the Supreme Court approved of the application of a state law that required the Jaycees to admit women as full members. The state's interest to remedy gender discrimination was compelling and admitting women was the least restrictive means; therefore, the right not to associate of the male members must give way. A unanimous Court likewise upheld the application of another state's statute to require Rotary Clubs to admit women members. *Bd. of Dirs. of Rotary Int'l v. Rotary of Duarte*, 481 U.S. 537 (1987).

But the Court balked when still another state applied its public accommodations statute to attempt to force the organizers of the St. Patrick's Day parade in Boston to allow a gay rights organization to march along. The parade organizers had a right not to associate with the gay rights organization and its message, a right that the government was required to respect. *Hurley v. Irish-Am. Gay, Lesbian & Bisexual Grp. of Bos.*, 515 U.S. 557 (1995). An openly gay man could not rely on state anti-discrimination laws to force the Boy Scouts of America to allow him to continue as a member and to serve as an adult leader of a troop. The forced association would violate the organization's freedom of expression and the rights of association of its members by detrimentally compromising Scouting's stated policy and official position against homosexuality. *B.S.A. v. Dale*, 530 U.S. 640 (2000).

Taken together, these holdings pose a complication for our constitutional diagram. These outcomes do not neatly fit into our regular bifurcated figure that differentiates between individual liberty and government power. Sometimes the individual right to associate is upheld against an invocation of government power. Sometimes the individual right not to associate is upheld against the invocation of government power. But sometimes the Constitution recognizes a government power to regulate associational rights and the government's regulations trump a claim of the right to associate or the right not to associate. These competing constitutional liberties to associate and not to associate plus the "sometimes" government power to regulate them might be depicted this way:

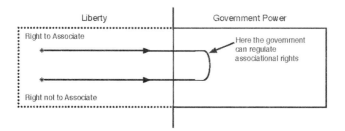

For clarity we left out the line dividing federal and state power because it is irrelevant for now. We have merely drawn a curvilinear line of progression from the constitutional right to associate to the constitutional right not to associate; both of these constitutional rights are located on the individual liberty side of our basic diagram. The middle area on the line diagram, which represents governmental policy-making power to regulate associational rights between the two competing individual rights, is located on the government power side of our basic diagram. Finally, although we have here focused on the right of association and the right not to associate, this constitutional analysis would apply to any other pair of competing constitutional rights, whenever two individuals are invoking the Constitution and the government is called upon to pick sides between them. *Cf. Rumsfeld v. FAIR*, 547 U.S. 47 (2006) (Court will make an independent determination whether associational rights are being violated).

6. PROTECTING CONSTITUTIONAL LIBERTY

In the usual constitutional case or controversy, what is happening is that the Supreme Court itself is defining and enforcing the individual liberty against the governmental action being challenged through the entry of a judicial decree—a court judgment and order that the governmental action is unconstitutional and invalid. It might take the form of a declaratory judgment or an injunction against the state official from enforcing the law. That really amounts to one branch of the government, the judiciary, protecting the citizen from another branch of the government, either the legislature or the executive. There also are significant occasions when the Congress and the Executive may act to protect and enforce individual liberty against governmental action.

Congress has exercised its broad Commerce Clause power, for example, to enact civil rights statutes prohibiting racial discrimination against those traveling in interstate commerce. *Heart of Atlanta Motel, Inc. v. United States,* 379 U.S. 241 (1964); *Katzenbach v. McClung*, 379 U.S. 294 (1964). Congress may also exercise its spending power, for another example, to prohibit discrimination by any grantee of federal funding or to affirmatively require minority business set asides in government projects funded with federal funds. *E.g., Sabri v. United States*, 541 U.S. 600 (2004); *Fullilove v. Klutznick*, 448 U.S. 448, 474 (1980). These and other enumerated congressional powers, however, are not without limits, as we shall see in Chapter 5 (Government Powers).

Additionally, the last sections of the Thirteenth, Fourteenth, and Fifteenth Amendments, and the last paragraph of the Nineteenth Amendment explicitly authorize Congress to enforce those Amendments by appropriate legislation. Those Amendments contain their own Necessary and Proper Clause. *See* Chapter 5, § 3 (Implied Federal Powers). If and when Congress does so, it is Congress itself that is protecting individual liberty by legislation. Congress has in fact passed various civil rights acts to protect individual constitutional liberties against governmental action. Congress has no power to change the substantive right, of course. What Congress is doing in these instances, however, is only creating enforcement mechanisms and remedies, such as criminal penalties or civil liability, against those who deprive others of their constitutional rights. *City of Boerne v. Flores*, 521 U.S. 507 (1997).

In all of these situations, the Executive Branch is called upon, in turn, to perform its constitutional responsibility by enforcing these federal statutes. The President has not just the power but the duty to "take Care that the Law be faithfully executed." U.S. Const. art. II, § 3. *See* Chapter 1, § 8 (Executive Power); Chapter 6, § 10 (Separation of Powers— Executive). That duty to execute the law includes the law of the Constitution as interpreted by the Supreme Court of the United States, as well as all constitutional laws Congress enacts to protect civil rights and civil liberties and to provide remedies for persons deprived of their constitutional liberty. Thus, the role of the President and the executive departments to protect civil rights and civil liberties is a necessary outgrowth of the congressional protection of individual liberty by legislation.

In our constitutional analysis, these congressional civil rights statutes and their executive enforcement are a constitutional exercise of federal power to protect and preserve individual liberty by opposing government power improperly exercised by some public official who is violating the Constitution. These congressional measures and their enforcement resemble the more familiar efforts of the Supreme Court and the lower courts in deciding cases to protect individual liberty. In this instance, the government is acting on the liberty side of our constitutional diagram through the Congress and the Executive, just as it more usually acts through the Judicial Branch.

To take into account this constitutional dynamic, visualize again the left side of our constitutional diagram, the side where we prohibited arbitrary and excessive government powers that improperly infringe upon freedom and individual liberty. We can insert under that left side of the constitutional diagram a brief summary description of the shared constitutional authority to protect individual liberty:

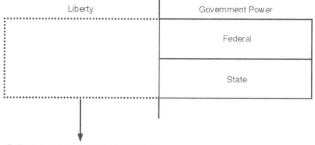

Liberty | Government Power

Federal

State

Defined and enforced in most instances by Court decision, but also enforced (but not defined) by the passage of "civil rights" legislation in Congress and by the President's actions carrying out court decisions and enforcing civil rights legislation

Notice once again the fundamental Madisonian contradiction comes into play: the Constitution calls the government into being and charges it with the protection of individual rights. The ultimate justification of the government is to provide the legal force necessary to protect individual rights, yet the government itself is the greatest threat to individual rights. American constitutionalism is all about resolving that ongoing dilemma. *See* Chapter 1 (American Constitutionalism).

7. CONGRESSIONAL ENFORCEMENT

Section 5 of the Fourteenth Amendment provides: "The Congress shall have power to enforce, by appropriate legislation, the provisions of this article." As was previously noted, this Section of this Amendment, and comparably worded sections found in several other Amendments, thus resemble the Necessary and Proper Clause authorization to enact appropriate legislation. U.S. Const. art. I, § 8, cl. 18; *Katzenbach v. Morgan*, 384 U.S. 641 (1966). The critical constitutional question for the congressional exercise of this power is: what is the meaning of the word "enforce"? Does it mean that Congress has the power merely to create criminal and civil penalties for those who violate a citizen's rights under the Constitution? Or does it mean that Congress itself can define and determine the scope of constitutional liberties by enacting legislation? In terms of our constitutional diagram, can Congress actually enlarge the scope of liberty under the Constitution? Or reduce it? Does the power to "enforce" the Fourteenth Amendment include the right to move

the all-important constitutional boundary line
between individual liberty and government power?

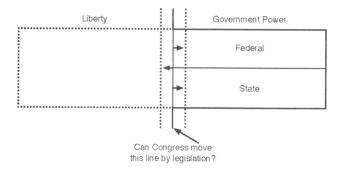

The refutation of this constitutional question
seems to be suggested in its restatement to ask:
whether Congress can pass a statute to make some
governmental action constitutional after the
Supreme Court has ruled it to be unconstitutional or
whether Congress can pass a statute to make some
governmental action unconstitutional after the
Supreme Court has ruled it to be constitutional? But
to master constitutional analysis one must become
accustomed to analyzing the obvious.

The intuitive answer to these questions for anyone
who is a student of American constitutionalism
would be that the congressional power to "enforce"
the Fourteenth Amendment is no more, nor no less,
than the power to create civil and criminal liability
against those persons who infringe the constitutional
liberties defined by the Supreme Court's
interpretation of the Constitution. The well-settled

constitutional concept has been that the Constitution is supreme over congressional law and that mere statutory law cannot alter the scope of constitutional liberty. After all, this was the basic premise of *Marbury v. Madison*, 5 U.S. (1 Cranch) 137 (1803), the historic decision establishing the power of judicial review. *See* Chapter 2 (Judicial Review).

The question, however, is not as easily disposed of as might be assumed. The three Reconstruction Amendments were a new and significant departure in American constitutionalism. For the first time, broad protections of individual liberties against *state* intrusion were put into the Constitution. For the first time, each of these three Amendments adopted the practice, which has since been followed as a routine matter in constitutional Amendments, of providing Congress with the power to enact appropriate legislation to enforce its provisions. *See* Chapter 1, § 11 (Amendments). The line of cases interpreting Section 5 of the Fourteenth Amendment limns this congressional power and provides still another perspective on constitutional analysis and our constitutional diagram.

In the *Slaughter-House Cases*, 83 U.S. (16 Wall.) 36 (1873), the Supreme Court eschewed an activist judicial role for defining the Privileges or Immunities Clause, the Due Process Clause, and the Equal Protection Clause in Section 1 of the Fourteenth Amendment. *See* Chapter 3, § 4 (History of Constitutional Liberty). The Supreme Court forthrightly came to recognize that the Fourteenth Amendment was intended as a limitation on the power of the states and an enlargement of the power of Congress, not the judicial power:

> It is not said the *judicial power* of the general government shall extend to enforcing the prohibitions and to protecting the rights and immunities guaranteed. It is not said that branch of the government shall be authorized to declare void any action of a state in violation of the prohibitions. It is the power of Congress which has been enlarged.

Ex parte Virginia, 100 U.S. 339, 345 (1879). Then in the *Civil Rights Cases*, 109 U.S. 3 (1883), the Supreme Court interpreted Section 1 of the Amendment to prohibit only state action, not private action, that violated those clauses and went on to articulate its understanding that Section 5 provided a remedial power in Congress that extended only to state actions in violation of Section 1. *See* Chapter 3, § 2 (Individual Liberty Versus Government Power).

If these early views of the respective roles of the Supreme Court and the Congress had prevailed, there would be no question that the definition of the scope of the individual liberties would primarily be in the hands of Congress rather than in the hands of the courts. This seems strange, even preposterous to us. Fast-forwarding through the constitutional analysis and constitutional history already described in Chapter 3 (Constitutional Analysis), our modern understanding of the central role of the courts to define and protect individual liberty was famously proclaimed by Justice Jackson:

The very purpose of a Bill of Rights was to withdraw certain subjects from the vicissitudes of political controversy, to place them beyond the reach of majorities and officials and to establish them as legal principles to be applied by the courts. One's right to life, liberty, and property, to free speech, a free press, freedom of worship and assembly, and other fundamental rights may not be submitted to vote; they depend on the outcome of no elections.

W. Va. State Bd. of Educ. v. Barnette, 319 U.S. 624, 638 (1943).

Tracing another interesting and informative digression serves to reinforce the proper understanding. The digression begins with the decision in *Lassiter v. Northhampton Election Bd.*, 360 U.S. 45 (1959), refusing to invalidate a state English-literacy requirement for voting under the Equal Protection Clause, at least in the absence of any evidence of a purpose or intent to discriminate. A few years later, in the Voting Rights Act of 1965, Congress outlawed the use of state English-literacy tests as a qualification for voting for persons who had gone to "American flag" schools, mainly people from Puerto Rico where instruction is not in English. The Supreme Court then upheld the federal statutory prohibition of state English-literacy tests in *Katzenbach v. Morgan*, 384 U.S. 641 (1966).

The *Morgan* decision expressly refused to overrule the *Lassiter* decision. Instead, Justice Brennan's opinion for the majority relied on two alternative theories of Congress's power under Section 5. The first theory was that Congress had the power to conclude that the Puerto Rican minority needed the right to vote to assure themselves nondiscriminatory treatment in various public services—extending them the right to vote was a remedy for the discrimination they would otherwise suffer. The second more radical and alternative theory was to suggest that Congress itself could have concluded that the English-literacy requirement was a violation of the Equal Protection Clause notwithstanding the Supreme Court's earlier holding that it was not a violation—that Congress could define and redefine the scope of individual constitutional liberty. Justice Harlan expressed exasperation for this second alternative theory in his dissenting opinion, to which the majority responded in turn by dropping a footnote surmising that the Section 5 power was only "to enforce" the Fourteenth Amendment. Therefore, Congress had no power whatsoever to restrict, abrogate, or dilute the individual guarantees of the Amendment—Congress could ratchet up the constitutional protection for individual liberty but could not ratchet it down. This application of Justice Brennan's so-called ratchet theory might be illustrated on our constitutional diagram this way:

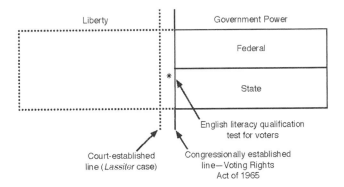

This ratchet theory is troublesome as a general proposition of constitutional law, and it also is troublesome specifically. As a general proposition, it is troublesome because it destroys or at least profoundly weakens the core American constitutional principle that the ultimate authority in defining constitutional rights is in the judiciary. Specifically, it is troublesome because if the Congress has the power to increase individual liberties, logic would demand that it also should have the power to decrease them. In terms of our constitutional diagram, if Congress can move the all-important boundary line between liberty and government power one way, then logically it should have the power to move it the other way.

The ratchet theory also ignores the inevitable externalities of affording individual liberty and freedom. We have already seen that constitutional liberties consist unavoidably of the balancing of the rights of an individual against the rights of other individuals, as was discussed above in § 5 (Competing Constitutional Liberties). Every protection of the constitutional freedom of one individual to act a certain way is a denial of the freedom of other citizens not to be subjected to that action or conduct. Protecting a woman's right to associate with an all-male organization prevents the male members from exercising their right not to associate with her. Protecting an organization's right not to associate with a person of a certain sexual orientation prevents that person from exercising a right to associate with the organization and its members. Even legislation authorizing non-English speaking voters, at least to some extent, lessens the voting strength and power of English-speaking voters. These comparisons are not made to take sides in these situations; the point is merely to remark on the reality of this logical mutuality in constitutional analysis.

The broad language Justice Brennan used in *Katzenbach v. Morgan* purporting to interpret Section 5 to authorize Congress to define constitutional rights was unnecessary to the decision and has been disavowed at different times since by the Supreme Court. Two particular disavowals are the most important. First, in *Oregon v. Mitchell*, 400 U.S. 112 (1970), a federal statute that lowered the minimum voting age from 21 to 18 in federal and state elections was struck down. Although badly divided on their rationales, a clear majority of the Justices rejected the theory that Congress had the power to invalidate state voting laws under Section 5, over Justice Brennan's own anguished dissent.

(The Twenty-sixth Amendment was ratified in 1971 to set the voting age at 18.)

A second, even more definitive, rejection of the ratchet theory of congressional power came in *City of Boerne v. Flores*, 521 U.S. 507 (1997). The Supreme Court struck down the Religious Freedom Restoration Act of 1993 (RFRA) for exceeding the congressional power under Section 5. In an earlier case, the Supreme Court had upheld state power to enact neutral and generally applicable laws against a claim of free exercise of religion when some drug counselors were fired for using peyote in a Native American religious ceremony and then were denied state unemployment benefits. *Employ't Div. v. Smith*, 494 U.S. 872 (1990). RFRA was an effort by Congress to restore a higher standard of judicial review for free exercise cases, in effect, to overrule *Smith* and cases like it, in order to statutorily protect greater individual liberty than the Supreme Court was willing to protect in the name of the Constitution.

Congress expressly relied on its Section 5 power to enact RFRA and the Supreme Court expressly relied on Section 5 to strike down the statute. The Supreme Court's reasoning is instructive. Congress has the wide latitude "to enforce" the provisions of the Fourteenth Amendment—the power to prevent or remedy constitutional violations. Congress does not have the power to determine what constitutes a violation—the power to substantively change the meaning of the Constitution is not for Congress but only for the Supreme Court. Congress could enact congruent and proportional legislation enforcing constitutional rights. Congress could not enact legislation that would change what the substantive constitutional right protects, even when the attempted change would have expanded individual liberty, as RFRA had unconstitutionally tried to do by expanding the right to the free exercise of religion. The *Katzenbach v. Morgan* precedent was not overruled, however, because there Congress could have been understood to have been exercising its remedial power after having determined that the English-literacy tests were being imposed by the states with a discriminatory intent, which was a clear violation of the Supreme Court's stated understanding of the Equal Protection Clause.

Following this approach, the Supreme Court struck down the Violence Against Women Act and squarely rejected the argument that Congress had the authority under Section 5 to create a civil remedy in damages for gender-based violent criminal attacks on women by individual malefactors who were private persons. Congress could not remedy harms that went beyond the scope of long-standing and settled Supreme Court interpretations of the Fourteenth Amendment that have applied its restrictions to state actors and to state actors only. *United States v. Morrison*, 529 U.S. 598 (2000). Even when it comes to the states *qua* states, the congressional power under Section 5 can be used to abrogate a state's Eleventh Amendment immunity against being sued in federal court by a private party, but only to the extent of remedying and enforcing— but not so far as redefining—the rights protected in Section 1 of the Fourteenth Amendment. *Bd. of Trs.*

of the Univ. of Ala. v. Garrett, 531 U.S. 356 (2001); *Kimel v. Fla. Bd. of Regents*, 528 U.S. 62 (2000).

Over time, the Supreme Court has impliedly rejected Justice Brennan's ratchet theory essentially on its own terms: to allow the Congress to define its own power under Section 5 by interpreting and defining the scope of the Section 1 rights of Due Process and Equal Protection would reduce the supremacy of the Constitution to the level of ordinary legislation and transform American constitutionalism into a parliamentary form of government. Thus ended the Supreme Court's digression with the ratchet theory of congressional power under Section 5 of the Fourteenth Amendment and for good reason.

8. LIBERTY FROM PRIVATE VIOLATIONS

One other facet of the congressional implementation of constitutional liberty deserves mention. Here we depart from our general constitutional analysis that defines constitutional liberty in opposition to government power. That constitutional analysis is fundamental and sound for the wide range of constitutional liberties. Deprivations of federal rights "under color of state law" are redressable under 42 U.S.C. § 1983, which creates a civil rights cause of action, but that statutory cause of action does not reach purely private defendants not acting on behalf of the state. The rights guaranteed under the Fourteenth Amendment thus are guaranteed against state violation—against "state action"—but the wrongful acts of purely private individuals unsupported by any state involvement do not make out a constitutional deprivation of the guarantees of privileges or immunities, due process of law, or the equal protection of the laws. *See* Appendix A § 3 (State Action). There are exceptions, however, that fit into our study of constitutional analysis here. *See also* Chapter 3, § 2 (Individual Liberty Versus Government Power).

The chief exception arises out of the Thirteenth Amendment, which on its own express terms does not simply set individual constitutional liberty against government power. The Thirteenth Amendment prohibits slavery and involuntary servitude in the United States and constitutes a prohibition against either the government or a private individual holding someone in slavery or involuntary servitude. This distinguishes the Thirteenth Amendment from most of the rest of the Constitution. It creates an exceptional kind of constitutional liberty, *i.e.*, a liberty that protects against intrusion and violation by private persons as well as the government. The Supreme Court has taken a somewhat restrained approach to its own powers to remedy private racial discrimination, compared to its willingness to defer to broad exercises of the congressional power in Section 2 to enforce the Thirteenth Amendment against private discrimination.

Jones v. Alfred H. Mayer Co., 392 U.S. 409 (1968), involved racial discrimination by the owner of realty who refused to sell the property to a black person. Suit was brought under 42 U.S.C. § 1982, a statutory provision which was originally part of the Civil Rights Act of 1866, that provides "all citizens" the "same right" to "inherit, purchase, lease, sell, hold, and convey real and personal property." The Court held that racial discrimination is a "badge of slavery" within the meaning of the Thirteenth Amendment. The Court held that this statute reached all racial discrimination, public discrimination and private discrimination.

This broad theory of the Thirteenth Amendment was also confirmed in *Runyon v. McCrary*, 427 U.S. 160 (1976), which involved the application of another Civil War era statute, 42 U.S.C. § 1981, which protects the right "to make and enforce contracts" without discrimination. The Supreme Court interpreted the statute to prohibit racial discrimination on the part of a private, commercially operated, non-sectarian school for refusing to admit a black student on account of race in that the refusal amounted to an interference with the right of the Black parents to contract with the private school to have their child attend the school.

Still another Reconstruction era statute, the Ku Klux Klan Act of 1871, currently 42 U.S.C. § 1985 (3), also relies on the congressional enforcement power to protect certain federal privileges and immunities that are fundamental—basically only the right to vote in a federal election and the right to interstate travel within the United States—against any and all conspiracies motivated by an invidious *animus*, even a private conspiracy among individuals to interfere with those federal rights. *Griffin v. Breckenridge*, 403

U.S. 88 (1971). This statute does not protect other federal rights that do depend on state action, however. The Supreme Court rejected the application of this statute to persons obstructing abortion clinics, for example, because it reasoned that the obstructers were not motivated by an *animus* towards women and because the right to an abortion was a constitutional right against only state interference. *Bray v. Alexandria Women's Health Clinic*, 506 U.S. 263 (1993).

All these decisions upholding the application of civil rights statutes to private discrimination are not analytically the same as the ratchet theory in *Katzenbach v. Morgan*, discussed above in § 7 (Congressional Enforcement) of this Chapter, although at first they may appear to be so. Rather, the Supreme Court is holding in each case that the Constitution itself forbids the private racial discrimination involved as being a "badge of slavery" forbidden by the Thirteenth Amendment, which reaches both governmental discrimination and private discrimination. So the congressional legislation, as interpreted, simply enforces or provides a remedy for the understood constitutional violation.

Once the Supreme Court justified these statutes under the congressional enforcement power in the Thirteenth Amendment, and moreover interpreted them broadly, those case developments took the pressure off the Court for spinning a theory of the Fourteenth Amendment to reach purely private discriminatory conduct, a theory that the Supreme

Court has formally and unmistakably disapproved. *United States v. Morrison*, 529 U.S. 598 (2000). A private person who conspires with state officials to interfere with individual constitutional rights can be punished as a matter of federal criminal law, of course. *United States v. Guest*, 383 U.S. 745 (1966). Moreover, Congress has exercised two of its enumerated powers, the power to regulate interstate commerce and the spending power, to enforce civil rights and civil liberties against private conduct that interferes with them. *See* Chapter 5 § 4 (Federal Commerce Power) & § 5 (Federal Taxing snd Spending Power). Finally, the Fifteenth Amendment authorizes Congress to enact appropriate legislation to protect the right to vote without racial discrimination and the Supreme Court has upheld various Voting Rights Acts aimed at the states and state misconduct in this regard under Section 2 of that Amendment. *South Carolina v. Katzenbach*, 383 U.S. 301 (1966); *see also City of Rome v. United States*, 446 U.S. 156 (1980). But additionally, in the *White Primary Cases*, the Supreme Court managed to find the requisite state action even when ostensibly private political parties organized themselves to keep blacks from voting by holding all-white preliminary elections antecedent to the primary and general elections. *Terry v. Adams*, 345 U.S. 461 (1953); *see also* Appendix A, § 3 (State Action) (private individuals acting in concert with the state may be held to constitutional standards). It has been observed repeatedly that voting is the most fundamental right because it functions to preserve all other rights. *E.g., Harper v. Va. State Bd. of*

Elections, 383 U.S. 663, 667 (1966); *see also* Appendix
A § 9 (Equal Protection—The Right to Vote).

The important constitutional workarounds that
allow Congress to enact legislation to protect
individual civil rights and civil liberties from being
violated by other private individuals include the
Thirteenth Amendment, the Fifteenth Amendment,
the Commerce Clause plus the Necessary and Proper
Clause, and the Spending Clause plus the Necessary
and Proper Clause. Those last two other
workarounds are covered in more detail in Chapter 5
(Government Powers).

9.   CONCLUSION

This Chapter ends on a caution. To try to
constitutionalize everything and somehow make
everything a constitutional right would be just as
mistaken as to try to deny everything that is a
constitutional right and to insist that we all live at
the will and mercy of the government. Neither logical
extreme would be true to our Constitution, which
eschews claims of absolute rights as well as claims of
absolute powers. This is the fundamental basis for
imagining the constitutional diagram in which
individual liberty is arrayed against government
power. There is some balance, some equilibrium,
some equipoise, in our American constitutionalism.
It is supposed to make sense.

The scope of individual liberty that the
Constitution protects is limited for good reasons.
First, of course, ours is a government of ordered
liberty. We are by our nature rights-bearing

individuals. But there are powers and authorities that only the government can perform. We need the government to protect life, liberty, and property. Only the power of the government to protect our rights is equal to the power of the government to deprive us of our rights. Second, we take for granted the division of life into the public sphere and the private sphere. The Constitution maps the boundary between public and private. Third, the Constitution is the law that governs the relationship of the individual with the government; it is the law for the government. Other forms of law—criminal law, tort law and property law—govern the relationship between individuals for the most part. Thus, some of the most important legal rights we have are non-constitutional rights.

The Constitution thus might be likened to one of those formless, backless gowns that are standard issue in a hospital: no matter how hard you pull on it and try to rearrange it, it does not cover everything and sometimes it does not cover things that are important to you.

CHAPTER 5

GOVERNMENT POWERS

In Chapter 3, you were introduced to the constitutional diagram that divided individual liberty from government power. In Chapter 4, the emphasis was on Constitutional Liberty on the left side of that constitutional diagram. The subject of this Chapter is Government Powers on the right side of the constitutional diagram. This dichotomy between individual liberty and government power is the self-disciplining insight of this NUTSHELL that will help you become a master of the study of constitutional law.

1. CONSTITUTIONAL POWERS

The 1787 Constitution of the United States constitutes a federal system of ordered liberty that contemplates a balance between individual liberty and government power. The people are sovereign—the ultimate source of all power and legitimacy. The Constitution is the fulfillment of the *Declaration of Independence of 1776*:

> We hold these truths to be self-evident, that all men are created equal, that they are endowed by their Creator with certain unalienable Rights, that among these are Life, Liberty and the pursuit of Happiness. That to secure these rights, Governments are instituted among Men, deriving their just powers from the consent of the governed * * *.

The Tenth Amendment describes the people's allocation of powers in these constitutional relationships: certain powers are delegated to the government of the United States, some powers are either prohibited or reserved to the states, and still other powers are reserved to the people. U.S. Const. amend. X. The "powers reserved to the people" correspond to the rights that were the subject of Chapter 4 (Constitutional Liberty). *See also* Appendix A (Leading Case Outline of Constitutional Liberty). Individual persons have rights. Governments have powers. The Constitution ordains and establishes and grants powers to the national government. State governments existed before the Constitution, but the Constitution limits their powers. This Chapter is about the "powers delegated" to the national government and the "powers prohibited" to the states by the Constitution. The emphasis here is on the right hand side of the constitutional diagram—the government powers side of our constitutional analysis:

Liberty	Government Power
	Federal
	State

National powers include express powers, implied powers, and inherent foreign powers. State powers are not created by the Constitution but have their source in the sovereignty of the people and are manifested by the sovereign state "police power" to regulate for their health, safety, morals, and general welfare. The Constitution prohibits particular exercises of the state police power that violate its guarantees of individual liberty or that interfere with the enumerated and delegated powers the Constitution allocates to the national government. The next Chapter will elaborate on the structure of the Constitution, to explain federalism—the ebb and flow of power between the national and the state governments—and to explain the separation of powers—the competition for power and influence among the three branches of the national government. That the concepts of federalism and separation of powers are equal parts constitutional law and political philosophy is reflected in how Supreme Court decisions have gone back and forth to favor federal interests during some eras and state interests during other eras and in how the Justices have chosen to side with the President sometimes and with the Congress other times. *See* Chapter 6 (Structure of the Constitution).

Implicit in all the cases involving the scope of federal power and state power is the preliminary conclusion that the liberty-versus-power balance has already been resolved in favor of government power and against individual liberty. Otherwise, if the attempt by the state or federal government to regulate and control private individuals falls within the area of constitutional liberty, then we never get to the issue about the allocation of power between the national government and the states. The individual liberty versus government power issue is always primary but only sometimes determinative. In some cases, however, the liberty versus government power issue is so obvious and predictable that it falls away and the Court simply begins with the power allocation issue to decide the federal power versus state power issue. In other cases, both fundamental issues require the Court's careful attention. That is the inherent logic of the constitutional diagram.

Consider the leading case of *United States v. Darby*, 312 U.S. 100 (1941). The Supreme Court upheld the federal Fair Labor Standards Act, which prohibited the shipment in interstate commerce of goods manufactured by employees who worked more hours than a statutory maximum or who were paid less wages than a statutory minimum. First, this holding sounded the death knell for substantive economic due process and the "right to contract" that had prevailed under earlier cases like *Lochner v. New York*, 198 U.S. 45 (1905), to strike down economic regulations of the marketplace. The statute was constitutional under the Fifth Amendment even though there may have been some employees and employers who would have been willing to contract for more hours or lower wages—the law did not deprive them of liberty. *See* Appendix A, § 8 (Substantive Due Process). Second, this holding affirmed the exercise of the congressional power under the Commerce Clause plus the Necessary and Proper Clause. Congress possessed the authority to regulate intrastate activities that affected interstate commerce even when its purposes coincided with a purpose available to the states under their police powers, *i.e.*, regulating wages and hours in manufacturing. In other words, just because the state legislatures could have adopted the same regulation under their police power was not a constitutional reason that Congress could not have done so in the first place under the Commerce Clause plus the Necessary and Proper Clause. Furthermore, the physical shipment of goods between states is obviously within the purview of the congressional power over interstate commerce. Third, this holding reconciled the statute with the Tenth Amendment to explain that the enumerated power under the Commerce Clause was delegated to the federal government and necessarily, therefore, could not be a power reserved to the states.

Thus, in order to uphold the statute, the Supreme Court had to decide two fundamental issues of constitutional law as depicted in our constitutional diagram. First, the Supreme Court had to decide that the statute did not violate individual liberty [1] but instead came within the proper scope of government powers. Second, the Supreme Court had to decide that the statute was a constitutional exercise of the federal power to regulate commerce among the states [2] and did not fall within the reserved powers of the states. The asterisk locates the conjunction of these two holdings:

Liberty		Government Power
	① ②*	Federal
		State

2.   EXPRESS FEDERAL POWERS

The words of the Constitution are a constituent act that create the national government and grants it powers. All the traditional powers of governments, consistent with American constitutionalism, are expressly provided in Article I, Section 8: to lay and collect taxes; to spend for the general welfare; to borrow money; to regulate commerce; to regulate immigration and naturalization; to regulate bankruptcy; to coin money; to fix standards of weights and measures; to regulate the mail; to regulate patents and copyrights; to establish federal courts; to define crimes; to declare war; to raise and support military forces; to regulate the militia; and to perform several other particular powers. To be sure, there are other clauses in the first Article, dealing with the writ of *habeas corpus*, *ex post facto* laws, and bills of attainder, that restrain the Congress. But it was intended that the Congress would wield all the great powers of legitimate governments.

As we will discuss, the federal powers over foreign affairs are plenary, but the federal powers over domestic affairs are limited and enumerated. Article I begins, "All legislative powers herein granted shall be vested in a Congress of the United States * * *." U.S. Const. art. I, § 1, cl. 1. The Tenth Amendment provides: "The powers not delegated to the United States by the Constitution, nor prohibited by it to the States, are reserved to the States respectively, or to the people." U.S. Const. amend. X. Therefore, any and every act of Congress must come within some authorization in the Constitution. The federal government is a government of limited and enumerated powers. In contrast, the state legislatures have a sovereign police power to enact any and all laws, so long as they do not violate the particular prohibitions of the Constitution. Congress has this expansive police power only in the narrow circumstances of legislating for the District of Columbia and other federal territories, and even then it is enumerated in so many words in the Constitution. U.S. Const. art. I, § 8, cl. 17.

Defending the proposed constitution against the complaint that it did not contain a bill of rights, Alexander Hamilton argued that the enumeration of national powers was the best protection of the people and their rights. "Here, in strictness, the people surrender nothing; and as they retain everything they have no need of particular reservations * * *." Continuing he asked rhetorically, "For why declare that things shall not be done which there is no power to do?" *Federalist Paper No. 84.*

As we shall come to appreciate, however, some of the enumerated powers of the federal government are at once exceedingly important and remarkably broad, particularly when they are coupled with the Necessary and Proper Clause. Nevertheless, for a federal statute to be "above the line" that separates federal power from state power in our constitutional diagram, there must be some arguable textual referent for it in some clause in the Constitution. Admittedly, Congress and even the Supreme Court sometime lose sight of this basic proposition now that the modern administrative role of the federal government is so taken for granted.

An important feature of express federal powers is that for a federal statute to be constitutional the statute must be within one of Congress's powers— only one. In the important case dealing with the Affordable Care Act of 2010, popularly and unpopularly known as "Obamacare," *NFIB v. Sebelius*, 567 U.S. 519 (2012), a controversial provision of the statute—the individual mandate— that required most Americans to purchase health insurance or pay a penalty tax was challenged. There were five votes that the individual mandate was not a valid exercise of the Commerce Clause plus the Necessary and Proper Clause, but there were five votes that the individual mandate was a valid exercise of the Taxing and Spending Clause plus the Necessary and Proper Clause. Chief Justice Roberts wrote an *ersatz* opinion for the Court along those lines siding with one foursome on the first issue and with the other foursome on the second issue. *See* 1 KINGS 3:16–28 (KJV). The remaining Justices formed two opposing foursomes. Parsing the opinions and counting Supreme Court noses: one foursome voted the individual mandate invalid on both bases and the other foursome voted the individual mandate valid on both bases. *Nota bene*: a simple majority upheld the individual mandate under one of Congress's powers, but not the other power, but that still means it was upheld. Never forget, however, that any and every exercise of a congressional power is valid if, and only if, it does not otherwise violate a constitutional right. To be valid, a federal statute has to be a constitutional exercise of one of Congress's powers. But a federal statute that violates any one of the provisions of the Constitution protecting individual rights is invalid.

3. IMPLIED FEDERAL POWERS

Perhaps the most expansive power the Constitution vests in Congress—or in any other branch for that matter—is the power "To make all Laws which shall be necessary and proper for carrying into Execution the foregoing Powers, and all other Powers vested by this Constitution in the Government of the United States." U.S. Const. art. I, § 8, cl. 18. This Necessary and Proper Clause is sometimes called the Elastic Clause or the Sweeping Clause. There are similar provisions in the Thirteenth, Fourteenth, Fifteenth, Nineteenth, Twenty-Fourth, and Twenty-Sixth Amendments.

In what some consider the greatest opinion of our greatest Chief Justice, *McCulloch v. Maryland*, 17 U.S. (4 Wheat.) 316 (1819), John Marshall wrote for a unanimous Supreme Court to uphold the power of the federal government to create the Bank of the

United States, although there is no specific reference to the power to create a national bank in the text of the Constitution itself. He insisted that "we must never forget, that it is *a constitution* we are expounding." He eloquently described the nature and character of our Constitution as a document containing the "great outlines" of government and its "important objects," a document granting "ample powers" and "ample means for their execution," a document governing a "vast republic" and the "exigencies of the nation," a document "to be adapted to the various crises of human affairs," a document "intended to endure for ages to come."

The Constitution creates a limited national government and grants it enumerated powers, *i.e.*, specified powers that are limited but supreme within their sphere. These enumerated and delegated powers do not amount to inherent powers, *i.e.*, the federal government cannot do anything and everything imaginable within the internal, domestic affairs of the country. The Necessary and Proper Clause, however, is a separate grant of incidental or implied powers. Congress has legislative discretion to choose the particular means to achieve its general enumerated powers. Chief Justice Marshall gave that clause this expansive interpretation: "Let the end be legitimate, let it be within the scope of the constitution, and all means which are appropriate, which are plainly adapted to that end, which are not prohibited, but consist with the letter and spirit of the constitution, are constitutional." *Id*. at 421.

The Court reasoned that the creation of a bank was the establishment of an instrumentality of government to aid in carrying out other powers granted to the federal government, such as the power to coin money and regulate currency, the power to tax and spend, the power to regulate interstate commerce, the power to raise and support the military, and so on. The bank was an "appropriate" means towards these government ends, and therefore it was a constitutional exercise of congressional power. The bank certainly is not "necessary" in any strict sense of the word—the first Bank of the United States had been allowed to lapse when the second was incorporated in 1816 and we have been without one since 1836—but it was "appropriate," and that is enough to be constitutional. Indeed, the language of modern amendments simply authorizes Congress to enforce the measure by "appropriate legislation." *See* Chapter 4, § 7 (Congressional Enforcement).

4.   FEDERAL COMMERCE POWER

Article I, Section 8, Clause 3 delegates to Congress the power "To regulate Commerce with foreign Nations, and among the several States, and with the Indian Tribes." This is the constitutional reference for many of the federal laws that regulate domestic affairs today.

The federal power over foreign trade and with American Indian tribes is plenary and complete. There is no comparable state power. The Tenth Amendment does not qualify the enumerated federal power. Thus the constitutional diagram of the governmental power to regulate foreign commerce and commerce with the tribes of Native Americans looks like this:

By comparison, the federal power to regulate "commerce among the states" is more complicated and more nuanced. In a famous early case, Chief Justice Marshall defined that "Commerce undoubtedly, is traffic, but it is something more; it is intercourse. It describes the commercial intercourse between nations, and part of nations, in all its branches, and is regulated by prescribing rules for carrying on that intercourse." *Gibbons v. Ogden*, 22 U.S. (9 Wheat.) 1 (1824). The Commerce Clause power was intended to create a kind of common market among the states—two centuries before the advent of today's European Union—to put an end to the trade barriers and tariffs that had developed among the newly-independent states and to place legislative control over that national market in the national legislature that alone was politically accountable to the people of the entire nation. The economic theory is the United States is a free-trade zone—the states form a common market—the economic unit is the nation. Every seller and every buyer in every state is an equal participant. The political theory is that the national legislature can be trusted to regulate in the best interests of the entire nation. In sharp contrast, state legislatures are to be mistrusted because they represent in-state interests against out-of-state interests. Therefore, Congress has the power to regulate interstate commerce inside the territory of the states, not just at their borders, as well as the power to regulate intrastate commerce that affects interstate commerce. In a famous dissent that later was adopted by a majority, Justice Holmes asked us to imagine there was no Constitution and no Congress. Then commerce among the states, like commerce among sovereign countries, would depend on the self-seeking policies of the individual states. Instead, under the Commerce Clause, that interstate trade and commerce encounters the public policy of the United States determined by the national legislature. *Hammer v. Dagenhart*, 247 U.S. 251, 281 (1918) (Holmes, J., dissenting) *adopted by United States v. Darby*, 312 U.S. 100, 117 (1941).

As the national economy has grown and become more integrated, as technology has advanced, the congressional power has merely kept pace with those developments. Indeed, consider that from John Marshall's horse-and-wagon economy to today's online e-commerce in goods and services, what has changed has not been the federal power to regulate; rather, the activities being regulated have been transformed. The modern commerce clause power is equal to the task of regulating the modern economy.

The scope of the modern federal Commerce Clause power has three dimensions. First, Congress may regulate the use of the channels of interstate commerce. Congress can prohibit the shipment in interstate commerce of goods manufactured by workers paid less than a federal minimum wage or employed for more than a federal maximum number of hours. *United States v. Darby*, 312 U.S. 100 (1941). Congress can prohibit racial discrimination in hotel accommodations that qualitatively and quantitatively diminish interstate travel for persons of color. *Heart of Atlanta Motel, Inc. v. United States*, 379 U.S. 241 (1964).

Second, Congress can regulate and protect the instrumentalities of interstate commerce or persons and things in interstate commerce, even though the harm may be caused only from intrastate activities. Congress can regulate intrastate rates of common carriers that discriminate and harm interstate transportation. *Hous., E. & W. Tex. Ry. v. United States*, 234 U.S. 342 (1914). Congress can criminalize local loan sharking activity that funds organized crime syndicates at the national level. *Perez v. United States*, 402 U.S. 146 (1971).

Third, Congress can regulate those activities that have a substantial relation to interstate commerce, *i.e.*, those kinds of intrastate activities that substantially affect interstate commerce. This third dimension of the congressional power over interstate commerce deserves some elaboration. When the Congress has relied on the Commerce Clause Power plus the Necessary and Proper Clause, the Supreme

Court has upheld federal regulations that practically bear some resemblance to state police power regulations. Indeed, in *United States v. Darby*, 312 U.S. 100 (1941), the Court held that Congress possessed the authority to regulate intrastate activities that affected interstate commerce even when the congressional purpose coincided with a purpose within the traditional police powers of the states, *i.e.*, regulating wages and hours in manufacturing. The Court went so far as to state that the Tenth Amendment was of no consequence whatsoever and amounted to a "truism" in that the Commerce Clause power was enumerated and delegated to Congress and by definition the congressional exercise of the power could not interfere with any reserved power of the states. Thus, with the Tenth Amendment read out of the analysis, the only significant limitations on the congressional commerce power are to be found in the Bill of Rights. *See* Chapter 4 (Constitutional Liberty).

During President Franklin D. Roosevelt's New Deal, the Supreme Court upheld a federal statute that explicitly regulated unfair labor practices "affecting commerce." Such an economic impact was enough to justify federal regulation as a necessary and proper exercise of the Commerce Clause power. *NLRB v. Jones & Laughlin Steel Corp.*, 301 U.S. 1 (1937). The Congress and the Supreme Court pushed the envelope of this theory in the famous case of *Wickard v. Filburn*, 317 U.S. 111 (1942), a decision worthy of our attention. Farmer Filburn owned and operated a small farm. It had been his practice to raise a small acreage of winter wheat and to sell a portion of it, to feed a portion to his poultry and livestock, to use some in making flour for his own family's consumption, and to keep the rest for seeding. Under the Federal Agricultural Adjustment Act of 1938, Filburn was allotted 11.1 acres. He knowingly violated his allotment to sow 23 acres and harvested 239 excess bushels of wheat from the 11.9 extra acres, again, for his own use and not intending to bring it to market. He refused to pay the assessed penalty of $117.11.

Our constitutional analysis duality comes into play on these facts. There is first and foremost a genuine liberty question whether either government, state or federal, can control the amount of wheat a farmer can grow on his own property for his own use. The Court's answer to this issue was that Farmer Filburn's "right" to grow how much wheat he wanted to grow on his own farm for his own use did not fall in the area of constitutionally-protected individual liberty. For purposes of regulating the overall national production of wheat, the government could control the amount of wheat a particular farmer grows, even for his own use. There was no deprivation of property without due process of law; the statute was not so arbitrary and capricious as to amount to a violation of individual liberty under the Fifth Amendment. Matters of the wisdom or effectiveness of the policy were for the legislature. The soundness of this conclusion can be demonstrated if one simply imagines how the individual liberty issue would be decided if Farmer Filburn had decided to grow marijuana, again only for his own consumption. *See Gonzales v. Raich*, 545 U.S. 1 (2005) (Congress's

Commerce Clause authority includes the power to prohibit the local cultivation and use of marijuana otherwise in compliance with state law).

But then the Supreme Court was called on to answer the second question of our constitutional analysis: did the national government have the constitutional power to reach so deeply into local affairs to regulate a single, solitary family farm? This presented an important issue of federalism. Even if we assume that a state government could impose such strict production quotas on individual farmers under its police power to regulate the market for wheat—given the Court's holding against Farmer Filburn on the individual liberty question—does the federal power to regulate interstate commerce reach this kind of private, individual, local activity that is wholly intrastate?

The Supreme Court's answer was to uphold the federal power to regulate. The power to regulate commerce includes a power to regulate prices, which, in turn, includes a power to regulate practices that affect prices, which, in turn, includes a power to regulate production for personal use. Farmer Filburn's extra 239 bushels may not appreciably affect the overall demand and supply of wheat in the country, but in the aggregate the total of home-grown wheat being grown by all the wheat farmers in the country was a significant variable factor in the marketplace that accounted for 20% of national production. Cumulatively, home-grown wheat overhangs the market, *i.e.*, it results in a reduction in market demand for wheat or, if higher prices induce it into the market, it results in an increase in market supply. Price is affected either way.

When Congress regulates a category of actors or activities and that whole category, considered cumulatively and aggregately, substantially affects interstate commerce, the courts have no power to immunize one single transaction within the category simply because the isolated actor or activity, considered alone, is itself too trivial or insignificant for regulation. What the Supreme Court is doing is to defer to Congress's interpretation of its own power; Congress enacts such legislation based on its interpretation of the balance between federal and state powers.

Another example of this inter-branch dialog is the Civil Rights Act of 1964, which prohibited private racial discrimination in any place of public accommodation "if its operations affect commerce." The statute was upheld as applied to a motel that had just over 200 rooms located near an interstate highway that had advertised nationally and that served about 75% out-of-state guests. *Heart of Atlanta Motel, Inc. v. United States*, 379 U.S. 241 (1964). The statute was also upheld as applied to a family-owned restaurant, not because its customers were interstate travelers, but because a substantial portion of its foodstuffs had traveled in interstate commerce before being purchased from a local supplier. *Katzenbach v. McLung*, 379 U.S. 294 (1964). Together, these Court holdings deferred to Congress to find there was a rational basis for concluding that private discrimination in public accommodations affected interstate commerce and the legislation was a reasonable and appropriate means to eliminate it, under the Commerce Clause and the Necessary and Proper Clause. This statute is an important workaround of the state action doctrine so far as it protects individuals from the harm caused by other private individuals. *See* Chapter 4, § 8 (Liberty from Private Violations). *See also* Americans with Disabilities Act, 42 U.S.C. § 12101, *et seq.* Once again, the Commerce Clause power supersized by the Necessary and Proper Clause power comes up huge.

Given such a broad interpretation of the federal Commerce Clause power, where is the constitutional limit? If the federal government can reach into an individual home of a small family farmer, have we not defined the scope of federal power so broadly so as to violate the fundamental principle that the federal government is a government of limited and enumerated powers? An old constitutional law professor used to muse, "The federal commerce power covers everything except a naked man in a tree, and it covers him when he climbs down." The logic and reasoning in *Wickard v. Filburn* makes us wonder whether our constitutional diagram should look like this:

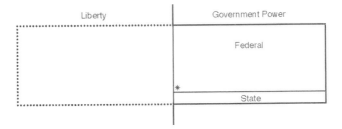

Note: The location of the asterisk shows the case of *Wickard v. Filburn* close to the liberty line and extending federal power deeply into local matters

Of course, the guarantees of individual liberty remain as important restraints on any and every exercise of government power, state or federal. Likewise, we must recognize that there is overlap between state and federal powers so that the great breadth of federal power does not automatically mean that state power is reduced to nothingness. Here is a simple thought experiment to keep distinct and separate the two fundamental questions in our constitutional analysis, the question of liberty versus government power and the question of federal power versus state power.

Assume that Congress passes a statute requiring all motorcyclists and bicycle riders to wear helmets. Suppose you are doubtful about the constitutionality of such a federal statute. Ask yourself this question: could a state or local government pass such a statute? If your answer is: "No, I don't think a state or city could do this," then your concern is about individual liberty. If your answer is: "Oh, yes, a state or city could do this," then you have no individual liberty question; your real concern is only for the proper distribution of power between the federal government and the states.

Or take a reverse situation where a state simply outlaws all two-wheeled motor vehicles on public highways. Suppose it applies this law so that motorcyclists cannot even drive into the state from other states. If you doubt the constitutionality of this state law, as well you might, ask yourself this question: could Congress outlaw all motorcycles on public highways? If your answer is: "No," then you are thinking in terms of individual liberty. You are asserting that constitutional liberty forbids either the federal government or the states from outlawing all motorcycles on public highways. But if your answer is: "Yes, Congress could do this," then you are thinking in terms of the distribution of power between state and federal governments. You are asserting that the state is placing a burden on interstate transportation, and that this violates the distribution of powers between the state and federal governments, but that the federal government could pass this law under the power to regulate interstate commerce.

The purpose of this thought experiment with these two hypotheticals is to make you aware of the constitutional analysis of any case when it contains both a substantial liberty issue and a distribution of government power issue, as did the case of *Wickard v. Filburn*. By asking whether *the other* government could engage in this regulation, you are isolating the individual liberty question from the distribution of governmental powers question. Likewise, you will better understand the essential nature of whatever constitutional doubts you have with respect to a particular statute.

Between 1937 and 1995, the Supreme Court did not strike down a single federal regulation for exceeding the scope of the Commerce Clause power. Then, in *United States v. Lopez*, 514 U.S. 549 (1995), the Supreme Court invalidated the Gun Free School Zones Act which had made it a federal crime to knowingly possess a firearm in a school zone. The defendant was a twelfth-grade student who had been convicted for bringing a handgun to his high school. The statute had nothing to do with "commerce" or any sort of economic enterprise. Nor was there a jurisdictional element that would have required proof that the particular firearm had been transported in interstate commerce. The Court rejected the government's nexus argument that tried to string together inferences that guns threaten the educational process and learning environment leading to a less-educated and less-productive citizenry workforce resulting in a harmful effect on the national economy. The logic of the government's argument, the Court insisted, would allow Congress a plenary power to regulate "any activity by an individual." But Congress has no police power. The broadest interpretation of the Commerce Clause power allows Congress to regulate intrastate activity that substantially affects interstate commerce, but the underlying regulated activity must be commercial. The Court noted that Farmer Filburn's home-grown wheat was "in commerce" in a way that

a student bringing a gun to a high school simply was
not.

The Supreme Court defended the constitutional
distinction between commercial and non-commercial
activities again in *United States v. Morrison*, 529
U.S. 598 (2000). The decision followed the same basic
analysis to invalidate a provision of the Violence
Against Women Act that had created a federal civil
remedy for victims of violent crimes that were
motivated by gender bias. The Court reasoned that a
gender-motivated crime, like the weapons offense in
the *Lopez* case, is not economic or commercial
activity, notwithstanding the statute's legislative
history and congressional findings that had followed
the government's same line of logic previously argued
and rejected in *Lopez*. No civilized system of justice
could fail to provide a remedy for the victim of the
brutal sexual assault in the case, but according to the
majority her remedy was to be found in the state
power over crimes and torts, not in the federal power
to regulate interstate commerce.

Reconsider the case dealing with the Affordable
Care Act of 2010, previously mentioned. *NFIB v.
Sebelius*, 567 U.S. 519 (2012). The individual
mandate provision of the statute required most
Americans to purchase a set amount of health
insurance or pay a penalty tax to the IRS. The Court
reasoned that the textual power to "regulate"
commerce did not include a power to create
commerce; the power to regulate assumes there
already is something to be regulated. Allowing
Congress to regulate individuals who are not doing

something (not purchasing health insurance) would go beyond all the Court's precedents. Significantly, although perhaps a variety of *dictum*, Chief Justice Roberts' opinion explicitly rejected the Government's economic and legal arguments based on the Commerce Clause and the Necessary and Proper Clause.

These holdings—*Wickard*, *Lopez*, *Morrison*, and *Sebelius*—demarcate the outer limits of the federal power under the Commerce Clause plus the Necessary and Proper Clause in the current thinking of the Supreme Court. The federal power is broad and deep but not without constitutional limitations. There is a judicially enforceable limit to the congressional tendency to nationalize more and more of the law in area after area of public policy. Some subjects, like the environment, seem necessarily to require national regulation. Still, much of the law that controls our daily lives today is state law, considering the scope and importance of criminal law, property law, contract law, tort law, family law, and other traditional exercises of the state police power. *See* Chapter 1, § 6 (Federalism); Chapter 6 (Structure of the Constitution).

Logically, of course, Congress can choose to exercise self-restraint and decide not to exercise its fullest powers over the economy. That Congress possesses the power does not mean Congress will exercise the power. However, Justice O'Connor once referred tongue-in-cheek to Congress's "underdeveloped capacity for self-restraint." *Garcia v. SAMTA*, 469 U.S. 528, 588 (1985). So what happens when Congress adopts the famous slogan "just do it"? How far can Congress go? As we have seen, ultimately, that is up to the Supreme Court in the exercise of its power of judicial review. As Justice Black once explained, "whether particular operations affect interstate commerce sufficiently to come under the constitutional power of Congress to regulate them is ultimately a judicial rather than a legislative question, and can be settled finally only by this Court." *Heart of Atlanta Motel, Inc. v. United States*, 379 U.S. 241, 273 (1964) (Black, J., concurring). Congress has demonstrated a willingness to push the envelope of its Commerce Clause power, and the Supreme Court generally has acquiesced albeit with some important and significant recent exceptions discussed above. The Court has demonstrated a willingness to strike down particular federal statutes that in the opinion of the Justices do not substantially affect commerce or the economy, leaving those subjects to the police power of the states. The constitutional analysis may be depicted in our constitutional diagram:

Liberty	Government Power
	Federal
	State

5. FEDERAL TAXING AND SPENDING POWERS

Justice Holmes once quipped that "taxes are what we pay for civilization." *Compania General de Tabacos de Filipinas v. Collector of Internal Revenue*, 275 U.S. 87, 100 (1927) (Holmes, J., dissenting). The first power on the list of enumerated power delegated to Congress in Article I, Section 8, of the Constitution is the power to tax and spend, one of the most important of all the federal powers. James Madison interpreted the clause narrowly to mean that Congress was limited to taxing and spending only in the exercise of one of its other enumerated powers. Alexander Hamilton interpreted the clause broadly as an additional power to tax and spend for any purpose Congress believed served the general welfare. In *United States v. Butler*, 297 U.S. 1 (1936), the Supreme Court adopted the Hamiltonian broad reading, and subsequent judicial opinions have consistently assumed a posture of deference towards changing congressional understandings of what is in the "general welfare." But the enumerated power to tax and spend, like the other enumerated Congressional powers, is nonetheless limited, as we shall see.

In one old and famous case, *Child Labor Tax Case*, 259 U.S. 20 (1922), the Court managed to strike down a federal tax on goods manufactured using child labor because the tax was considered to be a legislative pretext for regulating child labor. But that old holding was only following an interpretation of the Commerce Clause that is thoroughly discredited today, namely, that the federal commerce power did not allow federal regulation of manufactured goods produced with child labor. *Hammer v. Dagenhart*, 247 U.S. 251 (1918). Such federal regulations today are valid under the broad contours of the modern Commerce Clause power, and we can be confident that such federal taxes would be upheld, as well, under the modern Taxing and Spending Clause power. *United States v. Darby*, 312 U.S. 100 (1941); *Charles C. Steward Mach. Co. v. Davis*, 301 U.S. 548 (1937). That an otherwise valid exercise of the taxing and spending power cannot be a violation of the Tenth Amendment—because a delegated federal power cannot be a power reserved to the states—is obvious from our fundamental constitutional analysis, and the Supreme Court has overcome its own confusion in that regard.

Today, a federal tax will be upheld under the Taxing and Spending Clause if it in fact raises revenues or if it is intended in theory to raise revenues, regardless of any ulterior legislative motive of Congress to regulate, even when the practical effect of the tax may likely be to regulate the activity completely out of existence. The Court upheld against a Tenth Amendment attack a federal occupational tax that required persons engaged in the business of wagering and gambling to register and pay taxes on their illegal proceeds. *United States v. Kahriger*, 345 U.S. 22 (1953). The Tenth Amendment reserves to the states those powers not delegated to the federal government, but the Taxing and Spending Clause is a delegated federal power, so the Tenth Amendment is not any kind of restriction on the power to tax and spend for the general welfare. Disapproving some contrary language in earlier cases, the Supreme Court maintained that courts cannot invoke either the Tenth Amendment or their own views of the general welfare to limit the exercise of the congressional taxing power. That holding was about the federal versus state government power question in our constitutional analysis.

Of course, Congress cannot exercise the taxing and spending power—or any other power for that matter—in a manner that would violate the constitutional guarantees of individual liberty. For example, the Supreme Court held that an individual's assertion of his Fifth Amendment privilege barred his prosecution for violating the same federal occupational tax imposed on illegal gamblers because registering and paying the tax would have been self-incriminating under state and federal criminal laws against gambling. *Marchetti v. United States*, 390 U.S. 39 (1968). That holding was about the individual liberty versus government power question in our constitutional analysis. The Bill of Rights once again trumps the limited and enumerated powers of Congress.

Congress has relied on the Taxing and Spending Clause plus the Necessary and Proper Clause to work around the state action doctrine. *See* Chapter 3, § 2 (Individual Liberty Versus Government Power). Consider one important example: Title VI, 42 U.S.C. § 2000d, *et seq.*, prohibits discrimination on the basis of race, color, and national origin in programs and activities which receive federal financial assistance.

The consequence is that a private university, which is not otherwise covered by the Fourteenth Amendment, must nonetheless behave like a state university and refrain from those discriminations, or else the private university risks the loss of federal funding. Given the size of the federal budget, Congress can purchase a great deal of protection for individuals from discrimination by government-funded private actors. Indeed, the spending power can be deployed to prescribe wanted conduct or to proscribe unwanted conduct on the part of the recipient of federal funds. *E.g.*, *Sabri v. United States*, 541 U.S. 600 (2004) (upholding federal law criminalizing bribing state and local officials serving in governmental entities receiving federal funding); *Fullilove v. Klutznick*, 448 U.S. 448, 474 (1980) (requiring 10% of federal funding on local public works to be awarded to minority-owned contractors).

The modern Congress also has innovated to tie strings to exercises of its taxing and spending power in order to "encourage" the states to go along with policies Congress could not otherwise impose on them. Despite the fact that the Twenty-first Amendment reserves the power to regulate intoxicating liquors to the states, the Supreme Court upheld the power of Congress to threaten to withhold federal funding for highways from any state that did not raise its drinking age from 18 to 21. Apparently, the Court's concerns for separation of powers override its concerns for federalism. It will defer to the Congress in such matters, sometimes to the consternation of the states. *South Dakota v. Dole*, 483 U.S. 203 (1987). These conditional exercises of the spending power are constitutional so long as Congress is acting in the general welfare and the conditions are related to the purpose of the federal spending program, but the conditions cannot violate some other guarantee of individual liberty. It mattered not that Congress might lack the power to impose a national minimum drinking age directly. It was enough that the states could theoretically turn down the federal funding.

As was previously mentioned, in the important case of *NFIB v. Sebelius*, 567 U.S. 519 (2012), a five member majority interpreted the individual mandate provision—which required most Americans to purchase health insurance or pay a penalty tax—in such a way as to be a valid exercise of the Taxing and Spending Clause plus the Necessary and Proper Clause. The power to tax included a power to tax the passive decision not to buy health insurance. Congress's intention to influence people to purchase health insurance was permissible, since the only consequence of an individual's noncompliance with the mandate was to pay money into the Federal Treasury. Another provision of the Affordable Care Act, however, was not spared by the Court. Congress dramatically expanded the coverage and costs of Medicaid to the states, according to some estimates by $100 billion per year or nearly 40%. Here Congress went too far, however, to coerce the states into accepting the higher costs by threatening to withhold *all* Medicaid funding from the states, not just the additional funds for the expansion of the program, from the states that refused to comply. Chief Justice Roberts compared what he called this "economic dragooning" to be an unconstitutional kind of Godfather's offer the states could not refuse—he actually likened it to holding a gun to somebody's head. *Id*. at 528. What was remarkable about this decision is that it is the first and only time the Supreme Court invalidated a congressional exercise of the taxing and spending power to bribe the states. It is a powerful reminder that the congressional powers enumerated in Article I, § 8 are limited powers.

The scope of the Taxing and Spending Clause power, augmented by the somewhat shady congressional technique of "bribing" the states into doing the bidding of Congress, has the overall effect of increasing the federal power at the expense of state power. This can be depicted in our constitutional diagram this way:

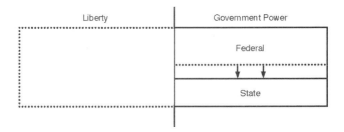

6.   FOREIGN AFFAIRS POWERS

The United States is a sovereign nation among the nations of the world. The Constitution contains some specific references to federal powers over foreign affairs. Article II enumerates various powers of the

President: to make treaties subject to the ratification of two-thirds of the Senate, to appoint and receive ambassadors, and to act as Commander-in-Chief of the armed forces. U.S. Const. art. II, §§ 2 & 3. Congress is given the powers to declare war, to enforce international law, and to regulate immigration and naturalization. U.S. Const. art. I, § 8, cls. 4, 10 & 11. In the history of these powers, the Executive Branch has dominated the arena of foreign affairs.

The nature of the federal power over foreign affairs is different than the federal power over domestic affairs. There are no inherent powers in domestic affairs, *i.e.*, the federal government is a government of limited and enumerated powers. *Kansas v. Colorado*, 206 U.S. 46 (1907). In foreign affairs, however, the federal government possesses extra-constitutional powers, pre-constitutional powers that are inherent in the national sovereign as a nation-state among the other nation-states of the world. The United States government exercises the "external sovereignty" of the nation to the exclusion of the states. This has been an aspect of international law and the world order since the Peace of Westphalia in the 17th century. According to the Supreme Court, national powers over foreign affairs were transferred from the Crown of England to the United States of America by the *Declaration of Independence*; the Union, not the states, was endowed with these powers that do not depend on the affirmative grants of powers in the Constitution. *United States v. Curtiss-Wright Exp. Corp.*, 299 U.S. 304 (1936). According to this theory, the powers to conduct foreign affairs—to declare war, to make peace and to enter into treaties—would be vested in the federal government even if there were no mention of them in the text of the Constitution. Our federal system—the relationship between our states and the federal government—is an internal domestic matter. It is not of concern to the nations of the world in their relations to the United States as a nation. *See* U.S. Const. art. I, § 10 (prohibiting states from entering into treaties).

The treaty power, like all the other powers in the Constitution, is necessarily subject to constitutional limitations. Beyond peradventure, "no agreement with a foreign nation can confer power on the Congress, or on any other branch of Government, which is free from the restraints of the Constitution." *Reid v. Covert*, 354 U.S. 1, 16 (1957). The rules of international law and provisions of international treaties are subject to the provisions of the Bill of Rights and other guarantees of individual liberty; neither a treaty nor an executing statute can be given effect in violation of the Constitution. This is contrary to international law, which places no limits on the purpose or the subject matter of international agreements other than that they may not contravene some peremptory norm of international law. But the Constitution, not international law, is the supreme law of the land within the legal system of the United States.

In *Missouri v. Holland*, 252 U.S. 416 (1920), Justice Holmes delivered an opinion for the Court upholding the Migratory Bird Treaty Act of 1918 against the state's challenge based on the Tenth Amendment, even though an earlier federal statute, before there was a treaty, had been struck down on that same ground. The treaty and the statute protected birds migrating between Canada and the United States. Between the federal government and the states, the treaty and the statute were "the supreme Law of the Land" and superseded all state laws about the migratory birds. U.S. Const. art. VI, cl. 2. The federal government possessed a power to regulate the migratory birds after the treaty that it did not possess before the treaty. Before the treaty, the first statute did not implement any federal power and it was invalid; after the treaty, the second statute did implement a federal power—the federal treaty power—and it was a valid exercise of that power plus the Necessary and Proper Clause power. The treaty power is one of the federal government's enumerated and delegated powers, so the second statute did not violate the Tenth Amendment's reservation of state powers to the states. *Q.E.D.*

In our constitutional analysis, therefore, for a treaty to be valid we must answer the liberty versus government power question in favor of government power. The vertical line between individual liberty and government power remains constant. Turning then to the subject of this Chapter, however, the federal treaty power can be exercised to increase federal powers and to diminish state powers, *i.e.*, the horizontal line separating federal and state powers can be moved. This can be drawn in our constitutional diagram:

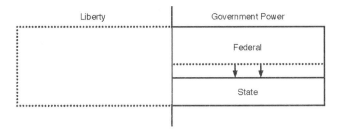

Effect of treaty-making power on federal
power—note it has no impact on liberty

7.   STATE POLICE POWERS

The   Founders   described   their   design   of
government powers in *Federalist Paper No. 45*:

> The   powers   delegated   by   the   proposed
> Constitution to the Federal Government are few
> and defined. Those which are to remain in the
> State   Governments   are   numerous   and
> indefinite. * * * The powers reserved to the
> several States will extend to all the objects,
> which in the ordinary course of affairs, concern
> the lives, liberties, and properties of the people,
> and   the   internal   order,   improvement,   and
> prosperity of the State.

There are many discontinuities between their time
and ours. Today, we take for granted the expansive
role that government plays in all aspects of our lives.
Federal powers are still delegated and enumerated,
but have grown apace, like the power over interstate
commerce; the power is still limited to "commerce
among the states," but that commerce has grown and

become more complex and integrated into a national economy that itself is now situated within a global economy. Wars and depressions and other crises have grown the modern administrative state into the Leviathan the federal government has become. But the increased prominence of the federal government has not correspondingly diminished the power of the states, which have also become modern governments with their own comprehensive programs and pervasive regulations.

The states possess a kind of sovereign power that the federal government does not possess: the state "police power"—the general power to regulate for the health, safety, morals, and general welfare of its citizens and for the common good of society. The only limitations on the police power of a state are found in the prohibitions in the United States Constitution and in the state's own constitution.

Article I, Section 10, contains some important federal prohibitions on state sovereignty. States may not enter any treaty, unilaterally wage war, coin money, or pass a bill of attainder, an *ex post facto* law or a law impairing the obligation of contracts. U.S. Const. art. I, § 10. States may not violate the civil rights and civil liberties guaranteed in the Constitution. The Fourteenth Amendment Due Process Clause incorporates most of the provisions of the Bill of Rights and applies them to the states, and that Amendment contains the Privileges or Immunities Clause and the Equal Protection Clause as well. U.S. Const. amend. XIV. The Supremacy Clause also is an important limitation on the state police power that provides that the Constitution and all valid constitutional federal laws and all treaties are the "Supreme Law of the Land" and consequently preempt any and every state law, including a state constitution, that is in conflict with the federal law. U.S. Const. art. VI. The Constitution also explicitly reserves some powers to the states, for example: the power to conduct elections for Congress and the President, the power to ratify proposed amendments, and the power to regulate intoxicating liquor. U.S. Const. art. I, §§ 2 & 3, art. II § 1, art. V & amend. XXI. The Constitution preserves the states and relies on them to structure the Union. *See generally* Chapter 6 (Structure of the Constitution).

Many state constitutions contain state bills of rights and protections of individual rights that go beyond the rights protected in the United States Constitution. Sometimes these state provisions guarantee wholly new and completely different protections that have no federal counterpart, like a state constitutional right to a free public education. Sometimes these state provisions resemble their federal counterpart but are interpreted more broadly, like a state free-speech provision that is interpreted by the state supreme court to protect obscene material, *i.e.*, material that is not protected under the First and Fourteenth Amendments to the United States Constitution. These state constitutional provisions are limits on the exercise of the state police power, but for our purposes they are not part of our study of constitutional analysis under the United States Constitution.

This sequence of state powers tracks the familiar Tenth Amendment typology of rights and powers and the fundamental principle of American constitutionalism that the source of all sovereignty is in the people: (1) powers are delegated to the federal government; (2) powers are reserved to the states; and (3) powers are reserved to the people, *i.e.*, the rights and individual liberties guaranteed by the United States Constitution. Instead of "power *to* the people" the more appropriate chant would be "power *from* the people." *See* Chapter 1 (American Constitutionalism).

For purposes of our constitutional analysis, the basic content of the residual state government powers in our constitutional diagram follows upon our two fundamental inquiries. *See* Chapter 3 (Constitutional Analysis). First, we take away the individual liberty and freedoms guaranteed by the Constitution. That balance of individual liberty versus government power was the subject of the last Chapter. *See* Chapter 4 (Constitutional Liberty). Second, we take away the enumerated and delegated powers of the federal government, a national government limited in its objects but supreme within its sphere, and consequently we divest the states of some of their original powers. It is this balance between federal power and state power that is the subject of this Chapter on Government Powers. What is left in the state government power portion of our constitutional diagram is the state police power as modulated by the Constitution:

Liberty	Government Power
	Federal
	State

8.   DORMANT OR NEGATIVE COMMERCE CLAUSE

Early on in our constitutional history, the Supreme Court struggled to reconcile the delegation of limited and enumerated powers to the federal government with the extant police power of the sovereign states. The question was whether the delegation of powers to the national government under Article I, Section 8, of the Constitution constituted an implied denial of the same powers to the states.

For some of the federal powers it appeared rather obvious that the nature of the power delegated did constitute a necessary denial of similar power to the states. Sometimes the text makes it redundantly certain, as for example the power to "coin Money" that in so many words is expressly delegated to the Congress and at once expressly denied the states. U.S. Const. art. I, § 8, cl. 5 & § 10, cl. 1. Sometimes the language of the delegation makes it certain, as for example when Article I, Section 8, clause 17, expressly provides Congress with the power "[t]o exercise exclusive Legislation in all Cases whatsoever" over what has come to be known as the District of Columbia. Other powers, like the postal power or the power to wage war must reasonably be interpreted to be exclusively federal. But at the same time, other federal powers, like the taxing and spending powers or the power to borrow money, must reasonably be interpreted to be concurrent, *i.e.*, the grant of the power to the federal government did not deny the same power to the state governments. Thus, determining the negative implications for the state police power from the federal delegated powers has been a matter for the Supreme Court to resolve on a clause-by-clause or power-by-power basis. For example, the Twenty-first Amendment carves out commerce in intoxicating liquor from the congressional authority and places it under the regulatory control of the states. U.S. Const. amend. XXI. However, the states' power to regulate does not go so far as to discriminate in favor of in-state producers and against out-of-state producers. *Granholm v. Heald*, 544 U.S. 460 (2005).

How and when to interpret a particular federal enumeration to effectuate an "implied prohibition" on the states is an important issue for our understanding of government powers in this Chapter. Consider the Commerce Clause power. What should be the effect of this delegated power in the absence of federal legislation, when Congress has not positively exercised its delegated power to legislate on the subject? How should the Supreme Court interpret the "great silences" of the Constitution? How should the Supreme Court interpret the sounds of silence on the part of Congress?

Logically, the Supreme Court had three possible interpretations of the Commerce Clause power to choose among: (1) the power is exclusively federal, like the war-making power, to impliedly prohibit any and all state regulations affecting interstate commerce; (2) the power is concurrent in the state and federal governments, without any implied prohibition on state power to regulate interstate commerce and therefore any state regulation is valid unless and until Congress actually exercises its commerce power to preempt the state law; or (3) the power is concurrent state and federal but with an implied prohibition that is judicially enforceable to invalidate some state laws even in the absence of federal legislation. Eventually, the Court would select choice (3) and would conclude that when the federal commerce power lies dormant the Commerce Clause still may act as a negative on some state legislation, *i.e.*, the constitutional provision itself is a self-executing limitation on the state police power and is judicially-enforceable. This "dormant" or "negative" Commerce Clause power creates the boundary in our constitutional diagram separating the federal commerce power from the state police power.

In his famous opinion in *Gibbons v. Ogden*, 22 U.S. (9 Wheat.) 1 (1824), Chief Justice Marshall, devout Federalist and determined nationalist, seemed to flirt with the first interpretation above and paused to comment that it had "great force" and that the Court was "not satisfied that it has been refuted," but the Court did not end up holding that the federal commerce power was exclusive. Nor did the Court accept the second interpretation above to the effect that the power to regulate interstate commerce was like the power to tax, and so any state commerce regulation was possible so long as it did not conflict with an actual federal commerce regulation. But the Court did not need to decide the legal effect of the dormant Commerce Clause, *i.e.*, the effect of the constitutional provision when there was no federal regulation. Instead, the Court held, as between the two litigating competitors, that the state steamboat license that gave the plaintiff-operator a monopoly was in conflict with a valid federal steamboat license that had in fact been issued to the defendant-operator and, therefore, under the Supremacy Clause the state license had to give way to the federal license.

Five years later, in what otherwise is merely a note case, Chief Justice Marshall squarely rejected the first interpretation above. *Willson v. Black Bird Creek Marsh Co.*, 27 U.S. (2 Pet.) 245 (1829). The state had legislatively authorized the building of a dam across a creek. Because the creek was navigable, there was no question that the federal government had power to control the uses of the creek and the building of a dam across it. But Congress had not in fact engaged in any such regulation. Chief Justice Marshall found that the authorization of the dam by the state could not be considered "as repugnant to the power to regulate commerce in its dormant state."

In a series of transition cases, the Supreme Court went back and forth to hold that some state regulations originated in the state police power and were valid but other state regulations originated in the federal commerce power and were invalid. Then the Supreme Court coalesced behind the distinction between those matters involving commerce in which the states continue to have constitutional power to regulate and those matters in which the Constitution itself forbids the states to regulate.

In *Cooley v. Bd. of Wardens*, 53 U.S. (12 How.) 299 (1851), the Court formally announced this rule of "selective exclusivity"—rejecting interpretations (1) and (2) above and basically settling on interpretation (3)—what we call today the dormant or negative Commerce Clause doctrine. The Court's basic distinction was between "national" interstate commerce and "local" interstate commerce. As to national matters, the states have no power per the Commerce Clause itself. But as to local matters, the states do have power. The justification for the distinction was the need for some kinds of interstate commerce always to be regulated on a uniform basis. These matters require exclusive control by Congress. But other kinds of interstate commerce require diversity to allow for local needs. These are the local areas that permit state control. In the case, a state statute that required ships to engage a local pilot when entering or leaving the port was deemed to be a local matter and a proper subject of state regulation. This basic distinction remains part of the constitutional analysis today, although there have been some refinements and adjustments, as will be discussed.

To represent this in our constitutional diagram, we continue to use a solid line for the federal powers, and we will use a wavy line to show the extent of the state powers. This is how we represent the basic nature of the government power—federal and state—to regulate interstate commerce:

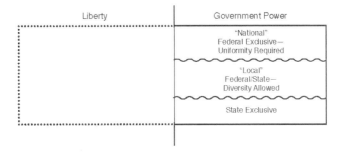

In too many cases to annotate them all here, the Supreme Court has refined this basic understanding of the dormant commerce power to elaborate on its intricacies. For a time, the Court pretended that there was a discernable distinction between state laws that "directly" regulated interstate commerce, and thus were invalid, and state laws that merely "indirectly" regulated interstate commerce, and thus were valid. But that fiction eventually gave way to a kind of balancing analysis. *See DiSanto v. Pennsylvania*, 273 U.S. 34, 43 (1927) (Stone, J., dissenting). The modern judicial understanding of the Commerce Clause is based on an essential economic concept and a fundamental political principle.

The essential economic concept is the common market, the idea that the United States is one country populated by one people who will prosper together as buyers and sellers in an integrated national market for goods and services. The internecine jealousies of the several states—as witnessed during the period between 1776 and 1787 under the *Articles of Confederation*—must be guarded against and cannot be allowed to Balkanize the economy with divisive fiscal aggressions like the customs and tariffs that characterize international trade between independent nations. Stop to appreciate the Framer's vision encapsulated by Justice Jackson in *H.P. Hood & Sons v. Du Mond*, 336 U.S. 525, 537–39 (1949):

> This principle that our economic unit is the Nation, which alone has the gamut of powers necessary to control of the economy, including the vital power of erecting customs barriers against foreign competition, has as its corollary that the states are not separable economic units * * *. The material success that has come to inhabitants of the states which make up this federal free trade unit has been the most impressive in the history of commerce, but the established interdependence of the states only emphasizes the necessity of protecting interstate movement of goods against local burdens and repressions * * *. Our system, fostered by the Commerce Clause, is that every

farmer and every craftsman shall be encouraged to produce by the certainty that he will have free access to every market in the Nation, that no home embargoes will withhold his export, and no foreign state will by customs duties or regulations exclude them. Likewise, every consumer may look to the free competition from every producing area in the Nation to protect him from exploitation by any. Such was the vision of the Founders; such has been the doctrine of this Court which has given it reality.

The fundamental political principle is that the Congress is the national legislature with the necessary and proper powers to control the national economy consistent with the interdependence of the states and that the Congress is politically accountable in a way that the state legislatures are not. Congressional accountability is national. State legislatures have an internal political check only insofar as in-state consumers and in-state producers are concerned. Out-of-state consumers and out-of-state producers do not vote and do not participate in the in-state political processes. Therefore, the dynamic of state politics allows for the untoward potential of state laws that might advantage in-state interests or disadvantage out-of-state interests in a way that the dynamic of national politics would simply not allow. The Supreme Court often has recognized this underlying political reality: "When the regulation is of such a character that its burden falls principally upon those without the state, legislative action is not likely subjected to those political restraints which are normally exerted on legislation when it affects adversely some interest within the state." *S.C. Hwy. Dep't v. Barnwell Bros., Inc.*, 303 U.S. 177, 184–85 n. 2 (1938).

An oft-quoted summary of the two levels of analysis describes how the determination is based on the nature of the state regulation:

> Where the statute regulates evenhandedly to effectuate a legitimate local public interest, and its effects on interstate commerce are only incidental, it will be upheld unless the burden imposed on such commerce is clearly excessive in relation to the putative local benefits. If a legitimate local purpose is found, then the question becomes one of degree. And the extent of the burden that will be tolerated will of course depend on the nature of the local interest involved, and on whether it could be promoted as well with a lesser impact on interstate activities.

Pike v. Bruce Church, Inc., 397 U.S. 137, 142 (1970) (citations omitted).

At the first level of analysis, a state law that discriminates against out-of-state competition will be struck down as economic protectionism and unconstitutional, as will a state law that acts extraterritorially to regulate commerce wholly beyond the borders of the state. For example, when a state prohibited the sale of out-of-state milk at a price lower than the state-controlled price of in-state milk, the discrimination against interstate commerce was struck down for contravening both the constitutional design of the national common market and the norm that the state police power cannot reach beyond its own state borders. *Baldwin v. G.A.F. Seelig, Inc.*, 294 U.S. 511 (1935).

At the second level of analysis, state laws that do not discriminate on their face or in their purpose are subject to a more forgiving judicial balancing that weighs the importance of the state interest against the burdensome effect on interstate commerce. These cases have an *ad hoc* quality: a state law that limited the number of rail cars in trains was invalid because it was burdensome on cross-country railroads and did not actually contribute to better safety, *Southern Pacific Co. v. Arizona*, 325 U.S. 761 (1945), while a state law setting a maximum width and weight of trucks was a valid measure to assure safety and protect state highways, *S.C. Hwy. Dept. v. Barnwell Bros., Inc.*, 303 U.S. 177 (1938).

A state law that is discriminatory in its purpose, means, or effects must pass a "least restrictive means" scrutiny, *i.e.*, the law can survive if and only if it is justified by a legitimate police power purpose and there is simply no other alternative that is less burdensome on interstate commerce. Requiring inspections of pasteurization facilities or imposing product ratings and uniform standards for outside facilities were less burdensome alternatives and, therefore, a city ordinance that required milk to be processed only within the city limits was struck down. *Dean Milk Co. v. Madison*, 340 U.S. 349 (1951). There are rare and infrequent cases when this higher standard is satisfied. *See Maine v. Taylor*, 477 U.S.

131 (1986) (upholding a ban on importing live bait fish that could infect local fish with parasites that could not otherwise be detected).

Our previous constitutional diagram needs to be revised. In the bottom "state power" segment, a state law that affects interstate commerce must have a legitimate state police power purpose and cannot have as its stated purpose the regulation of interstate commerce. As we have discussed earlier in this Chapter, however, the police power to regulate health, safety, morals, and general welfare is broad and malleable. An otherwise valid exercise of the police power that happens to affect interstate commerce is not for that reason alone invalid.

In the middle segment of government powers in our previous constitutional diagram, where federal and state power overlap, note that diversity is allowed but not constitutionally required. The states can regulate. But if the federal government decides to undertake regulation in this overlapping area, the federal regulation necessarily would preempt the state regulation. This necessarily follows from the Supremacy Clause. That is not remarkable, as we shall see. *See* Chapter 6, § 5 (Preemption).

What is remarkable is that in the top segment of government powers in our previous constitutional diagram, where the Court has interpreted the dormant or negative Commerce Clause to invalidate a state law—either because the state regulation is discriminatory or because the state interests are outweighed by the need for national uniformity—Congress can nevertheless override the Court by enacting a statute authorizing the state regulation, so long as the authorization is unmistakably clear. See *Leisy v. Hardin*, 135 U.S. 100 (1890). How can this legerdemain be accomplished? How can Congress by a mere statute change the Constitution? What happened to the requirements of Article V for constitutional amendments?

The Supreme Court has exercised its power of judicial review to interpret the Commerce Clause to mean the implied prohibition we call the dormant or negative commerce power when Congress is silent. But the Commerce Clause is a grant of power to Congress—not to the Court. Once Congress speaks, there is no need for the Court to interpret or imply anything. The statute is an act of Congress exercising its delegated power to adopt a federal policy favoring non-uniformity or discriminatory regulation by the states. The only limits on the congressional power to override the Court are the limits inherent in the Commerce Clause power itself.

An intratextual reading of the Constitution demonstrates that what is going on here is nothing *ultra vires* or improper. There are several explicit provisions in the Constitution in which the words of the constitutional prohibition itself give Congress the power to consent to what otherwise is prohibited. In a provision that is closely related to interstate commerce, the states are prohibited from laying export and import taxes "without the Consent of Congress." U.S. Const. art. I, § 10, cl. 2. Article I, Section 10, clause 3 contains a whole list of prohibitions against the states, including an important one about interstate compacts, and yet the states are prohibited from engaging in any of those activities only "without the Consent of Congress."

These other provisions demonstrate that congressional consent can be and has been written into the Constitution to allow Congress to affect the impact of the Constitution itself in certain particular instances. A similar kind of congressional power has simply been recognized under the Supreme Court's dormant or negative Commerce Clause doctrine. As with any other judicial interpretation or Court doctrine, at least until the interpretation or doctrine is revised, it is as if the text of the Commerce Clause itself contained these words: "The states are prohibited from regulating commerce in ways that are unduly burdensome or when national uniformity is required or when the effect is discriminatory, unless Congress consents." Our constitutional diagram can be revised to represent this interpretation of the Commerce Clause taking into account the dormant or negative commerce power and the congressional authority to override the Court:

Liberty	Government Power
	Federal/State Exclusively Federal as "National" or Discriminatory, Unless Congress Consents
	Federal/State State Can Control as "Local" Until Congress Preempts It
	State

There are two important observations about the power of Congress to consent to a state law that would otherwise violate the dormant Commerce Clause. First, actual exercises of the power are neither frequent nor forthcoming and many are of a quite venerable age. Indeed, the current general attitude is for Congress to federalize or nationalize more and more areas of public policy. This has been so since the New Deal. And, as we shall see, federal preemption of state laws is more the norm than congressional acquiescence in diversity of state regulations or state taxes. *See* Chapter 6, § 5 (Preemption). Second, one should not generalize about the congressional power to consent to the exercise of one of its delegated powers by the states. Some clauses explicitly allow for consent, like the Interstate Compact Clause. U.S. Const. art. I, § 10, cl. 3. Other clauses have been interpreted by the Supreme Court to imply a power of congressional consent—the dormant or negative Commerce Clause under discussion is the best example. But still other clauses delegate an exclusive power to Congress with a corresponding prohibition on the states from performing the specified function and the state prohibition is binding on the Congress, *i.e.*, a federal statute that purported to authorize the states to make treaties or coin money would be beyond the power of Congress and unconstitutional. U.S. Const. art. I, § 10, cl. 1. Likewise, Congress could not waive the Article IV guarantee of privileges and immunities to the citizens of the states or undo the Supremacy Clause to enact a statute that purported to make the law of a particular state supreme over future federal laws. U.S. Const. art. IV, § 2, cl. 1 & art. VI, cl. 2.

The dormant commerce power is an aspect of the relationship between the federal and state governments and, therefore, does not apply to limit the actions of private market participants. Likewise, there is a recognized exception for state proprietary activities, *i.e.*, when the state is merely acting as a market participant, and not acting in its sovereign governing role, the state enjoys the same marketplace freedom. The Commerce Clause does not apply to a private business; the Commerce Clause does not apply to a state or county or city behaving like a private business—buying and selling in the marketplace. So, for example, a state-owned and state-operated cement plant can discriminate and sell its product only to in-state residents. *Reeves, Inc. v. Stake*, 447 U.S. 429 (1980). However, the Privileges and Immunities Clause in Article IV, Section 2, also applies to such discriminations by states as market-participants against out-of-staters in terms of some protected privilege, like being employed by the state or "earning a livelihood." While the market participant doctrine is an interpretation of the Commerce Clause, it is not an interpretation of the Privileges and Immunities Clause. Therefore, to pass constitutional muster under that second clause, there must be a substantial reason for the discrimination, *i.e.*, some demonstration the out-of-staters are a peculiar cause of the mischief for which the only reasonable remedy is to treat them unequally. *Hicklin v. Orbeck*, 437 U.S. 518 (1978). At the same time, a substantial disparity to purchase a hunting license between residents and nonresidents was upheld because hunting is not a protected privilege or immunity under the aegis of that clause. *Baldwin v. Fish & Game Comm'n of Mont.*, 436 U.S. 371 (1978).

Sometimes the Court's distinctions are subtle. It struck down a local law that guaranteed a minimum waste flow to a local private waste facility, but went on to distinguish that ruling to uphold a waste flow ordinance that required local waste to be processed at a public waste facility. *Compare C & A Carbone, Inc. v. Town of Clarkstown*, 511 U.S. 383 (1994) *with United Haulers Ass'n, Inc. v. Oneida-Herkimer Solid Waste Mgmt. Auth.*, 550 U.S. 330 (2007). Understand that the economic activity is not the waste that has no value; the economic activity is the disposal of the waste. *Ore. Waste Sys., Inc. v. Dep't of Envtl. Quality*, 511 U.S. 93 (1994); *Fort Gratiot Sanitary Landfill, Inc. v. Mich. Dep't of Nat. Res.*, 504 U.S. 353 (1992).

The Supreme Court and Congress engage in an elaborate pantomime over the dormant commerce power. Congress is silent. The Court interprets that silence. Congress can always speak its mind. The Court must bow to the legislative will once expressed. The states must follow the federal lead of both Court and Congress. Some of the Justices have been critical to complain that this idea of a dormant or negative commerce clause is merely an elaborate judicial charade and the Court should not take an active role when Congress has chosen to be passive, but as we have seen, this doctrine has been around for the better part of two centuries. *See Dept. Revenue of Ky.*

v. Davis, 553 U.S. 328 (2008) (Alito, J., dissenting); *Okla. Tax Comm'n v. Jefferson Lines, Inc.*, 514 U.S. 175, 200 (1995) (Scalia, J. joined by Thomas, J., concurring in the judgment); *Direct Marketing Ass'n v. Brohl*, 814 F. 3d 1129, 1147 (10th Cir. 2016) (Gorsuch, J., concurring).

9. STATE AND LOCAL TAXATION

The Supreme Court's jurisprudence on the state and local power to tax interstate commerce has gone through an analytical development similar to the development just described for the state police power regulations under the dormant or negative commerce power. There are twin competing constitutional priorities: maintaining the free flow of interstate commerce in goods and services while at the same time allowing the states to extract equitable tax revenues to pay for the legitimate cost of government. Government services, like public schools, cost a lot of money. Taxes are how we pay for them. The emphasis is on fairness and proportionality so as to avoid the burden of multiple taxation.

For a time, the Court's decisions went off on formalistic distinctions between "direct and indirect" taxes and whether a tax unduly interfered with the "privilege" of conducting a business in interstate commerce. In 1977, the Supreme Court abandoned those formulas and adopted a four-part test that balances the practical consequences of a challenged tax on interstate commerce against the legitimate need for revenues to fund state government. A state tax is constitutional under the Commerce Clause if the tax is: (1) applied to an activity with a substantial nexus to the taxing state; (2) fairly apportioned to apply only to activities connected to the taxing state; (3) fair and equitable not to discriminate against out-of-staters or interstate commerce; and (4) fairly related to the governmental services provided by the taxing state. *Complete Auto Transit, Inc. v. Brady*, 430 U.S. 274 (1977).

The Supreme Court applies the basic four-part test with only minor variations to all the various types of state taxes. Different states rely on different kinds of taxes and combinations of taxes. The various types of state taxes include: sales tax; use tax; severance tax; property tax; income tax; gross receipts tax; and business or occupation tax. Their names generally imply what the tax applies to or how it is assessed. Relatedly, the Due Process Clause of the Fourteenth Amendment requires a "minimum connection" between the taxing state and the person or property or activity being taxed. *ASARCO Inc. v. Idaho State Tax Comm'n*, 458 U.S. 307 (1982). A discriminatory state tax might also run afoul of that Amendment's Equal Protection Clause or the Privileges and Immunities Clause in Article IV, Section 2. *Metro. Life Ins. Co. v. Ward*, 470 U.S. 869 (1985); *Toomer v. Witsell*, 334 U.S. 385 (1948). State taxes on foreign commerce must satisfy the same four-part test and cannot be discriminatory under either the Foreign Commerce Clause or the Import-Export Clause. U.S. Const. art. I, § 8, cl. 3 & § 10, cl. 2. The Export Clause prohibits the federal government from imposing any tax on exports. U.S. Const. art. I, § 9, cl. 5.

   As a general proposition, the measure of the state
tax must be reasonably related to the extent of the
contacts with the state, because the activities or
presence of the taxpayer in the state is the
justification for obliging the taxpayer to bear a just
share of the state tax burden. *Commonwealth Edison
v. Montana*, 453 U.S. 609 (1981). Once again, the
evolution of the national economy introduces new
constitutional issues for decision and constitutional
law has to catch up. In *Quill Corp. v. North Dakota*,
504 U.S. 298 (1992), the Supreme Court followed the
precedents and decided that the Constitution barred
states from collecting sales taxes from companies
that did not have a substantial connection to the
state, typically understood to be a physical presence
in the state; thus, advantaging out-of-state online
firms. But in *South Dakota v. Wayfair*, 138 S. Ct.
2080 (2018), the Justices reconsidered the
competitively problematic dynamic in which brick-
and-mortar stores located in a state were required to
collect and pay state sales taxes while their out-of-
state online competitors were not, so they could
charge lower prices. The Supreme Court overruled
Quill and abandoned the physical presence rule. The
Justices self-consciously considered the economic
reality of the contemporary online economy. States
may not discriminate against interstate commerce;
states may not impose undue burdens on interstate
commerce. But a state can impose fairly apportioned
taxes so long as there is a substantial nexus with the
taxing state. Large national online sellers who
engage in a significant quantity of business in a state

consequently maintain a virtual presence there and now are subject to being taxed there.

This brief summary oversimplifies a rather complex area of constitutional law. But for present purposes it is enough to note the similarities and the differences in the constitutional analysis under the dormant or negative Commerce Clause of state taxes and state regulations. A discriminatory state tax on interstate commerce, like a discriminatory state regulation, is very likely to be struck down as a violation of the dormant or negative Commerce Clause. A state tax is analyzed under the four-part test summarized in this Section, not under the two-level balancing analysis applicable to state regulations that was summarized earlier in this Chapter in the discussion of the Dormant or Negative Commerce Power. The doctrinal test for taxes is slightly different from the doctrinal test for regulations, although there is a strong resemblance. Finally, congressional approval will save a state tax that otherwise would be invalid under the dormant or negative Commerce Clause, just as congressional approval can save a state regulation. Consequently, our constitutional diagrams for state regulations of commerce in the previous Section of this Chapter provide a fairly accurate depiction of the constitutional analysis for exercises of the power of state taxation and need not be reproduced here. *See* Chapter 5, § 8 (Dormant or Negative Commerce Clause).

10. CONCLUSION

This Chapter's discussion of government powers illustrates the essential difference between federal powers and state powers. The federal government is a government of limited and enumerated powers. Congress does not have superpowers. But federal powers under the Commerce Clause and the Taxing and Spending Clause have been given broad interpretations, particularly when coupled with the sweeping authority of the Necessary and Proper Clause. Likewise, the other delegated powers in Article I, Section 8, have been given exceedingly broad interpretations. For a federal law to be valid, it must be a proper exercise of a constitutional power and not otherwise violate a right protected by the Constitution. The state police power to regulate for the health, safety, morals, and general welfare of the people is an attribute of state sovereignty that is limited only by the prohibitions of the Constitution. State legislatures are subject to the supremacy of the Constitution. For a state law to be valid, it must not be an improper violation of a constitutional prohibition. Judicial review is the saving grace of American Constitutionalism. *See* Chapter 1 (American Constitutionalism); Chapter 2 (Judicial Review). As we will learn in the next Chapter on constitutional structure, principles of federalism provide rules of recognition for discerning valid federal laws and invalid state laws and principles of separation of powers allocate federal powers among the three branches of the national government.

CHAPTER 6

STRUCTURE OF THE CONSTITUTION

In Chapter 3 (Constitutional Analysis), this NUTSHELL introduced a way of thinking about the Constitution that focuses on the primary relationship of the government with its citizens illustrated by the constitutional diagram. In Chapter 4 (Constitutional Liberty), we examined that relationship from the side of the individual. In Chapter 5 (Government Power), we examined that relationship from the side of the government. Having thus completed our examination of both sides of the constitutional diagram, now in this Chapter we shift our focus to the complex interrelationships among government institutions under the Constitution.

In this Chapter we will consider how the Constitution performs two fundamental and related functions: the establishment of the national government and the ordering of the relationship of the national government with the states. These are the two dimensions of government-to-government structural organization under the Constitution. Along the vertical axis, the national government and the states exist within the relationship of federalism. *See* Chapter 1, § 6 (Federalism). Along the horizontal axis, the three branches of the national government perform their legislative, executive, and judicial functions within the separation of powers. *See* Chapter 1, § 5 (Separation of Powers).

1.   FEDERALISM AND SEPARATION OF POWERS ILLUSTRATED

What has been called "the etiquette of federalism" is as elaborate and formal and, at times, even as melodramatic as any Victorian novel. *United States v. Lopez*, 514 U.S. 549, 583 (1995) (Kennedy, J., concurring). The previous two Chapters on individual liberty and government power both attest to these qualities. While we have said that only individuals have rights and only governments have powers, taken together, the Tenth Amendment and the Eleventh Amendment protect the states in a way that somewhat resembles the manner in which the Constitution protects the rights of the individual— through the powerful engine of judicial review. The protean nature of our federalism is incapable of being depicted once and for all in the basic constitutional diagram. It can only remind of us of the need to observe the boundary between federal power and state power and how important that boundary is under the Constitution:

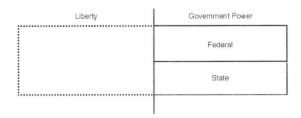

While the idea of the separation of powers is intrinsic in the design of the Constitution and perceptible in its Roman numeral organization, it is more a principle than a simplistic rule. One can imagine the powers of the national government to be rigidly defined and exclusively assigned to one of the three branches, so that they have distinct and impermeable boundaries. Some of the federal powers do fit into this tripartite paradigm. Some Justices think this way about separation of powers. Some Supreme Court decisions can be characterized as merely placing whatever power is at issue in the proper pigeonhole. Our constitutional diagram might depict this approach with the [L], [E] and [J] respectively demarcating the separate powers of the Legislative, Executive and Judicial Branches:

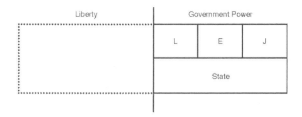

But such rough and crude pigeonholing can often cause harm to the pigeon. Indeed, one cannot reasonably fit all the federal powers so neatly into one of those three distinct federal components. Most Justices do not think this simplistically about separation of powers. And many more Supreme Court decisions exhibit a sense that the powers of the three branches exist in an organic and dynamic relation with each other and their relationships exhibit an uncertainty principle not unlike the Heisenberg uncertainty principle in particle physics.

One cannot measure once and for all where the power of one branch ends and where the power of another branch begins until one takes their measure in a particular case or controversy. Furthermore, their ongoing constitutional interactions are constantly changing how the three branches relate to each other. The Constitution calls into being a national political entity that speaking metaphysically—without trying to sound blasphemous or idolatrous—could be said to resemble the mystery of the Trinity: the constitutional mystery is that there are three (separate) branches in one (combined) government. The equilibrium of the three branches is always moving and changing. It is not static. Powers are best understood to be blended and shared. The branches are purposefully intermixed. *See The Federalist No. 66.* Therefore, we might redraw the constitutional diagram with the three branches of the federal government relating and interacting dynamically with each other inside the area of federal powers:

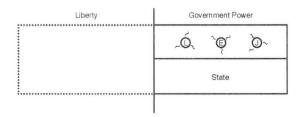

Everyone remembers something about the separation of powers and the "checks and balances" existing in our constitutional system within the federal governmental structure from their high school civics class. *See The Federalist No. 51* ("The Structure of the Government Must Furnish the Proper Checks and Balances Between the Different Departments"). But it is useful to recount a few examples to remind ourselves that the Constitution by express provisions and by necessary implications does describe the respective roles of the coordinate branches of the national government in this kind of organic and dynamic interaction. The separation of powers is manifested in specific clauses as well as in the deeper structure of the Constitution. Consider the interrelatedness of government powers among the Three Branches: Article I-Legislative, Article II-Executive, and Article III-Judicial. *See* Chapter 1 (American Constitutionalism); Chapter 5 (Government Powers). The Three Branches are in a constitutional perpetual motion—they never stop checking and balancing one another. Each branch has its own unique powers, its own constitutional moves, like the different moves the different pieces can make in a game of Chess.

Legislative. Congress possesses express power to legislate and enact laws necessary and proper to its enumerated powers. This includes the power to determine the budgets of the Executive and the Judiciary. Congress can override a presidential veto. It can impeach and remove from office members of the Executive and Judicial Branches. The Senate must confirm superior Executive officers and Article III judges. Congress has effective control over the subject matter jurisdiction of the federal courts. It has power to investigate the other parts of government and to supervise federal agencies. The

Congress is the most thoroughly democratic branch of the government—the most accountable to the people—and pragmatically it has extensive control over the activities of both the Executive and the Judiciary for this reason. Insofar as the Supreme Court is said to sometimes "follow the election returns," and perhaps to some immeasurable extent it does, Congress has this responsibility of indefinable magnitude that lies at the core of a republican form of government.

Executive. The President can veto bills approved by Congress. The Executive is charged with the enforcement of the laws and appoints Executive Branch and Judicial Branch officers. The President serves as Commander-in-Chief of the armed forces. The President has considerable influence and power over the budget and the course of other legislation. As the head of the Executive Branch, the President has considerable authority to determine the policies of the federal government. The "bully pulpit" of the office affords the President an unparalleled influence over the national government.

Judicial. Purportedly "the least dangerous branch," the Judiciary possesses the power of judicial review, the authority to interpret the Constitution and to strike down invalid statutes and improper Executive actions. The Judicial Branch decides cases and controversies between private citizens and between the government and citizens. This power to interpret the law of the Constitution and to apply the Constitution as the law for the government, state and federal, is the great invention of American

Constitutionalism. But the Congress and the states can propose and ratify amendments that ultimately trump the power of judicial review.

The Constitution thus sets in motion the three interrelated branches of the national government in a complex dynamic with the state governments. The three branches do not exist in splendid isolation. Rather, they function together in the same government matrix of separated powers. The national government and the states necessarily contemplate and complement each other in our federalism. The Framers of the Constitution designed a clockwork mechanism, an elaborate yet elegant machinery of government that would go of itself, but a government that would act predictably and according to their plan to secure liberty. They were self-consciously and deliberately practicing the "science of politics." *The Federalist No. 9.* They believed that there were principles of government— not unlike the principles of the natural sciences such as gravity—that were dimly perceived in ancient republics, principles that they could discover and implement in the Constitution. Indeed, James Madison understood federalism and separation of powers to be the most powerful protections against tyranny. *See The Federalist No. 51* ("The different governments will control each other, at the same time the each will be controlled by itself."). The government structure in the Constitution is sufficiently complex and sophisticated, however, that our two-dimensional constitutional diagram sometimes is inadequate to capture and display the entire dynamic quality of these constitutional principles. Nonetheless, the combination of the written descriptions and the basic constitutional diagrams will advance our project to master our subject.

2.   FEDERAL REGULATION OF THE STATES

One line of Supreme Court cases, perhaps better than any other, illustrates the importance of federalism and how competing philosophies of federalism would adjust the tensions between the national government and the states in different ways. The recurring issue in a line of cases was whether the Fair Labor Standards Act, a federal statute that regulated the wages, hours, and conditions of labor of workers in interstate commerce, could be applied to state and local government workers under the Constitution. Understand that the issue was whether Congress could regulate the states and state employees the same way Congress can regulate private employers and private employees under the Commerce Clause. In 1968, the Supreme Court answered "yes." *Maryland v. Wirtz*, 392 U.S. 183 (1968). In 1976, the Court changed its mind and said "no." *National League of Cities v. Usery*, 426 U.S. 833 (1976). In 1985, the Court changed its mind yet again and said "yes." *Garcia v. San Antonio Metro. Transit Auth.*, 469 U.S. 528 (1985).

The 1985 decision of this trilogy, a five-to-four decision that overruled the previous five-to-four decision, illustrates two competing visions of federalism. The majority opinion in *Garcia* was written by Justice Blackmun, who defected and switched sides between the two cases. The *Garcia* majority gave up on the idea that there were judicially discernable government functions of the states that were immune from federal regulation. Neither history nor tradition nor function could differentiate and distinguish such activities. Judicial enforcement of the Tenth Amendment reserved powers of the states against an exercise of the Commerce Clause power of Congress was deemed "unsound in principle and unworkable in practice." The *Garcia* majority read the constitutional blueprint to leave the role of the states in the federal system to the federal political process, the elected branches, and not to the unelected federal Judicial Branch. The states were left on their own to participate in the federal political process to protect state interests, and it is up to the Congress to take into account the status of the states in the exercise of its delegated and enumerated powers. The *Garcia* majority thus interpreted the Tenth Amendment in the context of federal regulation of the states identically as in the context of federal regulation of private individuals. *See United States v. Darby*, 312 U.S. 100 (1941) (exercise of the Commerce Clause power is unaffected by the Tenth Amendment). *See also* Chapter 5, § 4 (Federal Commerce Power).

The dissenters in *Garcia* adhered to a competing previous vision of federalism; they played the role of Antifederalist antagonists to the majority's Federalist protagonists. Justice Powell insisted that the Tenth Amendment was judicially-enforceable in favor of the states, just as other provisions of the Bill of Rights were judicially-enforceable in favor of individuals—who are just as "represented" as the states in the Congress. Justice O'Connor flat out denied the constitutional legitimacy of the notion that the states were left to Congress's "underdeveloped capacity for self-restraint." Then-Justice Rehnquist vowed on behalf of the dissenters to wait in time to pick up the needed fifth vote to overrule the overruling. But that has never happened. The current state of the law under the Commerce Clause can be depicted in our constitutional diagram by the downward arrows suggesting that Congress has the power to legislate and the states are obliged to comply with some federal regulations:

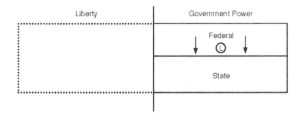

The sentiments of the dissenting side in *Garcia* prevailed, however, in a different later battle in this judicial civil war over federalism by creating a limited federalism restriction on the power of Congress over state and local governments themselves. In *New York v. United States*, 505 U.S. 144 (1992), the Court held that Congress could not exercise the Commerce Clause power to order state governments to enact and enforce a federal legislative agenda. Specifically, the federal statute that was invalidated had attempted to commandeer the legislative processes of the states by dictating to them that they adopt state legislation setting standards for the storage and disposal of low-level nuclear waste and also had attempted to coerce the states into taking ownership and being responsible for privately owned nuclear waste in their states. The statute operated directly upon the state governments *qua* states to coerce and compel them and dictate how they should govern their states in a federally prescribed manner, and that proved too much for the Supreme Court.

While Congress could encourage and even cajole the states into going along with the federal policy, Congress is lacking the power to coercively regulate the states as states. The federal legislature is not the boss of the state legislatures. Presumably, Congress could get away with passing a federal statute regulating the nuclear waste directly under the Commerce Clause or exercising its Spending Clause power to bribe the states with grants to comply with federal conditions or passing legislation under the dormant commerce power theory authorizing states that complied with federal standards to discriminate and prohibit the importation of the waste from other noncomplying states. *See* Chapter 5, § 4 (Federal Commerce Power) & § 5 (Federal Taxing and Spending Powers). The constitutional distinction resembles the doctrine of entrapment in criminal law: Congress can entice/encourage but cannot coerce/compel the states into affirmatively exercising their state sovereignty to enact legislation. This anti-commandeering principle applies to federal laws that prohibit what the state legislatures may enact into law, as well. A federal statute that effectively prohibited state legislatures from approving sports betting was struck down in *Murphy v. NCAA*, 138 S. Ct. 1461 (2018), under this line of cases. The Tenth Amendment anti-commandeering principle is violated by a federal law telling the states what laws they must not enact as well as telling them what laws they must enact.

The Court ruled again that this constitutional limit was exceeded by the 1993 amendments to the federal Gun Control Act. *Printz v. United States*, 521 U.S. 898 (1997). The amendments were struck down for imposing duties and responsibilities on state law enforcement officers in the background checking and licensing of handgun sales. Even seemingly minor duties that were imposed only temporarily and in the interim, until a federal system became operative, were not allowed. The procedures upset the equilibrium of federalism: Congress must depend on the federal Executive, not the state executive, to enforce its laws. The Constitution confers upon Congress the power to regulate individuals, not the power to regulate the governments of the states as governments—"the states *qua* states." Congress may not dragoon state executive branch officers into administering federal regulatory programs.

The Court explored these contours of federalism again in *Reno v. Condon*, 528 U.S. 141 (2000), to uphold the federal Driver's Privacy Protection Act, which limited how the states could disclose or sell information about registered drivers. This was a simple exercise of the commerce power; it did not coerce or control the manner in which the sovereign states exercised the police power to regulate private citizens; it did not commandeer state officials to enforce federal statutes; it only regulated states and private resellers in the market for personal information per the Commerce Clause. Therefore, there was no violation of federalism principles.

This anti-commandeering line of cases can be represented in our constitutional diagram with upwards arrows suggesting that the states may pushback against some federal statutes, *i.e.*, resist and even refuse these kinds of congressional commands:

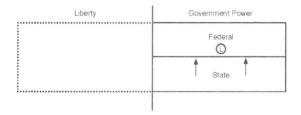

3.   STATE SOVEREIGN IMMUNITY

Federal courts are courts of limited jurisdiction: in order for a federal court to have subject matter jurisdiction to decide a case, the "case or controversy" must come within some provision in Article III defining the "judicial power of the United States," plus some jurisdictional statute enacted by Congress. *See* Chapter 2, § 2 (Case or Controversy

Requirement) & § 4 (Jurisdiction and Procedures). Personal jurisdiction must satisfy the dictates of the Due Process Clause of the Fifth Amendment. *See* FED. R. CIV. P. 4. The Eleventh Amendment also is in play.

The Eleventh Amendment was ratified to overrule *Chisholm v. Georgia*, 2 U.S. (2 Dall.) 419 (1793), which had contemplated a lawsuit in federal court brought by a non-citizen against a state for damages. The Amendment provides the states with a general immunity from being sued in federal court. That is the constitutional default. The language of the Amendment has been interpreted to apply to suits brought against a state by its own citizens as well as by a citizen of another state. *Hans v. Louisiana*, 134 U.S. 1 (1890). The concept of sovereign immunity, which the Amendment constitutionalizes, can be traced back to the notion that "the king can do no wrong" and has always co-existed in some tension with the concept of the rule of law. The Supreme Court has held that under the Constitution state governments also cannot be sued in state court without their consent. *Alden v. Maine*, 527 U.S. 706 (1999).

However, a suit brought against the state by the United States government or by another state is not barred. *Colorado v. New Mexico*, 459 U.S. 176 (1982); *United States v. Texas*, 143 U.S. 621 (1892). The full-bodied immunity is from private suits. The Amendment has no consequence for the Supreme Court's appellate jurisdiction. *McKesson Corp. v. Div. of Alcohol Beverages & Tobacco, Dep't of Bus.*

Regulation of Fla., 496 U.S. 18 (1990). The Eleventh Amendment immunity does not protect political subdivisions of the state, such as counties and municipalities. *Lake Country Estates, Inc. v. Tahoe Reg'l Planning Agency*, 440 U.S. 391 (1979). And a suit against a state official to recover damages from the individual official personally and not the state falls outside the Eleventh Amendment immunity, although the official may enjoy some level of common law immunity. *Hafer v. Melo*, 502 U.S. 21 (1991).

The most important exception to the Eleventh Amendment allows a federal court suit against a state for injunctive relief, an exception that makes possible most of modern constitutional law. The Supreme Court adopted a legal fiction that such a suit is against the state officer as an individual and not the state for purposes of the Eleventh Amendment, yet for purposes of the Fourteenth Amendment there is state action. *Ex parte Young*, 209 U.S. 123 (1908). This inside baseball ruling is a critical workaround the Eleventh Amendment. For example, the landmark decision in *Brown v. Bd. of Educ.*, 347 U.S. 483 (1954), and all the rest of the cases in your casebook protecting individual liberty from state infringement, were brought in federal court under this important, if anomalous, legal fiction.

The Eleventh Amendment immunity of the states in federal courts may be depicted in our constitutional diagram to contemplate prospective injunctive relief but to forbid retroactive money damages:

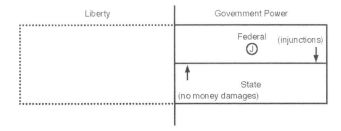

The Eleventh Amendment immunity is from private lawsuits for money damages. The constitutional bright line is between allowable prospective relief, even if compliance might cost the state money, and prohibited retroactive money damages. *Compare Milliken v. Bradley*, 433 U.S. 267 (1977) *with Edelman v. Jordan*, 415 U.S. 651 (1974). A state may waive its immunity and consent to be sued in federal court. *Atascadero State Hosp. v. Scanlon*, 473 U.S. 234 (1985). One of the historical purposes of the Fourteenth Amendment was to give Congress legislative power over the states. So Congress may create a cause of action against the states, even for retroactive damages, by expressly exercising its enforcement power in Section 5 of the Fourteenth Amendment. *Fitzpatrick v. Bitzer*, 427 U.S. 445 (1976). But it is not enough for Congress simply to invoke Section 5; the Supreme Court must agree that the abrogation of the Eleventh Amendment immunity is a proper exercise of that congressional power. The federal law must enforce one of the rights that are guaranteed by Section 1 of that Amendment. *City of Boerne v. Flores*, 521 U.S. 507 (1997). None of the other congressional powers found in Article I can be the basis for stripping the states of their Eleventh Amendment immunity, even in state courts. *Alden v. Maine*, 527 U.S. 706 (1999); *Seminole Tribe v. Florida*, 517 U.S. 44 (1996). The congressional power to enforce the Fourteenth Amendment against the states by creating a cause of action for retrospective money damages can be drawn in our constitutional diagram:

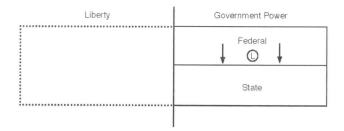

4.   RESERVED STATE POWERS

Although the decision amounts to a narrow factual holding, the opinions in *U.S. Term Limits, Inc. v. Thornton*, 514 U.S. 779 (1995), recorded an epic interpretative debate among the Justices over fundamental principles of federalism. A state popular referendum passed that amended the state constitution to provide that the election ballots in Arkansas would not include incumbent members of Congress who had served for three terms in the House of Representatives and for two terms in the Senate, respectively. The state defended the measure as merely a "ballot access" provision because the measure did allow write-in votes for the incumbent members of Congress. The majority understood the measure differently, to impose a *de facto* six-year term limit on Representatives and a *de facto* twelve-year term limit on Senators.

By a five-to-four vote, the Court struck down the state provision as a violation of the Qualifications Clauses for the House of Representatives and the Senate, U.S. Const. art. I, § 2, cl. 2 & § 3, cl. 3., and also held that it did not fall within the states' reserved powers under the Tenth Amendment. Adhering to fundamental principles of federalism, however, all the Justices agreed that the Constitution left it entirely up to the state whether to impose term limits on the Governor and members of the state legislature. Their constitutional divide was over how the referendum affected members of Congress elected from the state.

The majority, speaking through Justice Stevens, deemed the Qualifications Clauses to be exclusive and supreme. Because the textual provision setting qualifications for members of Congress was intended to be exclusive, the states were divested of any power on the subject. Under the Tenth Amendment, the states could not reserve a power that they did not already possess at the time of the ratification of the Constitution. Furthermore, the majority reasoned that the text, history, structure, and democratic principles in the Constitution would not allow the individual states to add or vary the qualifications for Congress. The people of one state could not alter the relationship specified in the Constitution between the people of the nation and their federal representatives.

The strident dissent, penned by Justice Thomas, took the majority to task for its constitutional analysis. The dissent interpreted the Constitution to express a different Tenth Amendment default: if the text is silent, then there is no bar to action either by the states or by the people. The federal government has only limited and enumerated powers. Each state was delegated the remainder of government powers not retained by the people. It was the people—not the states—that did the reserving and the retaining of powers to the states and to themselves, respectively. The dissent interpreted the Qualifications Clauses to establish only the minimum qualifications for election to Congress. The states thus have reserved powers—from the people—to add other qualifications unless the people of that state have retained the right to themselves in their state constitution. The people in the other states thus had no federal constitutional ground to complain about the Arkansas provision being challenged, according to the dissent.

A subsequent election provision adopted in Missouri "instructed" that state's Representatives and Senators to vote in favor of a congressional term limit amendments to the U.S. Constitution or else their refusal would be explicitly noted on the ballot for their next re-election. The Court reached the same result as it had reached earlier in the Arkansas case and divided along the same five-to-four voting alignment. *Cook v. Gralike*, 531 U.S. 510 (2001). This proved to be the last gasp of the term limits movement via ballot measures at the state level. Not surprisingly, proposed amendments to the U.S. Constitution to impose term limits do not garner much support among incumbent members of Congress. *See* U.S. Const. art. V (vote of two-thirds of both houses required to send amendments to the states). *See also* Chapter 1, § 11 (Amendments).

The Tenth Amendment line the Supreme Court has drawn emboldens the states only so far as the states enjoyed the relevant power before the Constitution:

Liberty	Government Power
	Federal
	State (10th Amendment reserved powers)

5. PREEMPTION

The Supremacy Clause provides:

This Constitution, and the Laws of the United States which shall be made in Pursuance thereof; and all Treaties made, or which shall be made, under the Authority of the United States, shall be the supreme Law of the Land; and the Judges in every State shall be bound thereby, any Thing in the Constitution or Laws of any State to the Contrary notwithstanding.

U.S. Const. art. VI, cl. 2. This language codifies a fundamental tenet of federalism: the Constitution and valid federal laws and treaties trump any and all state laws that are in conflict. The clause thus separates and distinguishes what is properly federal or national policy from what is properly state policy.

Preemption is determined by divining the congressional intent. *Gade v. Nat'l Solid Waste Mgm't Assoc'n*, 505 U.S. 88 (1992). Preemption can be express or implied. Section umpteen of the federal statute can expressly provide, in so many words, "This statute preempts state laws on the same subject." *See Geier v. Am. Honda Motor Co. Inc.*, 529 U.S. 861 (2000). Alternatively, when the statute does not say so in so many words, the courts can infer a preemption by implication. Implied preemptions can be either specific or comprehensive. "Conflict preemption" is found when, as a practical matter, it is impossible to comply with both the federal and state regulations that govern or when the state regulations logically create an obstacle to the achievement of the purposes and objects of Congress behind the federal statute. "Field preemption" is found when the scheme of federal regulation is so complete and so pervasive so as to make it reasonable for the courts to conclude that Congress intended federal law to govern the entire field or area and that Congress intended to leave no room for the states to regulate or supplement the subject matter.

Courts interpret the federal statute looking for these qualities of pervasiveness, the perceived need for national uniformity, and the importance of the national policy in terms of just how problematic state regulation would be. The cases often turn on subtle distinctions related to the subject matter being regulated, distinctions that sometimes are lost on some of the Justices themselves: interpreting a series of comprehensive federal statutes, the Court divided five-to-four to rule that regulation of the field of safety of nuclear facilities was preempted by federal law, but ordinary state tort negligence law could supplement the federal scheme for personal injuries caused by nuclear accidents because the field of remedies was not preempted. *Silkwood v. Kerr-McGee Corp.*, 464 U.S. 238 (1984).

Consider a pair of examples. In one case, the Supreme Court found a conflict preemption between a state statute that prohibited state agencies from buying goods and services from companies doing business in Burma and an after-enacted federal statute imposing various sanctions on Burma. *Crosby v. Nat'l Foreign Trade Council*, 530 U.S. 363 (2000). In another case, the Supreme Court concluded that federal law occupies the entire field of immigration law and the federal law of foreign relations preempts any and all state laws in that area; therefore, a state statute that required aliens to register *et cetera* was invalid. *Hines v. Davidowitz*, 312 U.S. 52 (1941). Finally, it is worth repeating Justice Black's caveat that preemption is highly contextualized: as he said, there is no "infallible constitutional test" nor any "exclusive constitutional yardstick," but rather the nine Justices put on their robes and hold a judicial séance to look for signs from the other side of government. *Id*. at 67. The conceptual comparison to the dormant or negative commerce power should be evident. *See* Chapter 5, § 8 (Dormant or Negative Commerce Clause).

If an area of public policy is preempted per the Supremacy Clause—whether through conflict preemption or through field preemption—that area of public policy is all federal and only federal. There is no room whatsoever for state policy in our constitutional diagram:

Liberty	Government Power
	Federal
	(Conflict preemption or Field preemption)

6. INTERGOVERNMENTAL IMMUNITY

In his famous opinion in *McCulloch v. Maryland*, 17 U.S. (4 Wheat.) 316, 421 (1819), Chief Justice Marshall got off the famous line "the power to tax involves the power to destroy"—a line he borrowed from Daniel Webster's oral argument and a line that often is misquoted or misunderstood to substitute the word "is" for the word "involves." *See* Chapter 5, § 3 (Implied Federal Powers). The decision struck down a state tax on the federally chartered Bank of the United States. Although this *dictum* has had a life of its own, today Justice Holmes's later riposte is more accurate: "The power to tax is not the power to destroy while this Court sits." *Panhandle Oil Co. v. Mississippi ex rel. Knox*, 277 U.S. 218, 223 (1928).

During the heyday of Chief Justice Marshall's heroic brand of federalism, there were reciprocal state and federal immunities from regulation and taxing of the other sovereign's property, functions, and agents. In the modern era, however, state employees pay federal income tax and federal employees pay state income tax. *Graves v. New York ex rel. O'Keefe*, 306 U.S. 466 (1939); *Helvering v. Gerhardt*, 304 U.S. 405 (1938). Real property owned by the federal government is generally exempt from state and local property taxes. *Van Brocklin v. Anderson*, 117 U.S. 151 (1886). Of course, Congress has the Supremacy Clause power to designate functions of the federal government that may not be subjected to state taxes, and Congress also has the power to consent to state taxes. *Davis v. Mich. Dep't of the Treasury*, 489 U.S. 803 (1989).

Justice Brennan once explained, "[T]he states can never tax the United States directly but can tax any private parties with whom it does business, even though the financial burden falls on the United States, as long as the tax does not discriminate against the United States or those with whom it deals." He went on to explain further, "[t]he rule with respect to state tax immunity is essentially the same, except that at least some nondiscriminatory federal taxes can be collected directly from the States even though a parallel state tax could not be collected directly against the Federal Government." *South Carolina v. Baker*, 485 U.S. 505, 523 (1988).

Our constitutional diagram is again "all federal," *i.e.*, Congress can tax the states and Congress can consent to be taxed by the states:

Liberty	Government Power
	Federal (Power to tax states and Power to consent to state taxes)

7.   STATE PRIVILEGES AND IMMUNITIES

The Privileges and Immunities Clause of Article IV, Section 2, provides: "The Citizens of each State shall be entitled to all Privileges and Immunities of Citizens in the several states." This constitutional language summarizes a provision in the *Articles of Confederation* designed to overcome untoward state provincialism and actual discrimination against out-of-staters. The basic idea is that a citizen of state A who ventures into state B is guaranteed the same fundamental privileges that state B affords its own citizens. For some purposes, being a citizen of the Union is deemed more important than being a citizen of a state. The constitutionality of one state's statutes affecting nonresidents cannot depend on the configuration of another state's statutes. *Lunding v. N.Y. Tax Appeals Tribunal*, 522 U.S. 287 (1998) (invalidated a state statute that denied nonresident taxpayers an income tax deduction for alimony payments).

Of course, a student at a state law school paying out-of-state tuition sitting in class next to a student paying in-state tuition might wonder what *that* is about. It turns out that the kind of equality that this comity clause protects is more modest: (1) only fundamental rights, privileges, and immunities are protected, like constitutional interests and the ability to earn a livelihood; (2) only discriminations without a "substantial reason" are forbidden when there is a less restrictive means of achieving the state's goals; and (3) only individuals who are United States citizens can claim the protection of the Privileges and Immunities Clause. *Hicklin v. Orbeck*, 437 U.S. 518 (1978). A state law that required nonresidents to pay 100-times more than residents to obtain a commercial fishing license was struck down. *Toomer v. Witsell*, 334 U.S. 385 (1948). But a 25-times higher license fee for non-residents than residents for recreational sport hunting of wild game was upheld. *Baldwin v. Fish & Game Comm'n of Mont.*, 436 U.S. 371 (1978). The constitutional difference is not between fish and elk, but between earning a living and just going hunting for the weekend. Restrictions on professional licensing of lawyers can run afoul of the Privileges and Immunities Clause, as for example, when the Supreme Court struck down a state supreme court rule limiting bar admissions only to state residents. *Supreme Court of N.H. v. Piper*, 470 U.S. 274 (1985).

Finally, distinguish the Privileges and Immunities Clause in Article IV from the Privileges or Immunities Clause in the Fourteenth Amendment, which does the somewhat different constitutional work of protecting fundamental rights of federal citizenship—federal privileges or immunities—like the right to interstate travel and to move from one state to another. *Saenz v. Roe*, 526 U.S. 489 (1999); *see* Chapter 3, § 4 (History of Constitutional Liberty). The two clauses are closely related and frequently confused: Article IV is properly invoked by nonresidents against a state they are merely visiting; the Fourteenth Amendment is properly invoked by recently moved, new residents against their new home state.

All this may be rendered simply in our constitutional diagram to depict two asterisks marking the protected Privilege and Immunity to earn a livelihood and the requirement of comity a state must afford its citizens and citizens of other states:

Liberty	Government Power
	Federal
	State
*	*
(Privilege or Immunity to earn a livelihood)	(Requirement of comity)

8. INTERSTATE COMPACTS

Among its other federalism prohibitions, Article I, Section 10, provides: "No state shall, without the Consent of Congress * * * enter into any Agreement or Compact with another state * * *." U.S. Const. art.

I, § 10, cl. 3. This constitutional provision is not followed literally, however. It was early recognized that states could reach some agreements and make basic contracts with each other that did not need to be submitted to Congress, the kind of ordinary agreements involving, for example, reciprocal recognition of professional qualifications for doctors and lawyers, the purchase and sale of property, and other such prosaic matters. In *Virginia v. Tennessee*, 148 U.S. 503, 519 (1893), the Supreme Court recognized this necessary and practical distinction by interpreting the Compact Clause to be limited to agreements "directed to the formation of any combination tending to the increase of political power in the states, which may encroach upon or interfere with the just supremacy of the United States." Like all other matters of federalism, the clause seeks to preserve the states but to keep them in their place in the Union.

The federalism exercise of the compact power has been widespread and not infrequent, although it has not been the subject of many headlines. For example, the New York Port Authority was created under an interstate compact approved by Congress. Compacts have been used widely in criminal law enforcement. There also have been compacts concerning flood-control measures. The Colorado River Compact relates to the allocation of the river water. These examples suggest the usefulness of the interstate compact.

How and when Congress may consent to an interstate compact is left to the legislative will of

Congress. But the Supreme Court has made it clear that through its power of judicial review the Court itself has "the final power to pass upon the meaning and validity of compacts." *West Virginia ex rel. Dyer v. Sims*, 341 U.S. 22, 28 (1951). In that decision, the Supreme Court invoked federal supremacy to reject the state supreme court's interpretation of the state constitution as being in conflict with the interstate compact and the congressional consent to the compact and, therefore, invalid. Otherwise, a state could renege on a done deal or try to change its terms unilaterally and after-the-fact.

Our constitutional diagram shows asterisks in both the Federal powers and the State powers because a compact among the states requires the approval of the affected states and Congress:

Liberty	Government Power	
	Federal	*
	State	*

(States' compacts with other States only with approval of Congress)

9. SEPARATION OF POWERS— LEGISLATIVE

Article I begins, "All legislative Powers herein granted shall be vested in a Congress of the United

States which shall consist of a Senate and a House of Representatives." U.S. Const. art. I, § 1. The greater part of Chapter 5 (Government Power) is a substantive account of the major federal legislative powers that are enumerated and delegated in the Constitution. *See also* Chapter 1, § 7 (Legislative Power). Here the emphasis is relational in the context of the separation of powers and the federal system of checks and balances:

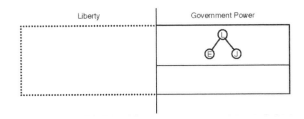

The Speech and Debate Clause protects legislative independence by providing that United States Senators and Representatives engaged in their legislative duties "shall not be questioned in any other Place." U.S. Const. art. 1, § 6. This provision creates an absolute immunity from civil or criminal suits. The immunity applies to members of Congress and their legislative aides, and covers the legislative process in all its particulars: speeches, voting, committee hearings and reports, *et cetera. Gravel v. United States*, 408 U.S. 606 (1972). The scope of the privilege only covers the "reasonable bounds of legislative tasks," however, so while a committee report to the Congress is covered, efforts to disseminate the same information more widely through the popular media to the public is beyond the protection and subject to suit. *Doe v. McMillan*, 412 U.S. 306 (1973). A member may be held accountable in civil damages for defamation that occurs beyond the legislative halls. *Hutchinson v. Proxmire*, 443 U.S. 111 (1979). A federal court generally will not enjoin the issuance of a congressional subpoena by a committee investigating any subject that might potentially be a subject of legislation—it would be difficult to imagine a larger discretion. *Eastland v. U.S. Servicemen's Fund*, 421 U.S. 491 (1975). The congressional immunity is backwards-looking to apply only to past legislative actions. A federal criminal prosecution of a member of Congress is still possible, however, for taking bribes to promise some future legislative acts, a promise to deliver a speech, a promise to vote, or a promise to solicit other votes in the future. *United States v. Heltoski*, 442 U.S. 477 (1979).

The congressional power to investigate, augmented by the sanction of contempt, is not provided for in so many words in the Constitution but is understood to be a concomitant power of the legislative process. It is part and parcel of the informing function of Congress—usually performed through committees—to evaluate the administration of existing laws as well as the need for further laws. These inquiries also can be justified by the need to investigate and to publicize corruption or maladministration in federal agencies. *Watkins v. United States*, 354 U.S. 178 (1957). In these situations, individual witnesses may enjoy some protections of their constitutional rights, such as the Fifth Amendment right against self-incrimination.

In two early New Deal era decisions, before FDR's Court-packing plan and before the Supreme Court became more hospitable to the far-reaching federal reforms dealing with the Great Depression, the Supreme Court invoked a general principle that Congress cannot delegate its essential legislative power, either to abdicate or to transfer its legislative authority to administrative agencies. *A.L.A. Schechter Poultry Corp. v. United States*, 295 U.S. 495 (1935); *Panama Refining Co. v. Ryan*, 293 U.S. 388 (1935). A delegation to a private person is considered the most obnoxious kind of delegation. *Carter v. Carter Coal Co.*, 298 U.S. 238 (1936). Only the Congress has the federal legislative power because only the Congress is politically accountable for its policy choices. Since then, no other federal statute has ever been struck down as a violation of the nondelegation doctrine. The announced standard requires that Congress enact "intelligible principles" to guide the agency—a standard that is remarkably vague and apparently easily satisfied. *Whitman v. Am. Trucking Ass'n*, 531 U.S. 457 (2001). While there have been a few scattered dissents over the years sounding in nostalgia for a stricter standard, the general consensus is that the current minimalist judicial doctrine pragmatically allows for the kinds of broad legislative delegations of rulemaking authority to federal agencies that, in turn, allow modern administrative and regulatory agencies to "do their own thing." While such agencies are sometimes referred to as the "fourth branch," in theory they fit into the tripartite separation of powers under the Executive Branch, although as part of that branch they are subject to congressional oversight.

For a time, the accountability gap created by broad delegations of legislative authority to federal administrative agencies was partly filled by hands-on congressional oversight via the legislative veto. That ended, however, with *INS v. Chadha*, 462 U.S. 919 (1983), when the Supreme Court struck down the device that had figured prominently in nearly two hundred different statutes in just as many different areas of federal policy. In that case, Congress had authorized the Attorney General to recommend the suspension of deportation of aliens, but Congress saved the statutory authority to "veto" the suspension by a simple majority vote of either the House of Representatives or the Senate. The Justices were not swayed that the device was "efficient, convenient, and useful" because they deemed it contrary to the Constitution. This ersatz law-making procedure short-circuited the Presentment Clause— in that the President did not have the opportunity to sign off on the matter or to veto it—and ignored the requirement of bicameralism—in that one house of Congress could act unilaterally without the other. U.S. Const. art. I, § 7, cls. 2 & 3; art. I, § 1 & § 7, cl. 2. The Congress had to go back to the old fashioned way—the 18th-century way—of introducing and passing a private bill to undo the Attorney General's decision to suspend an individual deportation. The dissent asked the rhetorical constitutional question, left unanswered by the majority: if Congress can delegate lawmaking authority to independent and executive agencies in the first place, then why cannot Congress reserve for itself a check on the exercise of that legislative power? Apparently, because the majority believed the Constitution said "no" but not in so many words.

Congress cannot execute the laws—that power is separated from the Legislative Branch and assigned to the Executive Branch alone—and Congress cannot grant an officer under its control a power that it does not possess. The Supreme Court will strike down a law that delegates executive power to Congress. *Metro. Wash. Airports Auth. v. Citizens for Abatement of Aircraft Noise*, 501 U.S. 252 (1991). In 1985, a complicated budget reduction statute established maximum allowable deficits and, if spending exceeded the statutory maximum, the statute required the Comptroller General, the head of General Accounting Office, to impose spending cuts according to the terms of the statute. The Comptroller General, however, was deemed a legislative official because a 1921 statute had authorized Congress to remove the Comptroller General by overriding the President's veto. By placing important responsibilities for execution of the budget act with an officer who was subject to removal only by Congress, the act unconstitutionally intruded on the executive function. Once Congress has exercised its legislative powers to make a policy choice, its constitutional role is completed and ended. *Bowsher v. Synar*, 478 U.S. 714 (1986).

Once the President makes and the Senate ratifies a treaty, it becomes the supreme law of the land. U.S.

Const. art. II, § 2 & art. VI. Congress has Necessary and Proper Clause authority to enact enforcement statutes when the treaty is not self-executing by its own terms. U.S. Const. art. I, § 8, cl. 18. Congress can enact statutes pursuant to a treaty without regard for the Tenth Amendment and the reserved powers of the states. *Missouri v. Holland*, 252 U.S. 416 (1920). But neither a treaty nor an enforcing statute can violate the individual rights protected in the Constitution. This is a limitation of our domestic constitutional law; international law norms do not recognize any such limitations on treaty making. Once ratified, a treaty is on the same level of law as a statute, *i.e.*, they are equivalent federal laws of equal regard. Therefore, if there is a conflict between a federal treaty and a federal statute, the constitutional rule of the road is that the later-in-time is controlling. So Congress effectively can terminate a treaty by enacting a contradictory statute. *Whitney v. Robertson*, 124 U.S. 190 (1888). Again, international law may not recognize this constitutional sequencing but the law of the Constitution is ascendant over international law in the courts of the United States.

While the Constitution sets out a procedure for entering a treaty, it is silent about ending a treaty. A plurality of the Supreme Court has opined that whether the President could unilaterally terminate a treaty was a nonjusticiable political question, as was the extent to which the Senate or the Congress could attempt to negate the action of the President. *Goldwater v. Carter*, 444 U.S. 996 (1979). The elected branches were left to their own constitutional devices. The Supreme Court stepped back from that political fight between the two elected branches.

In the field of foreign affairs, the Judicial Branch is appropriately quiescent. Historically and consistently, the Supreme Court has shown great, nearly complete, deference to the Congress over matters of nationalization and deportation. Policies over the entry of aliens and their right to remain in the United States are left to Congress. *Fiallo v. Bell*, 430 U.S. 787 (1977); *Galvan v. Press*, 347 U.S. 522 (1954). Once a person becomes a naturalized citizen, however, the courts have interpreted the Constitution to prohibit Congress from stripping the person of American citizenship unless and until the individual person renounces or gives it up in an affirmative and unambiguous decision. The government is not entitled to a kind of no-fault divorce in its relationship with its citizens. *Afroyim v. Rusk*, 387 U.S. 253 (1967). There is a Fifth and Fourteenth Amendment distinction, however, between natural-born citizens and naturalized citizens who are born or naturalized inside the territory of the United States, on the one hand, versus persons born abroad who are not Fourteenth-Amendment-first-sentence citizens, on the other. U.S. Const. amend. XIV. Persons born abroad have lesser rights of citizenship, and Congress has more power to set conditions and to expatriate them for failing to comply with the rules for qualifying and maintaining their citizenship. *Rogers v. Bellei*, 401 U.S. 815 (1971). And someone who becomes a naturalized citizen fraudulently may be stripped of their citizenship *nunc pro tunc. Knauer v. United States*, 328 U.S. 654 (1946).

Congress has a greater authority to stop an alien at the border than to deport an alien already in the United States in violation of immigration laws. At the border, whatever procedure the statute provides is sufficient; once inside the country the alien must be afforded procedural due process. *Compare United States ex rel. Knauff v. Shaughnessy*, 338 U.S. 537 (1950) *with Shaughnessy v. United States ex rel. Mezei*, 345 U.S. 206 (1953).

10. SEPARATION OF POWERS—EXECUTIVE

The President is smack-dab in the middle of the separation of powers. *See* Chapter 1, § 8 (Executive Power). The first sentence of the Executive article says, "The Executive Power shall be vested in a President of the United States of America"—*period*. U.S. Const. art. II, § 1. The President's power and influence in domestic affairs and in international relations cannot be exaggerated. The office of President of the United States is the most important office in the world today. His or her powers are amorphous and enormous. Presidential powers are relational to the other two branches:

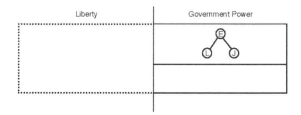

The President's powers are pan-constitutional. James Madison thought there was no federal power to create a national bank when he was in George Washington's cabinet, but he changed his mind later once he became President. Thomas Jefferson believed that he could not make the Louisiana Purchase without a constitutional amendment, but he went ahead without one. Abraham Lincoln defied the Supreme Court over the suspension of the writ of *habeas corpus* and appealed to the higher law of necessity to save the Union from the rebellion. All told, Presidents have sent American troops into combat more than 150 times over the last two centuries, yet Congress has formally declared war only five times.

Justice Jackson described the inconclusiveness and inconsistency of constitutional law on presidential powers in his landmark concurring opinion in *Youngstown Sheet & Tube Co. v. Sawyer*, 343 U.S. 579, 634–35 (1952) (Jackson, J., concurring):

Just what our forefathers did envision, or would have envisioned had they foreseen modern conditions, must be divined from materials almost as enigmatic as the dreams Joseph was called upon to interpret for Pharaoh. A century and a half of partisan debate and scholarly speculation yields no net result but only supplies more or less apt quotations from respected sources on each side of any question. They largely cancel each other. And court decisions are indecisive because of the judicial practice of dealing with the largest questions in the most narrow way.

In that case, Justice Jackson voted along with the majority to order President Truman to give up his attempt to nationalize the steel industry by taking over the plants to prevent a labor strike that the President believed would harm the country's military effort in the Korean conflict. Justice Jackson's analysis distinguished among three scenarios: (1) executive powers exercised with express or implied congressional authorization results in maximum presidential powers; (2) executive powers exercised alongside congressional silence creates a twilight zone; and (3) executive powers exercised inconsistently with an express or implied congressional prohibition results in minimal presidential powers. He sided with the steel mills and against the President because he determined that the case fell into the third category. Afterwards, the Justices had to pour a lot of bourbon down Harry S Truman to get him to feel better about the outcome— true story. Later cases have followed Justice Jackson's analysis, although it is better understood as a spectrum rather than three distinct and separate categories. *See Dame & Moore v. Regan*, 453 U.S. 654 (1981).

The Executive Branch has its own set of privileges akin to the Speech and Debate Clause privileges enjoyed by members of Congress. The Constitution conjures a cloak of invisibility for the President, an absolute immunity from damages liability predicated on official acts while in office. Separation of powers provides impeachment and removal as the only constitutional remedy for serious misconduct while in office. *Nixon v. Fitzgerald*, 457 U.S. 731 (1982). But presidential aides enjoy only a qualified immunity that shields them from liability for civil damages insofar as their conduct did not violate clearly established constitutional rights. *Harlow v. Fitzgerald*, 457 U.S. 800 (1982). Nonetheless, a President may be forced to answer in a civil case for damages based on conduct that allegedly occurred before the President's term in office and that was unrelated to any presidential duties—an important matter of timing and a distinction that former constitutional law professor William Jefferson Clinton would come to regret in his second term as President. *Clinton v. Jones*, 520 U.S. 681, 702 (1997) (Supreme Court famous-last-words: "it appears to us highly unlikely to occupy any substantial amount of petitioner's time.").

In the decision that was a proximate cause for the only presidential resignation in history, the Supreme Court rejected President Nixon's claim of an absolute immunity. *United States v. Nixon*, 418 U.S. 683 (1974). The Court affirmed the denial of the President's motion to quash a third-party subpoena *duces tecum* to produce tape recordings and documents relating to conversations with aides and advisors. While presidential communications are presumptively privileged under the doctrine of separation of powers, the privilege would give way to the government's need to obtain evidence in a criminal prosecution to serve the higher interest that the guilty not escape punishment and the innocent not suffer, at least in the absence of a need to protect military, diplomatic, or sensitive national security secrets. Procedural safeguards in the district court's *in camera* review of the materials were adequate protection of Executive Branch secrets. Likewise, by-then-former President Nixon later would lose his bid to keep privileged his Oval Office papers and tape recordings from being catalogued and archived by the government pursuant to the Presidential Recordings and Materials Preservation Act. The presidential immunity survived past the end of his presidency, but the qualified immunity was outweighed by the governmental needs to preserve legal evidence, to maintain historical materials, and to investigate the need for remedial legislation. *Nixon v. Adm'r of Gen. Servs.*, 433 U.S. 425 (1977).

The case of *Clinton v. City of New York*, 524 U.S. 417 (1998) represents a significant precedent for the separation of powers. Just as it had struck down the legislative veto device that had sought to add a new power to the Congress, the Supreme Court struck down the Line Item Veto Act, which had sought to provide a new power to the President. The statute had authorized the President to apply specified criteria to cancel individual spending items and limited tax benefits as a means to the greater end of balancing the budget. Speaking through Justice

Stevens, the Court characterized the cancellation procedures as authorizing the President, in effect, to amend acts of Congress by unilaterally repealing portions of them. Essentially, the President was substituting an Executive policy preference for the legislative policy preference. Thus characterized, it was obvious to the majority that the President acting unilaterally in this fashion was not following the prescribed separation of powers procedures that provide for bicameral congressional enactment, presentation to the President, signing or vetoing and returning to the Congress by the President, all spelled out in Article I, Section 7. (Aside: while neither the legislative veto nor the line item veto are provided for in the text of the Constitution, it is interesting to note that neither is the judicial veto we call judicial review.)

The side opinions were lively and scored debate points. Justice Kennedy cautioned that liberty is always at risk when Congress and the Executive get together to freelance about separation of powers. Justice Scalia dissented to insist that the statute amounted to legislative authorization to the President to impound funds, an Executive practice of longstanding legitimacy. Justice Breyer deconstructed the line item veto to imagine that the principal statute was incorporated into every single subsequent spending bill or tax reform bill and impliedly delegated discretion to the President to cancel particular provisions, unless Congress explicitly denied discretion in the subsequent bill—a delegation that was constitutional in his dissenting view.

The appointment and removal of Executive Branch office holders have generated considerable separation of powers issues. U.S. Const. art. II, § 2. For "principal or primary officers," Congress creates their position by legislation; the President appoints them; the Senate confirms them. For "inferior officers," the President acts alone to appoint them. Most persons who work for the federal government, however, are merely employees and their employment is subject to the terms of the applicable federal civil service statutes. The President also enjoys a power under the Recess Appointments Clause when the Senate is in recess that must be confirmed by the Senate by the end of the next Session of Congress, which allows the President to fill some positions at least temporarily. U.S. Const. Art. II, § 2, cl. 3. But the Senate must be in an actual recess. *See NLRB v. Noel Canning*, 134 S.Ct. 2550 (2014).

Removals, and constitutional fights over the power to remove an official, do raise important questions for the separation of powers. A noteworthy decision about the Independent Counsel Act is illustrative. *Morrison v. Olson*, 487 U.S. 654 (1988). The Supreme Court upheld that statute against elaborate arguments that it violated the separation of powers by invading Article II powers of the President. The Act authorized the Attorney General to apply to a Special Division composed of federal judges to have them appoint an Independent Counsel to investigate designated alleged wrongdoing by high Executive Branch officials. The legislative impulse was to avoid the conflict of interest inherent when a member of the

318 STRUCTURE OF THE CONSTITUTION CH. 6

Executive Branch is being investigated for criminal behavior. The Court concluded that the Independent Counsel was an inferior officer, not a principal officer. Congress could place the appointment power outside the Executive Branch in the Judicial Branch. The fact that the Attorney General, who was in the President's chain of command, could remove the Independent Counsel for just cause was enough to save the statute. That the President could not remove the Independent Counsel merely at will did not impede the President's ability to perform the Article II, Section 3, duty to "take Care that the Laws be faithfully executed." The Court concluded that the statute also was not an attempt by Congress to increase its power at the expense of the Executive Branch. Nor did the statute undermine the Executive Branch or disrupt the balance of power between the coordinate branches more generally.

Only Justice Scalia dissented. He insisted that the statute deprived the President of the essential, core power to prosecute crimes, a power the Constitution assigns without qualification to the Executive. The dissent's parade of horribles warned about the potential for abuses and excesses of an Independent Counsel effectively operating outside the Constitution and without meaningful limits. In the aftermath of several Independent Counsel investigations during the Clinton Administration, including the Whitewater Investigation by Kenneth Starr that led to the House Impeachment and Senate acquittal of President Clinton, Congress allowed the statute to expire in 1999. Whether or not this legislative dénouement vindicated Justice Scalia's dissent, Congress did seem to conclude that if the Independent Counsel was not unconstitutional, it should be or, at least, that it was a bad law. Of course, not all bad laws are unconstitutional, but all unconstitutional laws are bad. At her Senate confirmation hearing, Elena Kagan took pains to explain whether a statute was a "dumb law" was a different question from whether or not it was constitutional.

In *Free Enter. Fund v. Pub. Co. Accounting Oversight Bd.*, 561 U.S. 477 (2010) the Court qualified Morrison to this degree: one level of good cause protection was valid but more than one level of good cause protection from being removed by the President was not allowed.

For functional and constitutional reasons, the President is the sole organ of foreign relations, possessed of an inherent power nowhere else manifest in the Constitution. *United States v. Curtiss-Wright Exp. Corp.*, 299 U.S. 304 (1936). *See* Chapter 5, § 6 (Foreign Affairs Powers). The President can enter into agreements by Executive Order that have the force and effect of treaties but that need not be ratified by the Senate. And much of our foreign affairs are conducted on that basis. *United States v. Pink*, 315 U.S. 203 (1942). The President can enter into such binding agreements to resolve outstanding private claims by nationals of one country against nationals of the other country by settling the claims or assigning them to an alternative forum. *Dames & Moore v. Regan*, 453 U.S. 654 (1981). An Executive Agreement automatically trumps state laws under the Supremacy Clause and, if the President is exercising the exclusive inherent power over foreign relations, an Executive Agreement will trump earlier inconsistent congressional enactments. So great are the President's powers in foreign affairs that giving these agreements these effects does not violate the separation of powers. Congress is obliged to yield the right of way to the President in foreign affairs. *See Zivotofsky v. Kerry*, 135 S. Ct. 2076 (2015) (approving the President's direct defiance of an act of Congress pursuant to the Executive's exclusive power to recognize foreign nations and governments).

Important unresolved constitutional issues of Executive Branch powers, and perhaps nonjusticiable issues, center around the War Powers Resolution, passed by Congress in 1974, in the aftermath of the United States' involvement in the Vietnam conflict. 50 U.S.C. §§ 1541, *et seq.* The Resolution purports to place limits on the President's power to commit American troops abroad and imposes requirements on the Executive to consult and report to the Congress. Only Congress can "declare" war, of course, but the President has the power to "make" war in the capacity of Commander-in-Chief and in the context of the other textual and inherent Executive powers over foreign affairs. U.S. Const. art. I, § 8, cl. 11 & art. II, § 2, cl. 1. Presidents over the years have chosen to comply or not comply with the Resolution based more on their political standing at the time than anything else, but Presidents have uniformly insisted that the Resolution was not constitutionally binding on them.

Opponents of particular presidential adventures and opponents of presidential adventurism generally have vehemently insisted that Congress is within its constitutional powers to restrain the President. Who would have standing to bring the issue to a court? Would the issue be a justiciable case or controversy? On the merits, the situation would likely fit into Justice Jackson's third category: the President would be invoking Executive Branch powers in the face of an explicit limitation imposed by the Congress. So far, however, this is still only the stuff of class discussion and blue book essays.

The so-called "war on terror" has generated some unique constitutional law at the margins of Executive Power and foreign affairs. Congress has not declared war against terror in the only way the Constitution authorizes Congress to declare war. U.S. Const. art. I, § 8, cl. 11. But Congress has passed two different resolutions or "Authorizations for the Use of Military Force" (AUMF)—one AUMF against the terrorists responsible for the September 11, 2001, attacks and one AUMF applicable to the military action in Iraq. A U.S. citizen, captured as an "enemy combatant" and held in custody in the United States is entitled to a procedural due process hearing to determine his status as an unlawful combatant. The September 11th AUMF was sufficient authority to hold him in custody. *Hamdi v. Rumsfeld*, 542 U.S. 507 (2004). Detainees at the U.S. Naval Station in Guantanamo Bay, Cuba—aliens in custody abroad— have a constitutional right to a writ of *habeas corpus*. There is no constitution-free zone. *Boumediene v. Bush*, 553 U.S. 723 (2008). Reading these and other related opinions, one cannot help but acknowledge the Rule of Law at work. *See* Chapter 1, § 2 (Rule of Law).

11. SEPARATION OF POWERS—JUDICIAL

"The judicial Power of the United States" is created and defined in Article III, and the Constitution gives over to Congress the power to "ordain and establish" federal courts and the responsibility to prescribe their statutory subject matter jurisdiction within its confines. *See* Chapter 2, § 4 (Jurisdiction and Procedures). The President nominates and the Senate confirms Article III judges, who enjoy constitutional tenure "during good behaviour"— subject only to impeachment and removal—and whose salary is protected to further insure their independence. U.S. Const. art. III, §§ 1 & 2. *See* Chapter 1, § 9 (Judicial Power). Stop for a moment to appreciate how this recitation is a neat example of how national powers are blended and shared among the three branches. *See* Chapter 1, § 5 (Separation of Powers); Chapter 6, § 1 (Federalism and Separation of Powers Illustrated).

Chapter 2 (Judicial Review) provides a rather detailed account of the Third Branch within the separated powers. Some of that discussion bears repeating here to allow the reader to more fully appreciate the separation of the Third Branch *in situ* following the accounts of the other two elected branches in the preceding two Sections of this Chapter. Indeed, this entire book is about the federal Judicial Branch, in the sense that our constitutional analysis describes how the Supreme Court goes about exercising its awesome power to interpret the Constitution to guarantee individual liberty and to enforce the limits on government power. Of course, when the Supreme Court plays the role of constitutional referee in a fight between the Congress and the President, it is performing the judicial function within the separation of powers. At his Senate confirmation hearing, Chief Justice Roberts experienced a brief fit of humility to insist:

> Judges and Justices are servants of the law, not the other way around. Judges are like umpires. Umpires don't make the rules, they apply them. The role of an umpire and a judge is critical. They make sure everybody plays by the rules, but it is a limited role. Nobody ever went to a ball game to see the umpire.

In *The Federalist No. 78*, Hamilton memorably proclaimed: "The judiciary has no influence over either the sword or the purse; no direction either of the strength or of the wealth of the society; and can take no active resolution whatever. It may truly be said to have neither FORCE nor WILL, but merely judgment." In our constitutional diagram, this might be depicted to turn upside down the previous two diagrams so that the judicial branch is designated below the two elected branches, which do have the powers of the purse and the sword:

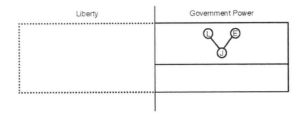

Likewise, when the Court holds that one or the other coordinate political branches has exceeded that branch's constitutional limitations, the Court is enforcing the separation of powers. The deep structure of the Constitution cannot be ignored. The theme of the proper role of the judiciary within the structure of the separation of powers will be amplified here with annotations to some of the leading cases.

Article III provides that the federal judicial power extends only to a "case or controversy." The paired terms are used interchangeably, although strictly speaking a "controversy" is more narrow than a "case" in that "controversy" includes only suits of a civil nature. *Aetna Life Ins. Co. v. Haworth*, 300 U.S. 227, 240 (1937). A "case or controversy" generally must be one that is appropriate for judicial determination, namely a real, live dispute as opposed to a hypothetical or academic disagreement; it must concern legal relations and real parties and carry adverse legal consequences as opposed to being merely advisory of the law in the abstract; it must be substantial and more than *de minimis*; it must be capable of being resolved fully and effectively by some judicial relief or judgment. *See* Chapter 2, § 2 (Case or Controversy Requirement).

The case or controversy requirement prevents the Supreme Court from issuing an advisory opinion merely to act like a lawyer giving legal advice to a client; rather, the Justices may only act formally like a court to resolve real disputes presented by adverse parties. *Muskrat v. United States*, 219 U.S. 346 (1911). Likewise, friendly lawsuits or feigned cases, in which the litigants are in collusion to desire the same result, do not present a constitutional case or controversy. *Moore v. Charlotte-Mecklenburg Bd. of Educ.*, 402 U.S. 47 (1971).

Taxpayers *qua* taxpayers generally do not have standing to raise general issues involving federal spending programs because of the small and indefinite interest they have in the case. *Frothingham v. Mellon*, 262 U.S. 447 (1923). The states likewise cannot bring such a suit as *parens patria* of its citizens. *Massachusetts v. Melon*, 262 U.S. 447 (1923). A state may sue the United States in its own right. *Missouri v. Holland*, 252 U.S. 416 (1920). And one state may sue another state. *Wyoming v. Oklahoma*, 502 U.S. 437 (1992). Federal taxpayers do have standing to challenge governmental spending as a violation of the Establishment Clause of the First Amendment, however, because that is a specific constitutional limitation on the taxing and spending power. *Flast v. Cohen*, 392 U.S. 83 (1968). But this exception is itself limited to the Establishment Clause limitation on the Taxing and Spending Clause. The Supreme Court has remarked that the fact that no one may have standing to sue is not reason alone to afford someone standing who does not otherwise qualify. *Valley Forge Christian Coll. v. Ams. United for the Separation of Church and State, Inc.*, 454 U.S. 464 (1982).

The whole idea of standing is that the right person is bringing the lawsuit so the courts should provide an appropriate remedy. The Article III minimum requirements for nontaxpayer standing are: (1) the plaintiff has suffered an injury in fact; (2) the injury is fairly traceable to the challenged action; and (3) the injury is redressable by the remedial powers of the court. *Duke Power Co. v. Carolina Env't Study Grp., Inc.*, 438 U.S. 59 (1978). These requirements often become stumbling blocks in so-called public law cases that bring a constitutional challenge against some governmental program or policy.

Besides these three Article III requirements for standing, there are some other prudential, court-created rules on standing that have more play in the joints. As a general rule, a third party cannot bring a lawsuit to vindicate the constitutional rights of another person, unless the third party is in a special relationship with the other person and there is some good reason that the other person cannot practically bring suit. For example, a physician will be allowed to challenge a state law that allegedly burdens women patients' right to seek an abortion. *Singleton v. Wulff*, 428 U.S. 106 (1976). In free speech cases, the substantial overbreadth doctrine allows a court to strike down a statute that might be constitutional as applied to the party before the court, if the court believes that the statute on its face will chill substantial free speech of others. *See Broadrick V. Oklahoma*, 413 U.S. 601 (1973). An association or organization can have standing to sue in its own right—or it can have standing to represent its members who would have standing—so long as the nature of the claim and the relief sought does not require the individual members to participate. *Warth v. Seldin*, 422 U.S. 490 (1975). A labor union might have associational standing to represent the rights of its members. *Int'l Union, United Auto., Aerospace, & Agric. Implement Workers of Am. v. Brock*, 477 U.S. 274 (1986).

An important feature of the separation of powers between the Congress and the Judicial Branch is the general prohibition on congressional standing. When several individual members of the House and Senate who had voted against the Line Item Veto Act brought suit to challenge its constitutionality once it passed, the Supreme Court ruled that they lacked standing to sue and dismissed the case. *Raines v. Byrd*, 521 U.S. 811 (1997). Being on the losing end of a congressional vote was not a case or controversy. The separation of powers prevented them from asking for a judicial do-over and prevented the courts from giving them one. Only someone who had suffered an injury-in-fact from a presidential cancellation of legislation could bring the suit. (It is instructive that in a decision the next year reaching the constitutional merits, *Clinton v. City of New York*, 524 U.S. 417 (1998), which involved a suit brought by proper party plaintiffs who did have standing, the line item veto statute was struck down as a violation of the separation of powers. *See* Chapter 6, § 10 (Separation of Powers—Executive).

A case or controversy must satisfy the ripeness doctrine. As the metaphor suggests, ripeness is a matter of timing. The doctrine serves to avoid premature adjudication and avoid the entanglement of the courts in abstract disagreements that may or may not mature into a genuine case or controversy. Especially for closely contested constitutional issues, the courts will wait to see a factual record to understand how a challenged law might be actually enforced. *Int'l Longshoremen's & Warehousemen's Union, Local 37 v. Boyd*, 347 U.S. 222 (1954).

If the ripeness doctrine is about a lawsuit brought too early, the mootness doctrine is about a lawsuit brought too late. If events subsequent to the filing of a lawsuit in effect resolve the dispute, the case must be dismissed as moot, at the trial level or on appeal, and even in the Supreme Court itself. Various subsequent events might moot a case. If the parties settle the matter, the controversy is no longer alive. If the challenged statute or regulation expires or is repealed, the controversy is over. Any change in circumstances that has the practical effect of ending the dispute is grounds for declaring the lawsuit moot. *DeFunis v. Odegaard*, 416 U.S. 312 (1974).

But if, because of inexorable time factors, cases would always be mooted by the time the issue was finally decided on appeal, the Supreme Court will go ahead and decide the case, because the issue is capable of repetition, yet otherwise evading of judicial review. In the famous abortion case, for example, human gestation takes only nine months compared to the considerably more lengthy time it takes to try a case, take an appeal, and petition for Supreme Court review; furthermore, an individual woman might become pregnant again in the future. *Roe v. Wade*, 410 U.S. 113 (1973).

The separation of powers is also respected by the Judicial Branch in the performance of its judicial powers through the nonjusticiability or political question doctrine. *See* Chapter 2, § 6 (Nonjusticiable Political Questions). That doctrine essentially is a principle of constitutional interpretation and a feature of judicial self-restraint that treats some matters to be wholly committed to Congress or the Executive Branch and off limits to the Judicial Branch because of the separation of powers. The Court will refrain from reaching the merits and dismiss the case if it finds: (1) a constitutional commitment of the issue to a coordinate branch; (2) a lack of judicially-manageable standards; (3) an initial policy determination calling for nonjudicial discretion; (4) the impossibility of deciding the case without disrespecting the other branches; (5) an unusual need to adhere to the political decision already made; and (6) the potential for embarrassment from multiple conflicting pronouncements by the different branches. *Baker v. Carr*, 369 U.S. 186 (1962). Admittedly, however, these categories are somewhat vague and uncertain.

The malleability of the political question doctrine and the Justices' willfulness to decide a paradigm political dispute—despite the high political stakes for the country and despite the negative institutional consequences for the Supreme Court—were on full display in the dramatic decision to reach the merits and end the Florida recount in the 2000 presidential election. *Bush v. Gore*, 531 U.S. 98 (2000). When something quite similar occurred in the 1876 presidential election, there was a political solution to the controversy outside the courts. The electoral votes of Florida, Louisiana, Oregon, and South Carolina were disputed; neither candidate had a majority of uncontested votes; Congress established an Electoral Commission consisting of five Representatives, five Senators, and five Justices; Rutherford B. Hayes was awarded the disputed votes—and the election—over Samuel J. Tilden. Knowing that history makes it curiouser and curiouser that the nine Justices took up the matter in 2000 without any mention whatsoever of the political question doctrine.

The judicial corollary to the political question doctrine, which preserves the power of judicial review, is that whether one of these six formulations applies to commit the issue to a coordinate branch and the scope of that commitment are matters for the courts to hear and decide. The decision of the House of Representatives to expel a member for wrongdoing was left where the Constitution presumptively placed that responsibility—with the members of the House. *See Powell v. McCormack*, 395 U.S. 486 (1969) (*dicta*). The Supreme Court declined to conduct a kind of procedural due process review of the Senate's rules for conducting an impeachment trial of a federal judge. *Nixon v. United States*, 506 U.S. 224 (1993). If the Supreme Court concludes that a case presents a nonjusticiable political question, that determination has the effect of leaving in place the decision of the coordinate political branch and that branch's underlying interpretation of its own constitutional powers.

The decision upholding the constitutionality of the federal Sentencing Guidelines in federal criminal law enforcement is highly instructive about separation of powers. *Mistretta v. United States*, 488 U.S. 361 (1989). In the old system, Congress legislatively defined the maximum allowable sentence, the district court judicially imposed a sentence within a range of years, and parole officials administratively determined the actual duration of imprisonment for someone convicted of a federal crime. Most of the power was lodged with the individual judge. The 1984 Act changed all of that to shift substantial power over sentencing, in effect, from the Judicial Branch to the Executive Branch, *i.e.*, the federal prosecutor's determination of what crime to charge is the most important variable affecting sentencing. The Sentencing Commission has promulgated elaborate sentencing formulas in the form of Sentencing Guidelines that were statutorily declared to be binding on the district judge and were calculated to yield determinate sentences that would be subject to appellate review for any departures up or down. The U.S. Sentencing Commission is an independent commission in the Judicial Branch; members are appointed by the President with the advice and consent of the Senate; at least three of the seven members must be federal judges selected from a list of nominees from the Judicial Conference of the United States; no more than four can be of the same political party; members serve six-year terms and are subject to removal by the President for good cause shown. The Commission is responsible for reviewing and revising the Guidelines on a regular basis—a Herculean task given their complexity and volume. The current set of Guidelines fill a manual with over 600 dense pages complete with parts, sub-parts, formulas, charts, checklists, *et cetera*. The Guidelines are revised annually.

The Supreme Court commented that the constitutional principle of separation of powers is not violated "by mere anomaly or innovation." *Id*. at 385. Congress would have transgressed the separation of powers by placing the Commission in the Judicial Branch only if the Commission's powers expanded the powers of the judiciary beyond constitutional bounds or undermined the integrity of the Judicial Branch. Neither concern applied. The Commission's powers were not judicial, so it could be made accountable to Congress and its members could be made subject to the President's limited removal power. Judges were allowed to accept the extra-judicial duty to serve as commissioners. The Commission was not a court, so non-judges could also serve. In short, Congress was allowed to delegate to an expert body located in the Judicial Branch the task of formulating and monitoring the Sentencing Guidelines. The majority gave the Guidelines a constitutional "thumbs up."

Only Justice Scalia dissented, but he was beside himself with separation of powers angst towards what he sneered amounted to a new and previously unheard of branch of government—"a sort of junior-varsity Congress." *Id*. at 426. He noted the telling difference between himself and the majority in this and in other separation of powers cases generally. He described the majority of the Court as apparently being ready, able, and willing to analyze whether or not the functions of the branches were being commingled too much in the individual cases, judging for themselves, balancing case-by-case. He insisted, in dramatic contrast, that the Framers of the Constitution had already decided how much commingling of powers was appropriate, advisable, and allowable and they had set out their conclusions in the document with considerable specificity and particularity. So it was not up to judges to do their own balancing analysis, but rather judges should be obliged to preserve the original balances written into the Constitution. The Constitution's structure, the Framers' original balances of powers, Justice Scalia insisted, does not allow for any body besides Congress to exercise the lawmaking power, the kind of lawmaking power the U.S. Sentencing Commission exercises, and the lawmaking power cannot be located within the Judicial Branch.

Subsequently, a fractured Supreme Court invalidated the statutory mandatory feature of the Sentencing Guidelines. A majority reasoned that the Sixth Amendment—not the Separation of Powers—was being violated because a judge applying the Guidelines was making factual findings that properly belonged to a jury under beyond the reasonable doubt standard. To save them, the Supreme Court ruled that the Guidelines would only be advisory for the sentencing judge and then subject to *de novo* review on appeal. *United States v. Booker*, 543 U.S. 220 (2005).

Congress is authorized to make exceptions to the Supreme Court's appellate jurisdiction. U.S. Const. art. III, § 2, cl. 2. This power to make exceptions goes so far as to repeal jurisdiction over a case that has been briefed and argued but not yet decided. *Ex parte McCardle*, 74 U.S. (7 Wall.) 506 (1869). Likewise, Congress has the power to ordain and establish lower federal courts and to grant or deny them subject matter jurisdiction within the outer limits of Article III. The congressional power does not go so far, however, as to reopen and re-determine the outcome of cases that have been fully and finally resolved by the courts. Congress once tried to undo an earlier Supreme Court interpretation of a statute that had resulted in the dismissal of certain cases by amending the statute to automatically revive motions to reinstate suits filed before the Court's decision, suits that had been dismissed with a final order and were no longer appealable. That intruded on the constitutional prerogative of the Third Branch and the separation of powers. *Plaut v. Spendthrift Farm, Inc.*, 514 U.S. 211 (1995). Congress does have the authority to make a valid statute retroactive to still pending cases which have not yet been finally resolved, however. *Bank Markazi v. Peterson*, 136 S. Ct. 1310 (2016).

12. CONCLUSION

The deep structure of the Constitution is reflected in all these holdings and opinions on federalism and separation of powers. The national government has vast powers, to be sure, but the national government is not all-powerful. The Constitution affords states the esteem due to them as sovereigns. Separation of powers prescribes the organization of the national government; separation of powers prescribes rules for how the three branches function independently; separation of powers prescribes how they relate together. But the Constitution is the rule of law for both the national government and the states. The Supreme Court of the United States performs its role as interpreter of the Constitution to give meaning to federalism and separation of powers.

The Supreme Court's power of judicial review is at the center of gravity of the Constitution. We can now appreciate how this power actually gives the Supreme Court a certain preeminence over the other institutions of government. Furthermore, we understand that it is the Court itself that interprets this constitutional role for the Court. Thus, the power of judicial review is an anomaly. Judicial review depends on the Court's own assumption of the role that the Constitution sets out for it. But the Court's role is not fully determined by the Constitution until the Court actually performs it. *See* Chapter 2 (Judicial Review).

Judicial review, properly understood, is structurally unlike the Executive veto in one essential way. The President can veto a bill and it is gone from the books, unless the veto is overridden by Congress, of course. U.S. Const. art. I, § 7. The judicial branch has no power whatsoever to amend or repeal a statute—those are exclusively legislative powers. *See* U.S. Const. art. I, § 1. When a court is said to "strike down" a statute, what it is actually doing is to exercise the *Marbury v. Madison* power to decline to enforce that unconstitutional statute. *See* Chapter 2, § 1 (Origins of Judicial Review). Additionally, the court has the *Ex parte Young* power to enjoin the executive from enforcing that unconstitutional statute against the party before the court. *See* Chapter 6, § 3 (State Sovereign Immunity). Unless and until the legislature itself repeals the disapproved statute, the law technically is still on the books but it exists in an unconstitutional limbo—indefinitely unenforceable. In theory, the Court can even change its mind about the statute and overrule its own precedent. *See* Chapter 7, § 3 (What is the Constitution?—Precedent or doctrine). Therefore, judicial review really amounts to a kind of judicially-imposed non-enforcement remedy or suspension policy, *i.e.*, something of a passive virtue of the Constitution. The judicial branch is not just the "least dangerous" branch per *Federalist Paper No. 78*, it remains the least understood. But we are getting way too far into the weeds. *See generally* Chapter 7 (Constitutional Theory).

The importance of this power of judicial review in the government structure and in all aspects of our nation's life is probably beyond full comprehension and full evaluation. Judicial review is the essential feature of constitutional law as we know it in this country. Not only does our Supreme Court have the power, in the name of the Constitution, to allocate the distribution of governmental responsibilities among the various branches of the federal government and the power to define the scope of federal and state responsibilities, but the Court has that most critical power of all, the power to guard and protect the great individual civil rights and civil liberties guaranteed under the Constitution. In a few words, this is what judicial review is all about. With great power comes great responsibility.

"Whoever hath an absolute authority to interpret any written or spoken laws, it is he who is truly the lawgiver, to all intents and purposes, and not the person who first spoke or wrote them." *Bishop Hoadly's Sermon, preached before the King* (1717). "But the Constitution is too important to be left to the Justices." THOMAS E. BAKER, "THE MOST WONDERFUL WORK"—OUR CONSTITUTION INTERPRETED 8 (1996).

CHAPTER 7
CONSTITUTIONAL THEORY

1. WHY THEORY?

Why not? Sorry, it is a professor's habit to answer a question with a question. But then again, this Chapter is all about trying to make some sense of in-class discussion and out-of-class readings in treatises and law reviews of a dialect that might be called "con law prof talk." When your professor mentions or you read jargonistic references to "originalism" or "constitutional moments" or "counter-majoritarian difficulty" or "civic republicanism" or "hermeneutics" or "illegitimate hierarchies" or "social constructs" or "anti-essentialism" or "postmodern epistemology" or "the Constitution in exile," *et cetera*, do you have a clue? You need to get one, if you go to a fancy law school or if your professor did—and that would include just about every law student in the United States. This Chapter will help. *See generally* Thomas E. Baker, *Constitutional Theory in a Nutshell*, 13 WM. & MARY BILL OF RTS. J. 57 (2004) (earlier, extended, and footnoted version of this Chapter).

Constitutional law is a challenging subject to master for several reasons. First, it is so important and has shaped our nation's history. Second, while it is an American invention, as a nation we have been continually reinventing constitutional law over the last two centuries. Third, the Supreme Court of the United States is a fascinating institution. Fourth, there is so much material when we contemplate over five hundred Talmudic volumes of U.S. REPORTS filled with majority, concurring, and dissenting opinions augmented by an endless scholarly commentary. Fifth, each October Term there are new decisions that elaborate, revise and sometimes overrule our past understandings. Sixth, constitutional law resembles a kind of civic religion that has transcendent and immanent qualities for our political life. This is tough law, tough to teach and to learn, tough to master.

Constitutional theory helps us to overcome this difficulty and master our subject. It helps us to understand Supreme Court decisions and the opinions of the Justices. It allows us to distinguish between a good argument and a bad argument. Constitutional theory helps us to understand where an argument is coming from and where it might lead. It helps us to see the big picture. We better understand how a doctrine came to be and how it might evolve. We see how different doctrines are related and how they fit into the overall organization of constitutional law. Constitutional theory allows us to talk about our subject with each other. It is the *patois* that constitutional law professors write and speak to other professors and to their students. If we manage to gain some perspective from the vantage of constitutional theory, we will better understand constitutional law. At least, that is what a con law prof would tell you while sober.

This Chapter provides a nutshell description of the leading theories and identifies some of the leading theorists on the Constitution. The unit of currency here is the academic law review article, not the Supreme Court decision. The citations here provide illustrative examples of the literature. However, these references should not be considered any kind of endorsement of the views expressed. Indeed, a close reading of this Chapter reveals how the constitutional commentary is profoundly contradictory and deeply disputatious. The discussion provides preliminary sketches of an intellectual landscape that is vast and often foreboding to the beginner. These theories are neither self-contained nor static. Rather, they overlap over time and they are evolving in different directions. They are plastic and therefore highly contestable and greatly contested. For example, Scott D. Gerber, at Ohio Northern, has demonstrated that all the prevailing methods of constitutional interpretation can be shown to recognize a right of privacy and, at the same time, all of them can be shown to deny it. He concludes that scholars and jurists too often prefer outcomes to theory. Scott D. Gerber, *Privacy and Constitutional Theory*, 17 SOC. PHIL. & POL'Y 165 (2000). One of the biggest raps against theory is that interpreters really only make up their minds about a set of particular issues that are important to them, like abortion, and only then pretend to be committed to some larger theory of the Constitution. Jack Balkin, one of the leading theorists of our day, differentiates between "positive constitutional theory"—the study of how the constitutional system actually works over time—and "normative constitutional theory"—the philosophy of how the system ought to work and how interpreters should interpret the Constitution. He understands that courts do not really care about constitutional theory but constitutional theorists, like him, necessarily must care about courts. Normative theorists are obliged to take most of constitutional law as legitimate—like a "given" in a mathematical proof—and then seek to reconcile existing doctrine with their particular theory. But the Justices seem rationally oblivious to academic theorizing. Jack M. Balkin, *What Brown Teaches Us About Constitutional Theory*, 90 VA. L. REV. 1537 (2004).

This Chapter is organized around three basic interpretative questions: Who has the authority to interpret the Constitution? What are the legitimate sources of meaning for interpreting the Constitution? How is the Constitution interpreted within different philosophical communities?

This Chapter is devoid of constitutional diagrams. Instead, we will repair to the lawyer's stock in trade—the use of words—and offer verbal descriptions of the extant theories. In this endeavor, we follow James Madison's example of humility and efficiency in *The Federalist No. 37*:

> Besides the obscurity arising from the complexity of objects, and the imperfection of the human faculties, the medium through which the conceptions of men are conveyed to each other adds a fresh embarrassment. The use of words is to express ideas. Perspicuity, therefore, requires not only that the ideas should be distinctly formed, but that they should be expressed by words distinctly and exclusively appropriate to

them. But no language is so copious as to supply words and phrases for every complex idea, or so correct as not to include many equivocally denoting different ideas. Hence it must happen that however accurately objects may be discriminated in themselves, and however accurately the discrimination may be considered, the definition of them may be rendered inaccurate by the inaccuracy of the terms in which it is delivered. And this unavoidable inaccuracy must be greater or less, according to the complexity and novelty of the objects defined.

Thus, what follows is necessarily abstract, highly conceptual, very theoretical, and even downright philosophical.

2. WHO INTERPRETS THE CONSTITUTION?

Since 1803, of course, the law school answer is the Supreme Court of the United States. *Marbury v. Madison*, 5 U.S. (1 Cranch) 137 (1803). *See* Chapter 2 (Judicial Review). But that is a rather incomplete answer, when you think about it. The President takes an oath to "preserve, protect and defend the Constitution." U.S. Const. art. II, § 1, cl. 7. Members of Congress likewise must take an oath "to support this Constitution," as do members of all three branches of the state governments. U.S. Const. art. VI, cl. 3. Thus, the first line of interpreters of the Constitution are federal and state officials in the exercise of their governmental powers. However, judicial review is the mainstay of constitutional theory. Constitutionalists fetishize it.

Logically, the theory of judicial review does not necessarily require judicial supremacy. Within the national government of separated powers, there have been historical claims on constitutional supremacy made by all three branches. Chief Justice Marshall so feared the threat of judicial impeachments from the Jefferson Administration that he privately suggested that he would prefer a power in Congress to set aside Supreme Court decisions. But that would have required a constitutional amendment, although there are commentators from the left and the right who advocate that very idea today. The foundational principles of American Constitutionalism would not allow Congress the last word on constitutional matters—doing so would undo the hierarchy of the written Constitution that renders the will of the people expressed in the organic document supreme over the will of the people's elected representatives expressed in legislation. *See* Chapter 1 (American Constitutionalism). This highlights the paradoxical, if not downright anti-democratic, nature of judicial review by which a court of nine unelected lawyers with lifetime tenure exercises the power to invalidate what the people's duly elected representatives have done. Much of constitutional theory tries to overcome this "counter-majoritarian difficulty." The conservative iconoclastic critic Lino Graglia has made a career out of pointing out that the real problem with judicial review is not the problem of being ruled by the dead hand of the past, rather the real problem, he insists, is being ruled by unelected

liberal judges imposing their subjective policy choices
on the rest of us by pretending that the platform of
the Democratic Party is mandated by the
Constitution. His Constitution in bas-relief leaves
most issues to the discretion of the legislature and
beyond the power of judicial review. Lino A. Graglia,
Rethinking Judicial Supremacy, 31 CONST.
COMMENT. 381 (2016). He believes that Congress and
state legislatures should be in charge and judges
should be bystanders for the most part.

Congress is continually obliged to assess the
constitutionality of its legislative actions. Indeed,
implicit in every act of legislation is a congressional
determination that the statute fits within one of its
enumerated, delegated powers. Under the Necessary
and Proper Clause in Article I, and for similar clauses
found in several of the amendments, the Supreme
Court has adopted a decidedly deferential posture
toward Congress's policy judgments. What Congress
reasonably thinks is necessary is constitutional.
McCulloch v. Maryland, 17 U.S. (4 Wheat.) 316
(1819). *See* Chapter 5 (Government Powers). In this
fashion, constitutional interpretation is a dynamic
process resembling a conversation among the
branches. Of course, it is up to the Supreme Court to
have the final say when Congress has exceeded its
powers of constitutional interpretation. When
Congress passed a statute seeking to set aside a
Supreme Court ruling by trying to provide greater
protection for religious liberty than the Court had
interpreted in the First Amendment, the statute was
struck down. The Court held that Congress was not
"enforcing" the Fourteenth Amendment, but rather

Congress was creating new rights or expanding existing rights in a way the Constitution would not allow—by invading the province of the judicial branch. *City of Boerne v. Flores*, 521 U.S. 507 (1997). More generally, these interbranch interactions frequently reveal a judicial deference to Congress reviewing questions of legislative facts in constitutional cases, although that deference not infrequently can also be opaque, indeterminate, and inconsistent. These disputes about facts really are disputes about the meaning of the Constitution and the power of the legislative branch. DAVID L. FAIGMAN, CONSTITUTIONAL FICTIONS: A UNIFIED THEORY OF CONSTITUTIONAL FACTS (2008). Judicial deference to legislative policy choices is a background quality of judicial review.

Numerous Presidents have had occasion to assert co-equal status with the other branches in their power to interpret the Constitution in showdowns between the Executive and the Congress or the Supreme Court. Thomas Jefferson followed his own counsel on the constitutional issues in his position as chief prosecutor in the treason trial of Aaron Burr. *United States v. Burr*, 25 F. Cas. 2 (C.C.D. Va. 1807). Andrew Jackson deemed himself the tribune of the people and vetoed the bill to continue the Bank of the United States for the announced reason that he thought it was unconstitutional, despite the fact that the Supreme Court had previously upheld its validity in the celebrated case of *McCulloch v. Maryland*, 17 U.S. (4 Wheat.) 316 (1819). Abraham Lincoln never accepted the Supreme Court's infamous decision in *Dred Scott v. Sanford*, 60 U.S. (19 How.) 393 (1865), and he openly defied Chief Justice Taney's ruling that he lacked power to suspend the writ of *habeas corpus* during the Civil War, *Ex parte Merryman*, 17 Fed. Cas. 144 (C.C.D. Md. 1861) (No. 9487). Franklin D. Roosevelt took on the Supreme Court by proposing to increase the number of Justices in his 1937 "Court-packing Plan," but Congress would not go along; tensions eased when the Justices seemed to lose some of their zeal for invalidating his programs around the same time; eventually he would succeed in packing the Court the old-fashioned way, through retirements and replacements. There have been equally historic occasions, however, when the President has acquiesced to judicial supremacy at the cost of loss of power to the Executive, such as when President Truman gave back the steel mills he had nationalized during the Korean conflict, *Youngstown Sheet & Tube Co. v. Sawyer*, 343 U.S. 579 (1952), or when President Nixon obeyed the order to turn over tape recordings of his conversations about the Watergate scandal that led to his resignation, *Nixon v. United States*, 418 U.S. 683 (1974). *See* Chapter 6, § 10 (Separation of Powers—Executive). Keith Whittington is convinced that in the long run this pattern of Executive acquiescence of the High Court's practice of judicial supremacy has benefited the Supreme Court, the Presidency, and the Nation. KEITH E. WHITTINGTON, POLITICAL FOUNDATIONS OF JUDICIAL SUPREMACY (2007). It is remarkable among the countries of the world how our chief executives have behaved themselves constitutionally and accepted severe judicial censures.

A great deal of constitutional-law-in-action takes place between the Congress and the Executive branch. Those complex interactions sometimes end up before the Court for review, but much of that activity is beyond the purview of the judiciary's responsibility to decide cases and controversies. *See* Chapter 6 (Structure of the Constitution). As we have seen, the Supreme Court's own understanding of its power of judicial review includes a recognition that there are some questions of constitutional law that are nonjusticiable political questions. In those areas, such as most aspects of foreign policy, the coordinate elected branches have the final word on how they should proceed constitutionally. *See* Chapter 2, § 6 (Nonjusticiable Political Questions). There may be no better example of this constitutional-law-in-action that takes place "off the books" and beyond the ken of judges than the long history of the blended powers of the President to nominate and the Senate to confirm Supreme Court Justices. The recent MMA-cage-like take downs in that arena reveal what Mark Tushnet has labeled "constitutional hardball." Mark V. Tushnet, *Constitutional Hardball*, 37 JOHN MARSHALL L. REV. 523 (2004). The national leaders of the two political parties are repeat players locked in the game theory of the "prisoner's dilemma," especially when the White House and the Senate have been controlled by different parties. This has been true ever since 1988 when "Bork" became a verb in the dictionary (MERRIAM-WEBSTER: "to attack or defeat a nominee or candidate for public office unfairly through an organized campaign of harsh public criticism and vilification"). Partisanship has escalated as each side takes turns retaliating against the other side and neither side is willing or able to be conciliatory. Remember the names Merrick Garland and Neil Gorsuch? And it keeps getting worse and worse.

The answer to the question "who interprets the Constitution?" plays out decidedly differently along the axis of federalism. *See* Chapter 6 (Structure of the Constitution). The dominance of the Supreme Court in matters of constitutional law was established early in the Republic. Acts of state legislatures were declared unconstitutional, *Fletcher v. Peck*, 10 U.S. (6 Cranch) 87 (1810); state criminal proceedings were made subject to Supreme Court review, *Cohens v. Virginia*, 19 U.S. (6 Wheat.) 264 (1821); and final decisions of the highest courts of the states were deemed reviewable in the Supreme Court under the Constitution, *Martin v. Hunter's Lessee*, 14 U.S. (1 Wheat.) 304 (1816). The Civil War killed the political theory of John C. Calhoun that the states had the right to resist national supremacy. When modern "Confederates" tried to revive the idea of "states' rights" to keep from having to desegregate their public schools, the Supreme Court would hear none of it. A unanimous opinion, signed by all nine Justices, declared "the basic principle that the federal judiciary is supreme in the exposition of the law of the Constitution, and that principle has ever since been respected by this Court and the Country as a permanent and indispensable feature of our constitutional system." *Cooper v. Aaron*, 358 U.S. 1, 18 (1958). *See* Chapter 2, § 1 (Origins of Judicial Review).

Thus, the answer to the "who" question is that all the governmental actors in the national and state governments are routinely called upon to interpret the Constitution in the performance of their governmental duties. But the Supreme Court usually has the last word, unless the Court itself concludes that the Constitution gives the last word to Congress or the President. The Court's papal-like authority was aptly described by Justice Jackson: "We are not final because we are infallible, but we are infallible only because we are final." *Brown v. Allen*, 344 U.S. 443, 540 (1953) (Jackson, J., concurring).

Like rock-and-roll, judicial review is here to stay, with all due respect to the late Justice Scalia, who steadfastly declined to comment on *Marbury v. Madison,* 5 U.S. (1 Cranch) 137 (1803), during his Senate confirmation hearing because he said the issue might come before the Supreme Court. ANTONIN SCALIA, A MATTER OF INTERPRETATION: FEDERAL COURTS AND THE LAW (1997). However, a noteworthy development beginning in the 1990s was the hard-core critique against the Supreme Court's power and performance. Robert Bork, the Reagan nominee who was not confirmed to the Supreme Court and one of the most conservative constitutionalists on the right, and Georgetown University's Mark Tushnet (now at Harvard), one of the most liberal constitutionalists on the left, both published book-length arguments against judicial review. ROBERT H. BORK, SLOUCHING TOWARDS GOMORRAH: MODERN LIBERALISM AND THE AMERICAN DECLINE (1996); MARK TUSHNET, TAKING THE CONSTITUTION AWAY FROM THE COURTS (1999). Bork would allow the Supreme Court to continue to decide constitutional cases but would amend the Constitution to authorize Congress to overrule an interpretation of the Constitution by a simple majority vote. Tushnet would go further to eliminate judicial review in the courts by a constitutional amendment, leaving the task of constitutional interpretation to Congress and populist politics. Others have queued up in the line of academics critical of judicial review. Larry Kramer joins these ranks to proclaim that the truest understanding of the Constitution is that the Court ought to reflect popular will and the wishes of the people themselves in a system of government based on the consent of the governed. And, if the Court fails to do so, then the people should reclaim their constitutional birthright forthrightly by political means. LARRY D. KRAMER, THE PEOPLE THEMSELVES (2004). Christopher Eisgruber believes that democratic institutions, like legislatures and elections, are only incomplete expressions of democracy and the Supreme Court should be heard to speak for Americans about justice. CHRISTOPHER L. EISGRUBER, CONSTITUTIONAL SELF-GOVERNMENT (2001). Jack Balkin argues that the American constitutional project is based on faith, hope, and a belief in our shared redemption—the Constitution will deliver us from evil. And our constitutional principles have varied over time because they amount to temporary political compromises. JACK M. BALKIN, CONSTITUTIONAL REDEMPTION: POLITICAL FAITH IN AN UNJUST WORLD (2011). These prominent heretics, and numerous other scholars and commentators who have joined in the intellectual fray, demonstrate how the dogma of judicial review still remains controversial and mysterious.

One might give in to a measure of op-ed snarkiness, however, about the philosophy of populist constitutional law. It might be said that the problem with participatory democracy is the participants! Any political scientist is familiar with the studies of elective politics which demonstrate beyond peradventure that the American people are not stupid voters but they are demonstrably and profoundly ignorant voters. The difference? Because most voters understand intuitively that the chance their individual vote will make a difference is so infinitesimally small, most voters act rationally to remain ignorant and uniformed about government policy. In the age of the social media, people believe all sorts of things that are not true and even crazy, and they vote based on their mistaken beliefs. Increased political participation does not improve election outcomes, so why should we hope for a better quality of constitutional outcomes from a more democratic constitutional process? Recall Winston Churchill's famous quip, "Democracy is the worst form of government, except for all the others." Our constitutional law has always been elitist not egalitarian, for better or for worse. That democratic constitutional law would be different does not guarantee that it would be better.

3.   WHAT IS THE CONSTITUTION?

This is a serious question: just what is included in the Constitution for purposes of interpretation? What are the sources and references that properly can be brought to bear to resolve a question of constitutional law? The content of the canon for constitutional interpretation, *i.e.*, what sources provide constitutional meaning, depends somewhat on the interpretative issue and varies somewhat from one interpreter to another. Several standard sources will be discussed here: text, original understanding, history and tradition, structure, precedent or doctrine, and philosophy or moral reasoning.

Lawyers write briefs and make arguments to judges, who are lawyers too. Legal argumentation limits and constrains; legal conventions help define the way judges think about the task of judging. Judges are obliged to write reasoned opinions giving the justifications for their decisions, unlike members of Congress or the President. The opinions must be more than an expression of the Justices' personal predilections and policy preferences. Decisions are expected to be sincere and consistent over time. Judicial candor is a prerequisite. The Supreme Court is a collegial court: only a majority can exercise the power of judicial review—it takes five votes. An individual Justice cannot do anything but fulminate without four more Justices in agreement. Every year, Justice Brennan used to raise his hand over his head and hold out his fingers announcing to his new law clerks that "the most important rule around here" was the Rule of Five. "Five votes," he would tell them, "five votes can do anything." They were never quite certain if he was telling them it took five votes to do anything or that with five votes you could do anything. He was a master at "massing the Court," *i.e.*, carefully drafting an opinion that would attract and hold onto a majority. *See* Chapter 4, § 1 (Constitutional Analysis *Redux*).

There has been a longstanding debate over how "principled" Supreme Court decision-making has been or can be. The debate has joined issue over whether there are "neutral principles" that distinguish law from politics, *i.e.*, that a judge can and should look outside the judge's personal values for reasons for a decision that transcend the individual judge or the particular case. Judges should not be merely result-oriented to decide a case the way they subjectively want it to come out. This is the basis for evaluating the legitimacy of Supreme Court decisions—neutral principles derived from the Constitution. Critics have been doubtful whether this is anything more than a judge confusing what seems sensible or natural to the individual judge with a mythical principle of natural law or whatever. They believe that all judging is result-oriented and they think that is a good thing because it assures good results in individual cases and in the run of cases. They defy anyone to go down the table of contents in a constitutional law casebook and try to sort and separate "principled decisions" from "result-oriented decisions." Critics say every person who does this would come up with different lists and the lists would say more about the person than about the decisions. The debate over "neutral principles" has been raging ever since the 1950s when Herbert Wechsler of Columbia University criticized the opinion in *Brown v. Bd. of Educ.*, 347 U.S. 483 (1954)—a decision everyone today would agree was the "right result"— and the debate has been rejoined over numerous controversial decisions over the years, decisions like the abortion case, *Roe v. Wade*, 410 U.S. 113 (1973), and the 2000 presidential election case, *Bush v. Gore*, 531 U.S. 98 (2000). *See* Herbert Wechsler, *Toward Neutral Principles of Constitutional Law*, 73 HARV. L. REV. 1 (1959).

Harvard University's Cass Sunstein sought to transform case-by-case result-orientedness from a vice into a preferred value in his writings about the Rehnquist Court, extolling what he called the model of "judicial minimalism," which he closely identified with Justice Sandra Day O'Connor. CASS R. SUNSTEIN, ONE CASE AT A TIME: JUDICIAL MINIMALISM ON THE SUPREME COURT (1999). The methodology of minimalism is to leave important questions unresolved, to go about deciding the particular case on the particular facts, to write opinions narrowly rather than broadly, and to write shallow opinions that are not so deep as to be over-theorized. According to this approach, an opinion is a good opinion if it is sufficient unto the case. It is a good thing for an opinion to be case-bound. A judicial opinion should not read like a lengthy and dense law review article full of elaborations and tangents of *dicta*. By this light, Chief Justice Warren's discursive opinion in *Brown v. Bd. of Educ.*, 347 U.S. 483 (1954) was a good opinion: it declared *de jure* segregation in public school to be unconstitutional, overruled *Plessy v. Ferguson*, 163 U.S. 537 (1896), postponed the issue of remedy for reargument, and left other kinds of public segregation for later cases. In a later book that is more temperate in its content then in its title, Sunstein goes even farther to warn against judicial fundamentalism and extremism. He accepts the legitimacy of a judge nudging the law in one direction or the other (left or right) but only marginally and not excessively. CASS SUNSTEIN, RADICALS IN ROBES: WHY EXTREME RIGHT-WING COURTS ARE WRONG FOR AMERICA (2005).

Text. Nearly everyone believes that the text of the Constitution—the four corners of the document as amended—is the necessary beginning place for constitutional interpretation. Logically, the textual claim that the Constitution is itself "the supreme law of the land," means that the basic law must have a singular and non-contradictory meaning at any given time. Of course, its changing meaning over time is a quality of constitutional law *qua* law. Frankly, an argument that the text need not be consulted or should be ignored ought to be looked on with considerable suspicion. Different levels of commitment to the text trigger different names for these interpreters, which may carry subtly different connotations, including: "literalist," "textualist," "strict constructionist," "interpretivist" and "documentarian." Along these lines, it is helpful to distinguish between interpretation—the judicial activity of determining the linguistic meaning of a provision in the Constitution—and construction—the judicial activity of translating that meaning into a legal test or doctrine or rule for decision. You should also understand that the text of the Constitution is not important because it is unique, rather it is unique because it is so important. The various tools for interpretation used in constitutional analysis are not distinctive to the Constitution, but they take on added importance in that practice because the stakes are so high. Of course, constitutional law does not project out from the text fully formed and three dimensional like some hologram avatar from a video game. Indeed, despite what many theorists claim, constitutional meaning is elaborately and gradually constructed over time. The text is processed. Andrew Siegel, from the Seattle University School of Law, has offered a new paradigm that understands constitutional law as what emerges as the end product of institutional arrangements, practices, norms, and habits of thought that are "nominal, historically contingent, and ever evolving"—the generative "constitutional culture." Andrew M. Siegel, *Constitutional Theory, Constitutional Culture*, 18 U. PA. J. CONST. L. 1067 (2016). The further insight is that interpretation and construction are not the exclusive function of the judicial branch. The political branches also interpret and then construct laws, administrative regulations, political conventions, and legal institutions. Before Americans invented the "large-C" written Constitution, the English understood the "small-c" unwritten constitution to be the actual arrangement of government institutions and how they actually functioned—the arrangement and interaction of the King and the Parliament and the courts.

A clause-bound textualist focuses exclusively on a specific clause to interpret it on its own terms. The Court usually tries to find the essential purpose behind the particular clause, like the Contract Clause. *Home Bldg. & Loan Ass'n v. Blaisdell*, 290 U.S. 398 (1934). Akhil Reed Amar, from Yale University, advocates the kind of "intratextualism" that Chief Justice Marshall used in *McCulloch v. Maryland*, 17 U.S. (4 Wheat.) 316 (1819), where he compared and contrasted similar language in different clauses to interpret the Necessary and Proper Clause within the structure of the Constitution. Akhil Reed Amar, *Intratextualism*, 112 HARV. L. REV. 747 (1999). Using this technique, an interpreter pays close attention to syntax, organization, and significant similarities and differences in the wording and phrasing of the Constitution. The Constitution contains both "ordinary language" and "legal language" that have ordinary meanings and legal meanings respectively, sometimes with broad meanings and sometimes with narrow meanings. Any accurate and authentic interpretation needs to take into account the vernacular of the Constitution. Michael B. Rappaport & John O. McGinnis, *The Constitution and the Language of the Law*, 59 WM. & MARY L. REV. 1321 (2018).

Much of the Constitution is government boilerplate. Representatives serve two-year terms; Senators serve six-year terms; we have regular congressional elections. Presidents do not try to run for a third four-year term. This experience leads to a common technique that distinguishes between specific-particularized clauses and general-broad clauses. The requirement that the President "have attained the age of thirty five years" is specific. U.S. Const. Art. II, § 1, cl. 5. But a professor might try to obfuscate even such a seemingly specific clause. If the requirement was intended to assure "maturity and experience" then a person who is only 30 might qualify with the proper résumé. If the requirement was intended to designate wise elders, then today a person should be about 50 according to adjustments in life span over the last two centuries. Does the additional requirement that the President be a "natural born Citizen" exclude anyone delivered by a Caesarean section? Does the use of the masculine pronoun "he" in Article II mean that only males can serve as President? You get the idea.

Then there are the majestic generalities of the Constitution—clauses that invoke fundamental values like "Due Process" and "Equal Protection" and invite the interpreter to read into them content about fairness and equality. Indeed, a WESTLAW search in the Talmudic UNITED STATES REPORTS for the terms "due process" or "equal protection"—just those four words from one amendment to the Constitution— yields nearly 6,000 "hits." How does a judge decide what is fair or equal? When does the interpreter give up on the text in the face of such implicit indeterminacy? What is the next move? Some noted constitutionalists insist that it is inevitable to read values into the Constitution, and when judges pretend they are not doing so, they are only fooling themselves. The most fundamentalist textualists would counter that if the answer is not found in the text then the matter is left to the elected branches and ultimately to the people. This theory thus would significantly limit the role of courts and judges. But the choice to read the text narrowly, to exercise judicial self-restraint, is itself an interpretive choice that requires some justification. The Constitution does not say to the reader, "read me strictly" or "read me loosely," and presumably it would do similar harm to the text to read a narrow clause broadly or to read a broad clause narrowly. To interpret individual liberty too narrowly or too broadly would be as unfaithful to the text as to interpret government power too broadly or too narrowly. We should expect from our interpreters what Harvard University's Lawrence Lessig calls "fidelity" to the original document that allows the interpreter to translate the text from its original 18th-century context into the context of today. Lawrence Lessig, *Fidelity in Translation*, 71 TEX. L. REV. 1165 (1993). The comparison to translating from one language to another is a helpful metaphor for interpretation. The translator tries to convey the full meaning of the document, what it says and what its author intended, seeking to avoid "losing something in the translation."

Now, go past translation. Imagine that you were assigned the task of updating and revising the text of the U.S. Constitution to accurately reflect the document's modern meaning. You reflect on the meaning of "meaning" and decide to approach your assignment as a kind of translator to translate the 18th-century text into 21st century terminology. As you begin the translation, however, you realize that the meaning of much of the original text has been replaced with a different meaning—the text has remained constant but its meaning has changed. You also come to realize that it is the words of the original text that have been imbued with the new meanings over the past two centuries by judicial interpretation and historical practice. The old words carry the new meaning. Therefore, you come to accept the irony that the most accurate contemporary wording of the Constitution is the original 18th-century text, which best carries forward all the accumulated changes in meanings down to the present. Confused? This thought experiment follows along with Jorge Luis Borges's short story about a writer attempting to translate Cervantes's *Don Quixote* who ends up simply repeating the novel verbatim. Professor Marco Jimenez cleverly recreates the U.S. Constitution word-for-word in like fashion in order to communicate its full meaning. Marco Jimenez, *Towards a Borgean Theory of Constitutional Interpretation*, 40 PEPP. L. REV. 1 (2012).

Originalism. Most of the attention in constitutional theory has been focused on the arguments for and against the theory of originalism since the 1980s, when Attorney General Edwin Meese called for a return to the "jurisprudence of original intent" and that became a standard for the Reagan Administration's Supreme Court appointments. Edwin Meese, III, *The Supreme Court of the United States: Bulwark of a Limited Constitution*, 27 S. TEX. L. REV. 455 (1986). There are several varieties of originalists. Some pore over historical materials to ascertain the "original intent," *i.e.*, how the Framers themselves subjectively would have decided the very issue before the Court. Others take as their polestar a more objective "original understanding" of the Constitution, *i.e.*, how the words of the Constitution would have been understood by a reasonable and informed interpreter at the time it was written. Originalism is an exercise in historiography. "Virtually all practitioners of and commentators on constitutional law accept that original meaning has some relevance to constitutional interpretation." Michael C. Dorf, *Integrating Normative and Descriptive Constitutional Theory: The Case of Original Meaning*, 85 GEO. L.J. 1765, 1766 (1997). Originalism is a family of related theories that understand the meaning of the Constitution to have been fixed in time at its origins. Hard-core originalists insist that interpretation is narrowly defined and properly understood as giving the text the meaning its authors intended at the level of generality they intended. Anything else, anything more, anything different, simply is not interpretation by definition. It is doing something else to the text, but it is not interpretation. It is the *reader*—who strictly speaking is not acting as an *interpreter*—substituting some other content of the reader's own choosing for the text. Interpretation is just one thing, one important thing, to an originalist. Relying on other modalities and referring to other sources of meaning is not interpretation.

The allure of originalism is to appeal to the wisdom of the Framers, who have become something like political saints. Nonbelievers turn this around to reject the "dead hand of the past"—even worse, being ruled by dead white men—as being profoundly anti-democratic. But the counter-majoritarian difficulty has always cast a shadow over judicial review whatever the interpretative methodology, and more importantly, if judicial review is justified by the will of the people expressed in the Constitution, then the judge must be duty-bound to find and carry out that will. True believers insist that originalism is the one best method to keep judges from freelancing and imposing their own subjective policy preferences under the pretext of interpreting the Constitution.

Serious challenges to originalism question whether the historical materials are adequate: sometimes the Framers did not debate the issue; sometimes they could not agree; sometimes they seemed to try to slant the materials they left behind; sometimes the text itself seems to direct the interpreter to go beyond the document, for example, the Cruel and Unusual Punishment Clause in the Eighth Amendment or the Ninth Amendment reference to "other rights" not enumerated there. Furthermore, just who qualifies as a Framer? The delegates at the Constitutional Convention who drafted and proposed the document? Delegates at the state ratifying conventions who made it law? Federalist supporters and Antifederalist opponents? The first Congress? Early Supreme Courts? Finally, there is the intriguing question that has filled the pages of the law reviews: what was the original intent about original intent, *i.e.*, how did the Framers expect courts to interpret the Constitution? William Baude's workaround is to simply and forthrightly proclaim that originalism is our current

constitutional law, *i.e.*, an admittedly inclusive
originalism is the objective positive law of the
Constitution. William Baude, *Is Originalism Our
Law?*, 115 COLUM. L. REV. 2349 (2015).

A problematic issue for originalism is to ascertain
the proper level of generality. For example, the issue
in *McIntyre v. Ohio Elections Commission,* 514 U.S.
334 (1995), was whether the First Amendment
protected anonymous political leafleting. Two
leading proponents of originalism on the Supreme
Court, Justice Thomas and Justice Scalia—both
purporting to be practicing originalism—each relying
on the same historical record—came to opposite
constitutional conclusions about the original
understanding. One of the difficult challenges for an
originalist is to distinguish between continuities and
disjunctions—between circumstances that are
constant and circumstances that are variable—
between the founding and our time and then to factor
them into the constitutional decision one way or the
other, either to constitutionalize the issue of public
policy or to leave it to the majoritarian legislative
processes.

Different schools of originalism adopt different
levels of generality. The lowest level of generality
would consider the specific understanding of the
Framers on the question, for example, in 1868 the
drafters of the Fourteenth Amendment did not
actually contemplate a due process and equal
protection guarantee that protected same-sex
marriage. At higher levels of generality, however,
other originalists might conclude that the drafters

sought to protect a fundamental right to marry in the abstract or that the drafters entrenched a principle against caste discrimination that extends to sexual orientation or that the drafters mandated an equality norm that must take its meaning from contemporary societal understandings of tolerance and autonomy and respect. *See Obergefell v. Hodges*, 135 S. Ct. 2584 (2015). There does not seem to be a one-size-fits-all level of generality to these issues and how the theory of originalism answers them. Peter J. Smith, *Originalism and Level of Generality*, 51 GA. L. REV. 1 (2017).

History & Tradition. Related to the historical quest for the original understanding is the interpretive approach to rely on history and tradition to give meaning to the Constitution. This approach is developmental. For example, the Supreme Court has recognized that an issue of separation of powers between the President and Congress is informed by historical practices and past institutional behavior on the part of past Congresses and past Presidents. Long-standing, systematic, and continuous practices by the Executive branch, in which the Congress has knowingly acquiesced, demonstrate a constitutional interpretation by those co-equal branches that the Supreme Court will accept as an interpretive gloss on the Executive Power vested in the President in Article II. *Dames & Moore v. Regan*, 453 U.S. 654 (1981). James Madison believed that the meaning of the Constitution could be "liquidated" by historical practices. First, the relevant clause had to be indeterminate; second, a course of deliberate practice had to develop; third, the indeterminacy had to be settled by the practice. This liquidating process was characterized by acquiescence from the dissenting side of the controversy and the public approval of popular ratification. William Baude, *Constitutional Liquidation*, 71 Stan. L. Rev. ___ (2019). Consider an early example. Madison unsuccessfully opposed congressional chartering of the first Bank of the United States for constitutional reasons while he served in the House of Representatives. Later, when he was President, he deemed that events had overtaken his earlier constitutional reservations and he signed a bill creating the second Bank of the United States. Thus, history and tradition form an admixture of constitutional meaning.

Broader societal traditions can shape the scope of individual rights, as well, although the difficulty again is ascertaining the appropriate level of generality. In *Michael H. v. Gerald D.*, 491 U.S. 110 (1989), the issue was the constitutionality of a state law presumption of paternity in favor of a husband when a child is born while the husband and wife are married and living together. The true biological father of the child was in court trying to establish his parental rights. For the majority, Justice Scalia argued that the specific history and tradition of how the law treated illegitimacy afforded the biological father no Due Process rights. In dissent, Justice Brennan argued that the general history and tradition of protecting the institution of the family and society's evolving sense of family pulled in the direction of recognizing a constitutional interest in the biological father. The two were interpreting the history and tradition of Due Process on different levels of generality and from different perspectives. They brokered the needs for stability and change in different ways. Justice Scalia's approach to finding rights in history and tradition deferred to the majoritarian *status quo* of settled values. Justice Brennan's approach was more aspirational and progressive. He was more willing to exercise judicial power to "draw its meaning from the evolving standards of decency that mark a maturing society." *Trop v. Dulles*, 356 U.S. 86, 101 (1958). He was a firm believer in a "living Constitution."

It is worth noting that the idea of an unwritten, evolving Constitution is politically agnostic, *i.e.*, conservatives were purposivists in the 19th century and liberals were purposivists in the 20th century. They both sought to interpret the text in mind with its higher purposes. In this regard, you should distinguish between the "intellectual history *of* constitutional theory" and "intellectual history *as* constitutional theory." The former is a study of the various theories over time and how they have influenced constitutional law—and its potential contribution is evidenced in this Chapter. The latter deploys the techniques of historians to interpret the document and determine its meaning—and its contribution is far more modest. Intellectual history, done properly, is a better aid to understanding other constitutional theories than it is a theory unto itself. Lawrence B. Solum, *Intellectual History as Constitutional Theory*, 101 VA. L. REV. 1111 (2015). Constitutional interpretation necessarily includes history because the document being interpreted was written at a specific time in the past with a particular historical context.

What might be called the Yale school of constitutional history is presented in the writings of Bruce Ackerman and Akhil Reed Amar. Those two scholars at Yale Law School have developed elaborate and sophisticated analyses theorizing that the people of the United States may act outside Article V to effect enduring constitutional change. They believe that history trumps text. BRUCE A. ACKERMAN, WE THE PEOPLE: FOUNDATIONS (1991); AKHIL REED AMAR, THE BILL OF RIGHTS: CREATION AND RECONSTRUCTION (1998). Ackerman distinguishes between ordinary politics and rare "constitutional moments" of higher politics when the government and the people are focused in a crisis over an important constitutional issue. He identifies the Founding, Reconstruction, and the New Deal as three "constitutional moments" in American history that signaled a revolutionary reform, a profound shift in constitutional understanding that was the equivalent of formal amendment. Amar maintains that the Framers empowered popular majorities to sit in judgment of government, and when necessary to dissemble the Constitution and implement radical reforms of a fundamental nature without having to go through the onerous super-majority procedures required to formally amend the Constitution. More traditional constitutionalists, like Lawrence Tribe, are taken aback by these theories. Laurence H. Tribe, *Taking Text and Structure Seriously: Reflections on Free-form Method in Constitutional Interpretation*, 108 HARV. L. REV. 1221 (1995). Popular sovereignty is formally provided and required in Article V, and these extra-textual theories are lacking in the proper respect an interpreter owes the text. When the Framers set out the sole constitutional way to amend the Constitution, they were not required to explicitly negate all other political theories for accomplishing change. Thus, most constitutionalists believe that Article V means what it says. Thomas E. Baker, *Exercising the Amendment Power to Disapprove of Supreme Court Decisions: a Proposal for a "Republican Veto,"* 22 HASTINGS CONST. L. QTRLY. 325 (1995).

Finally, the reality is that lawyers and judges are trained in law, not history, trained to make legal arguments, and trained to decide legal disputes. Indeed, what passes for historical understanding in briefs and judicial opinions often is snickered at by real historians as "law-office history" that is highly-selective, opportunistic, and adversarial, more of a search for telling rhetorical arguments than an authentic academic exercise in understanding the past. Alfred H. Kelly, *Clio and the Court: An Illicit Love Affair*, 1965 SUP. CT. REV. 119, 123 n.13 ("By 'law office' history, I mean the selection of data favorable to the position being advanced with regard to or concern for contradictory data or proper evaluation of the relevance of the date proffered."). Some historians would compare writing about the past to predicting the future, and they insist that "postdicting" the past is more like writing a novel than the rest of us who are not historians can really appreciate. But legal historian Neil Richards has made this salient point: we should expect the

Supreme Court to rely on history as it makes history, but we should not expect the Justices to make up history. Neil M. Richards, *Clio and the Court: A Reassessment of the Supreme Court's Uses of History*, 13 J.L. & POL. 809 (1997).

Structure. The deep structure of the Constitution is vertically arrayed in federalism—the relation between the national government and the states—and horizontally arrayed in separation of powers—the elaborate system of checks and balances among the three branches of the national government. *See* Chapter 6 (Structure of the Constitution).

Charles Black, who taught at the law schools at Yale and Columbia, used structural reasoning about the Constitution based on federalism and national supremacy to defend the Warren Court from critics who attacked its decisions from a states'-rights perspective. CHARLES BLACK, STRUCTURE AND RELATIONSHIP IN CONSTITUTIONAL LAW (1969). An early historic example of structural reasoning was the federalism and Supremacy Clause reasoning Chief Justice Marshall used in *McCulloch v. Maryland*, 17 U.S. (4 Wheat.) 316 (1819), to forbid the state to tax the federally chartered Bank of the United States out of business. The structure of federalism could not allow it. More recently, in *United States Term Limits, Inc. v. Thornton*, 514 U.S. 779 (1995), there was quite a debate between Justice Stevens and Justice Thomas over the structure of federalism regarding the power of the state to impose term limits on its members of Congress. For the majority, Justice Stevens said the structure of the

Constitution and principles of democratic theory forbade an individual state from adding to the qualifications in the Constitution. In dissent, Justice Thomas interpreted the Tenth Amendment and the structure of federalism to permit it.

Alexander Bickel, from Yale University, set out the root problem for structural reasoning in terms of the "counter-majoritarian difficulty" presented by judicial review. ALEXANDER BICKEL, THE LEAST DANGEROUS BRANCH: THE SUPREME COURT AT THE BAR OF POLITICS (1962). How is it that an unelected and largely unaccountable Supreme Court should wield the power to set aside the considered judgments of the people's elected representatives in the legislature? He suggested that judicial review thus was a kind of "deviant" practice in a democracy. There are few restraints on judges beyond self-restraint, a reality that has the potential to render the interpreters of the Constitution more important than the Constitution. A bad side effect of this tendency towards judicial oligarchy is that the democratic and participatory instincts of the people and their representatives can atrophy after they become accustomed to turning over difficult and divisive issue to the courts. This is an odd turn of events in a system of government built upon the consent of the governed. *See Declaration of Independence* (1776). Since Bickel wrote back in the 1960s, generations of scholars have debated the legitimacy of judicial review in terms of the counter-majoritarian difficulty.

Other constitutionalists insist that the counter-majoritarian difficulty is not so prevalent, that the Court gets out of whack with the other branches and the rest of the country only for brief, temporary periods and at irregular, even rare, intervals. They worry that the Justices are not counter-majoritarian enough, that they reflect majoritarian values too much and too often. Indeed, the University of Southern California's Rebecca Brown blames Bickel for leading constitutionalists to wander in the desert for forty years. Rebecca L. Brown, *Accountability, Liberty, and the Constitution*, 98 COLUM. L. REV. 531 (1998). She insists that his initial move—to emphasize democracy and accountability—was wrong. She emphasizes instead that the overarching goal of the Constitution is to protect individual rights. In that structure, judicial review is a value, not a vice. The Constitution does not have a problem with judicial review; it has a problem with majoritarianism. The real, ongoing threat to individual liberty is government power. Brown's thesis obviously fits the thesis of our constitutional analysis as is illustrated by our constitutional diagram depicting the fundamental constitutional question of balancing individual liberty versus government power. Barry Friedman, at NYU, insists that someone concerned about the divide between law and politics would learn more about the Supreme Court and understand constitutional law better by examining popular reactions to Supreme Court decisions than by the more common approach of examining how the Justices react to popular politics. In the long history of the Supreme Court, its interpretations of the Constitution have never strayed too far or too long from public opinion. This insight suggests that it may be less important than is generally believed who is on the High Court. The Justices are all subject to the influence of popular opinion, directly and indirectly, over time. BARRY FRIEDMAN, THE WILL OF THE PEOPLE (2009). The question in the mirror is whether a Court that does actually reflect public opinion is capable of protecting minority rights against majoritarian excesses, *i.e.*, does the Supreme Court actually have a majoritarian difficulty? Michel Dorf wants us to think of the Supreme Court like a third legislative chamber which possibly can be insufficiently counter-majoritarian at the expense of freedom and individual liberty. He concludes that the actual record of judicial review and a proper understanding of constitutional interpretation writ large allay that worry that the Court is part of the establishment of government lording over the individual. Michael C. Dorf, *The Majoritarian Difficulty and Theories of Constitutional Decision-Making*, 13 U. PA. J. CONST. L. 283 (2010).

Perhaps the leading proponent of a kind of structural reasoning was the late John Hart Ely, who wrote one of the most influential books about the Supreme Court and the Constitution. JOHN HART ELY, DEMOCRACY AND DISTRUST: A THEORY OF JUDICIAL REVIEW (1981). Writing in the late 1970s and early 1980s, Ely can be credited with being the godfather of the modern generation of interpretative scholars. He set himself up as the chief apologist for the Warren Court to put forth a "representation-reinforcing" theory of judicial review that justified judicial intervention to eliminate structural or procedural problems in the political system that frustrated majorities and kept underrepresented minorities from full participation. He and his mentor, Chief Justice Warren, singled out the decision in *Reynolds v. Sims*, 377 U.S. 533 (1964), requiring apportionment of state legislative districts by population to insure "one person-one vote" equality, as a paradigmatic ruling. By contrast, Ely could not find much good to say about *Roe v. Wade*, 410 U.S. 113 (1973) as a constitutional holding, although he deemed protecting a woman's choice to have an abortion to be the appropriate policy for the legislature. Of course, as does everyone else, Ely has his critics. His former colleague at Harvard, Laurence Tribe, insisted that Ely had not managed to escape substantive constitutional law by championing political process because the priority Ely gives process really amounts to a substantive value that posits, in effect, that more process and wider participation are always preferable and beneficial to the polity. Laurence H. Tribe, *The Puzzling Persistence of Process-Based Constitutional Theories,* 89 YALE L.J. 1063 (1980). The *éminence grise* of his generation of constitutionalists, Tribe maintained that value-free interpretation of the Constitution simply is neither possible nor in any way preferable. For example, the right to vote and who gets it and how it is exercised and regulated are all substantive questions. For Tribe, the whole enterprise of constitutional interpretation is about making choices to preserve important values. To his mind, that is not a detraction of constitutional law, it is its beauty. Partnered with Ely on Tribe's substantive side is James Fleming who believes the "*über-düber*" right to privacy or autonomy must be grounded in constitutional democracy. Individual citizens must deliberate about their institutions of government and public policy, but they must also deliberate within their government about their personal autonomy over how they conduct their daily lives. The two ideas of autonomy are related and interdependent. JAMES FLEMING, SECURING DEMOCRACY: THE CASE OF AUTONOMY (2006).

Finally, Professor Ozan Varol, at the Lewis & Clark Law School, has turned the rights-structure dichotomy upside down. Ozan O. Varol, *Structural Rights*, 105 GEO. L.J. 1001 (2017). He rejects the conventional wisdom that structural provisions in the Constitution establish and empower government institutions while rights provisions solely protect individual freedoms. Rather, he reimagines rights to generate and distribute government power as well. The implementation and protection of individual rights, for example, can indirectly result in greater legislative or executive power, directly expand the power of judicial review, and ultimately facilitate the empowerment of democratic self-government by the citizenry. Thus, he maintains that individual rights are more than parchment barriers and contribute vitally to governmental function and constitutional stability.

Precedent or doctrine. The Constitution is something different and apart from constitutional law. A good lawyer understands this distinction. This is illustrated in a backwards way by the perhaps apocryphal story told about a leading constitutional law professor at Harvard at the beginning of the 20th century, Thomas Reed Powell, who was fond of telling his students, "Never, ever read the Constitution because it will only serve to confuse you." Most teachers and students of constitutional law spend most of their time together analyzing Supreme Court opinions and talking about Court precedents or doctrines, *i.e.*, past interpretations of the Constitution that seem to promise coherent and consistent answers in later cases. Indeed, maybe it is a good idea in this Chapter on Constitutional Theory to remind the reader once again that there is still plenty of constitutional law that must be learned and mastered. Indeed, there are so many rules and doctrines that there is a market for student aids like NUTSHELLS. The Supreme Court opinions we study are chock full of balancing analyses, multi-factor tests, levels of scrutiny, tiers of analysis, *et cetera*, that provide a rule for decision. Constitutional doctrines define the boundary between individual liberty and government power. *See* Chapter 4, § 2 (Constitutional Law Doctrines). Doctrines promise some measure of consistency and objectivity in UNITED STATES REPORTS. This is the horizontal or temporal force of *stare decisis*, *i.e.*, the effect a past decision exerts on the current Court deciding the case before it. Even more importantly, doctrines promise to reduce the subjectivity and discretion of state-court judges and lower federal-court judges. This is the vertical or hierarchical force of *stare decisis*, *i.e.*, the effect a Supreme Court precedent exerts on a court below the Supreme Court. Whether or not doctrines actually deliver on those promises is another question. Nevertheless, the important constitutional doctrines about individual civil rights and civil liberties are identified and summarized at the end of this book in the Appendix A (Leading Case Outline of Constitutional Liberty).

Stare decisis in constitutional law is hierarchical in that all the rest of the courts in the country— federal and state—are obliged to follow Supreme Court pronouncements on the Constitution. This has been a central tenet of American Constitutionalism from the founding to the present day. It is a critical feature of judicial review. *See* Chapter 2 (Judicial Review). The Supreme Court is the umpire of the separation of powers game among the branches of the national government. The Supreme Court is the cop of the federalism beat enforcing the Supremacy Clause and protecting the sovereignty of the states. *See* Chapter 6 (Structure of the Constitution).

Stare decisis in constitutional law also has the relatively weaker force of precedent from prior decisions felt by Justices on a constitutional court of last resort. In this regard, be reminded of your basic understanding of how any particular appellate court uses its past precedents to decide a present case. The deciding court, when faced with an issue and the task of applying one of its past precedents in the present case, has the power and the responsibility first to determine what the earlier precedent means and second to determine whether it is controlling in the present case. What the individual members of the past court subjectively meant at the time it was decided or even how they might have decided the issue in the present case is not controlling.

There has been some interesting theorizing about the idea of so-called "super precedents"—the idea came out of the questioning of judicial nominees at Senate confirmation hearings. Are there landmark decisions that are so deeply woven into the warp and woof of our constitutional fabric that they should be deemed to be permanent precedents and no longer within the contemplation of ever being overruled? A super precedent might have been controversial once upon a time but no longer. Only a handful of precedents arguably have achieved this status. *Compare* Michael J. Gerhardt, *Super Precedent*, 90 MINN. L. REV. 1204 (2006) (endorsing the idea) *with* Randy E. Barnett, *It's a Bird, It's a Plane, No, It's Super Precedent: A Response to Farber and Gerhardt*, 90 MINN. L. REV. 1232 (2006) (skeptical of the idea). *Brown v. Bd. of Educ.* (1954) might be one good example on everyone's list of decisions that if any Supreme Court wannabe appeared to question he or she would not be nominated by any President of either party nor confirmed by any Senate controlled by either party. Even when they disagreed with each other about its application to the case *sub judice*, both the majority and the dissenters in *Parents Involved in Community Schools v. Seattle School District No. 1* (2007) cited and quoted the *Brown* precedent to claim authority and legitimacy for their side and to cast shade on the other side. Matthew E.K. Hall, *Bringing Down Brown: Super Precedents, Myths of*

Rediscovery, and the Retroactive Canonization of Brown v. Board of Education, 18 J.L. & POL'Y 655 (2010). Indeed, Professor Balkin has concluded, "*Brown* is a hallowed achievement that we must explain if we wish to remain within the mainstream of respectable academic opinion" and that decision "disciplines and normalizes our legal imaginations." Jack M. Balkin, *What Brown Teaches Us About Constitutional Theory*, 90 VA. L. REV. 1537, 1576 (2004). What other decisions might qualify as "super precedents" is subject to debate, of course.

Some scholars are outright disdainful of precedent because they believe it to be so manipulable as to be pretextual and of doubtful legitimacy. Others hold up *stare decisis* as not merely one legitimate mode of constitutional argument, but the preferred mode for judges and academics. Liberals and conservatives alike do seem ready, able, and willing to emphasize "good" precedents and deemphasize "bad" precedents in their own cause, however.

David Strauss of the University of Chicago maintains that constitutional law is nothing more or less than the accumulation of rules over time handed down by the Supreme Court in a process that very much resembles the judicial process of the Common Law. DAVID A. STRAUSS, THE LIVING CONSTITUTION (2010). He argues, like Professor Powell's tongue-in-cheek suggestion to his students, that the text of the Constitution is insignificant compared to the content of Supreme Court opinions in the pages of UNITED STATES REPORTS. That is how the principal actors in the system behave: Justices, lower court judges, attorneys, and professors and students of constitutional law. He would give up on searching for the original understanding *et cetera*. While this description does fit many of the behaviors of the principal actors, the theoretical implication would be profoundly unsettling: the Supreme Court would sit as an ongoing Constitutional Convention, final, infallible, and absolute. That would prove the undoing of many of the fundamental principles of American Constitutionalism: the republican form of government, the idea of limited and enumerated federal powers, the rule of law. *See* Chapter 1 (American Constitutionalism). For someone to say that constitutional law resembles the common law is one thing, but to say that the Supreme Court's interpretations are superior to the Constitution simply proves too much. *Cooper v. Aaron*, 358 U.S. 1, 18 (1958); *see* Chapter 2, § 1 (Origins of Judicial Review). The argument has been made that constitutionalism requires obedience even to mistaken interpretations, and judicial supremacy works in order to restrain lower courts and state officials. *See* Larry Alexander & Fred Schauer, *On Extrajudicial Constitutional Interpretation*, 110 HARV. L. REV. 1359 (1997). However, one also could turn that argument around and insist that it is unconstitutional for the Supreme Court to adhere to its own precedents because the Constitution itself designates the Constitution—not federal common law—as the "supreme Law of the Land." U.S. Const. art. VI, cl. 2. Professor Richard Epstein, who teaches at the University of Chicago and NYU, makes an alternative analogy to the civil law system, in which the statute or code is ascendant and the role of the court is merely adjudicative and adjunctive. Richard A. Epstein, *A Common Lawyer Looks at Constitutional Interpretation*, 72 B.U. L. REV. 699 (1992). First, the Court gives common meanings to words or clauses in the text to decide paradigm cases. Second, the Court extends those paradigms to cover new cases in a consistent and similar fashion. Third, the Court seeks to reconcile inconsistencies between competing paradigms. This allows for a creative and evolving judicial process for annotating the Constitution.

Following prior precedent promotes the even-handed, predictable and consistent development of legal principles and this applies, as well, to constitutional interpretation. It is an advantage not to have everything always "up for grabs" in every case. Constitutional law is different from other areas of the law, however. Justice Brandeis once explained how the Court must be even more willing to overrule its constitutional decisions than its interpretations of federal statutes because of the different risks of error under the separation of powers. If the Court gets a statute wrong, Congress can make a correction by ordinary legislation. If the Court gets the Constitution wrong, however, correction can be had only by the difficult and infrequent process of amending the Constitution. *Burnet v. Coronado Oil & Gas Co.*, 285 U.S. 393 (1932). But that has actually happened only four times in history and only once in the last 100 years. The Supreme Court certainly does seem willing, even sometimes eager, to overrule its prior decisions. Indeed, the Rehnquist Court and its predecessor the Burger Court rank first and second in overrulings on the all-time list. And the Roberts Court is catching up to them. But the Supreme Court not having the power to overrule a prior interpretation of the Constitution would simply be unimaginable and unacceptable. *E.g.*, *Brown v. Bd. of Educ.*, 347 U.S. 483 (1954), *overruling Plessy v. Ferguson*, 163 U.S. 537 (1896).

Thus, *stare decisis* is not an inexorable command in constitutional law. Generally, the determination to overrule a prior ruling takes into consideration whether the ruling has proved intolerable and unworkable in practice, whether the ruling has been the subject of the kind of societal reliance that an overruling would result in special hardships, whether related principles of law have so far developed that the ruling has become a mere remnant of abandoned doctrine, and whether facts have changed or have come to be seen so differently that the ruling has lost its justification and significance. In a self-conscious, jointly-authored plurality opinion, Justices O'Connor, Kennedy and Souter, reviewed the previous twenty years of judicial infighting and public debate over the right to an abortion to reaffirm the essential holding that had declared the right in the first place. They did so despite their remarkable admission that they likely would not have joined the majority in the original decision. *Planned Parenthood v. Casey*, 505 U.S. 833 (1992). Virginia University's Fred Schauer has suggested this is as it should be. Because its docket is dominated by cases of exceptionally high moral, political, and policy consequences, the Supreme

Court may actually be the last place we should expect an authentic and consistent practice of *stare decisis*. Fred Schauer, *Has Precedent Ever Really Mattered in the Supreme Court?*, 24 GA. ST. U. L. REV. 381 (2007).

That an individual Justice's attitude towards constitutional *stare decisis* depends on the Justice's interpretative methodology is demonstrated by Justice Brennan's practice, also followed by Justice Marshall and Justice Blackmun, to dissent in every affirmance of a death penalty because he believed capital punishment was in all circumstances a violation of the Eighth and Fourteenth Amendments. *E.g., McCleskey v. Kemp*, 481 U.S. 279, 320 (1987). As applied to a particular issue, the doctrine of *stare decisis* can be in conflict with any of the other methods of interpretation, of course. And it would be no doctrine at all if judges prepared to overrule a precedent were not obliged to give reasons. Often enough, the issue of constitutional law plays itself out in the debate over the meaning and significance of prior precedents. For example, by a vote of 6 to 3 and in rather dramatic fashion, the Justices overruled a 17 year-old contrary precedent and held that it was unconstitutional for a state to make it a crime for two consenting adults of the same gender to engage in certain sexual intimacies in the privacy of their home. *Lawrence v. Texas*, 539 U.S. 558 (2003), *overruling Bowers v. Hardwick*, 478 U.S. 186 (1986). Geoffrey Stone of the University of Chicago borrows a page from John Stuart Mill urging constitutional interpreters to exercise some humility about their own conclusions given the fact that other interpreters, following other interpretive methodologies, have in the past and will in the future reach very different conclusions. Geoffrey Stone, *Precedent, the Amendment Process, and Evolution in Constitutional Doctrine*, 11 HARV. J.L. & PUB. POL'Y 67 (1988).

Michael Stokes Paulsen, from the University of St. Thomas School of Law, would go further to reject any claim of binding precedent whatsoever and instead ask in every case whether the prior decision is right or wrong, whether it should or should not be followed in the case before the Court, based on independent constitutional criteria. Michael Stokes Paulsen, *Does the Supreme Court's Current Doctrine of Stare Decisis Require Adherence to the Supreme Court's Current Doctrine of Stare Decisis?*, 86 N.C. L. REV. 1165 (2008). These attitudes will be reflected in what Richard Fallon calls the Reflective Equilibrium Hypothesis. He maintains that it is appropriate and legitimate, even necessary and essential, that an interpreter reconcile his or her first-order theories of constitutional interpretation with his or her best judgments about appropriate results in particular cases. A judge must adopt good faith methodological premises—*a priori* principles—but also must elaborate, qualify, or revise those premises upon further reflection over their actual implementation and applications. Theory informs outcomes, but outcomes also inform theory. Richard H. Fallon, Jr., *Arguing in Good Faith about the Constitution: Ideology, Methodology, and Reflective Equilibrium*, 84 U. CHI. L. REV. 123 (2017). As a set of extreme examples, there are some notorious Supreme Court decisions that any legitimate decision must refute—

think of *Dred Scott v. Sandford* or *Plessy v. Ferguson*—and this "anti-canon" helps inform our interpretive theory, as well. Jamal Greene, *The Anticanon*, 125 HARV. L. REV. 379 (2011).

Supreme Court opinions sometimes do not meet the expectations of students of constitutional law and often frustrate even veteran Court-watchers. But this is the nature of the judicial opinion on a collegial court. It is something quite different from a law review article. (Aside: this book would not be the first to wonder if part of the problem is that some of the current Justices who have an academic background still behave too much like law professors.) Imagine how a law review article would read if it were one of 80 full-length articles written by a committee of nine tenured senior professors, at least five of whom had to agree on every word and reference, all written simultaneously over the course of nine months. That would be weird. Furthermore, consider how much more is at stake in an opinion for the litigants and for the rest of the country—the great weight of the responsibility to decide these important issues is difficult for the rest of us to imagine. An opinion has different audiences, as well. The Court not infrequently is dialoguing with one or the other coordinate branches or with policy makers at the state level. Occasionally, the Court speaks to scholars, historians, and interested others. But there are always three primary audiences: the parties before the Court, other judges including later Justices, and the citizenry. The Supreme Court has been likened to a "republican schoolmaster" tasked with providing the country with a high political

education. Bryan A. Garner, editor of the leading
BLACK'S LAW DICTIONARY, has criticized the style of
Supreme Court opinions for, among other things,
their verbosity, density, and opaqueness, which he
largely blames on law clerk ghostwriters. Brian A.
Garner, *Style of Opinions, in* THE OXFORD
COMPANION TO THE SUPREME COURT OF THE UNITED
STATES (Kermit L. Hall, et al. eds., 2d ed. 2005). He
singles out a few exceptional stylists: Chief Justice
Marshall, and Justices Holmes and Jackson. For
their ability to turn a phrase, posthumous honorable
mentions also go to Justices Black, Brandeis,
Cardozo, Douglas, Frankfurter, and Scalia, and Chief
Justice Rehnquist. Among current and recent
Justices, there have been some good writers and
some not-so-good writers. Chief Justice Roberts and
Justice Kagan are first-rate stylists. By comparison,
Justice Souter wrote sentences and paragraphs
rivaling James Joyce that went on and on seemingly
without end and sometimes without a point. Justice
Kennedy had a baroque style that was often difficult
to understand let alone appreciate. Indeed, Anthony
Kennedy's writing was so bad that puckish Antonin
Scalia could not resist mocking it, with uncollegial
humor. *E.g., Obergefell v. Hodges*, 135 S. Ct. 2584,
2630 n.22 (2015) ("If, even as the price to be paid for
a fifth vote, I ever joined an opinion for the Court that
began [with the majority's first sentence], I would
hide my head in a bag. The Supreme Court of the
United States has descended from the disciplined
legal reasoning of John Marshall and Joseph Story to
the mystical aphorisms of the fortune cookie."). Pay
close attention when your professor revealingly

singles out a particular opinion or an individual Justice for encomium. That is a poker tell that deserves your attention. Still, the task at hand for judges is to decide the case, to hold onto a majority, and to write an opinion with dispatch. Hence, the utilitarian and pragmatic non-style style of writing of a Justice Breyer or a Justice Alito is efficient. They get the job done, even if they are not likely to win an exemplary writing award from THE GREEN BAG. Professor Lino Graglia, of the University of Texas School of Law, once made the same point with this anecdote:

> The topic I have been assigned * * * reminds me of a conversation I had a little while ago with a professor of classics. After telling me how much he enjoyed teaching Thucydides, he expressed the view that it was terrible that law professors should be paid more than professors of classics. I told him the reason for this was clear: In his line of work he gets to read Thucydides while in mine I get to read Harry Blackmun, and surely he would agree, that is worth a few bucks. When I read Thucydides, I noted, I don't get paid either.

Lino Graglia, *The Open-ended Clauses of the Constitution*, 11 HARV. J. & PUB. POL'Y 87, 87 (1988).

Philosophy or Moral Reasoning. At the founding, political philosophy and moral reasoning took the form of natural rights and the laws of nature. These ideas explained the way Americans of that time thought about government, ideas Thomas Jefferson explained in the *Declaration of Independence*. *See*

Chapter 1, § 10 (Individual Rights); Chapter 2, § 1 (Origins of Judicial Review). Natural law in the Christian tradition consists of commands and prohibitions derived from divine revelation, like the Ten Commandments, as is illustrated in the writings of Thomas Aquinas.

But the Framers were Lockeans, not Thomists. Truth for them came from right reason—from the mind of man, not from the Godhead. They believed that there was a body of ethical imperatives inherent in human beings and discovered by human reason alone. They read John Locke, who imagined that in a pre-existing state of nature neither civil society nor government existed and each person was sovereign unto himself or herself. But Thomas Hobbes, another political philosopher of their era, had described life in the state of nature, without government or civil laws, as being "solitary, poor, nasty, brutish and short." Civil society is called into being by the social contract: individuals consent to government and yield some personal autonomy to society that in turn exercises this sovereignty to protect the individual's right to the pursuit of happiness, including the right to acquire and enjoy property that allowed a person to be independent and free to exercise other rights. The laws of nature, therefore, provide the link between the state of nature and civil society, or between natural rights and government. Government does not grant us rights—we have inalienable rights, God-given rights. The New World was analogous to the state of nature in their minds and it was incumbent upon them to write a radically new social compact; this covenant theme has a religious origin that evolved into political theory from the Mayflower Compact through the colonial charters and the *Declaration of Independence* and the subsequent experience with early constitution-writing in the states leading up to the Constitutional Convention of 1787. This cultural tradition comes down to the present day: African-American political activism from the mid-19th to the mid-20th century—from Frederick Douglas to Martin Luther King, Jr.— forcefully invoked a higher law philosophy against racial injustice. Think of MLK's historic "Letter from a Birmingham Jail." VINCENT W. LLOYD, BLACK NATURAL LAW (2016).

American exceptionalism—captured in our motto "*Novus Ordo Seclorum*" ("A New Order for the Ages")—has always been obsessed with our national virtue, often to the bewilderment of the rest of the world. The caveat, of course, is that while the Founders themselves recognized the inevitable decline of republics throughout history, they nonetheless imagined their Constitution as a great experiment that they hoped against history would resist corruption, decline, and decay. Such was their modest brand of exceptionalism. Recall Benjamin Franklin's famous quip in 1789, shortly before his death, as the new national government was being formed under the newly ratified Constitution: "Our new Constitution is now established, everything seems to promise it will be durable; but, in this world, nothing is certain except death and taxes."

The Declaration leads to the Constitution because the rights endowed equally in all persons necessarily require a well-governed society to guarantee law and order—*née* "ordered liberty." *See* Timothy Sandefur, *The Declaration of Independence, Annotated*, 9 CHAP. L. REV. 147 (2005). The Framers believed that the whole Constitution was a kind of bill of rights that limited the threat against liberty posed by government. *The Federalist No. 84.* Soon after the Constitution was ratified, the Supreme Court debated the idea that judicial review could be exercised to strike down statutes on the basis of natural law. In *seriatim* opinions, Justice Chase said "yes;" Justice Iredell said "no." *Calder v. Bull*, 3 U.S. (3 Dall.) 386 (1798). In theory, the Supreme Court has followed Justice Iredell to base its decisions only on formal legal interpretations of the Constitution. In practice, the Court's interpretations of the Constitution often seem to have a great deal to do with norms and values the Justices read into the text. This may have a lot to do with the institutional role of a Supreme Court Justice, who admittedly is part-judge and part-philosopher in a way that lower court judges simply are not.

Professor Solum, who teaches at Georgetown Law School, has started a campaign to identify and appoint men and women of "judicial character" who possess "judicial virtues," *i.e.*, courage, temperance, judicial temperament, intelligence, and practical wisdom, jurists who will practice the "virtue of justice" on the bench. He believes that only such a theory of judicial character can achieve constitutional integrity. Lawrence B. Solum, *The Aretaic Turn in Constitutional Theory*, 70 BROOK. L. REV. 475 (2005). Likewise, Lawrence Sager prefers the judge who seeks "justice" as a full partner with the Framers rather than merely their agent. LAWRENCE G. SAGER, JUSTICE IN PLAINCLOTHES: A THEORY OF AMERICAN CONSTITUTIONAL PRACTICE (2006).

In our time, Princeton political scientist Walter Murphy insisted that in a post-Freudian world there can be no naïve denial that a judge's personal values and life experiences influence the way the judge interprets the Constitution and decides cases. *See* WALTER F. MURPHY, JAMES E. FLEMING, SOTIRIOUS A. BARBER & STEPHEN MACADO, AMERICAN CONSTITUTIONAL INTERPRETATION (5th ed. 2014). Most jurists do not consciously separate their empirical assumptions about the world from their interpretations of the Constitution in any scientific way. Yet, science—including the science of politics— operates in ways opposite from law: science values progress and change while law values stability and precedent. Nevertheless, all these values must be reconciled together. DAVID L. FAIGMAN, LABORATORY OF JUSTICE—THE SUPREME COURT'S 200-YEAR STRUGGLE TO INTEGRATE SCIENCE AND LAW (2004). There is a spirited debate among academics and jurists, however, over the propriety of a judge overtly relying on political philosophy or moral reasoning.

Ian Bartrum has catalogued the four basic constitutional values that are broadly shared in the United States, the features of our government system that are essential to the American regime: a legal constraint on government institutions and actors; flexibility to allow adaptation to cultural and technological change; popular representative participation in governmental decision-making that includes majority and minority groups; an expression of a national identity based on a shared history and common aspirations. Think: the rule of law enforced by judicial review; the Necessary and Proper Clause and the states' police powers; the Guarantee Clause promise of a Republican form of government; and "We the People" in the Preamble brigaded with the Bill of Rights. Clarity, not truth, legitimates the exercise of judicial review. Judges must be expected to explain and justify the constitutional value choices they make when they adopt any of the available theories of interpretation—they must practice "value transparency." Ian Bartrum, *Constitutional Value Judgments and Interpretative Theory Choices*, 40 FLA. L. REV. 259 (2013). Along the same lines, the late Professor Philip Kissam identified three basic constitutional values: the exercise of power by government and individuals upon other individuals; the influence of prior generations felt by the current generation; and the commitment to democratic participation by all individuals. He too relied on these basic features of the American regime to take the measure of the extant theories of constitutional interpretation. His meta-theorizing or synthesizing led him to endorse three dimensional theories that best accounted for power, time, and Everyman. Philip C. Kissam, *Triangulating Constitutional Theory: Power, Time, and Everyman*, 53 BUFF. L. REV. 269 (2005) (endorsing the high theorizing of Philip Bobbit, *infra*, and Ronald Dworkin, *infra*).

The late Ronald Dworkin, who taught at NYU and Oxford University, was a leading proponent of a moral reading of the Constitution. RONALD DWORKIN, FREEDOM'S LAW: THE MORAL READING OF THE AMERICAN CONSTITUTION (1996). He insisted that the value-laden discourse of constitutional law, on the part of "liberals" and "conservatives" alike, takes place within a moral context of political decency and ultimate justice. Nothing else would be true to the rule of law. The Framers meant the Constitution to codify and enact general principles, what he calls "concepts" of right and wrong, but they did not intend for subsequent generations to adhere to their particular views on specific issues, their "conceptions" of specific policies. This is the only way to avoid the Scylla and Charybdis of majoritarianism and being ruled by the dead hand of the past. Emory University's Michael Perry would go even farther to embrace the indeterminacy of moral reasoning as the justification for judging, *i.e.*, that judges exercise discernment and judgment to interpret the Constitution and decide cases. MICHAEL J. PERRY, MORALITY, POLITICS, AND LAW (1988). He would celebrate a judge's reliance on the judge's own personal beliefs. Consequently, both scholars would place a great emphasis on the importance of judicial selection to vet and choose judges who are wise and fair and principled members of the interpretive community.

Michael McConnell, who teaches at Stanford University, is highly critical of this approach to constitutional interpretation. Michael W. McConnell, *The Importance of Humility in Judicial Review: A*

Comment on Ronald Dworkin's "Moral Reading" of the Constitution, 65 FORDHAM L. REV. 1269 (1997). He sees but three alternatives: (1) to read the Constitution in light of the Framers' expectations about specific applications; (2) to read the Constitution in light of the moral and political principles they intended to express; or (3) to read the Constitution in light of what we now think would be the best way to understand the abstract language. An originalist who seeks the original understanding of the Constitution, McConnell says that only the second alternative is proper. He thus lines up with Justices Scalia and Thomas. The first alternative folds to the dead hand of the past. The third alternative—the approach Dworkin and Perry endorse—would for all intents and purposes turn over the Constitution to the power of the judges. But judges are men and women—not angels—and in designing a constitutional government James Madison warned us to be mistrustful of what power does to men and women.

Whether Dworkin/Perry or McConnell has the better argument is left to the reader. As with other interpretative methodologies, your preference really depends on what kind of Constitution—and what kind of Supreme Court—you think we should have. The chief proponent of moral reasoning in constitutional interpretation on the Supreme Court was Justice Brennan:

> We current Justices read the Constitution in the only way that we can: as Twentieth-Century Americans. We look to the history of the time of

framing and to the intervening history of interpretation. But the ultimate question must be, what do the words of the text mean in our time? For the genius of the Constitution rests not in any static meaning it might have had in a world that is dead and gone, but in the adaptability of its great principles to cope with current problems and current needs. What the constitutional fundamentals meant to the wisdom of other times cannot be their measure to the vision of our time. Similarly, what those fundamentals mean for us, our descendants will learn, cannot be the measure to the vision of their time.

William J. Brennan, *The Constitution of the United States: Contemporary Ratification*, *in* INTERPRETING THE CONSTITUTION—THE DEBATE OVER ORIGINAL INTENT at 23, 27 (Jack N. Rakove ed., 1990). The paradox in this approach is that if words change their meaning over time then they are not the same words and the Constitution amounts to a string of homonyms.

4.   HOW TO INTERPRET THE CONSTITUTION?

As was just described, among the available and most prevalent sources of meaning for interpreting the Constitution are the text, original understanding, history and tradition, structure, precedent or doctrine, and philosophy or moral reasoning. Constitutional interpretation is characterized by an intellectual syncretism that relies on these sources to varying degrees and often in combination. Different interpreters rely on different sources, and often they differ in approach, emphasis, and outcomes. Even the same individual interpreter will sometimes use different sources to analyze different constitutional questions. Nonetheless, Harvard's Richard Fallon maintains that it is highly desirable and readily possible for a constitutional interpreter to be coherent and consistent by striving for some measure of commensurability to fit together and weigh against each other these various sources of meaning. Richard H. Fallon, Jr., *A Constructivist Coherence Theory of Constitutional Interpretation*, 100 HARV. L. REV. 1189 (1987). *See also* PHILIP BOBBITT, CONSTITUTIONAL FATE: THEORY OF THE CONSTITUTION (1982) (identifying various modalities of constitutional interpretation); GRANT HUSCROFT, ed., EXPOUNDING THE CONSTITUTION: ESSAYS IN CONSTITUTIONAL THEORY (2008) (a dialogical colloquium about constitutional interpretation).

That there are fashions and trends in constitutional theory can be suggested by a paragraph recap of the last half of the twentieth century. During the Chief Justiceship of Earl Warren, the Justices favored moral reasoning in big important cases by striving to reach the "right result." They found the value for the school desegregation case chiseled in the pediment on the front of their building: "Equal Justice Under Law." Those Justices also invested the Court's prestige to reform government processes: reapportioning state legislatures and reforming the criminal justice system. They practiced a lot of clause-bound interpretivism, focusing on the "right to Counsel" in the Sixth Amendment, for example, and then used the common law methodology to build up a considerable body of case annotations. Following suit, the Burger Court worked over a lot of precedents and doctrine, often distinguishing the dickens out of Warren Court opinions. Those Justices developed the nontextual "right to privacy" and made the states redo their capital punishment laws. The Rehnquist Court presided over what likely will go down in history as the heyday of originalism. Even nonoriginalist Justices on the Court wrote opinions full of historical references and relied on history and tradition to fill in gaps left by the Framers. Those Justices called a halt to the development of nontextual rights, refusing to extend precedents to protect euthanasia, for example, but nonetheless preserving the essence of the right to abortion. A closely divided Court pursued structuralism to decide numerous cases based on separation of powers and federalism, in which cases the majority often sided against Congress and with the states. During these three eras, however, all the prevalent sources were brought down off the shelf at one time or another, and individual Justices followed their own interpretative instincts. The prolific Cass Sunstein has written about the same phenomenon among professors in the universities. Cass R. Sunstein, *Foreword: On Academic Fads and Fashions*, 99 MICH. L. REV. 1251 (2001).

We will have to wait and see what fads and fashions will describe the handiwork of the Roberts Court, which continues to evolve as of this writing.

Justice Byron White, who sat on the Supreme Court for more than three decades, was fond of observing that every time a new Justice joins the Supreme Court it becomes a different court. During the John Roberts era, there have been six different "natural courts"—the term political scientists use to describe Justice White's insight: Roberts for Rehnquist in 2005; Alito for O'Connor in 2006; Sotomayor for Souter in 2009; Kagan for Stevens in 2010; Gorsuch for Scalia in 2017; and Kavanaugh for Kennedy in 2018. Thus far, the Roberts Courts (plural) have been characterized by frequently closely decided, usually but not always conservative decisions in the more controversial cases and a tendency to avoid writing grand opinions—often to the chagrin of the talking heads on the left and the right on the cable news channels. As some of its remaining elderly Justices age-out or retire and are replaced, the center of the Court may shift seismically, depending on the next few presidential elections. The expectation is that the Roberts Court will truly become the John Roberts Court with the 2018 appointment, however, when the Chief Justice will occupy what the newspapers like to call the "swing seat" previously occupied by Justice Kennedy and before him by Justice O'Connor. Chief Justice Roberts' personal constitutional jurisprudence is characterized by incrementalism and minimalism and a powerful sense of institutional loyalty for the Supreme Court *qua* court. The popular convention of referring to eras by the last name of the Chief Justice is sometimes accurate.

One technique that the modern Supreme Court regularly uses is "balancing." The metaphor is borrowed from the blindfolded goddess of justice holding a set of scales to weigh the opposing claims. Balancing two constitutional values in conflict, as when the Court balances an individual's right to associate against a group's right not to associate with the individual, is one form. *See* Chapter 4, § 5 (Competing Constitutional Liberties). Another form of the metaphor is to balance individual liberty versus government power, which is the primary issue for constitutional analysis depicted in the constitutional diagram. *See* Chapter 3 (Constitutional Analysis). But balancing can amount to little more than a conclusion or a stated preference: "we find in favor of the individual and against the government" does not reveal much analysis. It is an intellectual sleight of hand to divert our attention. Taking the metaphor literally, we would carefully assay the individual liberty and the government power and assign each a calibrated value in order to balance them: "the individual liberty is worth five utils and the government power is worth three utils so the government must lose this case." You will never read that in an opinion. That is the inherent problem with a "balancing analysis."

For some constitutional issues, balancing is required by the text itself as, for example, the Fourth Amendment that forbids only "unreasonable" searches and seizures or the Eighth Amendment that prohibits "excessive fines" and "cruel and unusual punishments." Many Justices generalize this balancing technique to prefer standards, as opposed to rules, for deciding constitutional cases. An example of a standard is "drive at a safe speed," and

an example of a rule is "do not exceed 55 m.p.h."
Kathleen Sullivan, former Dean of the Stanford Law
School, chronicled how this methodological difference
accounted for the strongest disagreements among the
Justices on the Rehnquist Court. Kathleen M.
Sullivan, *The Supreme Court, 1991 Term:
Foreword—The Justices of Rules and Standards*, 106
HARV. L. REV. 22 (1992). Justice O'Connor was very
fond of totality-of-the-circumstance analysis
applying a standard like whether a statute interferes
"too much" with the Constitution. On the other hand,
Justice Scalia mocked balancing to say that "the scale
analogy is not really appropriate, since the interests
on both sides are incommensurate. It is more like
judging whether a particular line is longer than a
particular rock is heavy." *Bendix Autolite Corp. v.
Midwesco Enters., Inc.*, 486 U.S. 888, 897 (1988)
(Scalia, J., concurring). Our constitutional analysis
obliges the Supreme Court to find the balance of
individual liberty versus government power in the
Constitution by defining the scope of the liberty and
the reach of the power. This is more than some
simplistic "balancing" test that announces nothing
more than the subjective preference of a majority of
five about who should win and who should lose. The
standard operating methodology the Court relies on
the most in our constitutional analysis is doctrine or
precedent, which is considerably elaborate and full of
nuance. *See* Chapter 4, § 2 (Constitutional Law
Doctrines). All those three-part tests and four-prong
analyses in Supreme Court opinions basically are
variations on the balancing technique; the Justices
use these tests to call on lower court judges to do the

balancing in the first place in the application of the identified factors.

Besides balancing, there are a few other snipe hunts in constitutional theory. Although they are a familiar part of the discourse, these false dichotomies really do not withstand a closer scrutiny. Consider "strict construction" and "liberal construction." When the Court interprets individual liberty strictly, then correspondingly it is interpreting government power liberally, and *vice versa*. What does a President mean to say that an ideal judge is a "strict constructionist"? "Judicial activism" and "judicial self-restraint," like beauty, are in the eyes of the beholder. When they get outvoted, dissenters use those terms to distinguish themselves from the majority. It is not activism to enforce the Constitution; it is not self-restraint to refrain from enforcing the Constitution; it is simply enforcing or not enforcing the Constitution. Besides, any attempt to measure "activism" is fraught with its own indeterminacy. The "activsmometer" device to measure activism is itself an imaginary construct combining constitutional ontology—what renders constitutional claims true or false—and epistemology—what renders constitutional claims known or unknown. Also consider the Due Process Clauses and the distinction between "substance" and "procedure." Only a lawyer's mind could come up with the distinction between a logical redundancy and a logical contradiction: between "procedural due process" (process-process!) and "substantive due process" (substantive process!). All of constitutional law is substantive except for procedural due process, but procedural due process is about the fundamental fairness in providing adequate notice and a reasonable opportunity to be heard. That idea of fairness is a substantive value. Finally, the literature used to make much of the distinction between "interpretivists" and "non-interpretivists." But even Thomas Grey, the Stanford professor who started all of us talking about interpreters along those lines has given up to admit that we are all interpretivists and we are all non-interpretivists now. Thomas C. Grey, *The Constitution as Scripture*, 37 STAN. L. REV. 1 (1984). Everyone always starts with the text. Everyone goes beyond the text sometimes. Be wary of the subterfuge of formalism, which Cass Sunstein warns against. A sophisticated question of legal theory cannot be resolved with a language lesson. Someone who insists that the very idea or definition of "interpretation" obliges judges to adopt their own preferred method of construing the Constitution is making this bluff. Cass R. Sunstein, *There Is Nothing That Interpretation Just Is*, 30 CONST. COMMENT. 193 (2015). That is a favorite trick of law professors. Logically, there must be such a thing as a correct interpretation of a text. But Supreme Court Justices are eclectics. Their opinions may seem full of opportunistic arguments, but there is an individualized method to their interpretative madness. There is greater interpretative coherency chambers-by-chambers than there is across the full bench. Kenneth Arrow won a Nobel Prize for this insight into social theory. *See* Frank H. Easterbrook, *Ways of Criticizing the Court*, 95 HARV. L. REV. 802 (1982) (applying Arrow's Theorem to defend the

Supreme Court from the criticism that it is divided too frequently and decides cases inconsistently).

Finally, a pretty good test drive for any interpretive theory is to ask how it would decide modern landmark decisions that pushed the envelope of theory at the time they were decided. *E.g., Griswold v. Connecticut*, 381 U.S. 479 (1965); *Brown v. Bd. of Educ.*, 347 U.S. 483 (1954). Doing so provides useful insights about the theory and its implications for constitutional law. Consider this paradox: short of a formal constitutional amendment, constitutional change is only possible—and we can debate the soundness of constitutional holdings and the persuasiveness of the constitutional reasoning in Supreme Court opinions—if and only if we believe that there actually is a difference, at least in theory, between the Constitution and what the Justices say it is. Landmark cases, historic decisions which have come to be recognized as essential to the American scheme of ordered liberty by everyone no matter their political persuasion, are markers laid down to measure the integrity and legitimacy of the competing theories of interpretation. They operate like an eye chart to test the constitutional vision of the interpreter. *See* William P. Marshall, *Progressive Constitutionalism, Originalism, and the Significance of Landmark Decisions in Evaluating Constitutional Theory*, 72 OHIO ST. L.J. 1251 (2011); Stephen Kanter, *The Griswold Diagrams: A Unified Theory of Constitutional Rights*, 28 CARDOZO L. REV. 623 (2006).

5. LIBERAL THEORY

The philosophy of liberalism is rooted in the Enlightenment with its emphasis on the rights-bearing individual. Liberal political theory calls the state into existence, and the citizen needs the state to protect individual rights. The state, at the same time, represents the greatest threat to the realization and enjoyment of our rights. The Framers were followers of John Locke, and their liberal constitutionalism depended on rationality to posit a sphere of individual liberty, guaranteed by property rights writ large, with a fixed government constituted by majority consent expressed in regular elections participated in by an enfranchised citizenry. What newspapers today call "liberals" and "conservatives" are all philosophical heirs of the Framers. Modern liberalism followed these assumptions towards the progressivism of the left.

Classical liberal theory dominated the United States in the period between World War II and the end of the 20th century, and constitutional law was no different. Scotty Powe, of the University of Texas, has carefully chronicled how liberal elite values were dominant in the work product of the Warren Court. LUCAS A. POWE, THE WARREN COURT AND AMERICAN POLITICS (2000). Among constitutionalists, there has been considerable evolution within American liberalism. Thomas Grey, of Stanford University, has charted this intellectual family tree to include: the Progressive movement; Legal Realism; Process-based jurisprudence; Civic Republicanism or Neo-republicanism; Critical Legal Studies; Law and

Economics; Law and Literature; Feminism with variations; Critical Race Theory with variations; and Pragmatism. Thomas Grey, *Modern American Legal Thought*, 106 YALE L.J. 493 (1996). Thus, the political left is a crowded place full of intellectual diversity. It also is a contested space populated by some who insist that they have moved beyond liberalism. Some critical scholars, like Georgetown's Robin West, would be more than ambivalent to be linked with liberalism because they are skeptical whether the values in the Constitution are the right values in the first place. Robin L. West, *Constitutional Skepticism*, 72 B.U. L. REV. 765 (1992).

Liberalism shifted emphases between these different paradigms. In the early 1900s, the Progressives consciously pursued the betterment of society through legislative agendas informed by social science. Then the Legal Realists came along to value social science and support government regulation of the economy. Law was utilitarian not normative. They saw a central role for judges and courts to arbitrate social disputes, although their insights into judging emphasized how judges were influenced by unconscious attitudes and personal experiences. The Processualists trusted in the expertise of the administrative agencies of the New Deal for the economy. Their emphasis on procedures played out in the Warren Court's jurisprudence to protect discrete and insular minorities and to reform the political processes in the states. An intellectual *ennui* with liberalism set in, and after the turbulent 1960s there was something of a backlash among the *cognoscenti.* Civic Republicans went off in the direction of history to try to recapture the neo-classical values of the Framers, who viewed themselves as the political heirs of the ancient republics of Greece and Rome. There they found a priority for community and the practice of civic virtue by the individual in the pursuit of the common good. Others took on a critical perspective that turned against the traditional left and went beyond legal realism to deconstruct and be critical of liberalism itself. There was a loud critique of illegitimate hierarchy and much trashing of traditional understandings about law. But the critical legal studies movement seemed to play itself out in the academy except for how it later was reflected among feminists and critical race theorists. Each of these competing paradigms has obvious implications for the Constitution and the role of the Supreme Court.

Laura Kalman, a historian at the University of California at Santa Barbara, has chronicled American legal liberalism, which she explains is characterized by a faith in the potential of courts, especially the Supreme Court, to effectuate large-scale reforms that improve the situation of underrepresented and oppressed groups. LAURA KALMAN, THE STRANGE CAREER OF LEGAL LIBERALISM (1996). She zeroes in on how law professors in particular are prone to join the "cult of the Court" and become judge-worshippers. Thus, conventional liberal constitutional law professors are likely to believe that unregulated markets do not serve the public welfare and that government regulation is necessary to correct unequal distributions of wealth and power. At the same time, those same professors would believe that the realm of individual rights must be as free of government interference as possible so that individuals will enjoy the highest level of personal autonomy. Government is to be trusted to pursue this egalitarianism. Their priority has been on civil rights and civil liberties in the larger goal of achieving social justice. They look on the Warren Court with nostalgia and admiration for its halcyon decisions expanding individual rights. The ultimate test of the Justices' work was how it furthered liberty and equality. But Earl Warren died even before Elvis, and the hopeful who expect the Supreme Court will make a comeback to lead the agenda for radical social change have dwindled to a few true believers. And even they have been stymied by persistent working majorities of Republican-appointed Supreme Court Justices ever since the Reagan Administration in the 1980s. Given that recent experience, Jamal Greene argues that the only thing for a progressive academic to do is to fight a rear guard action and theorize towards judicial minimalism, at least so long as conservatives are ascendant in the Third Branch. Jamal Greene, *How Constitutional Theory Matters*, 72 OHIO ST. L.J. 1183 (2011).

6. CONSERVATIVE THEORY

Just as modern liberalism followed Lockean liberalism to the left, modern conservative theory followed it to the right. Like the Framers, modern conservatives are protective of property rights and more comfortable with inequality in wealth and status, at least more so than modern liberals. As was our observation about liberalism, conservative constitutional theory is not monolithic. Conservative jurists and conservative academics generally are drawn to some form of originalism in constitutional interpretation. They tend to be textualists who are mindful of history and tradition more than precedent or doctrine. They are mistrustful of the liberal egalitarian agenda and far more deferential to majoritarianism than liberals, although they can be profoundly protective of the judicial prerogative, as well. They are skeptical of nontextual constitutional analysis in the pursuit of individual rights, but at the same time they are keen on nontextual structural interpretation to enforce separation of powers and federalism. The Rehnquist Court was their favorite band—their favorite members were Clarence Thomas, Antonin Scalia, and William H. Rehnquist.

Robert Bork, whose constitutional conservativism cost him a seat on the Supreme Court bench, defined the limited role of the conservative judge:

> In a constitutional democracy the moral content of the law must be given by the morality of the framer or the legislator, never the judge. The sole task of the latter—and it is quite large enough for anyone's wisdom, skill, and virtue— is to translate the framer's or the legislator's morality into a rule to govern unforeseen circumstances. That abstinence from giving his own desires free play, that continuing and self-conscious renunciation of power, that is the morality of the jurist.

ROBERT H. BORK, TRADITION AND MORALITY IN
CONSTITUTIONAL LAW 11 (1984). Bork would look just
as suspiciously at a "liberal judge" relying on moral
reasoning and a "conservative judge" relying on
natural law because both those sources allow judges
to find things in the Constitution that are not there,
at least not in Bork's constitution. However, recall
that 1,925 law professors signed a petition against
his nomination for the Supreme Court, a revealing
factoid about Bork and most law professors.
Furthermore, some conservative constitutionalists
like the late historian Harry Jaffa and Randy
Barnett of Georgetown University Law School
embrace the idea of natural rights and appeal to the
philosophy of the founding to argue the legitimacy of
that mode of constitutional interpretation. Randy E.
Barnett, *A Law Professor's Guide to Natural Law and
Natural Rights*, 20 HARV. J.L. & PUB. POL'Y 655
(1997); Harry V. Jaffa, *What Were the "Original
Intentions" of the Framers of the Constitution of the
United States?*, 10 U. PUGET SOUND L. REV. 351
(1987). Bork does have a point, however, to be
suspicious of the coincidence that liberals use moral
reasoning and conservatives use natural law to find
values in the Constitution sharing a striking
resemblance to the platforms of the Democratic and
Republican national parties, respectively. More
recently, Barnett has emphasized how the
Constitution rests on a foundation of individual
sovereignty rather than a collective popular
sovereignty—his somewhat libertarian emphasis is
on "We the People, each and every one." That is why
courts are necessary: to protect individual natural

rights from legislative infringement. RANDY E. BARNETT, OUR REPUBLICAN CONSTITUTION: SECURING THE LIBERTY AND SOVEREIGNTY OF WE THE PEOPLE (2016). We should worry more about the threat against freedom and liberty from government power—the primary focus of the constitutional diagram featured in this NUTSHELL—than we should worry about the counter-majoritarian difficulty behind judicial review. Excessive judicial self-restraint could allow the complete undoing of the republican Constitution. Hadley Arkes is another notable true believer in natural law whose lifetime project has been to rescue constitutional law from legal positivism and historicism. He resists much of modern constitutional law to return to that "old time religion" of cases like *Lochner v. New York* (1905). HADLEY ARKES, CONSTITUTIONAL ILLUSIONS AND ANCHORING TRUTHS: THE TOUCHSTONE OF THE NATURAL LAW (2010).

According to Michael Paulsen, who teaches at the University of St. Thomas School of Law, some conservative judges are majoritarians who consistently manage to defer to legislatures, but other conservative judges do not always accept that posture. Michael Stokes Paulsen, *The Many Faces of "Judicial Restraint,"* 1993 PUB. INT. L. REV. 3. Conservative jurists with a strong interpretivist approach will follow the text, history and tradition, and structure, even when those sources lead to the invalidation of the legislation. Other conservatives, whose interpretivism is mediated by an instrumentalist sense of constitutional law and the role of the Supreme Court, will take a gradualist

approach and be more reluctant to upset precedent
and settled doctrines. Consequently, a Supreme
Court composed of conservative Justices can behave
in an unpredictable, downright hostile, manner
toward legislatures. Kathleen Sullivan has identified
nine different conservative preferences that pull in
different directions on different constitutional issues:
(1) originalism; (2) textualism; (3) judicial restraint
and deference to legislatures; (4) libertarianism and
deregulation; (5) states' rights and decentralization;
(6) traditionalism; (7) precedent; (8) free-market
capitalism; and (9) law and order. Kathleen M.
Sullivan, *The Jurisprudence of the Rehnquist Court*,
22 NOVA L. REV. 743 (1998). The preferences on this
list are ambiguous influences, however. Some
conservative judges might approach tradition
proactively to help shape its evolution, claiming that
role for the courts. Other conservative judges might
eschew any such judicial role and insist that the
traditions already enshrined in the Constitution
trump newer, lesser traditions. These nuances are
evident in the political phenomenon of the Tea Party
Movement, which began as a reaction to the federal
response to the financial crisis of 2009. That grass
roots movement had a split personality of originalism
and populism for its constitutional theory. The past
is important and useful to its members in
determining constitutional meaning. But the
movement's constitutional salience was felt more
keenly by the political branches than by the judicial
branch. Its conservative agenda for federalism and
individual liberty affected the constitutional
philosophy of its congressional caucus. Rebecca E.

Zietlow, *Popular Originalism?: The Tea Party Movement and Constitutional Theory*, 64 FLA. L. REV. 483 (2012).

Conservatism is a big tent that covers many devotees of law and economics, public choice theory, and libertarianism. As the term suggests, law and economics uses economic principles to analyze legal questions. Adam Smith published his famous book, "The Wealth of Nations" in the year of American Independence. Its influence was immediate and profound. Americans understood that markets require supporting infrastructure from government, public goods that include justice, security, and liberty for individuals and their property. Barry R. Weingast, *Adam Smith's Constitutional Theory* (2017) (available on SSRN). Surprisingly, however, constitutional theory has failed to engage with the power and influence of economic elites in American politics and the legal system. Vanderbilt University's Ganesh Sitaraman has called for theorists to recognize the reality and the persistence of economic power in the United States. Ganesh Sitaraman, *The Puzzling Absence of Economic Power in Constitutional Theory*, 101 CORNELL L. REV. 1445 (2016). Public choice theory is more particular to apply principles of microeconomics to describe or predict the actual behavior of government actors. Libertarianism takes different forms with a common underlying philosophy that everyone should be allowed to be autonomous and free to do as they please so long as they do not infringe on the equal freedom of other individuals. It can get noisy inside the tent, too, when some conservatives clamor for proactive judicial review to protect property rights, under the Takings Clause for example, and other conservatives resist by decrying such "judicial activism." This contemporary argument echoes the debate over *Lochner v. New York*, 198 U.S. 45 (1905) and substantive due process. *See* Appendix A, § 8 (Substantive Due Process). Professor Epstein is representative in the way he basically complains about everything that has happened in the United States since the New Deal. In his *magnum opus*, THE CLASSICAL LIBERAL CONSTITUTION: THE UNCERTAIN QUEST FOR LIMITED GOVERNMENT (2014), Epstein argues that the Supreme Court improperly and mistakenly endorsed progressive political reforms that have eroded individual liberty and property rights. He calls for a return to Enlightenment-era values of limited government as the only legitimate and effective way to restore a republican and libertarian regime. The reference in his title to "classical liberalism" is to the political philosophy of the 18th century, not to what the NEW YORK TIMES calls "liberal" today.

Conservatives reject the liberal motto that the Constitution has to be "kept in tune with the times" and the courts should lead the way. Conservatives might turn that cliché around to say that judges are supposed to keep the times in tune with the Constitution.

7.   FEMINIST THEORY

The priority of feminist theory is to incorporate and integrate women's perspectives into the legal system. It is a perspective, however, that basically is critical of law as a patriarchal institution. University of Missouri-Kansas City professor Nancy Levit has identified and explained four different schools of feminist theory. NANCY LEVIT, THE GENDER LINE: MEN, WOMEN AND THE LAW (1998). "Liberal feminists" argue for the elimination of all gender-based classifications. Men are viewed as the legal reference or norm. Ruth Bader Ginsburg, before she became a Justice, argued for equality and against sexual stereotypes that limit opportunities for both women and men. "Cultural feminists" emphasize an innate difference between women and men. Formal equality is not desirable; rather the essential biological and social facts that women bear children and are primarily responsible for child-rearing oblige the legal system to accommodate these differences. Some "difference feminists" believe that ultimately men cannot be reconciled with feminism and therefore they pursue a separatist agenda. "Radical feminists" view men as oppressors and emphasize the subordination of women by male norms in law and society. They seek to address class-based oppression by reforming social institutions. They are not satisfied with equality but rather conceive of gender politics as a zero-sum game in which women must take power away from their exploiters at all costs.

Of course, many constitutional law issues relate to gender and sex. Building on the work of social scientist and cultural feminist Carol Gilligan, Vanderbilt University's Suzanna Sherry has argued that the Constitution as interpreted in the general liberal tradition is quintessentially masculine, but she saw a feminine perspective in Justice O'Connor's jurisprudence. Suzanna Sherry, *Civic Virtue and the Feminine Voice in Constitutional Adjudication*, 72 VA. L. REV. 543 (1986). Justice O'Connor disputed this characterization of her jurisprudence. Sandra Day O'Connor, *Portia's Progress*, 66 N.Y.U. L. REV. 1546 (1991). Feminist high theorizing thus has moved from a liberal-equality stage to a cultural-difference stage to a radical-dominance stage and to a postmodern-anti-essentialist stage that is skeptical of all social constructs of "truth" and which seeks to be inclusive and other-regarding of the diversity of women of color and lesbians in such a way that they are respected and empowered. Martha Chamallas, at the Ohio State University, has described these intellectual developments and chronicled the internal and external debates over feminist theory as well as the diversity of views within feminist thought. MARTHA CHAMALLAS, INTRODUCTION TO FEMINIST LEGAL THEORY (1999). As the number of women Justices increases, and as new female Justices are appointed, they can be expected to raise the consciousness of their male colleagues.

8. CRITICAL RACE THEORY

As the term suggests, critical race theory focuses on how race and ethnicity operate in the legal system in favor of white-dominated institutions and against racial out-groups. It is an effort to confront overt and covert racial domination and the system of white privilege. Mari Matsuda, who teaches at the University of Hawaii, lists these defining attitudes: belief that racism is endemic in society; skepticism towards all claims of neutrality and objectivity; contextual and historical analysis of law; recognition for the experiential knowledge of persons of color; eclecticism and interdisciplinary methodology; and a commitment towards the elimination of racial and all other forms of oppression. MARI J. MATSUDA ET AL., WORDS THAT WOUND: CRITICAL RACE THEORY, ASSAULTIVE SPEECH, AND THE FIRST AMENDMENT (1993).

Critical race theory is hyper-critical of constitutional law and Supreme Court decisions and doctrines relating to race. In the foreword to a foundational collection of critical race theory scholarship, compiled by professors at UCLA, Western State, Georgetown, and Columbia, respectively, the editors advocate an oppositional vision of racial justice that rejects the views of race in liberalism and conservatism and fundamentally calls into question the legitimacy of the Supreme Court as an institution that preserves the white racial hegemony over society and protects conscious and unconscious racism. KIMBERLÉ CRENSHAW, NEIL GOTANDA, GARY PELLER & KENDALL THOMAS, CRITICAL RACE THEORY: THE KEY WRITINGS THAT FORMED THE MOVEMENT (1995). For them, race is nothing more and nothing less than a social construct invented and perpetuated by the racial majority to subjugate the racial minority. Law is the principal means for constructing race and for abusing people of color. Of course, this raises the postmodern dilemma that if race is merely a social construct, then what critical race theorists claim about racism must also be a social construct. They practice "identity politics" to focus on group membership and group rights, but they favor multiculturalism, in which diversity is celebrated and not denied or ignored or assimilated.

Charles Lawrence, of the University of Hawaii, likens racism to a disease that cannot be cured with legal doctrine, at least not the legal doctrines of contemporary Supreme Court Justices. Charles R. Lawrence III, *The Epidemiology of Color-blindness: Learning to Think and Talk About Race, Again*, 15 B.C. THIRD WORLD L.J. 1 (1995). The narrative form of the genre of critical race theory scholarship may be sampled by reading a series of stories by Albany Law School's Anthony Farley. Anthony Paul Farley, *Thirteen Stories*, 15 TOURO L. REV. 543 (1999). Finally, the late Derrick Bell, one of the founders of critical race theory, was so pessimistic about the future of race relations that he predicted that minorities are prepared to continue their fight for equality, despite any real hope or realistic likelihood of succeeding, merely to preserve their own sense of dignity through struggle. DERRICK BELL, FACES AT THE BOTTOM OF THE WELL: THE PERMANENCE OF RACISM (1992).

9.   POSTMODERN THEORY

Postmodernism is an anti-theory theory characterized by an intellectual playfulness and a dressed-all-in-black sense of irony that make it difficult to decide if the theory is brilliant or absurd or both. Dennis Arrow demonstrated this in his rich satire of postmodern constitutionalism. Dennis W. Arrow, *Pomobabble: Postmodern Newspeak and*

Constitutional "Meaning" for the Uninitiated, 96 MICH. L. REV. 461 (1997). Nonetheless there are many true believers, like Ronald Krotoszynski from the University of Alabama, who take up the law review cudgels to defend postmodernism as being compelling and inevitable. Ronald J. Krotoszynski, *Legal Scholarship at the Crossroads: On Farce, Tragedy, and Redemption*, 77 TEX. L. REV. 321 (1998). A postmodern's view of the world, both descriptive and normative, is a matter of that individual person's perspectives, which are the product of culture, language, class, education, experiences, *et cetera*. There is no Archimedean point, no reference point, no view from somewhere. Reality does not exist. It is only perceived. It is a perspective without perspective.

Postmodernism calls into question the whole enterprise of "hermeneutics," *i.e.*, the study of the methods of interpretation that give meaning to texts. It questions the meaning of meaning. It denies reason to insist that belief systems about reality are merely social constructs, thus denying everything from science to politics. A postmodernist would admit that science and politics have great utility, however, so the theory is somewhat self-contradictory but devotees would not deem that to be a problem. There are no foundational principles. There is no such thing as knowledge. There is no such thing as truth except for the "truth" that there is no truth. Postmodernists thus reject the Enlightenment beliefs in knowledge, truth, reason, and free will. Of course, they admit that Enlightenment thinkers themselves actually did believe in those things. "Epistemology" is the branch of philosophy that studies the nature of knowledge, its presuppositions and foundations, as well as its extent and validity. Postmodern philosophy is subversive of the authority of philosophy by rejecting anything and everything foundational. Its anthem is John Lennon's song *Imagine* (imagining a world without religions or countries or property).

Peter Schanck of Marquette University admits that most people and even many academics find these ideas "inconceivable, ridiculous, or abhorrent," but he makes the convincing case that postmodernism has become one of the dominant theories in the legal academy. Peter C. Schanck, *Understanding Postmodern Thought and Its Implications for Statutory Interpretation*, 65 S. CAL. L. REV. 2505 (1992). This distressing observation has implications for the Supreme Court, which—like it or not—functions in a postmodern world and sometimes operates in a postmodern manner, according to Stephen Feldman of the University of Wyoming. Stephen M. Feldman, *The Supreme Court in a Postmodern World: A Flying Elephant*, 84 MINN. L. REV. 673 (2000). For Yale's Jack Balkin the constitutional question that remains to be answered in the postmodern era is how have changes in society—changes in technology, communications, lifestyles, and workways—changed people's understandings about the Constitution, individual rights and government power? J.M. Balkin, *What Is a Postmodern Constitutionalism?*, 90 MICH. L. REV. 1966 (1992).

Postmodernism undermines the traditional understanding of constitutional interpretation by insisting that meaning is not contained in the document, but only in the interpreter. Before he became Chief Justice, Charles Evans Hughes observed, "We are under a Constitution but the Constitution is what the judges say it is * * *." Yale's Owen Fiss still maintains that something resembling objectivity remains because Supreme Court Justices are members of an interpretative community, and they accept its disciplining rules to restrain their thinking and decision-making. Owen M. Fiss, *Objectivity and Interpretation*, 34 STAN. L. REV. 739 (1982). So, within the interpretative community of constitutionalists, what judges do to the Constitution is real enough. For example, an interpreter who says that Congress cannot regulate interstate commerce is either a member of that community, who is badly mistaken and in need of remedial education, or not a member and someone to be ignored altogether. Sanford Levinson of the University of Texas doubts if an authentic interpretative community exists for the Constitution, however, given the variety of interpretative methodologies that are around. Sanford Levinson, *Law as Literature*, 60 TEX. L. REV. 373 (1982). Furthermore, the everyday occurrence is that the Justices cannot agree on either an interpretative method or an interpretation in a given case. Premier postmodernist Stanley Fish, in exile at the Florida International University College of Law, insists that the Justices are not constrained by theory or by external rules but they behave the way they do because they are situated so deeply in the context of law and judging. Stanley Fish, *Fish v. Fiss*, 36 Stan. L. Rev. 1325 (1984). Interpretation is authority and authority is interpretation. The Constitution does not have one meaning or many meanings. Meaning is conferred on the Constitution only by interpretation. Thus, constitutional interpretation inevitably draws on text and context, so neither constitutional theory by itself nor politics by itself are sufficient to explain constitutional change. Judges must be faithful readers rather than academic theorists. They are uniquely well-trained and situated readers as members of the judicial guild. Their readings create a pragmatic moment in politics and law. Indeed, the law-politics divide may be a source of anxiety for some, but the importance of the distinction is exaggerated and the distinction itself is blurred and unstable. At a constitutional minimum, a judge's reading of the Constitution is privileged over the readings of members of the political branches. That is the purchase of judicial review. B. Jesse Hill, *Resistance to Constitutional Theory: the Supreme Court, Constitutional Change, and the "Pragmatic Moment,"* 91 TEX. L. REV. 1815 (2013).

10. DOES THEORY MATTER?

Honk if you think constitutional theory is a lot of B.S. *See generally* HARRY G. FRANKFURT, ON BULLSHIT (2005). UC Berkeley's Daniel Farber and Vanderbilt's Suzanna Sherry have written a highly provocative book that says that just about all the other professor-theorists mentioned in this Chapter are full of it. DANIEL A. FARBER & SUZANNA SHERRY,

DESPERATELY SEEKING CERTAINTY: THE MISGUIDED QUEST FOR CONSTITUTIONAL FOUNDATIONS (2002). They insist that constitutional law ain't rocket science: grand unified theories ought to be saved for explaining the origin of the universe. Farber and Sherry prefer the way Supreme Court Justices actually behave in real life to decide cases pragmatically and to write under-theorized opinions about the Constitution. They seriously doubt that the highfalutin stuff in the law reviews is really any better for reaching sound decisions and controlling judicial discretion. They argue that no single foundational idea can account for all of American constitutional history. They and other constitutionalists have argued that the entire enterprise of constitutional theorizing might be furthered by paying more attention to how the Constitution actually gets implemented by the institutions of government than by imagining any more new-and-improved interpretative philosophies.

If you are wondering whether all this theorizing is merely academic, in one sense you are correct: law professors take constitutional theory far more seriously than do judges. Richard Posner, who was a federal judge on the Seventh Circuit and a law professor at the University of Chicago, argues against the entire enterprise of constitutional theory, and he is especially dismissive of what he calls "academic moralism" that lacks both intellectual cogency and emotional persuasiveness. Richard A. Posner, *Against Constitutional Theory*, 73 N.Y.U. L. REV. 1 (1998); Richard A. Posner, *The Problematics of Moral and Legal Theory*, 111 HARV. L. REV. 1637

(1998). He would have judges take a pragmatic approach to judging to overcome the fact that constitutional law is lacking in premises from which judges of different political views can reason to conclusions on which they can agree. Posner insists that to the extent the Supreme Court is a constitutional court it is a political body. So the Justices should practice modesty in their decisions by thinking and acting pragmatically. Richard A. Posner, *Foreword: A Political Court*, 119 HARV. L. REV. 31 (2005). Along these same lines, a former law professor and a judge on the Fourth Circuit wrote a book critical of the most prominent theories of constitutional interpretation discussed here. J. HARVIE WILKINSON III, COSMIC CONSTITUTIONAL THEORY: WHY AMERICANS ARE LOSING THEIR INALIENABLE RIGHT TO SELF-GOVERNANCE (2012). Judge Wilkinson insists that what we need is not more theorizing but an escape from theory. Otherwise, he fears an eventual judicial hegemony that will destroy our capacity for self-government. This will result from the inherent subjectivity of the extant theories. Likewise, Justice Breyer says all he can do is to look for a pragmatic resolution of each case, that will best serve the underlying purpose of the relevant constitutional provision consistent with a common sense respect for democratic self-government. He understands the Constitution to "contain unwavering values that must be applied flexibly to ever-changing circumstances." He believes that doing so will make the Constitution work better for those whom it affects. STEPHEN BREYER, MAKING OUR DEMOCRACY WORK—A JUDGE'S VIEW (2010).

These jurists' devotion to judicial pragmatism is perhaps better understood as their judicial disposition than as a full-throated constitutional theory. Otherwise, they would be contradicting themselves to reject constitutional theory and replace it with pragmatism—everyone says "it takes a theory to beat a theory." Pragmatism is a useful disposition in a judge because a judge is one step removed from an academic theorist writing an article. A pragmatic judge views theories not as ends in themselves but as pragmatic means for constitutional decision-making and opinion writing. Marc O. DeGirolami & Kevin C. Walsh, *Judge Posner, Judge Wilkinson, and Judicial Critique of Constitutional Theory*, 90 NOTRE DAME L. REV. 633 (2014). The jury is still out on Justice Breyer, however, who dabbles with the dark arts of proportionality review in his latest book and who seems to be under the influence of the jurisprudence of the European Union, at least when he does not feel bound by precedent. STEPHEN BREYER, THE COURT AND THE WORLD: AMERICAN LAW AND THE NEW GLOBAL REALITIES (2016). *See also* Chapter 3, § 5 (What Constitutional Analysis is Not).

Yale's Jed Rubenfeld is one professor who is impatient with all the academic theorizing. JED RUBENFELD, FREEDOM AND TIME: A THEORY OF CONSTITUTIONAL SELF-GOVERNMENT (2001). He reconceptualizes constitutionalism as democracy—really the commitment over time to self-government in the past, the present, and the future. He argues that none of the prevailing constitutional theories distinguishes between interpreting and rewriting the

Constitution and, at the same time, none of the theories accounts for the undeniable influence of evolving normative values that go beyond the text and are contrary to original understandings. He insists that all the theories have asked the wrong question and that the right question is why should the Constitution have any legitimacy over time, *i.e.*, why should we even try to interpret and obey it? Hmm. Perhaps we should be reminded here of what Alexander Bickel, the Yale professor, once wrote. ALEXANDER BICKEL, THE MORALITY OF CONSENT 77 (1975):

> And yet we do need, individually and as a society, some values, some belief in the foundations of our conduct, in order to make life bearable. If these too are lies, they are * * * true lies; if illusions, then indispensable ones. To abandon them is to commit moral suicide.

Constitutional theory should be appreciated only as a means to an end, and not an end in and of itself. Constitutional theory helps jurists, scholars, and students to assign meaning to the past, and it shapes arguments over the future of constitutional law. One must recognize the limitations of theory, however. Certainly, there is not much to be gained from attempts to explain that part of constitutional law that merely reflects the individual Justice's political views. But theory helps us to see consistencies in analysis, regularities in holdings, commonalities among Justices, and agreements across ideological divides. Thus, theory is valuable context, a way of collecting and organizing and making sense of the output of the Supreme Court. Legal theory and constitutional theory certainly matter to law professors, as is evidenced by the enormous output of tracts from the tenure track. All the leading law reviews regularly publish symposia on constitutional theory. There are books and articles too numerous to mention about constitutional theory and its discontents. *See* Forewords to the Second and Third Editions (bibliographic references).

NYU's Barry Friedman has described *The Cycles of Constitutional Theory*, 67 LAW & CONTEMP. PROBS. 149 (2004). The same normative arguments are deployed at different times by different constitutional protagonists. For example, during the heyday of *Lochner v. New York* (1905), conservatives embraced a purposive interpretation of a living Constitution protecting *laissez faire* capitalism, but later marched with their pitchforks and torches against what they feared to be a Frankenstein monster created by the Warren Court. For another example, progressives once endorsed the judicial activism of the Warren Court and applauded its liberal outcomes, but some of those same progressives shifted to argue in favor of judicial minimalism during the more conservative era of the Rehnquist Court. The eventual task of the constitutional theorist, according to Friedman, must be to recognize the ideological valence of these decisions and these shifting theories. Otherwise, theory and theorists seem naïve or irrelevant. Furthermore, a constitutional theory may be out of the mainstream and still have value as a theory. An out-of-favor theory might be described as "the Constitution in exile." (That term sometimes refers to a hard-core group of fundamentalist originalists who believe that the powers of the national government should be rolled back to what they were before FDR's New Deal, which began the dramatic increase in modern federal regulation and led to the modern administrative state.) But any and every theory is favored by some and disfavored by others. The contribution of the constitutional theorist is to convincingly describe shared values despite widespread disagreement about conclusions and outcomes. Stephen E. Sachs, *The "Constitution in Exile" as a Problem for Legal Theory*, 89 NOTRE DAME L. REV. 2253 (2014). Theorizing thus can be a means to the end of constitutional self-government.

Contemplating these various theories together suggests how theorists and their theories further the enterprise of constitutional interpretation in what philosophers of language call "meta-linguistic negotiation." The meaning of shared terms are contested adversarially and negotiated cooperatively; a term or concept like "Republican virtue" is debated towards some better understanding of what it is and how it works. The theory works itself pure. This is not so much the scientific method as it is the method of social science. It seems obvious that all these theories are related and interdependent. A good argument can be made that understanding how the normative theories of constitutional decision-making are arrayed in a hierarchy reveals two important insights. First, theories are pervasively dependent upon each other—as is ultimately illustrated by pragmatism, the least theoretical interpretative theory, which necessarily relies on rival theories for content. What counts pragmatically as a "good" result depends on how one sorts "good" and "bad" results. Second, constitutional interpretation is "inescapably a complex morally governed act." R. George Wright, *Dependence and Hierarchy Among Constitutional Theories*, 70 BROOK. L. REV. 141 (2004). This is the intuition we all share: that any theory that yields objectively moral results is a good theory; therefore, we should aspire to a constitutional progressivism that emphasizes moral outcomes. Theoretical disagreements are disagreements over which is the proper theory: every theory—every approach to constitutional decision-making—must be justified by normative arguments that support the theory. Andrew Coan, *The Foundations of Constitutional Theory*, 2017 WISC. L. REV. 833. Professor Coan distinguishes between approaches to constitutional decision-making and the normative claims underlying them. He also proposes a taxonomy categorizing the extant theories into four distinct categories he labels metaphysical, procedural, substantive, and positivist. Each of the approaches in each of these categories of theory has its own strengths and weaknesses.

Constitutional law is a dialogue, however, an ongoing conversation. As we have seen, however, everyone seems to be talking at the same time and past each other. Theories of constitutional dialogue have proliferated in recent years. Christin Bateup has catalogued these theories in the United States and abroad. She offers a dynamic fusion of two models of dialogue: the equilibrium model, which emphasizes the role of the judiciary, particularly the

Supreme Court, to facilitate society-wide discussions of constitutional issues, and the partnership model, which focuses on the institutional interactions of the political branches with the judicial branch. These models, together, offer the best normative vision for the power of judicial review in contemporary constitutionalism. Christine Bateup, *The Dialogic Promise: Assessing the Normative Potential of Theories of Constitutional Dialogue*, 71 BROOK. L. REV. 1109 (2006).

Borrowing another idea from linguistic theory, Ian Bartrum emphasizes the multiplicity and ubiquity of metaphors in constitutional theories. Those metaphors in theory and in practice allow for growth and creativity. In this fashion, constitutional practitioners more resemble poets than logicians. Ian C. Bartrum, *Metaphors and Modalities: Meditations on Bobbitt's Theory of the Constitution*, 17 WM. & MARY BILL RTS. J. 157 (2008). One simply cannot speak about the Constitution without using metaphors, often opposing metaphors—"the Constitution is an anchor" and "the Constitution is a sail." In that regard, speaking about the Constitution can faintly resemble how devout Old Testament Jews were so in awe of the deity that they avoided naming "G-d." Metaphors help us to make sense of the world without having to solve its mysteries. But metaphors can obfuscate and confuse us, as well. Judges and courts can invoke metaphors and forget they are only metaphors, merely figures of speech.

To "psych out" your con law prof, you might read some of his or her articles on the subject. You are part of the intended readership, although other law professors are the primary intended audience. To understand an individual Justice's interpretative philosophy, pay attention to the "interpretative moves" the Justice makes. Look for the Justice's solitary opinions, separate concurring opinions or dissenting opinions, to read a purer version of the Justice, and pay special attention to those occasions when a Justice says "if I were in the legislature, I would vote the other way, but because I am a judge I vote the way I do." Those are the clearest examples of a Justice following an interpretative theory beyond the common first-year student's cynicism that judges really only decide which result they like and make up a phony rationale after the fact. To master constitutional law for the final exam and the bar examination, you have to behave as if it is *law*. If you have a theoretical bent and want to look for a constitutional theory of your own, Richard Fallon of Harvard offers you some selection tips. Richard H. Fallon, Jr., *How to Choose a Constitutional Theory*, 87 CALIF. L. REV. 535 (1999). But be reminded that an effective constitutional theory should impose genuine constraints on its adherents. Constitutional theory is both descriptive and prescriptive. Theory should matter. By the time you finish the course on constitutional law, you should know enough about the subject to be able to evaluate the claims made on behalf of the various theories. There is what is called a "rule of recognition"—the ultimate rule for selecting a legal rule or constitutional theory. Law, even constitutional law, is normative. So select a theory that not just makes sense to you but makes sense for the entire polity, for "We the People." Larry Alexander, *Constitutional Theories: A Taxonomy and (Implicit) Critique*, 51 SAN DIEGO L. REV. 623 (2014).

Whether theory does matter, whether theory does distinguish constitutional law from politics, still remains the central question. Should unelected and life-tenured judges behave differently from elected officials? Is the Constitution merely a litmus of politics, in a dispute like the 2000 Election Case, that turns red for Republicans and blue for Democrats? *Bush v. Gore*, 531 U.S. 98 (2000). Not that long ago, a Court-watcher could point to maverick Justices who regularly voted against the political persuasion of the president who appointed them, even in important cases, *e.g.*, Justice Frankfurter and President Roosevelt, Justice Clark and President Truman, Justice Stevens and President Ford, Justice Kennedy and President Reagan, Justice Souter and President Bush. If the Justices choose up teams as Republican conservatives and Democratic liberals has the Supreme Court become less independent and less trustworthy? There is some empirical evidence that this transition is actually taking place. Going back to the 1950s, in closely divided decisions—5-to-4 and 5-to-3 decisions—there recently have been dramatic increases in both the percentage of liberal votes cast by Justices appointed by Democratic presidents and the percentage of conservative votes cast by Justices appointed by Republican presidents. In the last decade, Justices only infrequently vote against the ideology of the president who appointed them. *See* Lee Epstein & Eric A. Posner, *Supreme Court Justices' Loyalty to the President*, 45 J. LEG.

STUDIES 401 (2016). Such a party affiliation is familiar in Congress, of course. But the institutional question to ask is whether the public will continue to have respect and confidence in a Supreme Court whose members behave like elected politicians, who seem to deserve parenthetical party labels after their names in newspaper stories, *e.g.*, "Sonia Sotomayor (Dem.)" or "Neil Gorsuch (Rep.)". A study reported in the NEW YORK TIMES in July 2018 revealed an ideological disconnect between the typical American (the middle 50% of Americans) and all the current Justices. The conservative Justices are more conservative than the typical American and more conservative than the typical Republican; the liberal Justices are more liberal than the typical American and more liberal than the typical Democrat. Finley Peter Dunne's fictional Irish bartender, Mr. Dooley, once famously observed "there's wan thing I'm sure about. * * * That is, no matther whether th' constitution follows th' flag or not, th' supreme coort follows th' iliction returns."

Some believe that we may be witnessing the ascendancy of the attitudinal model on the High Court. LINCOLN KAPLAN, AMERICAN JUSTICE 2016: THE POLITICAL SUPREME COURT (2016). That political science attitudinal theory—popular with 1L students—is that a Supreme Court Justice's decisions reflect his or her background and politics, best indicated by the views of the President who appointed him or her. The traditional legal model— which characterizes this NUTSHELL and more importantly the bar exam—endorses the Rule of Law over the rule of judges. Constitutional law is *law*. The

Constitutional Law course is a course about *law*. Pay attention at how your professor moves back and forth between these two opposed philosophies—the attitudinal model and the traditional legal model. Admittedly, more and more contemporary constitutional law professors have replaced legal philosophy with baser politics. They have gone over to the Dark Side of the Force. They no longer emphasize interpretative methodology or judicial legitimacy. Instead, they pay attention only to the outcomes of cases that they approve or disapprove based on their likes and dislikes. For them, there is really no difference between what the Justices are doing and what the members of Congress are doing across First Street, Northeast. That sweeping turn to politics is itself another constitutional theory that claims to be reality-based, that depends on empiricism for some decisions and at the same time admits to uncertainty and arbitrariness in other decisions. It is legal realism with a vengeance. Andrew Coan, *Toward a Reality-Based Constitutional Theory*, 89 WASH. U. L. REV. 273 (2011). Many of its judicial practitioners explicitly embrace pragmatism. Professor Coan offers a "thought experiment" along these lines: suppose an imaginary constitutional amendment providing that "originalism is not our law" and instructing the Supreme Court to interpret the entire Constitution "to accommodate the practical exigencies of human affairs and the evolving standards of decency that mark the progress of a maturing society." Andrew Coan, *Amending the Law of Constitutional Interpretation*, 13 DUKE J. CONST. L. & PUB. POL'Y 83,

85 (2018). This amendment would turn judges loose to pursue their own sense of the political Pareto optimal.

As we have seen, constitutional theory does not inevitably lead to only conservative outcomes or only liberal outcomes—there are both kinds of theories and some other theories purport to be apolitical. During the House impeachment and the Senate trial of President Clinton in 1998, both sides of the aisle accused the other side of constitutional hypocrisy and flip-flopping their constitutional arguments. Constitutional theory does not seem to lead to certain answers to constitutional questions, as much as it seems to provide competing arguments for going about deciding them. The ultimate usefulness of any theory is to help differentiate between good arguments and bad arguments and to make it more likely that the interpreter will reach not just a *good* interpretation, but the *best* interpretation of the Constitution. The slightest admission that there are some arguments that are bad arguments—and everyone would have to admit that there are plenty of wrong answers to constitutional questions— demonstrates the logical fallacy behind the skepticism that in constitutional law "anything goes." A cynical justification is that constitutional theory does not operate to imagine and create constitutional doctrine but rather it merely operates to validate it after the fact. This claim of retrospective operation offers only as much validation as legal realism and the attitudinal model of judging, however.

One ultimate and tangential and provocative answer to the question whether theory matters is to wonder if the Constitution itself really matters! You may believe, like many respondents in contemporary public opinion polls, that the U.S. government has become dysfunctional in the 21st century. Our politics are polarized because of Duverger's Law, a proposition of sociology that theorizes that the Constitution's election provisions ineluctably result in a two-party system. Our institutions seem ineffective. In election after election, the two major parties take turns promising meaningful change. But once elected Presidents and Congressional majorities of both parties fail to achieve any measure of progress towards solving our social problems, which appear to be worsening and seem to be becoming more and more alarming. There is an existential and apocalyptic literature, epitomized by political scientist Sotirios Barber's book, CONSTITUTIONAL FAILURE (2014), which shifts the blame for all this apparent dysfunction from politics and politicians to the Constitution and the Framers. Barber argues that the Constitution is the plan of our government and if the government is failing then the only logical conclusion is that the plan is a failure and rightly to blame. The contemporary world reminds us that nations do fail. DARON ACEMOGLU & JAMES A. ROBINSON, WHY NATIONS FAIL: THE ORIGINS OF POWER, PROSPERITY AND POVERTY (2012); JARED DIAMOND, COLLAPSE: HOW SOCIETIES FAIL OR SUCCEED (2005). Neither the United States nor its Constitution is divine or eternal. Some American Edward Gibbon may one day write about "The

History of the Decline and Fall of the American Empire," but he or she has not likely been born yet. THE LIMITS OF CONSTITUTIONAL DEMOCRACY (Jeffrey K. Tulis & Stephen Macedo, eds., 2010). Understand that such a dystopian vision is not the prediction being made here and now. In *Federalist No. 39*, James Madison declared his abiding belief in our Republic:

It is evident that no other form would be reconcilable with the genius of the people of America; with the fundamental principles of the Revolution; or with that honorable determination which animates every votary of freedom, to rest all our political experiments on the capacity of mankind for self-government.

Nonetheless, even the most devout constitutionalists must admit that the Constitution contains some profound flaws—some provisions are just plain stupid. CONSTITUTIONAL STUPIDITIES, CONSTITUTIONAL TRAGEDIES (William N. Eskridge & Sanford V. Levinson, eds., 1998) (a roster of leading constitutionalists nominate various clauses). Not content to leave matters there, Sanford Levinson, who has spent his career provoking constitutionalists over the legitimacy and techniques of their craft, has compiled a series of proposed reforms to make the government more effective, more just, and ultimately more democratic. SANFORD LEVINSON, OUR UNDEMOCRATIC CONSTITUTION: WHERE THE CONSTITUTION GOES WRONG (AND HOW WE THE PEOPLE CAN CORRECT IT) (2008). But one problem with his *tour de force* critique is that he runs into a brick wall: an entrenched feature of the Constitution is that it is one of the most difficult constitutions to amend in the world. If Forest Gump was a constitutional law professor, he might observe, "Stupid is as stupid does." There have been only 27 amendments in more than eleven score years. That record does not encourage hopefulness for political self-correction. Indeed, the one conclusion we might draw from the dearth of amendments is that constitutional conflicts in the United States are virtually always resolved through the processes of constitutional interpretation rather than by formal constitutional revision. Think of the most controversial issues in recent memory: abortion, affirmative action, death penalty, executive powers, flag burning, gay marriage, prayer in public schools, for a few examples. Their resolution has been reached in the interpretations of the Constitution by the Supreme Court, not in the Article V process of ratifying amendments. *See* Bruce Ackerman, *The Living Constitution*, 120 HARV. L. REV. 1737 (2007). That is another good reason to learn to appreciate constitutional theorizing, which is the subject of this Chapter. The Constitution is the text; constitutional law is the subtext.

One thing—and maybe only one thing—is certain from this Chapter survey of constitutional theory. The generic law review article *leitmotif*—that the subject under consideration (whatever the subject) is "under-theorized"—does not apply to constitutional law. *See* Charles A. Sullivan, *The Under-Theorized Asterisk Footnote*, 93 GEO. L.J. 1093 (2005). Indeed, the opposite claim could be made: that academics have over-theorized the discipline. This is self-evident to any reader who peruses an opinion in the pages of UNITED STATES REPORTS and then picks up a stack of law review commentary on the same.

Wallace Stevens once composed a poem titled *Thirteen Ways of Looking at a Blackbird* in which he offered that many perspectives and descriptions in that many stanzas. At a minimum, there are only "Nine Ways of Looking at the Constitution" at any given moment in time that really and truly matter. But there are a hundred con law professors for every one of the nine *rarae aves* all pretending to be John James Audubon.

11. CONSTITUTIONAL ANALYSIS POSTSCRIPT

A brief verbal summary of our constitutional analysis fits into this last Chapter on constitutional theory. *See* Chapter 3 (Constitutional Analysis). Imagine you are in the constitutional law examination or writing a seminar paper. Imagine you are working on your law review note. Imagine you are taking the bar exam. Imagine that you have graduated and passed the bar, and you now are a practicing attorney representing a client and presenting a case in court. You are *not* going to begin your brief or your oral argument: "Mr. Chief Justice and may it please the Court, now you see we start off with this great big box that contains all the governmental power there is. Then we saw off a large portion of that box—take those powers away from the government—and those are by definition individual constitutional liberties * * *" and so on!

The purpose of the use of our constitutional diagram in our constitutional analysis has been to develop a better understanding of the questions and a mastery of the answers for constitutional law issues. Our constitutional analysis has become second nature by now. For the most part—and most importantly—constitutional analysis involves the tension between individual liberty versus government power. *See* Chapter 4 (Constitutional Liberty). Individual liberty and government power exist in a zero-sum ratio, more liberty for the individual means less power for the government, and less liberty for the individual means more power for the government. The Judicial Branch stands as the great guardian of our civil liberties and civil rights by exercising its power of judicial review to interpret the Constitution in the course of deciding cases or controversies. The Supreme Court occupies the apex of the Third Branch and performs the role of ultimate and final constitutional court. *See* Chapter 2 (Judicial Review).

Once the individual liberty versus government power question is resolved in favor of the power of the government to regulate or tax, in our federal system, we must consider the next issue of distribution of powers between the federal and state governments. *See* Chapter 5 (Government Powers). The federal government is a government of limited and enumerated powers delegated to it by the Constitution. Except in foreign affairs, the federal government may not exercise any power without a constitutional delegation of power to it. The states possess the sovereign police power. *See* Chapter 6 (Structure of the Constitution).

A valid exercise of federal power, however, always is supreme over state power. Exclusive federal powers are constitutionally beyond the states' police power. When both the federal government and the states have power to control the same situations, federalism depends on the nature of the power. For some concurrent powers, the states are allowed to govern unless and until Congress legislates to preempt the entire field or to preempt the particular matter. For some other powers, the delegation of the power to the federal government is itself a negative implication against state power that the judiciary will enforce, even when Congress is dormant, to strike down some state regulations. But Congress subsequently may exercise its federal power to consent to those exercises of the state police power.

Within the area of federal power, the structure of the Constitution calls for the separation of powers in a system of checks and balances. Among the three co-equal branches, the Supreme Court is perhaps more equal than the others in constitutional matters. The Supreme Court of the United States is not infallible, as we have learned, but it does have the final say on constitutional issues of individual rights versus government power, federalism and separation of powers.

To emphasize one last time, the primary and foremost question of constitutional analysis is the

individual-liberty-versus-government-power   issue.
The   constitutional   analysis   gets   around   to
considering principles of federalism or separation of
powers if and only if that threshold question is
resolved in favor of government power. The *raison
d'être* of the Constitution of the United States is to
guarantee civil rights and civil liberties. Appendix A
(Leading Case Outline of Constitutional Liberty)
describes and summarizes how the Supreme Court
has interpreted the Constitution to achieve this—the
document's highest purpose and the Court's most
important role. Indeed, Alexis de Tocqueville was not
the first nor the last to marvel at this remarkable
arrangement:

> When, after a detailed examination of the
> organization of the Supreme Court, we come to
> consider the whole body of prerogatives granted
> to it, it soon becomes clear that a mightier
> judicial authority has never been constituted in
> any land. The Supreme Court has been given
> higher standing than any known tribunal, both
> by the nature of its right and by the categories
> subject to its jurisdiction.

ALEXIS DE TOCQUEVILLE, DEMOCRACY IN AMERICA
149 (J.P. Mayer ed., 1969).

12. CONCLUSION

What the pseudonymous Publius (Alexander
Hamilton) wrote in *Federalist Paper No. 15* to his
readers is a fitting final comment to the reader of a
book on *Constitutional Analysis*:

If the road over which you still have to pass should in some places appear to you tedious or irksome, you will recollect that you are in quest of information on a subject the most momentous which can engage the attention of a free people, that the field through which you have to travel is in itself spacious, and that the difficulties of the journey have been unnecessarily increased by the mazes with which sophistry has beset the way. It will be my aim to remove the obstacles to your progress in as compendious a manner as it can be done, without sacrificing utility to dispatch.

APPENDIX A

LEADING CASE OUTLINE OF CONSTITUTIONAL LIBERTY

The emphasis throughout this book has been on the primary and most important function of the Constitution, i.e., to define and protect individual liberty against government power. The constitutional diagram depicts this dynamic balance of ordered liberty. This Appendix keeps the promise made in Chapter 4, § 2 (Constitutional Law Doctrines) to provide a leading case outline of Supreme Court precedents dealing with constitutional liberty. The holdings and doctrines highlighted here define civil rights and civil liberties under the Constitution—these cases give content and meaning to the individual liberty side of our constitutional diagram. The reader should be reminded that the theme of individual liberty also played a prominent role in Chapter 2 (Judicial Review), Chapter 3 (Constitutional Analysis) and Chapter 4 (Constitutional Liberty). Those chapters and this Appendix correspond to the topics in the typical "Constitutional Law II" law school course that emphasizes individual rights.

The reader also should be reminded again that the Constitution performs three other essential functions besides defining and preserving individual liberty: to establish the national government; to control the relationship between the national government and the states; and to enable the government to perpetuate itself. See *Chapter 3, § 1 (Functions of the Constitution). The leading Supreme Court decisions about establishing the national government and controlling the relationship between the national government and the states are discussed in considerable detail and depth in Chapter 5 (Government Powers) and Chapter 6 (Structure of the Constitution). The perpetuation-of-government function is the subject of Chapter 1, § 11 (Amendments). Those discussions will not be repeated here. Thus, for a full appreciation of the leading Supreme Court precedents for those other aspects of constitutional law—which are covered in the typical "Constitutional Law I" law school course—the reader should refer to those designated chapters.*

Finally, students enrolled in a stand-alone "Constitutional Law" course or some advanced elective course are obliged to match topics covered in their particular course syllabus with the relevant chapters. Again, this Appendix emphasizes only the leading Supreme Court cases defining and protecting individual liberty. The focus in this Leading Case Outline of Constitutional Liberty is on the left side of our constitutional diagram, i.e., giving content to individual freedom and liberty.

1. NATURE OF LIBERTY

In his inspired and inspiring majority opinion striking down a compulsory flag salute requirement in public schools as a violation of students' rights of conscience, Justice Jackson gave voice to liberty:

> The very purpose of a Bill of Rights was to withdraw certain subjects from the vicissitudes of political controversy, to place them beyond the reach of majorities and officials and to establish them as legal principles to be applied by the courts. One's right to life, liberty, and property, to free speech, a free press, freedom of worship and assembly, and other fundamental rights may not be submitted to vote; they depend on the outcome of no elections.

W. Va. State Bd. of Educ. v. Barnette, 319 U.S. 624, 638 (1943). This stirring quotation would be an apt caption for our constitutional diagram that visually illustrates the balance between individual liberty versus government power. Indeed, this has been from the beginning and continues to be today the most durable feature of American constitutionalism, the lived experience of "We the People." Abstract commitments achieve meaning through political traditions and practices. The U.S. Constitution is designed to protect liberty. "The Constitution is itself in every rational sense, and to every useful purpose, a Bill of Rights" to establish a national government of limited and enumerated powers. *The Federalist No. 84.* Its structural features—separation of powers and federalism—function to protect liberty indirectly but significantly. And, of course, the Constitution protects liberty by securing rights, notably in the Bill of Rights.

The Constitution secures positive liberty, *i.e.*, imposes affirmative duties on the government. The Preamble promises to "secure the blessings of liberty." Article IV, Section 4 guarantees a republican form of government in the states. *Et cetera*. Other textual provisions protect us against government encroachment on our privileges and immunities, Article IV, § 2. Most directly, however, the Constitution secures negative liberties. Read the clauses in the Bill of Rights and note how they read like the Ten Commandments. The Constitution says to the government, "Thou shalt not * * * violate these rights." Liberty enables individual freedom. Freedom of the individual is the personal autonomy to exercise the power of free will—free from any government interference or sanction.

These essential themes can be traced back to the *Declaration of Independence*: "We hold these truths to be self-evident, that all men are created equal, that they are endowed by their Creator with certain unalienable Rights, that among these are Life, Liberty and the pursuit of Happiness." Drawing on biblical language, Abraham Lincoln insightfully described the *Declaration of Independence* as an "apple of gold," and the Constitution as the "frame of silver" around it. To be an American is to be free, to be a rights-bearing individual, to be a member of the United States polity, *i.e.*, a full participant in constitutional self-government. The highest title in a constitutional republic is not "Senator" or "President," rather the highest rank is "citizen."

2. INCORPORATION OF
THE BILL OF RIGHTS

The Bill of Rights applies only to the federal government. This was the original understanding. *Barron v. Baltimore*, 32 U.S. (7 Pet.) 243 (1833). Strictly speaking, it is still the proper and formal and literal understanding.

Incorporation doctrine. The Supreme Court, however, has interpreted the Fourteenth Amendment Due Process Clause and the liberty that it protects to incorporate and include various provisions of the Bill of Rights, thus making those protections, though not those provisions themselves, applicable to the states. This has been accomplished by judicial decisions, by numerous Supreme Court decisions going all the way back to the end of the 19th century. *Chicago, Burlington, & Quincy R. R. Co. v. City of Chicago*, 166 U.S. 226 (1897).

Although some individual Justices, notably Justice Black, argued for a once-and-for-all total incorporation of the entire Bill of Rights, the process has been selective to focus on specific clauses case-by-case. *Adamson v. California*, 332 U.S. 46 (1947). While "selective incorporation" has been the approach in individual cases, however, the process of selecting and incorporating has been nearly total and is virtually complete today. *See Moore v. City of East Cleveland*, 431 U.S. 494 (1977) (White, J., dissenting) (surveying the case law).

The modern test whether to incorporate a provision from the Bill of Rights into the Fourteenth

Amendment is whether the right is "fundamental to the American scheme of justice." *Duncan v. Louisiana*, 391 U.S. 145, 149 (1968). Furthermore, once a provision in the Bill of Rights is deemed incorporated into the Fourteenth Amendment and applied to the states, it has the same content and imposes the same limitations on the states as it imposes on the federal government. *Malloy v. Hogan*, 378 U.S. 1 (1964). A handful of individual Justices have disagreed with this idea to argue that an incorporated right in the Fourteenth Amendment should apply less strictly against a state than the actual provision of the Bill of Rights has against the federal government. *E.g.*, *Johnson v. Louisiana*, 406 U.S. 356, 366 (1972) (Powell, J., concurring); *Duncan v. Louisiana*, 391 U.S. 145, 181 (1968) (Harlan, J., dissenting). And at least one Justice seems to be hinting that some clauses, particularly the Establishment Clause, could and should somehow be un-incorporated. *See Zelman v. Simmons-Harris*, 536 U.S. 639, 679–80 (2002) (Thomas, J., concurring). Finally, it is possible that in the future the Privileges or Immunities Clause in the Fourteenth Amendment might be revitalized to do the conceptual work of incorporation that the Due Process Clause performed. *See Saenz v. Roe*, 526 U.S. 489 (1999) (relying on that dormant provision to strike down a state statute). For now, however, the Justices are seemingly content with using the Due Process Clause. *See McDonald v. City of Chicago*, 561 U.S. 742 (2010).

Nonetheless, most but not all provisions have been incorporated. Most recently, the Second Amendment was incorporated in 2010. *McDonald v. City of Chicago*, 561 U.S. 742 (2010). The provisions that have not been incorporated make for a shorter list, as one reads down the first eight amendments. The Third Amendment prohibition on quartering troops has not been the subject of a Supreme Court holding to make it applicable to the states. The clause in the Fifth Amendment requiring an indictment by a grand jury is the only clause in that amendment that has not been incorporated. The Seventh Amendment right to jury trials in civil suits over $20 has not been incorporated. The Eighth Amendment excessive fines prohibition has not been applied to the states, but the Equal Protection Clause of the Fourteenth Amendment may amount to the same thing. The Ninth and Tenth Amendments do not apply to the states at all and, for that reason, some constitutionalists do not even consider them to be part of the Bill of Rights strictly speaking, although they were proposed and ratified together with the other eight amendments in 1791. These few last remaining provisions that have not been incorporated are not likely ever to be incorporated.

Reverse incorporation. There also has been an important instance of "reverse incorporation." The Bill of Rights does not contain an Equal Protection Clause. This Fourteenth Amendment provision has been read into the Due Process Clause of the Fifth Amendment to make it applicable to the federal government. *Bolling v. Sharpe*, 347 U.S. 497 (1954). Consequently, the constitutional principle of equality is enforceable against the national government.

3.   STATE ACTION

Constitutional liberty and government power usually exist in a zero-sum ratio: more government power results in less individual liberty and more individual liberty results in less government power. This is the perpetual dilemma of our constitutionalism: how to empower the government sufficiently to perform its essential tasks, and, at the same time, how to limit it from overreaching the individual. This is the constitutional analysis of the constitutional diagram. *See* Chapter 3 (Constitutional Analysis).

A private citizen robbing another private citizen is taking property without due process of law, but there is no constitutional violation because the government did not do the taking. This is simply a crime, prohibited by the criminal law, or a tort, remedied by a civil law suit. With few exceptions, liberty under our Constitution is defined as freedom from encroachments of governmental power. This principle was first stated in a case finding no violation of the Fourteenth Amendment in racial discrimination practiced by hotels, railroads, and theaters, all privately owned and operated. This is the State Action doctrine. *The Civil Rights Cases*, 109 U.S. 3 (1883). The term "*state* action" is something of a misnomer, however, in that the requirement applies to the national government and local governments as well as to the states.

(The current federal prohibition against discrimination on a racial basis in these type settings is not a constitutional right, but is based upon the

1964 federal Civil Rights Act passed under the power to regulate interstate commerce. *Katzenbach v. McClung*, 379 U.S. 294 (1964); *Heart of Atlanta Motel v. United States*, 379 U.S. 241 (1964). *See* Chapter 4, § 6 (Protecting Constitutional Liberty).)

Exception. The Thirteenth Amendment is the principal exception to the requirement of state action. The Thirteenth Amendment is written differently from the other amendments: it abolishes the institution of slavery so far as the government and individuals are concerned. Thus, in theory and in practice (although the cases are rare today), a private person can violate the Thirteenth Amendment by holding another person in slavery or involuntary servitude.

State action is a threshold issue, supposedly determined without looking ahead at the merits of the constitutional claim. When a state legislature passes a law, when a Governor enforces a statute, or when a state court issues an order, those are obvious examples of state action and the constitutional analysis moves straight to the merits to balance individual liberty against government power *a lá* the constitutional diagram. *Shelley v. Kraemer*, 334 U.S. 1 (1948). Early on, the Court created the concept of acting "under color of law" by which it could be held that a public official acting in an unconstitutional way nevertheless constituted governmental action if the official was acting within the ostensible scope of official authority. *Ex parte Virginia*, 100 U.S. 339 (1879).

When state action is in doubt, the Supreme Court has eschewed any formal test for finding state action and instead has followed a totality of the circumstances approach "sifting facts and weighing circumstances" on an *ad hoc* or case-by-case basis. *Burton v. Wilmington Parking Auth.*, 365 U.S. 715, 722 (1961). The qualifications of the doctrine are found in wavering and often overlapping lines of Supreme Court precedents that evaluate the presence and participation of the government in the action being challenged. The same entity might be a state actor for some purposes and not for others—the specific nature of the action that is being challenged is controlling. *Compare Polk County v. Dodson*, 454 U.S. 312 (1981) (individual public defender acting as defense counsel is not a state actor) *with Branti v. Finkel*, 445 U.S. 507 (1980) (public defender acting as a supervisor to hire and fire assistants was a state actor).

Public function. If private persons are engaged in activities that are traditionally, exclusively reserved to the government, then the Constitution applies. Examples include conducting an election for public office, *Terry v. Adams*, 345 U.S. 461 (1953), and organizing and maintaining a company town, *Marsh v. Alabama*, 326 U.S. 501 (1946). A privately owned shopping mall may resemble a downtown shopping district, but it is not a state actor for purposes of a First Amendment right of access for demonstrators. *Hudgens v. NLRB*, 424 U.S. 507 (1976).

Court enforcement of private agreements. A court order entered by a state judge pursuant to some rule of the state's common law is state action. *Shelley v. Kraemer*, 334 U.S. 1 (1948). But the line is not easily drawn between private action and state action. Following a testator's will to establish a public park is state action; therefore, the park cannot be racially segregated. *Evans v. Newton*, 382 U.S. 296 (1966). But applying state law to order that the same park revert to the heirs rather than continue on a desegregated basis is not state action that violates the Fourteenth Amendment. *Evans v. Abney*, 396 U.S. 435 (1970).

Symbiotic and financial arrangements. When a privately owned coffee shop refused to serve African-Americans, the racial discrimination was held to be a violation of the Fourteenth Amendment because the shop was located in a parking garage owned by a public parking authority that leased the space and directly benefited financially from the arrangement. *Burton v. Wilmington Parking Auth.*, 365 U.S. 715 (1961). This principle was applied to strike down a state program supplying textbooks to "segregation academies," racially discriminating private schools, because that tangible aid significantly facilitated, reinforced, and supported the invidious discrimination. *Norwood v. Harrison*, 413 U.S. 455 (1973). The Court distinguished without overruling an earlier precedent that had allowed a textbook lending program to private religious schools because those schools furthered the constitutional value of the free exercise of religion. *Bd. of Educ. v. Allen*, 392 U.S. 236 (1968). Following the money does not automatically mean there is state action, however, even when the private entity is dependent on public funding. *Rendell-Baker v. Kohn*, 457 U.S. 830 (1982) (private school firing employees); *Blum v. Yaretsky*, 457 U.S. 991 (1982) (private nursing home transferring and discharging residents). Once Congress statutorily created Amtrak to further governmental transportation objectives and then retained permanent federal authority over it, Congress could not statutorily exempt it from First Amendment free speech claims. *Lebron v. Nat'l R.R. Passenger Corp.*, 513 U.S. 374 (1981).

Licensing and regulation. A state Liquor Control Board regulation requiring local organizations to follow their national by-laws was state action that violated the Equal Protection Clause insofar as the national by-laws were racially exclusive and could not be enforced, but the fact that the private local fraternal lodge had a liquor license was not enough to trigger the Fourteenth Amendment and require it to admit members and serve guests on a nondiscriminatory basis. *Moose Lodge No. 107 v. Irvis*, 407 U.S. 163 (1972). A public utility that enjoyed a governmental monopoly was not a state actor when it discontinued service because the company's policy was merely approved—not ordered or required—by the state commission that licensed and regulated the utility. *Jackson v. Metro. Edison Co.*, 419 U.S. 345 (1974).

Non-financial facilitation. State action sometimes depends on who is suing whom and for what. A suit against a private warehouseman for conducting a forced sale of property seized in an eviction did not make out state action, even though the sale itself was permitted under the self-help rules of the state's commercial code. *Flagg Brothers, Inc. v. Brooks*, 436 U.S. 149 (1978). There was state action in a suit challenging state procedures for securing a prejudgment writ of attachment by filing an *ex parte* petition with the clerk of court and having the sheriff execute the writ, followed by a state court order of attachment. *Lugar v. Edmonsdson Oil Co., Inc.*, 457 U.S. 922 (1982). When a private litigant in a civil lawsuit invokes courtroom procedures to exercise peremptory challenges and excludes prospective jurors on the basis of their race, the opposing litigant can invoke the equal protection rights of the excluded jurors. *Edmonson v. Leesville Concrete Co.*, 500 U.S. 614 (1991). The same rule obtains in a criminal case, even when it is the defendant who is practicing the discrimination. *Georgia v. McCollum*, 505 U.S. 42 (1992).

Political authorization. A state is permitted to be neutral regarding private racial discrimination, *i.e.*, the state need not enact anti-discrimination laws. A state likewise can chose to repeal a state anti-discrimination statute and return to a neutral position. But a state cannot create a state right to discriminate on the basis of race. *Reitman v. Mulkey*, 387 U.S. 369 (1967). Furthermore, a state cannot restructure its political institutions and change the rules of state politics based on the racial nature of the public policy. *Compare Washington v. Seattle Sch. Dist. No. 1*, 458 U.S. 457 (1982) (removing the policy of student busing from the local school board level to the level of the state constitution did violate the Fourteenth Amendment) *with Crawford v. Bd. of*

Educ., 458 U.S. 527 (1982) (amending the state constitution to overrule an interpretation of the state supreme court did not violate the Fourteenth Amendment). However, in *Schuette v. Coalition to Defend Affirmative Action*, 572 U.S. 291 (2014), Justice Kennedy, speaking for the plurality, concluded that nothing in the United States Constitution allowed the federal judiciary to set aside an amendment to the Michigan Constitution that prohibited affirmative action in public education, employment, and contracting. These decisions have more to do with what is or is not a violation of the Equal Protection Clause than with the state action doctrine; a state statute, a state constitutional provision, and a state initiative or referendum are all state actions. *See Romer v. Evans*, 517 U.S. 620 (1996) (invalidating a state constitutional amendment passed by referendum).

Mirror-image. In an odd holding, the Supreme Court has ruled that when the state actor is performing the bidding of a private actor the otherwise private actor need not obey the Constitution. When the NCAA investigated and effectively required a public university to fire a coach, the NCAA was not a state actor and the rules of procedural due process did not apply in its investigation. *NCAA v. Tarkanian*, 488 U.S. 179 (1988). In a later case, however, the Supreme Court ruled that a non-profit association organized to regulate interscholastic sports among public and private high schools in a single state was a state actor when it imposed sanctions on a private high school member, given the pervasive entwinement of public institutions and public school officials in the association. *Brentwood Acad. v. Tenn. Secondary Sch. Athletic Ass'n*, 531 U.S. 288 (2001).

Bottom line. In order to apply the Constitution to a private party, the court ultimately must be satisfied that the claimed constitutional deprivation resulted from the exercise of some right or privilege having its source in state authority and that the private party being charged with the deprivation can be fairly described as a state actor. *Edmonson v. Leesville Concrete Co.*, 500 U.S. 614 (1991). Finally, one cannot ignore the ebb and flow of state action holdings over time: different Justices and different courts have raised or lowered the threshold. Additionally, one's constitutional intuition is that it is easier for the Court to find state action in an Equal Protection case dealing with racial discrimination, which lies at the core of the purpose and function of the Fourteenth Amendment.

4.   PROCEDURAL DUE PROCESS

"[I]t is procedural due process that is our fundamental guarantee of fairness, our protection against arbitrary, capricious, and unreasonable governmental action * * *." *Bd. of Regents v. Roth*, 408 U.S. 564, 589 (1972) (Marshall, J., dissenting). The remedy for a violation of procedural due process is to be afforded more procedure: adequate notice and a meaningful opportunity to be heard. A positive outcome is not guaranteed.

Read the Fifth Amendment and the Fourteenth Amendment—they contain identical Due Process

Clauses. In their procedural dimension, they do not absolutely guarantee "life, liberty and property" but rather they guarantee "process" before the government—state or national—deprives a person of those interests. The remedy is not to be granted a substantive right or to be guaranteed a particular outcome. Rather, the remedy for a denial of procedural due process is to be afforded more process, another hearing that might result in the same deprivation of liberty or property. For a long time, the Supreme Court was hung up on the distinction between a "right," which entitled a person to procedural due process, and a "privilege," which did not. Then the Court took something of an *ad hoc* pragmatic approach to evaluate just how important the interest being contested was to the individual. Those approaches were at best conclusory.

Basic analysis. The modern procedural due process analysis asks and answers two simple questions. The first question is did the state deprive someone of something that is "life" or "liberty" or "property"? If the answer is "yes," then the second question is "what process is due?" The decided emphasis is on procedure not substance, *i.e.*, whether the underlying decision-making process is fair, not on whether the ruling or decision is an arbitrary or unconstitutional outcome. If a state legislature passed a Draconian law making it a capital crime to exceed the speed limit, imposing the death penalty in a particular case would not be a violation of procedural due process, assuming the usual constitutionally-required criminal procedures were followed at the trial. Of course, such a statutory penalty would violate the substantive protection of the Eighth Amendment Cruel and Unusual Punishment Clause, incorporated in the Fourteenth Amendment Due Process Clause, as being unconstitutionally disproportionate to the crime. *See Coker v. Georgia*, 433 U.S. 584 (1977) (death penalty not permitted for the crime of rape). *See supra* § 2 (Incorporation of the Bill of Rights). Furthermore, the state does not have a constitutional duty to protect the life, liberty, and property of its citizens against deprivation by other individual private actors. That state officials could have done more to protect an individual does not violate the Fourteenth Amendment. *Castle Rock v. Gonzales*, 545 U.S. 748 (2005); *DeShaney v. Winnebago Cty. Dep't of Soc. Sers.*, 489 U.S. 189 (1989).

Life. If the state affords a person the full panoply of procedural due process, it can deprive that person of life itself. The Cruel and Unusual Punishment Clause allows the state to follow constitutional criminal procedures and then impose capital punishment on a murderer. *Gregg v. Georgia*, 428 U.S. 153 (1976). The Constitution has little to say about when life begins, *Roe v. Wade*, 410 U.S. 113 (1973), or how life should end, *Vacco v. Quill*, 521 U.S. 793 (1997). *See infra* § 7 (Equal Protection— Right to Die). Constitutional law courses focus more on "liberty" and "property" and the nature of the individual interest being deprived. The Supreme Court has taken a definitional approach to these protected interests.

Liberty. Liberty has its origin in the Constitution, in the substantive rights afforded by the Bill of

Rights and the Fourteenth Amendment. *See* Chapter 4 (Constitutional Liberty). Government action that physically restrains a person, imprisonment, is the paradigm interference with liberty. The government can deprive a person of liberty by interfering with the exercise of other constitutional rights or by other lesser interferences with a person's autonomy and freedom of choice and action. The mere showing that a non-tenured teacher at a state college was not rehired, without more, is not a loss of liberty. The teacher can always apply for another teaching position. The teacher might have suffered a substantive due process harm if, for example, the firing was punishment for exercising a substantive right like the Freedom of Speech, *i.e.*, the state college could not fire the teacher for a constitutionally improper reason. *Perry v. Sinderman*, 408 U.S. 593 (1972). However, a teacher cannot merely make a free speech claim and expect a court to automatically require a rehiring. *Mount Healthy City Sch. Dist. Bd. of Educ. v. Doyle*, 429 U.S. 274 (1977).

The line drawn in the cases to differentiate protected liberty from constitutionally unprotected interests is sometimes difficult to see. It was a deprivation of liberty for the sheriff to post a notice in liquor stores forbidding the sale of liquor to a named person. *Wisconsin v. Constantineau*, 400 U.S. 433 (1971). It was not a deprivation of liberty for the police to circulate a flyer identifying persons on the list as active shoplifters. *Paul v. Davis*, 424 U.S. 693 (1976). The distinction was that in the first case the person's status was changed because persons on the list could not purchase liquor; in the second case, persons on the list could still make purchases. Damage or harm to reputation is not alone enough to trigger the Fourteenth Amendment, since state law tort remedies may provide adequate post-deprivation procedure. *See Ingraham v. Wright*, 430 U.S. 651, 701 (1977) (Stevens, J., dissenting). Once a person has been afforded full criminal procedural safeguards and has been duly convicted, being automatically included on a publicized list of sex-offenders is not a due process deprivation. *Connecticut Department of Public Safety v. Doe*, 538 U.S. 1 (2003).

Property. Property is more than a personal abstract need or desire; it is mutual, not unilateral; it is a legitimate claim of entitlement of the kind people rely on in their everyday lives; it is not created by the Constitution, rather it is created by some independent source such as state law, like the law of contracts or the law of property or by statutory entitlements or licenses. An untenured professor whose year-to-year contract is not renewed at the end of the year has not been deprived of property. *Bd. of Regents v. Roth*, 408 U.S. 564 (1972). By comparison, a tenured professor enjoys the protected contract status of not being summarily dismissed but a tenured professor can be dismissed for good cause. Thus, tenure is a kind of property right.

What procedure is due? Basically, procedural due process guarantees adequate and effective notice plus a fair and reasonable opportunity to be heard. What particular procedures are required and the standard of proof or level of certainty also must be determined. When the hearing must take place—before or after the deprivation—is a crucial issue. The Supreme Court has developed a balancing test—really a "juggling test" in that there are three factors that determine what procedure is due and when: (1) the private interest being affected; (2) the risk of error in the procedures that were followed and the probable value of additional or substitute procedures; and (3) the government's interest.

The first factor is almost always on the individual's side in favor of earlier and more procedures. The third factor is mostly on the government's side in favor of lesser and later procedures. The second factor can break either way, depending on the nature of the interest at stake. These three factors are not the be-all or end-all of due process analysis, however, as the Court has proclaimed that the "straightforward test of reasonableness under the circumstances" is the ultimate measure of procedural fairness. *Dusenbery v. United States*, 534 U.S. 161 (2002).

The essential features of procedural due process include: (1) receiving adequate and effective notice of the pending action; (2) appearing before a neutral decision-maker; (3) appearing personally and making an oral presentation; (4) presenting evidence and witnesses; (5) confronting and cross-examining witnesses and responding to other evidence introduced by the government; (6) hiring and being represented by an attorney; and (7) being afforded a decision based only on the record with a statement of reasons and some explanation. In criminal matters, additional procedures would include: (1) compulsory process; (2) pre-trial discovery; (3) a public trial; (4) a jury; (5) a greater burden of proof on the government; (6) a transcript; and (7) basic appellate review procedures. On the criminal side, of course, the provisions of the Bill of Rights in the Fourth, Fifth, Sixth, and Eighth Amendments apply in a federal prosecution, and their incorporated versions apply in a state prosecution.

Two leading cases illustrate the operative balancing analysis. In *Goldberg v. Kelly*, 397 U.S. 254 (1970), the Court decided that a state had to hold a pre-termination hearing and provide a quasi-judicial evidentiary hearing before cutting off public assistance payments to a welfare recipient. The Court emphasized the "brutal need" of basic survival on the side of the individual over the interests of conserving fiscal and administrative resources on the government's side. In *Mathews v. Eldridge*, 424 U.S. 319 (1976), the Court held that a less formal hearing was adequate procedure for the termination of Social Security disability benefits because the nature of the determination was essentially a medical decision that was based on written evidence and medical reports. The majority determined there was something of a constitutional difference between disability benefits and welfare benefits, so far as the individual was concerned. The savings of administrative costs in the programs weighed on the government's side.

Emergency. There is an emergency exception of uncertain dimension to the general requirement of procedural due process. When harm to the public is threatened and the individual interest being infringed is deemed to be of significantly less importance, the government may take immediate summary action pending a later hearing. The clearest example is a governmental seizure of some contaminated or mislabeled foodstuff that threatens serious harm. *Ewing v. Mytinger & Casselberry, Inc.*, 339 U.S. 594 (1950). There has to be a genuine emergency calling for immediate action; for example, the government could not justify a seizure of real property used in a drug transaction without a pre-seizure notice and hearing. *United States v. James Daniel Good Real Prop.*, 510 U.S. 43 (1993). In a public employment setting, the government generally is required to afford at least an informal pre-termination hearing for someone who has achieved a level of civil-service-status job security. *Cleveland Bd. of Educ. v. Loudermill*, 470 U.S. 532 (1985). If the continued employment of the individual presents a significant hazard or harm to the government, however, an immediate suspension without pay pending a hearing would be permissible. *Gilbert v. Homar*, 520 U.S. 924 (1997).

Procedural due process applies in a variety of settings in day-to-day affairs: discipline in public schools, *Goss v. Lopez*, 419 U.S. 565 (1975); self-help remedies between debtors and creditors, *Mitchell v. W.T. Grant Co.*, 416 U.S. 600 (1974); medical commitments, *Parham v. J.R.*, 442 U.S. 584 (1979); state court rules and procedures, *BMW of N. Am., Inc. v. Gore*, 517 U.S. 559 (1996); deprivation of driver's licenses, *Bell v. Burson*, 402 U.S. 535 (1971);

forced sale of property for unpaid property taxes, _Jones v. Flowers_, 547 U.S. 220 (2006).

5. BILLS OF ATTAINDER

There are two bill of attainder clauses, one applies to the U.S. Congress, Art. I, § 9, cl. 3, and the other applies to the state legislatures, Art. I, § 10, cl. 1. Their historical understanding is settled and their modern applications are rare. Historically in England, a "bill of attainder" was a statute that sentenced an individual or a group of individuals to death and a "bill of pains and penalties" was a statute that sentenced an individual or a group of individuals to some other punishment, such as imprisonment, banishment, or the confiscation of property. Both of these historical practices are subsumed in the two bill of attainder clauses.

The two clauses generally protect the individual from legislative punishment. Thus, there is a family resemblance between the bill of attainder clauses and the due process clauses, _i.e._, judicial procedures must be followed before the government imposes a punishment on a person. There also is a separation of powers notion to the prohibition of bills of attainder that prohibits the legislative branch— federal or state—from constitutionally misbehaving and exercising judicial powers and performing like a court.

The key question is whether a statute in fact determines "guilt" and inflicts a "punishment" without all the procedural protections of a judicial trial. For example, _United States v. Brown_, 381 U.S.

437 (1965), struck down a federal law making it a crime for a member of the Communist Party simply to be a union official. The defendant was convicted although the Government did not charge and did not prove that he had advocated any illegal activity by the union. In a famous case—famous because it involved a defrocked President—the Court upheld the Presidential Recordings and Materials Preservation Act against former-President Nixon's challenge under the Bill of Attainder Clause. *Nixon v. Adm'r of Gen. Servs.*, 433 U.S. 425 (1977). The statute's specificity to apply to the former President by name did not render it a bill of attainder. Being the only chief executive ever to have resigned the office, he constituted a category of one. The statute did not inflict an historically or functionally unconstitutional "punishment" prohibited by the clause. Rather, Congress had several legitimate justifications for confiscating the former-President's recordings and papers: to preserve evidence in ongoing criminal prosecutions; to allow public access to the materials; and to maintain the historical archive of his presidency. The Government's confiscation of the former-President's tangible personal property—his recordings and documents—was a taking, however, and after a lengthy trial the parties agreed to a settlement for just compensation of $18 million. *See infra* § 7 (Takings).

6. IMPAIRMENTS OF CONTRACTS

Article I, Section 10 prohibits the states from, *inter alia*, passing any "law impairing the obligation of contracts." The Due Process Clause of the Fifth

Amendment imposes a similar restriction on the U.S. Congress, although the Supreme Court has remarked that the federal restriction is relatively somewhat "less searching." *Pension Benefit Guar. Corp. v. R.A. Gray & Co.*, 467 U.S. 717 (1984). The Court distinguishes between the "obligation" of contract, which cannot be impaired, and the "remedy" of contract, which is subject to the state's police power to regulate. That means that when two parties enter into a contract they do so against a background of state laws. When a state statute affects a public contract, an agreement between the state and a private entity, the obvious risk of self-dealing by the state triggers a less deferential and more searching judicial review. *See U.S. Trust Co. v. New Jersey*, 431 U.S. 1 (1977).

Two cases help us understand the protection afforded to an individual under the Contract Clause. They nicely illustrate the constitutional diagram that demarcates the boundary between individual liberty and government power. During the Great Depression, the Supreme Court upheld a state statute that declared a temporary moratorium on mortgage foreclosures but allowed the mortgagor to collect rent. *Home Bldg. & Loan Ass'n v. Blaisdell*, 290 U.S. 398 (1934). The Court famously remarked, "While emergency does not create power, emergency may furnish the occasion for the exercise of power." The reserved powers of the state may be exercises to impose reasonable regulations on contract remedies. This holding was reaffirmed but the case was distinguished in *Allied Structural Steel Co. v. Spannaus*, 438 U.S. 234 (1978). The state statute was declared unconstitutional because it imposed a requirement that a company afford a pension to employees in the state even after the company had closed all its operations and left the state, contrary to the express terms of the employment contract. The unconstitutional statute operated as a permanent and "substantial impairment" of the company's contract with its past employees; the company's contractual and economic expectations were legitimate and reasonable; imposing a permanent requirement of a pension was a severe economic cost to the company; and there was no emergency to justify such an impairment of the employment contract. So, the company won and it did not have to pay its past employees the statutory pension.

7. TAKINGS

The Framers were Lockeans who considered the right to property to be one of the most important rights protected by natural law. As sovereign governments, states have the power of eminent domain. When the federal government exercises eminent domain, the taking must be necessary and proper to the effectuation of one of its limited and enumerated powers. The text of the Fifth Amendment, which applies to the federal government, requires that private property can be taken only for a public use and just compensation must be provided. The principle has been incorporated into the Fourteenth Amendment Due Process Clause and applied to the states as well. *Chicago, Burlington, & Quincy R.R. Co. v. City of Chicago*, 166 U.S. 226 (1897). There is an important distinction between the government acquiring property for public use and the government regulating the private use of property.

Takings by possession. The paradigm example of a constitutional taking is the exercise of the power of eminent domain, by which a parcel of privately owned land is the subject of a judicial condemnation proceeding resulting in an order of a forced sale to the state at a fair market price in order to build a road or a park. The taking is total and permanent; the private ownership and individual property rights are completely extinguished. "Public use" is broadly understood: it is proper for a city to condemn an area, to pay compensation, and then to permit the private redevelopment of that urban area. In *Kelo v. New London*, 545 U.S. 469 (2005), the Court approved the city's taking of non-blighted real property to turn over to private developers under what the Court called "a carefully considered development plan." The requirement of a "public use" was satisfied by a "public purpose." The private development was expected to increase the city's tax base and that was enough.

A taking of personal property, like a taking of real property is still a taking. "The Government has a categorical duty to pay just compensation when it takes your car, just as when it takes your home." *Horne v. Dep't of Agric.*, 135 S. Ct. 2419 (2015). That is why the Government had to pay former-President Nixon for the value of his personal property interest in the documents and recordings made during his administration. *See supra* § 5 (Bills of Attainder).

Interest on funds is property and a state transfer of interest on funds is a taking. But the measure of just compensation is zero when the principal funds do not generate any interest. *Brown v. Legal Found. of Wash.*, 538 U.S. 216 (2003); *Phillips v. Wash. Legal Found.*, 524 U.S. 156 (1998).

Takings by possession also may be partial and temporary. The duty to compensate arises regardless of whether the physical taking is partial or total and whether it is temporary or permanent. For example, when government aircraft used the immediate navigable airspace over a chicken farm to take off and land at a nearby military airport so low and so frequently that chickens could no longer be raised there, the Supreme Court held it was a compensable taking. The owner's loss, not the taker's gain, is the usual measure and market value of the taking. *United States v. Causby*, 328 U.S. 256 (1946). Intangible property rights are protected by the Takings Clause but the nature of the property is determinative. For example, an important aspect of a private marina is the right to exclude others, so when the government imposed a navigational servitude authorizing a right of access for the general public it was a taking. *Kaiser Aetna v. United States*, 444 U.S. 164 (1979). But when the state supreme court ruled that there was a public right of access under the state constitution to engage in free speech at a privately owned shopping center that was otherwise open to the public, it was not a taking. *PruneYard Shopping Ctr. v. Robins*, 447 U.S. 74 (1980). Physical takings and regulatory takings are distinct under the Constitution.

Takings by regulations. The modern regulatory state had to be reconciled to historical understandings and traditional assumptions about the individual's right to use and enjoy property. Legitimate regulations routinely interfere with property rights and it would be as constitutionally impossible as it would be fiscally impossible to require the government to pay everyone to comply with every regulation that affects private property. The police power to provide for the health, safety, morals, and general welfare of society carries an authority to govern citizens without having to bribe them into obeying the law.

There is a constitutional difference, however, between a regulation that merely regulates and a regulation that goes so far to amount to a constitutionally compensable taking. While the question is one of degree, it is not simply an accounting question but more the occasion to weigh the various factors and interests. *Pa. Coal Co. v. Mahon*, 260 U.S. 393 (1922). On a case-by-case basis, the court will evaluate the economic impact on the owner from the challenged regulation, whether it interferes with reasonable investment-backed expectations, and the character of the governmental regulation. *Penn Cent. Transp. Co. v. New York*, 438 U.S. 104 (1978). If a regulation denies any and all economically beneficial and productive uses of the property, a court will find a taking because there is the economic equivalent of a physical appropriation. *Lucas v. S.C. Coastal Council*, 505 U.S. 1003 (1992).

Although a particular use of property may have occurred in a particular locale earlier in time, the inevitable encroachments of later, more common uses of property can justify the abatement of the earlier use if its nature comes to approach that of a common law nuisance. As the city of Los Angeles spread, a long-established clay mine and kiln could be prohibited and shut down without the payment of compensation, even though the prohibition resulted in a reduction in value of the property from $800,000 to $60,000. *Hadacheck v. Sebastian*, 239 U.S. 394 (1915). The same principle of no compensation was applied when cedar rust disease required the destruction of older growth cedar trees because of the threat posed to newly established apple orchards being started up in the same vicinity. *Miller v. Schoene*, 276 U.S. 272 (1928).

Zoning laws can go too far and cross this divide between regulation and taking. Still, the concept of the public welfare is broad and inclusive. "The values it represents are spiritual as well as physical, aesthetic as well as monetary. It is within the power of the legislature to determine that the community should be beautiful as well as healthy, spacious as well as clean, well-balanced as well as carefully patrolled." *Berman v. Parker*, 348 U.S. 26 (1954). Typical zoning regulations that separate residential areas from business areas, for example, are permissible governmental regulation without constituting a taking of property even though values in the properties affected are lowered. *Euclid v. Ambler Realty Co.*, 272 U.S. 365 (1926). Residential property may be zoned to exclude multiple dwelling houses from areas of one-family dwellings. *Village of Belle Terre v. Boraas*, 416 U.S. 1 (1974). However, zoning laws that effectively intrude on the family structure, as the family chose to structure itself, run afoul of the Fourteenth Amendment. A housing ordinance that prohibited a grandmother from living with her two grandsons who were first cousins rather than brothers could not withstand constitutional analysis. *Moore v. City of East Cleveland*, 431 U.S. 494 (1977).

Cutting-edge zoning laws that impose substantial conditions on the use of private property will be upheld if the conditions substantially further legitimate governmental purposes. There must be an essential nexus and some rough proportionality between them. Under this approach, requiring a public easement for beach access was a compensable taking, but requiring a green space for flood control was a noncompensable regulation. *Compare Nollan v. Cal. Coastal Comm'n*, 483 U.S. 825 (1987) *with Dolan v. City of Tigard*, 512 U.S. 374 (1994). Taking away only one stick in the bundle of property rights is not enough to amount to a taking. It ultimately depends on the temporal and geographic effects on the parcel as a whole: for example, a temporary moratorium on all development was not a taking because the owner was not deprived of all economically viable uses during the moratorium and the fee simple parcel would recover its market value when the moratorium ended. *Tahoe-Sierra Preserv. Council v. Tahoe Reg'l Planning Agency, Inc.*, 535 U.S. 302 (2002).

8.   SUBSTANTIVE DUE PROCESS

Soon after the Constitution was ratified, the Supreme Court debated the idea that judicial review could be exercised to strike down state laws on the basis of natural law. In *seriatim* opinions, Justice Chase said *yes*; Justice Iredell said *no. Calder v. Bull*, 3 U.S. (3 Dall.) 386 (1798). In form, the Supreme Court bases its decisions only on particular clauses and specific interpretations of the Constitution. In substance, the Court's interpretations of the Constitution often seem to have a great deal to do with norms and values the Justices read into the text. *See* Chapter 7 (Constitutional Theory). This interpretative dynamic is nowhere better demonstrated than in the case annotations interpreting the Due Process Clauses.

In the earliest interpretation of the Due Process Clause in the Fourteenth Amendment, the Supreme Court expressed doubt that the clause had any significant or appreciable substantive content. *Slaughter-house Cases*, 83 U.S. (16 Wall.) 36 (1872). But after interpreting the term "persons" to include corporations, the High Court gradually came around to the idea that the liberty protected by that clause could be infringed by state laws that interfered with private property rights. *Santa Clara County v. S. Pac. Ry.*, 118 U.S. 394 (1886). The individual right to liberty being protected was understood to limit the police power of the states to regulate businesses. *Allgeyer v. Louisiana*, 165 U.S. 578 (1897).

From about 1900 to 1935, the Supreme Court routinely struck down economic and social regulations as being an unreasonable and arbitrary interference with the "freedom to contract" (not to be confused with the Contract Clause, discussed above). The court was using a common law methodology to apply a market-oriented philosophy of *laissez faire* capitalism. A leading decision, which is the "poster child" for this concept, held unconstitutional a state law that limited the workday of bakery employees to ten hours and the workweek to sixty hours. *Lochner v. New York*, 198 U.S. 45 (1905).

Substantive economic due process. Changes in the Court's membership and a political and economic sea change in the country called this concept into question and it thrust the Supreme Court into the political vortex during the New Deal era. As Justice Holmes pointed out, "pretty much all law consists of forbidding men to do some things they want to do, and contract is no more exempt from law than other acts." *Adkins v. Children's Hosp.*, 261 U.S. 525, 568 (1923) (Holmes, J., dissenting).

The Court eventually abandoned this approach of strict judicial review of economic regulations, adopting in its place a low level judicial review marked by greater deference to the legislatures. Thus, state retail price controls on milk were upheld, despite their interference with the so-called liberty to contract. *Nebbia v. New York*, 291 U.S. 502 (1934). Eventually, the Supreme Court formally disavowed the "liberty of contract" approach and pronounced that "courts do not substitute their social and economic beliefs for the judgment of legislative bodies, who are elected to pass laws." *Ferguson v. Skrupa*, 372 U.S. 726, 730 (1963).

Footnote Four. The Supreme Court managed a 180° role reversal. It got out of the business of protecting economic rights and into the business of protecting civil rights and civil liberties. The theory behind the maneuver can be traced to a famous footnote in an otherwise not-so-famous case: footnote four in *United States v. Carolene Products Co.*, 304 U.S. 144, 153 n.4 (1938). There, the Supreme Court announced a weak form of judicial review of economic regulations to defer to the legislature and uphold statutes that have a rational basis, going so far as to assume facts that would make the regulation appear reasonable. To prevail, the government need only give some adequate reason for its regulation. At the same time, however, the Supreme Court announced a strong form of judicial review that would presume certain laws to be unconstitutional and shift the burden of justifying the regulations onto the government to show that the regulation was a justifiably narrow and necessary means of achieving a particularly compelling governmental purpose. Three justifications triggered this strict scrutiny judicial review: to protect rights provided in the Constitution; to guard against legislation that unduly restricts or limits participation in the political process; and to act as the champion of discrete and insular minorities who are disadvantaged in the traditional majoritarian processes of government.

The first two justifications deal with fundamental constitutional rights, such as the rights provided in the Bill of Rights and incorporated into the Fourteenth Amendment. The third justification focuses on the constitutional phenomenon of "suspect classes." It is the classification, not the members of the class, that is suspect and deemed to be constitutionally irrelevant to any governmental purpose. Such traits are immutable and permanent—obvious and readily apparent to allow for discrimination. Members of such a class have been burdened with legal disabilities, or have been subjected to a history of purposeful unequal treatment, or have been relegated to a position of political powerlessness so as to deserve greater judicial protection from the majoritarian political process. Race is the quintessential suspect classification and subject to the strictest level of judicial review. Gender has enough in common with race to be labeled a "quasi-suspect" classification that, as we shall see, is analyzed under an intermediate level of scrutiny.

Getting back to regular, every day judicial review, a court has to be convinced that a statute is irrational, *i.e.*, constitutionally crazy, to strike it down. Few laws that survive the legislative process are crazy. So most things government does are constitutional. Not all bad laws are unconstitutional, but all unconstitutional laws are bad laws. Thus, substantive economic due process is a negligible impediment to legislative power. Indeed, rational level judicial review is a formula for upholding legislation. From time to time, however, the Supreme Court will flex its judicial review muscle and strike down a law as being irrational and unconstitutional based on what might be called substantive equal protection. *E.g.*, *City of Cleburne v. Cleburne Living Ctr.*, 473 U.S. 432 (1985). These instances are sometimes referred to as "rational review with teeth." However, these occasional decisions do not take us back all the way to the heyday of substantive economic due process discussed above.

Strict scrutiny. Substantive due process has a fundamental rights version that calls for the strong form of judicial review. If a statute burdens the exercise of a fundamental constitutional right, like the provisions in the Bill of Rights that have been incorporated, then the due process analysis requires that the statute be narrowly-tailored to promote a compelling government interest. This strong form of substantive due process review was first associated with a non-textual right of privacy, derived from the penumbras and emanations of the Bill of Rights. Under this analysis, the Court upheld the constitutional right to obtain information and access to contraceptive devices and techniques. *Griswold v. Connecticut*, 381 U.S. 479 (1965). Eventually, the Court would re-think this justification and relocate the textual anchor for the right of privacy in the Due Process Clause protection of liberty in the Fourteenth Amendment. This is the basis for the constitutional protection of personal autonomy to obtain an abortion. *Roe v. Wade*, 410 U.S. 113 (1973).

The same style of strict judicial scrutiny applies under Equal Protection when the statute burdens the exercise of a fundamental right by a certain category or class of persons. The major protections of personal freedoms other than the preferred freedoms of conscience protected in the First Amendment are more commonly protected under the concept of equal protection of the laws, as set out in the next section.

9.   EQUAL PROTECTION

Your constitutional law professor will tell you that the single most important concept in the Constitution for the protection of individual rights is the principle of the "equal protection of the laws" expressed in the Equal Protection Clause in the Fourteenth Amendment and implied into the Due Process Clause of the Fifth Amendment by the doctrine of reverse incorporation. The government—state or federal—runs afoul of this principle when it draws lines, when it classifies people, when two groups of citizens are identified and distinguished and then treated differently for no good reason or for some bad reason. In other words, a constitutional violation is not made out by the simple fact of different treatment. Equality does not require that the government treat everyone the same. For example, government properly treats someone convicted of a crime differently than a law-abiding person. Rather, the equality principle is more subtle to require that similarly situated persons be treated similarly. For example, it is a *per se* violation of the Equal Protection Clause to assign white children and black children to attend separate public schools, even if the schools are equal in every tangible way, because the school children are similarly situated, constitutionally speaking. *Brown v. Bd. of Educ.*, 347 U.S. 483 (1954).

Standards of review. Most, though not all, Supreme Court Justices conceive there are three distinct standards of Equal Protection, three levels of judicial review or scrutiny: rational, intermediate, and strict. At each of these three levels, the analysis breaks down into the "purpose-means" test, a two-step evaluation of the justification or *purpose* of the challenged governmental action and how closely and carefully the government's *means* achieves its purpose.

Over-inclusiveness and under-inclusiveness. Sometimes, but not often, a governmental purpose is deemed invalid. But it is more likely that a classification will be struck down because of a poor "fit" between the means and the purpose. A classification might be under-inclusive when it does not cover all the stated purpose or over-inclusive when it reaches beyond the stated purpose or it might be both under-inclusive *and* over-inclusive. The *Japanese Internment Cases* during World War II provide a textbook example: the government classified resident aliens of Japanese descent and Japanese-Americans for relocation camps. The classification was racial/national origin—a suspect classification—and the purpose was to protect against espionage and sabotage—a compelling purpose. The classification was over-inclusive in that not all of the persons in the category were disloyal or threats to national security; indeed the program was terribly over-inclusive in this regard. The classification was almost remarkably under-inclusive at the same time because the government did not impose the same penalties and restraints on

Americans of Italian and German descent, even though the war was being waged against those countries as well. This is merely a "textbook example," however, given the fact that the Supreme Court actually upheld the program at the time. *Korematsu v. United States*, 323 U.S. 214 (1944). It is worth noting, however, that the Supreme Court disavowed this horrible precedent in the strongest words: "*Korematsu* was gravely wrong the day it was decided, has been overruled in the court of history, and—to be clear—'has no place in law under the Constitution.' 323 U.S. at 248 (Jackson, J., dissenting)." *Trump v. Hawaii*, 138 S. Ct. 2392 (2018).

Each level of Equal Protection review has its own buzzwords and its own distinct line of precedents.

Rational standard of review. At the minimal level of judicial scrutiny, the means chosen—the classification—must merely be rationally related to a purpose that is within the legitimate exercise of the state police power to regulate for the health, safety, morals, and general welfare of society. A traffic regulation that prohibits paid-for advertising on the side of a truck but allows advertising for the truck owner's business is a classification that is reasonably enough related to traffic safety to be constitutional. Never mind that the advertising for the truck owner's business is just as distracting and as much a hazard. The legislature is entitled to take one step at a time to deal with a problem. *Ry. Express Agency, Inc. v. New York*, 336 U.S. 106 (1949). Most laws are not irrational so most laws are upheld at rational-level review. The Court is so deferential that "if any state of facts reasonably can be conceived that would sustain it, the existence of that state of facts at the time the law was enacted must be assumed." *Lindsley v. Nat. Carbonic Gas Co.*, 220 U.S. 61 (1911).

Wealth classifications are subject to rational level review. Welfare regulations that establish a maximum benefit payment do not violate the equal protection rights of families with greater need. *Dandridge v. Williams*, 397 U.S. 471 (1970). State public-school funding formulas that provide more funds per student to some districts than others are constitutional, since the poor are not a suspect class and education is not a fundamental constitutional right. *San Antonio Indep. Sch. Dist. v. Rodriguez*, 411 U.S. 1 (1973).

Age discriminations likewise are subject to rational level review. State mandatory retirement laws that set maximum ages for state police are valid without regard to the fitness of individual officers. *Mass. Bd. of Ret. v. Murgia*, 427 U.S. 307 (1976). The same is true of mandatory retirement provisions for state court judges. *Gregory v. Ashcroft*, 501 U.S. 452 (1991).

This deferential standard mirrors substantive economic due process in that the reviewing court is obliged to begin with a presumption that the measure is valid and to hypothesize any conceivable rationalization to uphold the law. In social and economic policy, the legislature's choices may be based on rational speculation that is unsupported by evidence or empirical data. *Allegheny Pittsburgh Coal Co. v. Cty. Comm'n of Webster Cty.*, 488 U.S. 336 (1989). Still, there are occasional decisions that end up striking down state laws at this lowest level of scrutiny when the Court concludes that there simply is no purpose for the classification other than to discriminate. For example, a state cannot tax out-of-state businesses at a higher rate than in-state businesses. *Metro. Life Ins. Co. v. Ward*, 470 U.S. 869 (1985). As was previously mentioned, these cases are sometimes referred to as "rational review with teeth."

Strict scrutiny review and racial classifications. At the other end of the spectrum, racial classifications are deemed invidious and suspect and subjected to the strictest scrutiny. In the school desegregation decision, the Supreme Court vindicated itself to hold that racial segregation in state public schools was a *per se* violation of the Fourteenth Amendment. *Brown v. Bd. of Educ.*, 347 U.S. 483 (1954) ("*Brown I*"). This case overruled the Court's earlier interpretation of the Equal Protection Clause that had required only "separate but equal" treatment along racial lines in *Plessy v. Ferguson*, 163 U.S. 537 (1896). That pernicious holding had given life to the system of racial apartheid known euphemistically as "Jim Crow" after the title of a 19th-century minstrel song. The Supreme Court finessed over the absence of an Equal Protection Clause in the Fifth Amendment to hold that the public schools in the District of Columbia must also be desegregated under that Amendment's Due Process Clause. *Bolling v. Sharpe*, 347 U.S. 497 (1954). This interpretative move is called "reverse incorporation." *See supra* § 2 (Incorporation of the Bill of Rights).

The sequel to *Brown I* came the next year to hold that the local United States District Courts would exercise their equity powers to supervise the desegregation of the public schools with "all deliberate speed." *Brown v. Bd. of Educ.*, 349 U.S. 294 (1955) ("*Brown II*"). Although the opinion in *Brown I* had focused on public education and emphasized its important function, the principle was extended to all aspects of public life, wherever the government had segregated the races, including libraries, swimming pools, parks, *etc.*, in a series of *per curiam* opinions without anything more being said.

Brown II, on the other hand, showed the Supreme Court to be at best naïve and at worst timid, at least with the benefit of hindsight. Ten years later the Justices finally declared that the time for all deliberate speed had run out. *Griffin v. Cty. Sch. Bd. of Prince Edward Cty.*, 377 U.S. 218 (1964). Four decades later, the district courts were finally getting to the point of lifting desegregation decrees and declaring unitary status to return control over the schools to local officials. *Bd. of Educ. of Oklahoma City Pub. Sch. v. Dowell*, 498 U.S. 237 (1991).

Remedial court powers. The remedial powers of the federal courts are equal to the task of eliminating invidious *de jure* segregation. In order to eliminate the effects of past discrimination root and branch, court-ordered remedies can rely on racial classifications in pupil assignments, altering attendance zones, teacher and staff assignments, building plans, transportation or busing, *etc. Swann v. Charlotte-Mecklenburg Bd. of Educ.*, 402 U.S. 1 (1971). In short, all the techniques that were used to create a segregated dual school district can be used to remedy the lasting effects from *de jure* segregation. *Missouri v. Jenkins*, 515 U.S. 70 (1995). In creating a remedy for racial discrimination in public schools, school districts that have not been guilty of racial discrimination cannot be forced to participate in remedying the unconstitutional discrimination of other school districts. Remedial measures cannot cross district lines unless the past segregation being remedied did so. *Milliken v. Bradley*, 418 U.S. 717 (1974). At the university level, a state cannot satisfy its duty to dismantle a previously *de jure* segregated system by simply declaring a free-choice enrollment policy. *United States v. Fordice*, 505 U.S. 717 (1992). Apparently, a state is not required to maintain its historically black institutions of higher education (sometimes abbreviated HBCs) as such. Nor is it forbidden to do so. *Id*. (Thomas, J., concurring).

De jure versus de facto. The Supreme Court has adhered to a distinction between *de jure* segregation and *de facto* segregation; only *de jure* segregation—characterized by a governmental purpose or intent to discriminate—violates the Fourteenth Amendment and authorizes a court to exercise its equitable remedial powers. *Keyes v. Sch. Dist. No. 1*, 413 U.S. 189 (1973). This question of fact can be inferred from the circumstances; evidence that a governmental policy, such as using a qualifying test, has a disproportionate racial impact is relevant but not controlling on the issue. *Washington v. Davis*, 426 U.S. 229 (1976). If the challengers make out a *prima facie* case of an invidious purpose or intent to adopt a policy initially or to continue a policy with an untoward effect, then the burden shifts to the government to demonstrate that the same political decision would have resulted had the impermissible purpose not been part of the decision-making, a standard that is difficult to meet. *Village of Arlington Heights v. Metro. Housing Dev. Corp.*, 429 U.S. 252 (1977). On some factual records, however, there is no possible logical inference other than that the officials who were administering a facially neutral policy were in fact pursuing the policy with "an evil eye and an unequal hand." *Yick Wo v. Hopkins*, 118 U.S. 356 (1886).

Reverse discrimination or affirmative action. The validity of a policy of reverse discrimination or affirmative action divides the country and the Supreme Court is conflicted on the constitutional question, as well. In a somewhat enigmatic and even eccentric separate concurring opinion in *Regents of the University of California v. Bakke*, 438 U.S. 265 (1978), Justice Lewis Powell straddled the issue to agree with a set of four Justices that race could be taken into account in university admissions decisions to achieve a constitutionally protected value of student diversity but agreed with a different set of four Justices that the admissions procedures in the case *sub judice* were invalid. He explained that "a diverse student body" was a constitutionally permissible—but not a constitutionally required— goal in higher education that was part and parcel of the admitting faculty's academic freedom, itself an aspect of "special concern of the First Amendment." He squarely rejected all the other justifications offered, including eliminating the effects of past social discrimination. In a holistic way, race could be one factor—a "plus"—but not the only factor in an admission decision. UC Davis could not set aside a number of seats to be filled only by applicants of identified racial minorities.

After a long period of tacking back and forth, the Court established several important doctrinal base lines in *Adarand Constructors, Inc. v. Pena*, 515 U.S. 200 (1995): first, any governmental preference based on race is subject to strict judicial scrutiny; second, the standard of review is not dependent on the race of those benefited or burdened; and third, the standard is the same for federal programs under the Fifth Amendment and for state programs under the Fourteenth Amendment. So-called benign racial classifications are constitutionally no different from invidious racial classifications. The "equal protection of the laws" is an individual right to demand that any governmental actor must justify any racial classification to determine whether the classification is narrowly tailored to achieve a compelling governmental interest. However, the majority did take pains to insist that race-based policies could pass constitutional muster, that strict judicial scrutiny is *not* "strict in theory, but fatal in fact."

In 2003, in two companion cases arising from the same public state university, a majority basically adopted the approach Justice Powell had taken back in 1978. Applying strict scrutiny equal protection analysis, the Supreme Court upheld the race-conscious admissions procedures at the law school but struck down the race-conscious admissions procedures at the undergraduate school at the University of Michigan. Both cases held that attaining a diverse student body is a compelling state interest. But the difference between them was whether the respective admissions procedures were specifically and narrowly tailored. The validated procedures at the law school used race as only one of the factors in an individualized, holistic review of the law school applicant's entire file. *Grutter v. Bollinger*, 539 U.S. 306 (2003). By contrast, the invalidated procedures at the undergraduate school of the university automatically awarded 20 points or one-fifth of those needed to guarantee admission to the university, solely on the basis of race, to every single undergraduate applicant who was an "underrepresented minority." *Gratz v. Bollinger*, 539 U.S. 244 (2003). In a noteworthy and somewhat mysterious *dictum* in the law school case, the majority, speaking through Justice O'Connor, announced an imaginary sunset provision in the Fourteenth Amendment to say that admissions preferences in higher education ought to disappear in 25 years' time. Whether or not that *dictum* will survive Justice O'Connor's 2006 retirement remains to be seen between now and 2028. A case involving the University of Texas has demonstrated that the same divisions persist among the different Justices now sitting on the High Court. They keep remanding the case back to the lower court to re-apply the law, apparently out of disappointment with how the lower court keeps misapplying the Supreme Court's Equal Protection doctrine. The current strict scrutiny baseline is that a college or university must demonstrate there is no race neutral way of achieving a diverse student body. *Fisher v. Univ. of Tex.*, 136 S. Ct. 2198 (2016); *Fisher v. Univ. of Tex.*, 570 U.S. 297 (2013). The close decisions on this issue will embolden challengers who oppose affirmative action in higher education and guarantee future petitions for *certiorari* raising that issue.

The Roberts Court seems to have taken a hard line against voluntary integration in the public schools, which the majority believes amounts to the constitutional equivalent of *de jure* segregation. *Parents Involved in Cmty. Sch. v. Seattle School Dist. No. 1*, 551 U.S. 701 (2007). There is a constitutional duty of a *de jure* segregated school district to desegregate; however, a school district that has never segregated or a school district that has achieved unitary status and is no longer segregated cannot voluntarily integrate its schools based on race. The distinction is the difference between using race to remedy past *de jure* segregation ("desegregation") and using race to achieve some racial balance, for example, for each school to reflect the racial percentages in the community or to impose a limit on the percentage of students from different races in a school ("integration"). The programs in Seattle and Louisville were not remedying past intentional discrimination. Only remedial desegregation would satisfy strict scrutiny in elementary and secondary schools. The elementary and secondary schools could not rely on the justification of diversity—that compelling purpose is limited to institutions of higher education only. The majority and the dissent quarreled strongly over the meaning and implications of *Brown v. Bd. of Educ.* in a way that portends continued future disagreement.

Intermediate level review. Somewhere between rational level review and strict scrutiny review, there is an intermediate level of Equal Protection review defined with rather general, in-between terminology. At this intermediate level, the government's purpose has to be "important"—something somewhere between "compelling" and "legitimate"—and the classification has to be "substantially related" to the asserted governmental interest—a relatedness somewhat less than "necessary" and somewhat more than "reasonable." Consequently, the outcomes in cases applying intermediate scrutiny are less predictable than the cases applying rational level review—which usually uphold the government classification—or the cases applying strict scrutiny—which usually invalidate the government classification. Classifications concerning gender, illegitimacy, and alienage generally fit under the intermediate standard of Equal Protection.

Gender. In a preliminary case, a plurality of the Supreme Court tentatively decided to equate gender with race and to apply strict scrutiny, but that approach did not last. *Frontiero v. Richardson*, 411 U.S. 677 (1973). All gender classifications, whether in favor of men against women or in favor of women against men, must be substantially related to the

achievement of some important governmental
purposes. Therefore, a challenge can be brought by a
woman or a man claiming to be the victim of
discrimination based on her or his gender. A statute
that prohibits the sale of beer to men but allows the
sale to women of the same age has an important
enough purpose: public health and traffic safety, but
the discriminatory classification simply is not
substantially related enough to achieve that purpose.
The available automobile accident data did not
support the discrimination. *Craig v. Boren*, 429 U.S.
190 (1976). Intermediate level review produces
results both ways. For example, the Court, without a
majority opinion, upheld a state statute defining
"statutory rape" even though the statute made males
alone criminally liable for having intercourse with an
under-aged female. *Michael M. v. Superior Court*,
450 U.S. 464 (1981). However, the Court believed
that Congress deserved sufficient judicial deference
to authorize the registration of males but not females
for the military draft. *Rostker v. Goldberg*, 453 U.S.
57 (1981). The same *de jure/de facto* distinction
applies in gender cases that applies in racial cases.
There must be unconstitutional *animus*, *i.e.*, a
purpose or intent to discriminate for one gender and
against the other gender. *Personnel Admin. of Mass.
v. Feeney*, 442 U.S. 256 (1979). Furthermore, the
Supreme Court will apply the same intermediate
level review to affirmative action policies and
programs purporting to remedy past gender
discrimination. *Miss. Univ. for Women v. Hogan*, 458
U.S. 718 (1982). Finally, in *United States v. Virginia*,
518 U.S. 515 (1996), the Court held that a state could

not withhold from women a unique educational program and, therefore, the Virginia Military Institute must be opened to women. The majority was careful to note it was not deciding that any and all "separate but equal" gendered institutions violated the Constitution, but only that VMI's particular program did not have the "exceedingly persuasive justification" required of single-sex programs. A recent case demonstrated how the Court applies a remedy for gender discrimination to achieve constitutional equality. The majority held that the norm of equal protection was violated by a gender-based distinction in the statutes applicable to acquisition of U.S. citizenship by a child born abroad to one parent who was U.S. citizen and another parent who was a citizen of another nation, under which only one year of continuous physical presence in the U.S. was required before unwed mothers could pass citizenship to their children, but five years of continuous presence were required of unwed fathers. In an opinion by Justice Ginsburg, the Court decided to level down and not up, however, and ruled that the constitutionally appropriate remedy was to apply the five-year requirement prospectively to children born of unwed mothers, rather than to extend the benefit of one-year requirement to fathers. *Sessions v. Morales-Santana*, 137 S. Ct. 1678 (2017).

Illegitimacy. A state may not classify illegitimate children and impose exceptional legal burdens on them. The sins of the parents cannot be visited on their children per the Fourteenth Amendment. A state cannot prohibit acknowledgment of illegitimate children in order to permanently deny them benefits.

Weber v. Aetna Cas. & Sur. Co., 406 U.S. 164 (1972). But the state's legitimate interest (pun intended) in the accurate and efficient determination of paternity may allow for differences in various legal procedures between legitimate and illegitimate children, such as the requirements for qualifying for intestate succession. *Lalli v. Lalli*, 439 U.S. 259 (1978). The cases recognize that the states are entitled to deal differently with the circumstances and evidentiary proof between establishing maternity and paternity, but DNA technology may end up eroding what is left of the distinction. *See Clark v. Jeter*, 486 U.S. 456 (1988) (evidentiary needs). In some ways, illegitimacy classifications related to paternity determinations are also gender classifications, as far as the father is concerned. The Equal Protection analysis for gender and illegitimacy merge together. *Caban v. Mohammed*, 441 U.S. 380 (1979). Intermediate scrutiny is the order of the day.

Alienage. Aliens are persons and thus entitled to the protections of Due Process and Equal Protection, even though they are not citizens. Federal classifications are analyzed under the Fifth Amendment; state classifications are analyzed under the Fourteenth Amendment. The federal government has been delegated broad powers over naturalization and immigration, powers that are denied the states. The Supreme Court's decisions are more or less consistent with the deferential standard of equal protection. Federal programmatic classifications that deny aliens the same governmental benefits that are afforded citizens are constitutional so long as they meet the rational basis threshold. *Mathews v. Diaz*,

426 U.S. 67 (1976). State governments have no constitutional role in foreign affairs, immigration, or naturalization, however. Therefore, state classifications that discriminate against aliens usually are subjected to more searching review. A state law that altogether denied a free public education to the children of illegal aliens was invalid. *Plyler v. Doe*, 457 U.S. 202 (1982). A state law that deals with a particularized governmental function can classify, however, under a lower threshold. For example, a state disqualification of public school teachers who are resident aliens and eligible but who refuse to become naturalized citizens was valid. The teachers performed a government function and were representatives of the state, so the state could insist on citizenship as a qualification. *Ambach v. Norwick*, 441 U.S. 68 (1979).

Fundamental rights. A law that burdens the exercise of some fundamental constitutional right— like a law that is based on a suspect classification— also is subjected to something like strict scrutiny review. The law is presumed unconstitutional. This is part of the constitutional paradigm of the famous "footnote four" in *United States v. Carolene Products Co.*, 304 U.S. 144, 153 n.4 (1938). *See supra* § 8 (Substantive Due Process). Again, it is exceedingly difficult for the government to meet this standard. Fundamental rights can be found in the text of the Constitution, particularly in the provisions of the Bill of Rights. The rights that have been incorporated into the Fourteenth Amendment are all fundamental. *See supra* § 2 (Incorporation of the Bill of Rights). There are other rights, however, that are not expressly provided in the text of the Constitution that the Supreme Court understands to be fundamental. Thus, fundamental rights can be textual rights or nontextual rights.

A fundamental right is one that is "implicit in the concept of ordered liberty," *Palko v. Connecticut*, 302 U.S. 319, 325 (1937), or "deeply rooted in this Nation's history and tradition*,*" *Moore v. East Cleveland*, 431 U.S. 494, 503 (1977) (Powell, J., concurring). Once they go beyond the text, the key analytic is for the Justices to locate the proper level of history and tradition to determine what is fundamental and what is not. It is not uncommon for the Justices to disagree with each other on this aspect of American constitutionalism. *See Michael H. v. Gerald D.*, 491 U.S. 110 (1989) (Justice Scalia versus Justice Brennan). The First Amendment does not mention the "right of association" in so many words, but the Supreme Court has long interpolated the right to associate with other individuals as being a necessary corollary of the rights that are mentioned in the text. *NAACP v. Alabama ex rel. Patterson*, 357 U.S. 449 (1958). Once a fundamental right is identified, the Court is obliged to give it definition and scope. History and tradition are its guide, *i.e.*, the Justices observe how the right has manifested itself over time and how society has respected the right. There is a paradoxical quality to nontextual fundamental rights. A liberty that has been historically respected and widely respected will be deemed fundamental and worthy of judicial protection. But such a liberty that has been so respected has less need for judicial protection.

Access to the courts. The fundamental right of access to the courts requires that an impecunious criminal defendant who is convicted must be afforded a transcript and an attorney on appeal, even though there is no substantive constitutional right to an appeal in the first place. *Douglas v. California*, 372 U.S. 353 (1963); *Griffin v. Illinois*, 351 U.S. 12 (1956). This right is separate and apart from the Sixth Amendment right to counsel, which has been incorporated into the Fourteenth Amendment. *Gideon v. Wainright*, 372 U.S. 335 (1963). Some entitlements are anchored to the Sixth and Fourteenth Amendments, like the right to have a psychiatrist's assistance in an insanity plea. *Ake v. Oklahoma*, 470 U.S. 68 (1970). But other protections, like inmate access to prison law libraries, are linked to the more general right of access. *Bounds v. Smith*, 430 U.S. 817 (1977). The right of access to the courts can apply in civil cases, as well, although it seems to have less gravity. *See United States v. Kras*, 409 U.S. 434 (1973) (upholding filing fees in bankruptcy proceedings).

The right to vote. There are numerous textual references to voting found throughout the Constitution and in various amendments. There is a fundamental individual right to vote that exists alongside a countervailing compelling government power to regulate elections. The Fourteenth Amendment requires apportionment of state legislative districts by population to insure "one person-one vote" equality. *Reynolds v. Sims*, 377 U.S. 533 (1964). This standard applies to any election of any public official by popular vote. *Hadley v. Junior*

Coll. Dist., 397 U.S. 50 (1970). In congressional districts, there is no *de minimis* level of malapportionment—absolute mathematical equality is required so far as it is attainable. *Karcher v. Daggett*, 462 U.S. 725 (1983). There is a little more constitutional leeway in state legislative districts. *White v. Regester*, 412 U.S. 755 (1973). Because it is a fundamental individual right, even a political majority does not have the authority to deviate from this standard. *Lucas v. Forty-Fourth Gen. Assembly of Colo.*, 377 U.S. 713 (1964). Reapportionment of state legislative districts must occur upon the constitutionally required decennial census at a minimum, but may be more frequent. *See* U.S. Const. art. I, § 2. Political gerrymandering—by which a political party with a majority in the state legislature redraws districts with an eye towards favoring itself—is a justiciable issue. *League of United Latin Am. Citizens v. Perry*, 548 U.S. 399 (2006). Who has Article III standing to bring such a claim presents a contentious threshold question. *Gill v. Whitford*, 138 S. Ct. 1916 (2018) (remanding for further proceedings to allow plaintiffs to demonstrate a burden on their individual votes). Poll taxes, no matter how small, violate the Fourteenth Amendment. *Harper v. Va. State Bd. of Elections*, 383 U.S. 663 (1966). Property owning qualifications are suspect. *Hill v. Stone*, 421 U.S. 289 (1975). Candidates have a qualified right of access to be on the ballot and their followers have a right to vote for them. Nonetheless, state election laws can serve compelling purposes to assure the seriousness of a candidate, to control the size and reduce the confusion of a ballot, and to assure that the eventual winner has majority support. *Ill. State Bd. of Elections v. Socialist Workers Party*, 440 U.S. 173 (1979). The individual right to vote is so important—and perceived threats to the integrity of an election are taken so seriously—that the Supreme Court was willing to intervene in the 2000 presidential election in an exigent manner to resolve one of the most contested political disputes in history, at considerable cost to the prestige and credibility of the Court as an institution. *Bush v. Gore*, 531 U.S. 98 (2000). That controversial decision invoked, *inter alia*, the one-person-one vote principle.

Right to travel. The right to travel might be linked to several places in the text of the Constitution: the Privileges and Immunities Clause in Article IV, the Privileges or Immunities Clause in the Fourteenth Amendment, the Commerce Clause, the Due Process Clauses in the Fifth and Fourteenth Amendments, and even non-textually to the preceding *Articles of Confederation*. In *Saenz v. Roe*, 526 U.S. 489 (1999), the majority tentatively associated the right of a citizen of one state to be treated as a welcomed visitor in another state with the Privileges and Immunities Clause in Article IV; and associated the right of a citizen to move permanently from one state to another state with the Privileges or Immunities Clause in the Fourteenth Amendment; but declined to associate the fundamental right of a citizen of one state to enter and leave another state with any particular clause. No matter. The right to travel from one state to another state, particularly the right to pick up and move from one state to another, is so elementary as to be fundamental. Therefore, an unduly long residency requirement to qualify for basic state benefits, like welfare assistance or medical care, is unconstitutional. *Mem'l Hosp. v. Maricopa Cty.*, 415 U.S. 250 (1974)*; Shapiro v. Thompson*, 394 U.S. 618 (1969). Approximately 30 days is allowable to qualify to register to vote. *Dunn v. Blumstein*, 405 U.S. 330 (1972). But it is permissible to require city employees to be residents of the city. *McCarthy v. Phila. Civil Serv. Comm'n*, 424 U.S. 645 (1976). A reasonable period of in-state residency can be a qualification for lower university tuition, but a permanent bar is unconstitutional. *Vlandis v. Kline*, 412 U.S. 441 (1973). A state may not apportion state benefits based on how long a person has been a resident. *Zobel v. Williams*, 457 U.S. 55 (1982). Finally, all these decisions relate to domestic travel. The individual interest is lesser and the federal power is greater to regulate foreign travel, going so far as to prohibit it for certain countries or particular persons. *Haig v. Agee*, 453 U.S. 280 (1981).

Privacy and personal autonomy. There is no generalized absolute right to privacy of a libertarian dimension to do whatever one chooses so long as it does not harm someone else. Long ago, Justice Holmes famously denounced the "shibboleth" that there is anything in the Constitution like "the liberty of the citizen to do as he likes so long as he does not interfere with the liberty of others to do the same." *Lochner v. New York*, 198 U.S. 45, 65 (1905) (Holmes, J., dissenting). The state police power regularly interferes with individual decision-making, often in matters that are significant and important to the individual. Certain highly personal decisions, however, have been deemed to be so important to individual liberty—so crucial to personhood—that they deserve extraordinary judicial protection. The judicial precedents can be traced back to substantive due process decisions. Their modern counterpart in Equal Protection/fundamental rights jurisprudence became obvious in *Griswold v. Connecticut*, 381 U.S. 479 (1965), which struck down a state law forbidding the use of contraception based on a right of marital privacy that the state was obliged to respect. The privacy rationale later was significantly extended to unmarried couples. *Eisenstadt v. Baird*, 405 U.S. 438 (1972). That move made the right to privacy an individual right.

Then in 1973, in *Roe v. Wade,* 410 U.S. 113 (1973), the Supreme Court declared state laws in Texas and 30 other states criminalizing abortion to violate the constitutional right of privacy. That this was the most controversial decision since *Brown v. Bd. of Educ.* was reflected in how many cases found their way to the Supreme Court in the years following the decision, as different state legislatures challenged the High Court's privacy paradigm. The Constitution does not require the state to pay the expenses of an abortion for an indigent woman even when the woman has a right to an abortion. *Harris v. McRae*, 448 U.S. 297 (1980). States and the federal government may regulate the manner and circumstances of an abortion, up to a constitutional level. Government may pursue policies that disfavor abortion, but only up to a constitutional point. *Rust v. Sullivan*, 500 U.S. 173 (1991); *Webster v. Reprod. Health Servs.*, 492 U.S. 490 (1989); *Planned*

Parenthood of Cent. Mo. v. Danforth, 428 U.S. 52 (1976). No one besides the pregnant woman can make the decision for her: not a physician, not a spouse, not a parent. In the case of an unemancipated child, even parent notification requirements must be qualified with a judicial bypass procedure to assure the patient's autonomy is not compromised. *Ohio v. Akron Ctr. for Reprod. Health*, 497 U.S. 502 (1990).

A plurality opinion, jointly authored by Justices O'Connor, Kennedy, and Souter, reaffirmed the basic holding in *Roe v. Wade*, but also substantially revised the doctrine. *Planned Parenthood of Se. Pa. v. Casey*, 505 U.S. 833 (1992). The Fourteenth Amendment places limits on the state's power to interfere with a person's basic decision-making about family, parenthood, and bodily integrity. The state may not by purpose or effect impose an undue burden on a woman's constitutionally protected decision to terminate her pregnancy. Ordinary state medical regulations are appropriate so long as they serve the state's interest to protect the health and safety of the woman. The state may likewise promote its interest in the potential life of the fetus with appropriate regulations so long as they serve the state's interest in the life or health of the woman. The state may require informed consent for the procedure, as it does for any other medical procedure, and the state may require that certain information on abortion and childbirth be provided. The state can require record keeping so long as the record keeping does not afford a third party, like a spouse, the opportunity to interfere with the woman's decision. But if the physical health or psychological health or emotional health or mental health of the woman indicates an abortion and she makes that decision, the state cannot interfere in any significant way, *i.e.*, the state cannot impose an undue burden on the pregnant woman's decision to terminate her pregnancy. That standard was violated by state requirements that abortion providers have admitting privileges at a local hospital and that abortion facilities meet standards for ambulatory surgical centers. Those requirements created a substantial obstacle for women seeking a pre-viability abortion. *Whole Woman's Health v. Hellerstedt*, 136 S. Ct. 2292 (2016).

That the operative and controlling constitutional value is the woman's autonomous decision-making is further illustrated by the Supreme Court's decision applying the undue burden test to strike down a state ban on so-called partial-birth abortions, *i.e.*, very late-term abortions. The state statute did not have an exception for the pregnant woman's health and suffered from some other medical overbreadth in what it prohibited. *Stenberg v. Carhart*, 530 U.S. 914 (2000). In a subsequent case involving the same named physician, however, a five-to-four majority upheld the federal Partial Birth Abortion Ban Act. That decision upheld a prohibition of a defined abortion procedure (intact dilation & evacuation) that was deemed by Congress to be too close to infanticide. And, for the first time, the Court validated a statute that did not require an exception for the pregnant woman's health. *Gonzales v. Carhart*, 550 U.S. 124 (2007) (The federal law was an exercise of the Commerce Clause power; in a separate concurring opinion joined by Justice Scalia, Justice Thomas wondered out loud if it was a proper exercise of that power).

Heteronormativity. In 1986, by the narrowest of margins, the Supreme Court ruled that homosexual sodomy was not a fundamental right and that homosexuals were not a suspect class. *Bowers v. Hardwick*, 478 U.S. 186 (1986). After he retired from the Court, Justice Powell, who had cast the deciding and controlling fifth vote, publicly acknowledged his change of mind but the case remained on the books. Nevertheless, the Supreme Court managed to strike down a state referendum that prohibited all legislative, executive, or judicial action at any level of state or local government to protect homosexual persons or gays and lesbians. A majority deemed the measure to be unconstitutional *per se* in contravention of the fundamental principle of the "equal protection of the laws." *Romer v. Evans*, 517 U.S. 620 (1996). In 2003, the Court emphatically rejected the 1986 decision and declared that it was wrong when it was decided and it should be overruled. The new majority held that there was no legitimate state interest whatsoever for a criminal statute that prohibited two consenting adults of the same gender from engaging in certain sexual practices in the privacy of their own home. The majority declared that the Due Process Clause protected their right of privacy—their personal dignity and autonomy within that intimate precinct—against the state's unconstitutional regulation. *Lawrence v. Texas*, 539 U.S. 558 (2003). Their expression of intimacy was a liberty that was protected under the Due Process Clause of the Fourteenth Amendment and by necessary implication by the Due Process Clause of the Fifth Amendment. This line of cases was continued in later cases dealing with same-sex marriage, discussed in the next sub-section.

Marriage. Marriage is something of a non-textual fundamental right in and of itself, although many state regulations are deemed appropriate because they are justified by sufficiently compelling state interests. *Zablocki v. Redhail*, 434 U.S. 374 (1978). Minimum-age laws, laws against bigamy, and laws regulating marriage between closely related individuals do not give the courts pause. In contrast, the Supreme Court had an easy time striking down a state law forbidding interracial marriages as a violation of the Equal Protection Clause. *Loving v. Virginia*, 388 U.S. 1 (1967). The subject of same-sex marriage, however, has generated some noteworthy precedents. First, in *United States v. Windso*r, 570 U.S. 744 (2013), the Court struck down the Defense of Marriage Act, which as a matter of federal law defined marriage as a legal union between one man and one woman. The majority ruled that definition violated the Fifth Amendment liberty of same-sex couples lawfully married under the relevant laws of the states where they lived. The federal measure was deemed to be unconstitutional because it was demeaning to the same-sex couples and humiliating to their children. Next, rather predictably and seemingly inevitably, *Obergefell v. Hodges*, 135 S. Ct. 2584 (2015) followed. Once again, the textual reference was individual liberty. The majority held that the Fourteenth Amendment required a state to license a marriage between two persons of the same sex. The majority also held that the Fourteenth Amendment required a state to recognize a same-sex marriage that was licensed and performed in another state. These requirements were part and parcel of the fundamental right to marry protected by the Due Process Clause and the Equal Protection Clause. The dissenters in these same-sex marriage cases raised an interesting question that may arise in future challenges to state marriage laws: whether someday plural marriages will be included in the scope of the fundamental right to marry.

Right to die. Under the Fourteenth Amendment, a competent person has a constitutionally protected liberty to refuse unwanted medical treatment. This liberty is inherent in the bodily integrity of the individual. Assuming *arguendo* that a competent person would have a constitutional right to refuse lifesaving hydration and nutrition, the Supreme Court nevertheless held that a state could establish procedural safeguards for when the person has become incompetent and the decision is being made by a surrogate. A state may define formal procedures and forms for a person to follow in the decision to terminate life-sustaining measures. Alternatively, the state may also require a hearing and impose a standard of proof by clear and convincing evidence on a surrogate decision-maker, even if the surrogate is the next of kin or guardian of the incompetent patient. The Constitution, however, does not require the state to repose decision-making authority on anyone besides the patient. *Cruzan v. Dir., Mo. Dep't of Health*, 497 U.S. 261 (1990).

Even so far as the competent individual is concerned, a state may prohibit anyone from causing or aiding a suicide. Such a law does not violate a medical patient's fundamental right of liberty protected in the Due Process Clause of the Fourteenth Amendment. *Washington v. Glucksberg*, 521 U.S. 702 (1997). Nor does a ban on physician-assisted suicide violate the Equal Protection Clause, despite the fact that those patients on life-support systems can exercise their right to refuse treatment, either by themselves or through state procedures for surrogates. The longstanding distinction between withdrawing life support systems and assisting suicide is a classification that is consonant with constitutional "equal protection of the laws." *Vacco v. Quill*, 521 U.S. 793 (1997).

Postscript. Looking back over this entire section, explaining the variable levels of scrutiny and all the differential balancing tests, is it any wonder that some Justices have thrown up their hands in the face of all this complexity and nuance in the Equal Protection jurisprudence? "There is only one Equal Protection Clause. It requires every state to govern impartially. It does not direct the courts to apply one standard of review in some cases and a different standard in other cases." *Craig v. Boren*, 429 U.S. 190, 211–12 (1976) (Stevens, J., concurring). Alas and alack.

10. FREEDOM OF SPEECH AND PRESS

Perhaps because the United States was the first nation ever in history to be argued into existence, many constitutionalists on and off the Supreme Court deem the First Amendment to be preferred over other freedoms. Certainly, the freedoms in the First Amendment qualify as fundamental rights deserving of extraordinary judicial protection. Justice Cardozo called freedom of conscience "the matrix, the indispensable condition of nearly every other form of freedom." *Palko v. Connecticut*, 302 U.S. 319, 327 (1937). The theory of the First Amendment is based on some basic values of American constitutionalism: the pursuit of truth and enlightenment; the achievement of individual self-actualization and fulfillment; and the participation in self-government both as a citizen-participant and an outlier-opponent. Thus, speech is protected as a means to an end and as an end in and of itself. *Whitney v. California*, 274 U.S. 357, 375 (1927) (Brandeis, J., concurring). The Supreme Court has dealt with the freedom of conscience categorically in several overlapping and interrelated lines of precedent.

Clear and present danger doctrine. The First Amendment is not limited to prohibiting prior restraints, although that was one of its historic 18th century functions. Speech that creates a "clear and present danger" can be punished, however, such as a person *falsely* shouting "Fire!" in a crowded theater and causing a panic—to mention Justice Holmes' famous example. *Schenck v. United States*, 249 U.S.

47 (1919). Normally, there is no regulatory role for the government to play in the marketplace of ideas. Even when the speech involved is against the government—especially then—the best test for truth is the power of an idea to get itself accepted. *Abrams v. United States*, 250 U.S. 616, 630 (1919) (Holmes, J., dissenting). "Every idea is an incitement." *Gitlow v. New York*, 268 U.S. 652, 673 (1925) (Holmes, J., dissenting). But the government does have a power to forbid or even to proscribe "advocacy of the use of force or of law violation" if and only if the speech "is directed to inciting or producing imminent lawless action and is likely to incite or produce" such lawlessness. *Brandenburg v. Ohio*, 395 U.S. 444, 447 (1969). That decision illustrates Justice Holmes's insistence that the First Amendment must protect "not [just] free thought for those who agree with us but freedom for the thought we hate," *United States v. Schwimmer*, 279 U.S. 644, 655 (1929) (Holmes, J., dissenting), in that the speech being protected in *Brandenburg* was a televised racist diatribe delivered at a rally of the Ku Klux Klan using the most odious racial epithet. Indeed, this modern test is exceedingly protective of advocacy of illegal conduct and so is the Supreme Court, as demonstrated by its reversal of a conviction of a leader of a demonstration who was arrested for shouting to an unruly mob of protestors "We'll take the fucking street later." *Hess v. Indiana*, 414 U.S. 105 (1973). In today's perilous world, the government's interest in combatting terrorism and protecting the homeland is an "urgent objective of the highest order;" therefore, a federal law that

prohibited providing expert advice, training, service, and personnel was not vague and did not violate the speech or association rights of plaintiffs who sought to support designated terrorist groups with financial contributions, legal training, and political advocacy for the groups' otherwise lawful humanitarian and political activities. *Holder v. Humanitarian Law Project*, 561 U.S. 1 (2010).

Prior restraint. Historically and functionally, a prior restraint is constitutionally different than a criminal or civil punishment after the speech. While the threat of after-the-fact punishment is said to "chill" speech—to make the speaker more reluctant to speak—a prior restraint "freezes" the dialogue to keep the speaker from speaking the speech. Prior restraints are presumed unconstitutional and the government carries a heavy burden of justification. When the Nixon administration sought a court injunction against the NEW YORK TIMES and the WASHINGTON POST for publishing government reports about the military policies of the United States in Vietnam, reports that were rated "top secret," the Supreme Court ruled against the government. *N.Y. Times Co. v. United States*, 403 U.S. 713 (1971). An earlier precedent had struck down a state statute for authorizing state courts to abate, as a tortious public nuisance, "a malicious, scandalous or defamatory" newspaper or magazine. *Near v. Minnesota ex rel. Olson*, 283 U.S. 697 (1931). Parallel federal and state statutes that prohibited the publication or broadcast of conversation that had been illegally intercepted could not be applied to a radio station that itself had not obtained the recordings illegally. Their broadcast in the context of a collective-bargaining negotiation involving local public school teachers was a matter of unusual public concern. The Court remarked that laws that punish the publication of truthful information "seldom" can satisfy constitutional standards. *Bartnicki v. Vopper*, 532 U.S. 514 (2001). In the context of foreign intelligence operations, however, the Court approved the imposition of a constructive trust on the proceeds of a "kill-and-tell" book written by a CIA operative who breached his contract to apply for pre-publication clearance and approval. *Snepp v. United States*, 444 U.S. 507 (1980).

The public forum. "Wherever the title of streets and parks may rest, they have immemorially been held in trust for the use of the public, and time out of mind, have been used for the purposes of assembly, communicating thoughts between citizens, and discussing public questions." *Hague v. Comm. for Indus. Org.*, 307 U.S. 496, 515 (1939) (Roberts, J., concurring). Those are the places we own in common. Those are the places we gather. Those are the places we meet. Those are the places we confront one another. In the leading case, the Supreme Court defined three different types of public forums with different First Amendment rights of access. *Perry Educ. Ass'n v. Perry Local Educators' Ass'n*, 460 U.S. 37 (1983). In a traditional public forum, like a street or a park, the public has a right of access and the government can enforce a content-based exclusion only if the exclusion is necessary to serve a compelling state interest and is narrowly drawn. Time, place, or manner restrictions are permitted, however, so long as they are content-neutral and narrowly tailored to serve a significant government interest, and if there are ample alternative channels of communication. In a limited-purpose public forum, the government is not required to open the area to free speech activity, but as long as it does so, it must treat the area like a traditional public forum. In a non-public non-forum, in addition to time, place, or manner regulations, the government may reserve the area for its intended purposes and make exclusions that are content-based but not viewpoint-based.

The metaphor to streets and parks has been extended. At issue in the 1983 *Perry* case was access to public school teachers' mailboxes by a rival union vying to represent the teachers. The rival union was refused a right of access when the Court decided the mailboxes were in the third category. In numerous, sometimes difficult-to-distinguish cases decided since then, the Court has applied these categories and rules. The public sidewalks surrounding the Supreme Court building are a traditional public forum and the government could not prohibit picketing there, but inside the building and the building grounds were not a public forum and the prohibition was valid in those places. *United States v. Grace*, 461 U.S. 171 (1983). A statute that prohibited displaying signs near a foreign embassy that held that government in "public odium or disrepute" violated the rule against content-based exclusions. *Boos v. Barry*, 485 U.S. 312 (1988). A government-owned airport terminal, open to the public, was not a public forum. *Int'l Soc. for Krishna Consciousness, Inc. v. Lee*, 505 U.S. 672 (1992). The

Court upheld a city ordinance that prohibited picketing focused on a particular private residence— as opposed to a march through a neighborhood. *Frisby v. Schultz*, 487 U.S. 474 (1988). There was a compelling state interest to prevent voter intimidation and election fraud that allowed a content-based restriction on the display or distribution of campaign materials within a limited area around a polling place. *Burson v. Freeman*, 504 U.S. 191 (1992). A third-party candidate for Congress, who was excluded from a debate sponsored by a public television broadcaster for the candidates from the two major parties, did not have a right of access to participate. *Ark. Educ. Television Comm'n v. Forbes*, 523 U.S. 666 (1998).

Reasonable time, place, or manner restrictions. A licensing scheme that gives an administrator too much subjective discretion to grant or deny a permit to use a public forum based on the identity of the speakers or the content of their message will be struck down. *Niemotko v. Maryland*, 340 U.S. 268 (1951). An ordinance that allowed the official to vary the cost of a permit based on estimates of the cost to maintain public order during the event or protest effectively allowed for an unconstitutional content-based restriction on unpopular messages. *Forsyth Cty. v. Nationalist Movement*, 505 U.S. 123 (1992). Although one can ignore an unconstitutional ordinance and conduct a protest without applying for a permit or hold a protest after being turned down for a permit, in sharp contrast, one cannot ignore a judicial injunction based on the same unconstitutional ordinance and then invoke the First

Amendment as a defense to being held in contempt of court. *Compare Shuttlesworth v. City of Birmingham*, 394 U.S. 147 (1969) *with Walker v. City of Birmingham*, 388 U.S. 307 (1967). A city regulation designed to limit excessively amplified music was narrowly tailored and need not be the least restrictive means to be a valid manner restriction. *Ward v. Rock Against Racism*, 491 U.S. 781 (1989). These content-neutral, time place, or manner regulations must contain adequate standards to guide the official's decision and render it subject to effective judicial review. *Thomas v. Chic. Park Dist.*, 534 U.S. 316 (2002). A town could not regulate different kinds of signs differently based on the content of the signs. *Reed v. Town of Gilbert*, 135 S. Ct. 2218 (2015).

A court-issued injunction, unlike an ordinance, necessarily applies to certain persons or groups with a particular viewpoint, but so long as the injunction does not burden any more speech than is necessary to serve a significant government interest, the injunction is a reasonable time, place, or manner regulation. On a proper showing of past misconduct, therefore, a state court can issue an injunction to restrain the behavior of abortion protesters outside a clinic. *Madsen v. Women's Health Ctr., Inc.*, 512 U.S. 753 (1994). A state statute to the same effect, if narrowly drawn to resemble an injunction, is constitutional. *Hill v. Colorado*, 530 U.S. 703 (2000). In contrast, a state statute that required crisis pregnancy centers, who opposed abortion, to provide patients with information about the availability of low-cost or state-provided abortions was presumptively unconstitutional. *Nat'l Inst. of Family & Life Advocates v. Becerra*, 138 S. Ct. 2361 (2018). Such content-based laws must pass strict scrutiny, *i.e.*, the law must be narrowly tailored to serve a compelling state interest.

Likewise, anti-fraud laws must be carefully tailored to pass First Amendment scrutiny. Charitable solicitation is protected activity and the state cannot set a minimum percentage or ratio of the proportion of funds that must be spent on charitable purposes as opposed to fundraising expenses and fees. *Village of Schaumburg v. Citizens for a Better Env't*, 444 U.S. 620 (1980). A state law that authorized a waiver of a 25% limitation on expenses if it prevented the charitable organization from soliciting contributions was struck down because the regulation improperly assumed that high fundraising costs are a strong indicator of fraud. *Sec'y of State of Md. v. Joseph H. Munson Co.*, 467 U.S. 947 (1984). Like other forms of public deception, however, fraudulent charitable solicitation is unprotected speech and the state may punish false or misleading representations designed to deceive donors about how their donations would be used. *Illinois ex rel. Madigan v. Telemarketing Assocs., Inc.*, 538 U.S. 600 (2003). A statute that prohibited the distribution of anonymous campaign literature did not pass the exacting scrutiny required of any measure that regulates core political speech. *McIntyre v. Ohio Elections Comm'n*, 514 U.S. 334 (1995). The Court used a balancing analysis to strike down an ordinance that required door-to-door solicitors to obtain a permit: the individual and societal interests in traditional religious proselytizing, anonymous canvassing, and grassroots political activity far outweighed the government's admittedly important interests in the prevention of fraud and crime and the protection of residential privacy, which could be better achieved with more narrowly tailored regulations. *Watchtower Bible & Tract Soc'y of N.Y. v. Village of Stratton*, 536 U.S. 150 (2002).

Government subsidies and tax deductions may not compromise First Amendment values. A state statute that exempted print media but not cable television from a sales tax was valid and not a content-based discrimination. *Leathers v. Medlock*, 499 U.S. 439 (1991). But New York's "Son of Sam" statute that confiscated on behalf of the victim any proceeds earned by the convicted criminal from works about the crime was unconstitutional for being content-based and not narrowly tailored. *Simon & Schuster, Inc. v. Members of N.Y. Crime Victims Bd.*, 502 U.S. 105 (1991). Federal regulations that restricted recipients of federal funding from engaging in abortion counseling were upheld as a decision to fund one activity to the exclusion of another; the program subsidized pregnancy care and constitutionally refused to fund abortion; the government was using private parties to speak its message. *Rust v. Sullivan*, 500 U.S. 173 (1991). The Supreme Court upheld regulations of the National Endowment for the Arts that imposed "decency and respect" standards on grantee artists. *N.E.A. v. Finley*, 524 U.S. 569 (1998). Congress could not impose the limitation on the government-funded Legal Services Corporation forbidding its attorneys from representing clients challenging the constitutionality of welfare laws. *Legal Servs. Corp. v. Velasquez*, 531 U.S. 533 (2001). Compelled subsidies collected by the government are valid if the subsidies are ancillary to a comprehensive regulatory scheme; for example, when agricultural growers of a certain crop are required to contribute to a central fund for generic advertising for the crop. *Compare United States v. United Foods, Inc.*, 533 U.S. 405 (2001)(striking down the program for mushroom growers) *with Glickman v. Wileman Brothers & Elliot, Inc.*, 521 U.S. 1145 (1997) (upholding the program for fruit growers). Congress may not impose a condition on a federal grant recipient that requires the recipient to publicly affirm the government's belief or viewpoint that the recipient does not share. This would be impermissible as a direct regulation and it is no more proper as a condition on the receipt of federal funds. *Agency for Int'l Dev. v. Alliance for Open Soc'y Int'l, Inc.*, 570 U.S.205 (2013). As a general rule, when the government erects a permanent monument on public property it is engaging in government speech—there is no private speech taking place—and neither the protections nor the restrictions of the Free Speech Clause apply. (There may be some Establishment Clause limits, however.) *Pleasant Grove City v. Summum*, 555 U.S. 460 (2009). The Court held that a state's specialty license plate program constituted government speech; therefore, the state could refuse to issue plates with content it did not condone. *Walker v. Tex. Div., Sons of Confederate Veterans, Inc.*, 135 S. Ct. 2239 (2015). The First Amendment is a limit on government and not a grant of power.

Thus, the First Amendment limits government regulation of private speech but the First Amendment does not restrict the government from speaking for itself pursuant to its other governmental powers. An example is the Surgeon General's required package warnings on tobacco products.

That the First Amendment was ratified so close in time to the original constitutional grant of congressional power in the Copyright Clause, U.S. Const. art. I, § 8, cl. 8, is some indication that the Framers deemed the limited monopoly of copyright to be compatible with principles of free speech. Furthermore, while the First Amendment protects the freedom to speak or to not speak, the statutory copyright protection is really about the more limited right to use the speech of others. *Compare Wooley v. Maynard*, 430 U.S. 705 (1977) (upholding an individual's right to disassociate oneself from a state's motto on an automobile license plate) *with Eldred v. Ashcroft*, 537 U.S. 186 (2003) (upholding a statutory extension of the copyright term of years). The First Amendment did not prohibit Congress from granting exclusive use of the word "Olympic" to the U.S. Olympic Committee. *S.F Arts & Athletics, Inc., v. U.S. Olympic Comm.*, 483 U.S. 522 (1987). The so-called disparagement clause in the Lanham Act violated the First Amendment so far as it prohibited the registration of a racially offensive trademark that disparaged a person or group (the band name "The Slants") because that application of the statute amounted to an unconstitutional viewpoint discrimination. *Matal v. Tam*, 137 S. Ct. 1744 (2017).

Fighting words. At least in theory, states are permitted to ban so-called "fighting words, those personally abusive epithets which, when addressed to the ordinary citizen, are, as a matter of common knowledge, inherently likely to provoke violent reaction." *Cohen v. California*, 403 U.S. 15, 20 (1971). In that case, the Supreme Court set aside the defendant's conviction for disturbing the peace by appearing in a courthouse wearing a jacket with the slogan "Fuck the Draft." Those were not fighting words because the slogan was not directed at any particular person or group of persons. The Court denied the state the power to banish that "unseemly expletive" because "one man's vulgarity is another's lyric" and because the Freedom of Speech Clause protects the expression of both cognitive and emotive content. The Court struck down a "hate speech" ordinance for being content-based and view-point based to single out and punish racially-offensive speech against minorities without punishing other kinds of hateful speech. *R.A.V. v. City of St. Paul*, 505 U.S. 377 (1992). This is an important feature of the Free Speech jurisprudence that is often misunderstood in today's social media: so-called "hate speech" is not a juridical category of unprotected speech. In other words, racist epithets and insults are still protected by the First Amendment. Of course, the rules of polite society and common decency are otherwise. In numerous cases in which the Supreme Court has sided with the speaker to protect the controversial speech, the speaker has used the most vile terminology. For example, look up for yourself exactly what the KKK leader said to his fellow Klansmen—the odious racial epithet that was protected by a unanimous Supreme Court albeit in a *per curiam* opinion—in *Brandenburg v. Ohio*, 395 U.S. 444, 446 n.1 (1969). Although the Supreme Court held that the prosecution could not introduce evidence of a criminal defendant's white supremacist beliefs at a capital sentencing hearing, the Court later distinguished that case and allowed the imposition of an enhanced sentence on a black defendant who intentionally selected his victim on account of the victim's white race. *Compare Wisconsin v. Mitchell*, 508 U.S. 476 (1993) *with Dawson v. Delaware*, 503 U.S. 159 (1992). The Justices have made this evidentiary distinction: a state can criminalize cross burning with a specific intent to intimidate another person because "true threats" are unprotected hate speech or fighting words, but a statute that made any burning of a cross in public to be *prima facie* evidence of intent to intimidate cannot pass constitutional muster. *Virginia v. Black*, 538 U.S. 343 (2003).

Broadcast media. The Supreme Court acted expeditiously to strike down a state statute that granted a political candidate a right of access to a newspaper to reply to personal criticism. The content of a newspaper is under the absolute editorial control of the newspaper according to the First Amendment. *Miami Herald Publ'g Co. v. Tornillo*, 418 U.S. 241 (1974). By comparison, similar regulations of the electronic media, television and radio, could be upheld. Technological differences in the different media justify differences in the First Amendment analysis and outcomes. The FCC's "fairness doctrine," which previously required broadcasters to provide adequate and balanced coverage of public issues reflecting opposing views, was held to be constitutional by the Supreme Court. The theory was that the government allocates the scarce spectrum, and a licensee undertakes responsibility to the public who "owns" the airwaves. *Red Lion Broad. Co. v. FCC*, 395 U.S. 367 (1969). The regulation was eventually repealed, not by a court decision but by the regulatory agency itself as a matter of public policy not constitutional law. An FCC regulation of "indecent" content that limited the time and manner of the broadcast—a regulation of non-obscene and therefore protected material—was upheld regarding George Carlin's comedy monologue on "Filthy Words," the seven words you cannot say on radio or television. *FCC v. Pacifica Found.*, 438 U.S. 726 (1978). The government can still run afoul of the First Amendment, however, when for example it went so far as to prohibit Public Broadcasting Service television stations from engaging in any and all editorializing on public issues. *FCC v. League of Women Voters*, 468 U.S. 364 (1984). Furthermore, the FCC lost a case involving so-called "fleeting expletives" when it sanctioned a television network for failing to filter extemporaneous vulgarities during a live award show. The agency's standard violated due process for being vague. *FCC v. Fox Television Stations, Inc.*, 567 U.S. 239 (2012).

The less rigorous standard of review that applies to broadcasters does not apply to cable television because the spectrum scarcity rationale does not apply to the cable medium. There are an infinite number of channels, although it often seems there is nothing good on to watch. *Turner Broad. Sys., Inc. v. FCC*, 512 U.S. 622 (1994). Applying an intermediate standard of review, the Court subsequently upheld the "must carry" regulations that required cable companies to carry local broadcast television stations. *Turner Broad. Sys., Inc., v. FCC*, 520 U.S. 180 (1997).

The press and the criminal justice system. Freedom of the Press includes a right to publish the news that is a fundamental right and a right to gather the news that is a less protected liberty. A grand jury is entitled to subpoena a reporter for the sources of a news story, and the reporter cannot claim a First Amendment immunity. *Branzburg v. Hayes*, 408 U.S. 665 (1972). Any greater protections for newsgathering are to be found in various statutes, not the Constitution. But the source of a story may sue a reporter for damages when the reporter breaches a promise of confidentiality. *Cohen v. Cowles Media Co.*, 501 U.S. 663 (1991). The Fourth Amendment standard of reasonableness, and not the First Amendment, is controlling for searches and seizures conducted at newspapers and newsrooms. *Zurcher v. Stanford Daily*, 436 U.S. 547 (1978). Congress subsequently enacted the Privacy Protection Act, 42 U.S.C. § 2000aa, to provide statutory protection in these circumstances.

The strong presumption against prior restraints applies to orders by courts restraining the press from reporting on criminal trials. A so-called "gag order" must be based on the nature and extent of pre-trial news coverage, available alternative measures, and the likely effectiveness of any restrictions. There is an absolute right to report anything that transpires in open court. *Neb. Press Ass'n v. Stuart*, 427 U.S. 539 (1976). When a newspaper (a defendant in a libel case) obtained information during civil discovery, however, the trial court could impose limitations on the publication of the material for good cause shown. *Seattle Times Co. v. Rhinehart*, 467 U.S. 20 (1984). The extra-judicial speech of criminal defense attorneys may be limited during trial if the speech has a "substantial likelihood" of creating "material prejudice," but the bar regulations cannot be vague and misleading to the attorney. *Gentile v. State Bar of Nev.*, 501 U.S. 1030 (1991).

Criminal trials are presumptively open to the press and the public under a First and Fourteenth Amendment right of access; even though a criminal defendant has a Sixth Amendment right to a public trial, there is no corollary right to a closed trial. *Richmond Newspapers, Inc. v. Virginia*, 448 U.S. 555 (1980). A statute that required the exclusion of the press and the public during the victim's testimony in cases concerning sexual charges is unconstitutional for not requiring particularized findings on a case-by-case basis. *Globe Newspaper Co. v. Superior Court*, 457 U.S. 596 (1982). *Voir dire* of prospective jurors is presumptively open. *Press-Enterprise Co. v. Superior Court*, 464 U.S. 501 (1984). Pre-trial suppression hearings are likewise assumed to be open. *Waller v. Georgia*, 467 U.S. 39 (1984). The First Amendment does not grant the press the constitutional right to televise a criminal trial, but a state may adopt that public policy and require that trials be televised, even over the objection of the defendant. Most states have done so, although they have adopted procedures to protect the integrity of the proceedings. *See Chandler v. Florida*, 449 U.S. 560 (1981).

Commercial speech. Commercial speech is an expression related solely to the economic interests of the speaker and the audience; commercial speech proposes a commercial transaction in an area traditionally subject to police power regulation by the state. The Supreme Court applies the four-part analysis from *Cent. Hudson Gas & Elec. Corp. v. Pub. Serv. Comm'n*, 447 U.S. 557 (1980), to regulations of commercial speech: (1) whether the expression is protected by the First Amendment; (2) whether the government interest is substantial; (3) whether the regulation directly advances the governmental interest; and (4) whether the regulation is not more extensive than is necessary to serve that interest. A state regulation that prohibited electric utilities from promotional advertising regarding energy use failed to satisfy these criteria.

The greater police power to ban an activity or a product cannot and does not include a lesser power to ban advertising of the product. *Rubin v. Coors Brewing Co.*, 514 U.S. 476 (1995). Indeed, a ban on speech advertising a product is in some sense a greater power in that it allows the state to avoid the difficult policy choice to ban products and services like liquor and gambling. *See Posadas de P.R. Assocs. v. Tourism Co. of P.R.*, 478 U.S. 328 (1986). The Court struck down a state law banning advertisements of retail liquor prices. *44 Liquormart, Inc. v. Rhode Island*, 517 U.S. 484 (1996). A federal statute that prohibited a North Carolina radio station, where lotteries were illegal, from broadcasting Virginia lottery advertising into Virginia was constitutional as applied. *United States v. Edge Broad. Co.*, 509 U.S. 418 (1993). But the same statute could not be applied to forbid a radio or television station in Louisiana, where private casino gambling was legal, from broadcasting casino advertising in Louisiana that would reach into nearby surrounding states where such gambling was illegal. *Greater New Orleans Broad. Ass'n, Inc. v. United States*, 527 U.S. 173 (1999).

The four-part analysis affords commercial speech an intermediate level of protection; it is the same analysis that applies to time, place, or manner regulations. *Fla. Bar v. Went For It, Inc.*, 515 U.S. 618 (1995). The fourth factor—whether the regulation is not more extensive than is necessary to serve the government's interest—requires only a "reasonable fit." It is a requirement of narrow tailoring; it is not the more exacting requirement of "least restrictive means" that applies when a content-based restriction is being analyzed on the compelling interest or strict scrutiny track of First Amendment analysis. *Bd. of Trs. v. Fox*, 492 U.S. 469 (1989).

Keeping the consumer ignorant of market information cannot justify a regulation of commercial speech. Complete bans on advertising are reviewed with special care and are not likely to survive scrutiny. A complete ban on promotional advertising of electric utilities was struck down in the leading case of *Central Hudson* itself. A ban on "for sale" signs in front of houses is content-based and unconstitutional. *Linmark Assocs., Inc. v. Township of Willingsboro*, 431 U.S. 85 (1977). A law banning most other kinds of signs in a residential area was struck down. *City of Ladue v. Gilleo*, 512 U.S. 43 (1994). Trade names may be sufficiently misleading as to be prohibited in an industry like optometry. *Friedman v. Rogers*, 440 U.S. 1 (1979). Prohibitions on advertising for constitutionally protected activities will be struck down. Abortion advertising cannot be prohibited. *Bigelow v. Virginia*, 421 U.S. 809 (1975). The same applies to advertising other kinds of contraceptives. *Carey v. Population Servs. Int'l*, 431 U.S. 678 (1977). A city could not ban news racks from sidewalks that contained commercial advertising without banning news racks that contained newspapers. *City of Cincinnati v. Discovery Network, Inc.*, 507 U.S. 410 (1993). Content-based signage regulations trigger strict scrutiny and do not survive. *Reed v. Town of Gilbert*, 135 S. Ct. 2218 (2015).

As might be expected, restrictions on attorney advertising have been litigated extensively. A ban on advertising prices of routine legal services was struck down. *Bates v. State Bar of Ariz.*, 433 U.S. 350 (1977). Newspaper advertisements containing illustrations, so long as they were not false or deceptive, were protected. Appropriate forced disclosure requirements may be reasonably imposed on attorneys to inform the public. *Zauderer v. Office of Disciplinary Counsel*, 471 U.S. 626 (1985). Targeted, direct-mail advertising is protected. *Shapero v. Ky. Bar Ass'n*, 486 U.S. 466 (1988). The bar may impose greater restraints on in-person solicitations than on mail solicitations. *Compare Ohralik v. Ohio State Bar Ass'n*, 436 U.S. 447 (1978) *with In re Primus*, 436 U.S. 412 (1978). An otherwise truthful representation of fact, that an attorney is also a certified public accountant, cannot be censored by the Bar. *Ibanez v. Fla. Dep't of Bus. & Prof. Regulation, Bd. of Accountancy*, 512 U.S. 136 (1994).

Defamation and privacy in tort. Like speech critical of the government, speech critical of government officials is protected speech. State tort law about defamation and privacy, like state criminal law, must provide constitutional "breathing room" to this kind of speech to protect some amount of false speech in order to assure that the Freedom of Speech can perform a checking function on government. Therefore, state tort common law rules cannot presume damages to reputation from protected speech, and it is not enough only to allow a defense of truth to the speaker. That the statement is true is a constitutional defense, however.

In *New York Times Co. v. Sullivan*, 376 U.S. 254 (1964), the Court constitutionalized defamation law to require that a public official must show "actual malice" or "constitutional malice" with convincing clarity to recover damages, *i.e.*, that the defendant made the statement either knowing it to be false or with reckless disregard of whether it was false or not. "Convincing clarity" is a standard of proof beyond a preponderance of the evidence but less than beyond a reasonable doubt. "Reckless disregard" is more than mere negligence; it is an awareness of a high degree of probability that the statement is untrue.

In the *Sullivan* case, the Court relied on what might be called the doctrine of constitutional facts to review the evidence against the new constitutional standard without remanding and without deferring to the fact-finding of the lower court. This independent appellate review of the facts is essential as a means of assuring the higher degree of protection afforded free speech and press. Thus, in addition to the traditional responsibility of judges to "say what the law is," at least in a First Amendment context, trial and appellate judges are called upon to review the application of the law to the facts in evidence without necessarily deferring to the jury or the lower court the same way they must defer regarding findings of historical fact. *Bose Corp. v. Consumers Union of the U.S., Inc.*, 466 U.S. 485 (1984). *See* Chapter 4, § 4 (Constitutional Law and Constitutional Facts).

There is no immunity from civil discovery against inquiring into the "editorial process" of the press. *Herbert v. Lando*, 441 U.S. 153 (1979). The "minimum contacts" requirement of Due Process applies to *in personam* lawsuits for defamation. *Calder v. Jones*, 465 U.S. 783 (1984). But a state may allow recovery for actual damages caused in all other states if there is a single publication in the forum state. *Keeton v. Hustler Magazine, Inc.*, 465 U.S. 770 (1984). The Court has rejected any arguable distinction between fact and opinion. *Milkovich v. Lorain Journal Co.*, 497 U.S. 1 (1990).

A "public official" is any government official with responsibility or authority for the conduct of public affairs. *Rosenblatt v. Baer*, 383 U.S. 75 (1966). A candidate for public office likewise is covered. *Monitor Patriot Co. v. Roy*, 401 U.S. 265 (1971). The constitutional malice standard applies to the public official's performance of public responsibilities as well as any aspect of the official's private life that may impact official duties in any way. *Garrison v. Louisiana*, 379 U.S. 64 (1964). If there is a logical stopping point to what is relevant to evaluate an official's character, it does not readily come to mind.

In *Curtis Publishing Co. v. Butts*, 388 U.S. 130, 164 (1967), the Supreme Court extended the requirement of constitutional malice to a defamation suit against the athletic director of a university. The defendant was in the category of "public figures," persons who are not public officeholders but who are "intimately involved in the resolution of important public questions or, by reason of their fame, shape events in areas of concern to society at large." These are public figures for all purposes.

In *Gertz v. Robert Welch, Inc.*, 418 U.S. 323, 352 (1974), the Supreme Court again extended the constitutional malice standard to apply to a third category of "limited public figures," private persons who are not public officials and not "all-purpose public figures;" limited public figures are public figures only for a particular incident or event. The plaintiff was an attorney in a high-profile case but the Court concluded that without more he was not a limited public figure because he "plainly did not thrust himself into the vortex of this public issue, nor did he engage the public's attention in an attempt to influence its outcome." Otherwise-private persons must really go out of their way to bring attention and notoriety to themselves before they will be designated even a limited public figure. *Time, Inc. v. Firestone*, 424 U.S. 448 (1976). There is no "public figure" exception to the fair use limitations of the federal Copyright Act. *Harper & Row Publishers, Inc. v. Nation Enters.*, 471 U.S. 539 (1985). If a reporter deliberately alters a speaker's words but effects no material change in meaning, the speaker has not suffered any constitutionally compensable injury. *Masson v. New Yorker Magazine, Inc.*, 501 U.S. 496 (1991).

A plurality opinion effectively extended the constitutional malice standard to defamation suits involving "a matter of public concern," if that label fits the context, form, and content of the speech at issue. But a credit report, published and distributed to a limited number of subscribers, that contained an incorrect statement that a construction contractor had filed for bankruptcy was not that kind of protected speech. Presumed actual damages and punitive damages could be recovered without a showing of constitutional malice. *Dun & Bradstreet, Inc. v. Greenmoss Builders, Inc.*, 472 U.S. 749 (1985).

In *Philadelphia Newspapers, Inc. v. Hepps*, 475 U.S. 767, 775 (1986), the Court provided a two-step sequence of questions to sort through the constitutional analysis: (1) is the plaintiff a public official or a public figure? and (2) is the speech itself a matter of public concern? If the answer to both questions is affirmative, then constitutional malice and falsity must be proven. If the answer to the first question is negative but the answer to the second question is affirmative, then at least negligence and falsity must be proven. If the answer to both questions is negative, then state tort law is controlling.

The First and Fourteenth Amendments prohibit a state tort suit based on an invasion of privacy theory for a news report that identified the victim of a sexual assault by name, when the name was obtained in official court records that were available to the public. *Cox Broad. Corp. v. Cohn*, 420 U.S. 469 (1975). Nor could a state statute impose civil liability for publishing the name of a rape victim obtained from a police report that was a public document. *Fla. Star v. B.J.F.*, 491 U.S. 524 (1989). But a different state tort suit, a right of publicity, could constitutionally impose liability on a television station for showing on the nightly news the entire act of a circus performer who got shot out of a cannon. *Zacchini v. Scripps-Howard Broad. Co.*, 433 U.S. 562 (1977). A "false light" tort theory that involved a matter of public interest, like a story linking a play about a crime to the facts and people involved in the crime, is more like a defamation theory and so constitutional malice is required. *Time, Inc. v. Hill*, 385 U.S. 374 (1967). Constitutional malice is also required in a tort suit for the intentional infliction of emotional harm that is brought by a public official or a public figure. *Hustler Magazine v. Falwell*, 485 U.S. 46 (1988). The Court sided with religious protesters at a military funeral who displayed hateful and outrageously offensive signs attacking the deceased soldier and his family. The speech was deemed a matter of public concern; therefore, the family could not recover for the intentional infliction of emotional harm. *Snyder v. Phelps*, 562 U.S. 443 (2011). Once again, Congress enacted statutes regulating the time, place, and manner of protests at national cemeteries, which most assuredly pass constitutional muster.

Right of Association. The freedom to associate with others to exercise the rest of our political rights is implied in the First Amendment and incorporated in the Fourteenth Amendment, and a person's associations are protected from direct and indirect interference by the government. A state could not compel the NAACP to reveal the names of everyone on its membership rolls, especially when compelled disclosures had resulted in past reprisals against individuals. *NAACP v. Alabama ex rel. Patterson*, 357 U.S. 449 (1958) (notice the state action analysis was that the state's disclosure requirement would have facilitated untoward treatment by private individuals against members). *See also supra* § 3 (State Action). Some inquiries into knowing membership in the Communist Party are permitted, however, because it is *sui generis* to be linked to the foreign threat of violent overthrow of the government. *Barenblatt v. United States*, 360 U.S. 109 (1959). Requiring a loyalty oath by government workers to swear to support and defend the

Constitution is constitutional. *Cole v. Richardson*, 405 U.S. 676 (1972). But government employees generally have a right to freedom of belief and association to belong to a political party and, therefore, the government would infringe those rights to practice patronage in public employment based on party membership. For some policymaking or confidential positions, however, like a governor's speech-writer, the government may demonstrate that party affiliation is an appropriate and necessary requirement and an exception to the general principle. *Branti v. Finkel*, 445 U.S. 507 (1980). The more general principle was extended to related employment practices of hiring, promotion, transfer, and reinstatement of most regular employees of the government. *Rutan v. Republican Party of Ill.*, 497 U.S. 62 (1990). The principle also applies to government contracting practices with independent contractors. *O'Hare Truck Serv., Inc. v. City of Northlake*, 518 U.S. 712 (1996); *Bd. of Cty. Comm'rs v. Umbehr*, 518 U.S. 668 (1996). As a preliminary matter, a governmental employee enjoys general free speech rights. *Compare Connick v. Myers*, 461 U.S. 138 (1983) (valid firing for insubordination) *with Rankin v. McPherson*, 483 U.S. 378 (1987) (invalid firing for speech about a matter of public concern). There is an obvious and compelling governmental interest, however, behind the federal Hatch Act that prohibits federal employees from taking an active role in political campaigns. *U.S. Civil Serv. Comm'n v. Nat'l Ass'n of Letter Carriers*, 413 U.S. 548 (1973). As far as free speech is concerned, the First Amendment protects a public employee's right, in certain circumstances, to speak out as a citizen addressing a matter of public concern. But when public employees make statements pursuant to their official duties, they are not speaking as citizens and the First Amendment does not protect them from discipline. *Garcetti v. Ceballos*, 547 U.S. 410 (2006). The motive of the public employer, not the employee, is controlling because the First Amendment prevents the government employer from retaliating against an employee based on a mistaken belief. The employee bears the burden of proving an improper motive. *Heffernan v. City of Patterson*, 136 S. Ct. 1412 (2016). The First Amendment protected a public employee who provided truthful, sworn testimony, compelled by a subpoena, outside the course of his ordinary job responsibilities. *Lane v. Franks*, 573 U.S. 228 (2014).

When a state required a closed primary but a political party allowed independents to vote, the party's and its members' rights of association prevailed. *Tashjian v. Republican Party of Conn.*, 479 U.S. 208 (1986). A blanket primary, in which all persons, whether or not affiliated with a party, can vote for any candidate on a ballot listing every candidate, violates the right of association. An open primary, in which each voter can vote but there are separate ballots for each party, is constitutional. *Cal. Democratic Party v. Jones*, 530 U.S. 567 (2000).

The right of association has a positive dimension and a negative dimension: individuals have a freedom to choose with whom to associate and with whom not to associate. Indeed, a whole host of membership organizations exist primarily to include some and exclude others. Come to think of it, that is the whole point of a club. An association cannot be held responsible for harms caused by its members. Mere association with a group, absent a specific intent to further its unlawful aims, is not enough. *NAACP v. Claiborne Hardware Co.*, 458 U.S. 886 (1982). However, various civic associations have lost their freedom of association challenges to state regulations that required them to admit women to membership because of the compelling state interest to end gender discrimination. *Bd. of Dirs. of Rotary Int'l v. Rotary Club of Duarte*, 481 U.S. 537 (1987); *Roberts v. U.S. Jaycees*, 468 U.S. 609 (1984). Such organizations are neither personal nor exclusively engaged in First Amendment activity; they are more commercial and social affiliations. Therefore, they are subject to state anti-discrimination laws. *N.Y. State Club Ass'n, Inc. v. City of New York*, 487 U.S. 1 (1988). Congress could threaten to withdraw federal funding to institutions of higher education that denied access to military representatives for recruiting purposes. And the colleges and universities could not be heard to complain that they were acting in opposition to the U.S. military's policies concerning homosexuals. *Rumsfeld v. Forum for Acad. & Institutional Rights, Inc.*, 547 U.S. 47 (2006).

However, states failed in similar efforts on behalf of homosexuals in two cases. The associational rights of organizers of a St. Patrick's Day parade to select who could and who could not march were given priority over a gay and lesbian group that wanted to take part. *Hurley v. Irish-American Gay, Lesbian &*

Bisexual Grp. of Boston, 515 U.S. 557 (1995). The Boy Scouts could disassociate themselves and their organization from an openly gay scout leader. *B.S.A. v. Dale*, 530 U.S. 640 (2000). These two decisions are somewhat called into question, however, by more recent cases involving rights of the LGBTQ community. *See supra* § 9 (Equal Protection— Heteronormativity).

In the case of an "integrated" state bar, for which membership and dues are mandatory for lawyers, the right not to be associated with some of the political positions taken by the bar association may entitle individual members a prorated rebate or reduction in dues. *Keller v. State Bar of Cal.*, 496 U.S. 1 (1990). Charging mandatory student activity fees at a state university is constitutional, at least so long as the programs and speakers are being funded with viewpoint neutrality. *Bd. of Regents of the Univ. of Wisc. Sys. v. Southworth*, 529 U.S. 217 (2000). In *Janus v. American Federation*, 138 S. Ct. 2448, 2459 (2018), a closely divided Supreme Court ruled that public-sector employees who do not belong to unions cannot be forced to pay union contract-negotiating fees: "The First Amendment is violated when money is taken from nonconsenting employees for a public-sector union; employees must choose to support the union before anything is taken from them." *Abood v. Detroit Bd. of Educ.*, 431 U.S. 209 (1977), which had gone the other way on the issue, was rejected and overruled.

Student speech. The subject of student speech has received regular attention from the Supreme Court, although the Court's holdings have not kept up with the Court's rhetoric. Upholding the right of high school and junior high school students to wear black armbands to protest the undeclared war in Vietnam, the majority proclaimed, "It can hardly be argued that either students or teachers shed their constitutional rights to freedom of speech or expression at the schoolhouse gate * * *." *Tinker v. Des Moines Indep. Cmty. Sch. Dist.*, 393 U.S. 503 (1969). A Brennanesque plurality opinion without a clear rationale held that a local school board could not remove certain books from school libraries because of their content. *Bd. of Educ. v. Pico*, 457 U.S. 853 (1982). But a student could be suspended for delivering a speech at a high school assembly full of sexual double *entendres. Bethel Sch. Dist. No. 403 v. Fraser*, 478 U.S. 675 (1986). Public school educators may exercise broad editorial control over the content of a high school newspaper published as part of the school's curriculum. *Hazelwood Sch. Dist. v. Kuhlmeier*, 484 U.S. 260 (1988). Students could be disciplined for unfurling a banner conveying a message reasonably interpreted to promote illegal drug use ("Bong Hits 4 Jesus"). *Morse v. Frederick*, 551 U.S. 393 (2007). Thus, all in all, Justice Black's dire dissenting prediction in *Tinker* of the "beginning of a new revolutionary era of permissiveness in the country fostered by the judiciary" has not come to pass. Successive Supreme Court majorities have sided with school principals and against the students.

Symbolic speech. Symbolic speech or symbolic conduct can be First Amendment expression.

Protected speech can be non-verbal. Justice Souter once mused that the First Amendment "unquestionably shielded" such abstractions as the "painting of Jackson Pollock, music of Arnold Schönberg, or the *Jabberwocky* verse of Lewis Carroll." *Hurley v. Irish-American Gay, Lesbian and Bisexual Grp. of Boston*, 515 U.S. 557 (1995). If the state's regulation is related to the content of the expression, then regular First Amendment analysis applies: the regulation is presumed to be unconstitutional and the compelling interest, strict scrutiny standard must be satisfied. If the state's regulation is not related to the expression, then a lower standard applies, reminiscent of the intermediate standard for commercial speech and reasonable time, place, or manner regulations: the regulation must further an important or substantial governmental interest and the restriction on speech must be no greater than is necessary to serve the government's interest. This two-track analysis is the current doctrinal paradigm.

This doctrinal paradigm is easier to describe than it is to understand at times. When public school students were punished for wearing black armbands to protest the government's involvement in Vietnam, the case was on the strict scrutiny track and the students won. *Tinker v. Des Moines Indep. Cmty. Sch. Dist.*, 393 U.S. 503 (1969). When a protester burned his own draft card to indicate the same disapproval for the same policies, the government won under the lower level protection. *United States v. O'Brien*, 391 U.S. 367 (1968).

Flag desecration statutes have been struck down at the state and federal levels. Flag burners are expressing their dissatisfaction with the country and its policies, and their message ranks at the very top of the First Amendment value system. Political speech lies at the core of protected free speech. The government cannot take away that message of protest, cannot censor that dissenting point of view, cannot limit the use of the flag to only the patriotic and pro-government side of such a debate. *United States v. Eichman*, 496 U.S. 310 (1990); *Texas v. Johnson*, 491 U.S. 397 (1989). Proposals to amend the Constitution to overrule these decisions have not reached the two-thirds level of congressional support necessary to get to the state legislatures. *See* U.S. Const. art. VI.

Campaign financing. Individual rights to participate in the body politic bear something of a family resemblance to the Speech and Debate Clause that affords members of Congress important immunities from being "questioned in any other place" for participating in the legislative process. U.S. Const. art. I, § 6, cl. 1. These are the protected means to the greater end of constitutional self-government. Political speech is core fundamental protected speech. *Eu v. S.F. Democratic Cent. Comm.*, 489 U.S. 214 (1989). The rights of candidates, voters, and political parties to associate and to participate in elections are fundamental. *Tashjian v. Republican Party of Conn.*, 479 U.S. 208 (1986). Campaigns and elections are at the core First Amendment-protected speech and government regulations are subjected to strict judicial scrutiny. *Republican Party of Minn. v. White*, 536 U.S. 765 (2002).

Nevertheless, there are compelling justifications for the states to regulate voting and elections, in order to protect the integrity of the electoral process against the actuality or the appearance of corruption. When the Federal Election Act, as amended, came before Supreme Court, the 234-page *per curiam* opinion detailed the lengthy statute and applied strict scrutiny to draw a constitutional distinction between campaign contributions and campaign expenditures. *Buckley v. Valeo*, 424 U.S. 1 (1976). Money talks in politics. Limitations on *contributions* to a candidate or a campaign are marginal and tolerable restrictions on campaign speech. But limitations on *expenditures* by a campaign directly and immediately reduce the quality and quantity of campaign speech and cannot be permitted. The government regulation of campaign speech cannot be about the purpose of equalizing political voices; a statute is invalid if it restricts the freedom of speech of some elements of society in order to enhance the relative voices of others. The *Buckley* Court did expressly approve public funding of campaigns.

Campaign finance regulations are among the most complex and detailed laws imaginable; they are the stuff of a course on Election Law. The Court upheld the Bipartisan Campaign Reform Act of 2002, including the "soft money" ban as well as regulations on the source, content, and timing of political advertising. *McConnell v. FEC*, 540 U.S. 93 (2003). Then, in *Citizens United v. FEC*, 558 U.S. 310 (2010), the Court ruled that corporations and unions have the same political speech rights as individuals under the First Amendment so their political expenditures were likewise protected from regulation. At the same time, the majority generally supported disclosure requirements on contributions and expenditures. The Court later also invalidated the so-called Millionaire's Amendment, a provision that raised the contribution limits for those running against a self-financed candidate. *Davis v. FEC*, 554 U.S. 724 (2008). Judicial elections have a slightly different trajectory. In *Republican Party of Minnesota v. White*, 536 U.S. 765 (2002), the Court struck down a limitation on a judicial candidate from "announcing" a view on a legal or political issue but left in place a prohibition on making "pledges or promises" during a campaign. But in *Williams-Yulee v. Fla. Bar*, 135 S. Ct 1656 (2015), the Court upheld a prohibition on judicial candidates from personally soliciting campaign contributions.

Obscenity. The Supreme Court takes a definitional and categorical approach to erotica, *i.e.*, written or visual speech about sex. "Pornography" is not a constitutional law term of art—the legal term for unprotected erotic speech is "obscenity." If the material is found to be obscene, then it is not protected speech because it does not have any redeeming social value. *Roth v. United States*, 354 U.S. 476 (1957). Justice Stewart once made a remark about obscenity that he was stuck with for the rest of his career: "I know it when I see it * * *." *Jacobellis v. Ohio*, 378 U.S. 184, 197 (1964) (Stewart, J.

concurring). The definition of obscenity has varied over the years; the current working definition is:

(a) whether "the average person, applying community standards" would find the work, taken as a whole, to appeal to prurient interest; (b) whether the work depicts or describes, in a patently offensive way, sexual conduct specifically defined by the applicable state law; and (c) whether the work, taken as a whole, lacks serious literary, artistic, political, or scientific value.

Miller v. California, 413 U.S. 15, 24 (1973). Even when there is no risk of exposing juveniles and unwilling viewers, however, the state legislature can assume obscenity is harmful and exercise the police power to prohibit and punish obscenity towards the goal of assuring a general community quality of life. *Paris Adult Theatre I v. Slaton*, 413 U.S. 49 (1973). And, at least in theory, the usual constitutional hostility towards prior restraints can be ameliorated with adequate and sufficient procedures including prompt judicial review. *Freedman v. Maryland*, 380 U.S. 51 (1965).

The first factor applies a community standards test and depends on the jury to make the first determination whether the community will tolerate the materials on trial. But when a state court jury found the popular 1971 movie *Carnal Knowledge* obscene, the Justices unanimously reversed the case outright without remanding for further proceedings. *Jenkins v. Georgia*, 418 U.S. 153 (1974). Trial judges and appellate courts are still responsible for performing an "independent review" of the First Amendment issue. The second factor was elaborated to include patently offensive representations or depictions, whether actual or simulated, of sexual activity, *i.e.*, "hard-core" sexual material as defined in the state statute as written or construed. The third factor calls for a reasonable person test under a national standard. *Pope v. Illinois*, 481 U.S. 497 (1987). The same three-part definition of obscenity applies in federal prosecutions without identifying or defining what measure of community is supposed to be reflected in the "community standards" for a federal prosecution. There is no uniform nationwide community; at the same time, there is no constitutionally defined smaller geographical unit. *Hamling v. United States*, 418 U.S. 87 (1974).

"Pandering"—commercial promotions that appeal in a lewd and lascivious way to the morbid sexual curiosity of the customer—is relevant evidence of pruriency, even when the actual materials may be less than obscene. *Splawn v. California*, 431 U.S. 595 (1977). Books containing no pictures but only words can be found obscene and hence unprotected. *Kaplan v. California*, 413 U.S. 115 (1973). Mere possession of obscene material in the privacy of one's home cannot be made a criminal offense. *Stanley v. Georgia*, 394 U.S. 557 (1969). But there is no constitutional protection either to buy or to sell such materials even for private use. *United States v. Orito*, 413 U.S. 139 (1973); *United States v. Reidel*, 402 U.S. 351 (1971).

Zoning laws can either concentrate or disburse adult X-rated businesses, under an intermediate scrutiny, in order to reduce the secondary effects of the businesses and their customers on crime rates and property values and the like without substantially reducing otherwise-protected speech. *City of Renton v. Playtime Theatres, Inc.*, 475 U.S. 41 (1986); *Young v. Am. Mini Theatres, Inc.*, 427 U.S. 50 (1976). Live nude dancing—as distinguished from the crime of public nudity—is barely protected (pun intended) by the First Amendment. *Barnes v. Glen Theatre, Inc.*, 501 U.S. 560 (1991). But a municipality could not completely ban all nude dancing. *Schad v. Borough of Mount Ephraim*, 452 U.S. 61 (1981). And Congress could not practice internet zoning to prohibit "indecent" and "patently offensive" material on the World Wide Web. *Reno v. ACLU*, 521 U.S. 844 (1997). The Court has favored technology fixes over direct regulation, *i.e.*, the availability of blocking and filtering technologies rendered direct federal regulation overbroad and not narrowly tailored. *Ashcroft v. ACLU*, 542 U.S. 656 (2004). In a recent decision of uncertain future significance, Justice Kennedy fulsomely went on and on about the significance of social media to individual free expression. He revealed himself to be a tech utopian. The actual holding struck down a state statute that prohibited convicted sex offenders from using social media. A concurring opinion joined by four Justices sought to tamp down the majority's unfocused enthusiasm about the World Wide Web and the internet. *Packingham v. North Carolina*, 137 S. Ct. 1730 (2017).

Three recent cases taken together explore the outer reaches of protected speech and the understandings of the current Justices. Depictions of violence may be offensive and awful but are nonetheless protected speech so long as they are not prurient and obscene. The Court struck down a federal statute criminalizing the commercial creation, sale, or possession of depictions of animal cruelty, like dog fighting, for being substantially overbroad. *United States v. Stevens*, 559 U.S. 460 (2010). The Court ruled that a state law that imposed a civil fine on anyone who rented or sold a violent video game to a minor was unconstitutional. *Brown v. Entm't Merchs. Ass'n*, 564 U.S. 786 (2011). Under this precedent, for example, the *Active Shooter* video game—in which the player simulated being a school shooter—would be protected under the First and Fourteenth Amendments, although the public hue and cry against it convinced the marketer to stop selling it. One of the main purposes of protecting freedom of speech is to facilitate the discovery of truth in the marketplace of ideas. It was somewhat curious, therefore, that the Supreme Court went out of its way to strenuously protect a liar and his lies. The holding struck down a federal statute punishing false claims of having been awarded military honors and medals. *United States v. Alvarez*, 567 U.S. 709 (2012). Aside: in these three recent decisions, the majority denied that the Supreme Court had the authority to define new additional categories of unprotected speech by balancing the value of the speech versus the harm it caused. *But see Chaplinsky v. New Hampshire*, 315 U.S. 568 (1942) ("Allowing the broadest scope to the language and purpose of the Fourteenth Amendment, it is well understood that the right of free speech is not absolute at all times and under all circumstances. There are certain well-defined and narrowly limited classes of speech, the prevention and punishment of which have never been thought to raise any Constitutional problem.").

Minors can be protected from exposure to variable obscenity or material that might otherwise be protected for adult use. *Ginsberg v. New York*, 390 U.S. 629 (1968). A fractured Court left in place a congressional statute requiring public libraries that received federal funds to install software to block obscene or pornographic images to prevent minors from accessing inappropriate sexually explicit materials online, in part, because the filters could be disabled at the request of adult patrons. *United States v. Am. Library Ass'n*, 539 U.S. 194 (2003). When children are the subject of the material itself, the government's interests are compellingly greater and the value of the material is constitutionally *de minimis*. Therefore, child pornography is even less protected and subject to more regulation: pruriency is measured by a deviant user, not the average person; the depiction need not be patently offensive; and the material need not be considered as a whole. *New York v. Ferber*, 458 U.S. 747 (1982). The "privacy-in-the home" immunity for possession does not apply to child pornography. *Osborne v. Ohio*, 495 U.S. 103 (1990). However, the Supreme Court struck down, as substantially overbroad on its face, a federal statute that prohibited the use of computer-generated images of children, because no actual children were exploited or abused in the productions. *Ashcroft v. Free Speech Coal.*, 535 U.S. 234 (2002).

11. FREE EXERCISE AND NON-ESTABLISHMENT

The First Amendment contains two provisions in one grammatical clause that appear to be in tension with one another: "Congress shall make no law respecting an establishment of religion, or prohibiting the free exercise thereof." U.S. Const. amend. I. The Supreme Court has recognized this tension and the interpretative challenge to steer "a neutral course between the two Religion Clauses, both of which are cast in absolute terms, and either of which, if expanded to a logical extreme, would tend to clash with the other." *Walz v. Tax Comm'n*, 397 U.S. 664, 668–69 (1970).

The original text of the Constitution contains an additional provision concerning religion, Article VI, clause 3, which imposes an oath or affirmation requirement on members of the Congress and on all state officials, but which goes on to provide that "no religious Test shall ever be required as a Qualification of any Office of public Trust under the United States." A state requirement that a person declare a belief in God in order to become a notary public violated this provision. *Torcaso v. Watkins*, 367 U.S. 488 (1961). Likewise, a state law that prevented priests and ministers from serving as delegates to the state constitutional convention was invalidated. *McDaniel v. Paty*, 435 U.S. 618 (1978). Finally, it is noteworthy that the various provisions for requiring oaths all offer a person of sensitive conscience the option of affirming rather than swearing. *See* U.S. Const. art. I, § 3, cl. 6; art. II, § 1, cl. 8; art. IV, cl. 3; amend. IV.

Religion. The Constitution nowhere defines religion or says what qualifies as one. The Supreme Court has avoided giving the word "religion" in the First Amendment any formal constitutional definition. But in a case interpreting the Selective Service Act, for purposes of someone qualifying as a conscientious objector, the Court held the test was whether the given belief is sincere and meaningful and occupies a place in the life of the person that parallels the place orthodox belief in God plays in the life of a religious person who would qualify for the exemption. *United States v. Seeger*, 380 U.S. 163 (1965). Even though another objector actually crossed out the references to religion on the official government form requesting the exemption, the Court concluded the objector's sincere beliefs against participating in war were "in his own scheme of things, religious." *Welsh v. United States*, 398 U.S. 333, 340 (1970). Furthermore, an individual may claim a personal religious belief even though it is inconsistent with and contradicts the dogmas and doctrines of that person's religion. For example, it is enough that an individual person has a sincere religious belief against working in a munitions plant, and it does not matter that the person's religion does not formally teach that belief or officially require that duty. *Thomas v. Review Bd. of Ind. Emp't Sec. Div.*, 450 U.S. 707 (1981).

The Supreme Court has long made one thing perfectly clear: the government is only entitled to determine if the beliefs being espoused are sincerely held, and the government has no business judging their truth or falsity. Under the Constitution, the factual or theological correctness of a person's beliefs are between that person and whomever or whatever the person believes in. *United States v. Ballard*, 322 U.S. 78 (1944). The state can apply otherwise-neutral rules of state law to resolve legal disputes between competing factions of a religious community—like a dispute over the ownership of church property—but the state cannot take sides in the any underlying theological dispute. *Presbyterian Church in the U.S. v. Mary Elizabeth Blue Hull Mem'l Presbyterian Church*, 393 U.S. 440 (1969). Hierarchical and ecclesiastical disputes are beyond the domain and jurisdiction of the state and federal courts under the Constitution. *Jones v. Wolf*, 443 U.S. 595 (1979); *Serbian E. Orthodox Diocese for the U.S. & Can. v. Milivojevich*, 426 U.S. 696 (1976). The Free Exercise Clause and the Establishment Clause both contemplate that a religious group has an absolute authority to select and appoint its religious ministers without any government interference. *Hosanna-Tabor Evangelical Lutheran Church & School v. EEOC*, 565 U.S. 171 (2012).

Non-Establishment. The Establishment Clause is incorporated into the Due Process Clause of the Fourteenth Amendment and applies to the states as well as the federal government. *Everson v. Bd. of Educ.*, 330 U.S. 1 (1947). When an individual district court judge surprisingly attempted to revise history to rule that the Clause should not have been applied to the states, the Supreme Court promptly entered a stay and without qualification reaffirmed the long-standing and consistent precedent to incorporate the Establishment Clause. *Wallace v. Jaffree*, 472 U.S. 38 (1985). *But see Zelman v. Simmons-Harris*, 536 U.S. 639, 677–78 (2002) (Thomas, J., concurring) (eccentrically questioning the incorporation precedents). *See supra* § 2 (Incorporation of the Bill of Rights).

Under the Constitution, there is a foundational proposition that "the judicial power of the United States" extends only to "cases" and "controversies." U.S. Const. art. III, §§ 1 & 2. One of the controlling requirements is standing: "A plaintiff must allege personal injury fairly traceable to the defendant's allegedly unlawful conduct and likely to be redressed by the requested relief." *Allen v. Wright*, 468 U.S. 737, 751 (1984). In an Establishment Clause case, these considerations take on a peculiar meaning in the context of taxpayer standing. In *Frothingham v. Mellon*, 262 U.S. 447 (1923), the plaintiff sued as a federal taxpayer, not merely as a citizen. The Supreme Court ruled that the plaintiff lacked standing. The Court reasoned that the federal taxpayer's "interest in the moneys of the treasury—partly realized from taxation and partly from other sources—is shared with millions of others, is comparatively minute and indeterminable, and the effect upon future taxation, of any payment out of the funds, so remote, fluctuating and uncertain" that she lacked the requisite standing to bring the lawsuit. Thus, the general rule is there is no federal taxpayer standing to challenge federal programs. The landmark decision in *Flast v. Cohen*, 392 U.S. 83

(1968), established an important exception to the long-standing general rule against taxpayer standing. The Supreme Court held that a federal taxpayer did have standing to bring a lawsuit to enjoin federal subsidies to parochial schools under the Elementary and Secondary Education Act as a violation of the Establishment Clause. The Establishment Clause was understood to limit the taxing and spending power of Congress. This standing rule did not apply to a challenge against a HEW program to sell federal property. *Valley Forge Christian Coll. v. Americans United for Separation of Church & State, Inc.*, 454 U.S. 464 (1982). Nor did it apply to allow standing to a federal taxpayer's challenge to an Executive Order creating a federal program. *Hein v. Freedom from Religion Found., Inc.*, 551 U.S. 587 (2007). State taxpayers also lacked standing to challenge a tax credit. *Ariz. Christian Sch. Tuition Org. v. Winn*, 563 U.S. 125 (2011).

Different philosophies of the constitutional relation between church and state animated the founding generation and continue to animate individual Justices. The separationist view holds that religion and government exist in a profound tension; from the religion side, separation prevents worldly corruptions from harming the church; from the government side, separation safeguards private and public secular interests against being co-opted by ecclesiastical influences. The non-preferentialist view believes that both religion and government are served by diffusing and decentralizing policies; government might aid religion so long as the government does not prefer any one religion over the others or religion over non-religion; religions should multiply and prosper and be allowed to compete as factions, so that no one religion can dominates the others. These different philosophies play out differently, alone and in combination, in different cases. Individual Justices often disagree with each other and the same Justices sometimes contradict themselves from case to case. Sometimes, government action that assists religion generally but does not "endorse" religion is upheld. Providing a truly neutral moment of silence in public school might be okay. *See Wallace v. Jaffree*, 472 U.S. 38 (1985). Sometimes, government action is struck down because it amounts to too much of a "coercion." A clergy-led prayer at a high school graduation is not okay. *Lee v. Weisman*, 505 U.S. 577 (1992). Sometimes, the Court simply looks for an answer to an issue in the "history and tradition" of how religion and government have related in this country. Having a chaplain say a prayer to open sessions of a state legislature is okay. *Marsh v. Chambers*, 463 U.S. 783 (1983). In *Town of Greece v. Galloway*, 572 U.S. 565 (2014), all nine Justices agreed that the issue of legislative prayer in *Marsh* was decided rightly. They all agreed it was permissible. But they divided on the issue whether the town commission's practice of inviting local clergy members to open its meetings with a prayer was constitutional. Five Justices said "yes" and four Justices said "no." The dissenters accused the town commissioners of favoring Christian prayer givers over others and making the others in attendance reasonably feel excluded in an unconstitutional manner. In *Trump v. Hawaii*, 138

S. Ct. 2392 (2018), a majority rejected an Establishment Clause challenge to an Executive Order that limited entry and immigration from a list of designated countries that were predominately Muslim, by deferring to the President's constitutional and statutory authority over foreign affairs.

The doctrinal three-part test for Establishment Clause cases takes its name from the lead case, *Lemon v. Kurtzman*, 403 U.S. 602 (1971). The "*Lemon* Test" provides that any statute or government program: (1) must have a secular legislative purpose; (2) must have a principal or primary effect neither to advance nor to inhibit religion; and (3) must not foster an excessive government entanglement with religion. The *Lemon* Test has long been a constitutional doctrine in flux: there have been many instances when the Court has decided an Establishment Clause case without applying the test, yet the test is still used to decide some cases; several Justices have called for its outright overruling, yet the test apparently is still favored by some Justices and has not been overruled or discarded. In 1997, a majority of the Justices announced a revision of the three-part analysis to place greater emphasis on the inquiry into the purpose and effect of the program and to fold the excessive entanglement factor back into that inquiry. The fact that this revised, accomodationist approach was generally more tolerant of government programs that aided religion and would countenance considerably greater entanglements was demonstrated by the holding to approve in 1997 the very same government program that the Court had disapproved in 1985, a program that sent public school teachers into parochial schools to provide remedial education to disadvantaged students. *Agostini v. Felton*, 521 U.S. 203 (1997), *overruling Aguilar v. Felton*, 473 U.S. 402 (1985). We are left without a "Grand Unified Theory" of the Establishment Clause. Different categories of Establishment Clause cases trigger different analytical approaches. But the *Lemon* Test remains the default doctrine, a precedent in the background.

A lack of any secular purpose was determinative to strike down a state law that required the Ten Commandments to be posted in public school classrooms, *Stone v. Graham*, 449 U.S. 39 (1980), and invalidated a state law that required public schools to teach the religious theory of "creation science" alongside evolution, *Edwards v. Aguillard*, 482 U.S. 578 (1987). A Sunday closing law was upheld, however, despite its strong religious identification because of the neutral and valid secular purpose of providing a uniform day of rest in the workplace. *McGowan v. Maryland*, 366 U.S. 420 (1961). The fact that Sabbatarian's who observe Saturday as their Sabbath day were economically disadvantaged by the state's designation of Sunday—because they had to close their businesses two days a week—did not matter to the Supreme Court.

The primary effect of the challenged law cannot be either to advance or inhibit religion, *i.e.*, there cannot be even a symbolic endorsement of a particular religion or of religion generally. A state statute that guaranteed every employee not to have to work on the employee's Sabbath was struck down for its primary effect of advancing that religious practice. *Estate of Thornton v. Caldor, Inc.*, 472 U.S. 703 (1985). But the Court upheld the Equal Access Act, a federal statute that prohibited schools from denying access to their facilities for non-curricular groups because of their religious, political, or philosophical views. The statute benefited all groups equally without singling out religious groups or religion in general. *Bd. of Educ. of Westside Cmty. Sch. v. Mergens*, 496 U.S. 226 (1990). A school district that opened its facilities to non-curricular groups could not single out religious users for exclusion. *Lamb's Chapel v. Ctr. Moriches Union Free Sch. Dist.*, 508 U.S. 384 (1993). The same ruling applies to after-school usages of public school facilities. *Good News Club v. Milford Cent. Sch.*, 533 U.S. 98 (2001). Much the same restrictions apply to the policies for funding organizations at state universities. Equal aid to religious and non-religious groups is permissible. The funding is understood to be a kind of free speech intangible public forum characterized by a right of access. Viewpoint discrimination is not tolerated and religion is a viewpoint. *Rosenberger v. Rector & Visitors of the Univ. of Va.*, 515 U.S. 819 (1995).

What is left of the excessive entanglement prong is concerned with the pernicious consequences for religion from comprehensive, ongoing, and intrusive monitoring by the government. Any program that creates the potential for excessive entanglement also could be the near occasion for political strife and divisiveness over public policies towards religion. *Comm. for Pub. Educ. & Religious Liberty v. Nyquist*,

413 U.S. 756 (1973). Government could not pay the salaries of teachers in parochial schools, even if they taught only secular subjects like science and mathematics, because the government would necessarily be required to monitor their teaching and conduct surveillance of their interactions with students in an excessive entanglement. *Sch. Dist. of City of Grand Rapids v. Ball*, 473 U.S. 373 (1985).

The public schools have been a contested area in numerous Establishment Clause cases. A public school policy that required a "non-denominational" prayer be recited was held to be unconstitutional in an early decision. *Engel v. Vitale*, 370 U.S. 421 (1962). A public school could not require that the Lord's Prayer be prayed or that the Bible be read as a devotional even without comment. Of course, the Bible could be read and studied in a literature class or for a class on comparative religion. *Sch. Dist. of Abington Twp. v. Schempp*, 374 U.S. 203 (1963). When the legislative history of requiring a moment of silence for "meditation or silent prayer" made it obvious that the policy was intended to reintroduce prayer into the public school, the Court struck it down for that reason. *Wallace v. Jaffree*, 472 U.S. 38 (1985). A clergy-delivered prayer at a public high school graduation violated the separation of church and state. *Lee v. Weisman*, 505 U.S. 577 (1992). Prayers at public high school football games, even voluntary student-delivered prayers, are unconstitutional when there is significant involvement by school officials. *Santa Fe Indep. Sch. Dist. v. Doe*, 530 U.S. 290 (2000).

The Court struck down a release program allowing students to attend religious instruction on the school's campus during the school day, but just a few years later upheld a release program that allowed students to leave campus for religious instruction. *Zorach v. Clauson*, 343 U.S. 306 (1952); *Illinois ex rel. McCollum v. Bd. of Educ.*, 333 U.S. 203 (1948).

In a series of confused and confusing decisions, the Supreme Court has ruled that religious symbols are allowed on government property so long as the display does not convey a government endorsement of religion. So there has to be just the right arrangement of Christmas nativity figures, Menorahs, reindeer, Santa Clauses, and Frosty-the-Snowpersons. *Cty. of Allegheny v. ACLU*, 492 U.S. 573 (1989); *Lynch v. Donnelly*, 465 U.S. 668 (1984). In *The Ten Commandments Cases* (2005), the Justices divided five-to-four in two companion cases: to allow a display of the Ten Commandments on the grounds of the Texas State Capitol, *Van Orden v. Perry*, 545 U.S. 677 (2005), and to disallow a display of the Ten Commandments in a county courthouse in Kentucky, *McCreary Cty. v. ACLU*, 545 U.S. 844 (2005). Interestingly, four Justices believed both displays violated the Establishment Clause and four other Justices believed that both displays were proper. Only Justice Breyer saw a constitutional difference between the two displays. His solitary emphasis was on how long the Texas Capitol display had been there and how it had not generated any controversy until very recently, in sharp contrast to the Kentucky courthouse display. His historical concern was to avoid religious divisiveness.

Sometimes the Court goes off on a Freedom of Speech tangent in one of these public display cases, as it did to hold that the state violated the Klu Klux Klan's rights by excluding their display of a large cross on a park across from the state capitol. *Capitol Square Review & Advisory Bd. v. Pinette*, 515 U.S. 753 (1995).

General tax exemptions for charitable and educational organizations, like a state property tax exemption, are constitutionally applied to religious organizations. *Walz v. Tax Comm'n*, 397 U.S. 664 (1970). But the tax exemption cannot be available only to a religious organization. *Tex. Monthly, Inc. v. Bullock*, 489 U.S. 1 (1989). So tax exemptions for eleemosynary institutions—religious and non-religious organizations alike—are constitutionally permissible but not constitutionally required. This idea of neutrality also was evident in *Mueller v. Allen*, 463 U.S. 388 (1983), which upheld a state tax credit that applied to expenses of public and parochial school students alike.

Programs of aid to parochial schools have generated considerable constitutional litigation. The opinions are full of contentious rhetoric and it is sometimes difficult to reconcile their outcomes. The two basic norms are the "no aid" principle and the "equal aid" principle. Over time, the "equal aid" principle has gained more prominence. Providing public transportation to students is constitutional. *Everson v. Bd. of Educ.*, 330 U.S. 1 (1947). Providing textbooks in secular subjects is constitutional. *Bd. of Educ. v. Allen*, 392 U.S. 236 (1968). The state can

send remedial teachers onto the campus of a
parochial school to provide instruction. *Agostini v.
Felton*, 521 U.S. 203 (1997). The government may
provide a sign interpreter for a deaf student at a
parochial school. *Zobrest v. Catalina Foothills Sch.
Dist.*, 509 U.S. 1 (1993). For a time, there was a
constitutional ban on state-provided instructional
materials that could be adapted for religious
instruction, but that ban was lifted by the Supreme
Court. *Mitchell v. Helms*, 530 U.S. 793 (2000),
overruling Meek v. Pittenger, 421 U.S. 349 (1975).
The key fact was that the aid-in-kind, *e.g.*, books,
computers, projectors, *etc.*, was awarded based on the
individual enrollment decisions of private citizens—
parents and students chose where they would attend
school and they chose private parochial schools—and
the aid-in-kind could not be easily diverted to
religious use. A plurality—but only a plurality—
hinted that so long as the state funds public schools
it can afford financial support to private parochial
schools, but there were five "no" votes for that idea in
the concurring and dissenting opinions. Finally, in an
important decision for the future of this area of
constitutional law, a closely divided Supreme Court
held that a state could pay tuition aid vouchers
directly to parents who then could decide to send
their children to private religiously affiliated schools.
The purpose of the program was to benefit poor
children who were stuck in inadequate public
schools; the program was neutral because individual
parents, not the government, made a genuine and
independent private choice where to send their
children to school. The financial aid vouchers were

paid directly to the parents who then decided to endorse them to the private parochial schools. *Zelman v. Simmons-Harris*, 536 U.S. 639 (2002). Indirect aid through the parents is thus constitutional in a way that direct aid to the schools apparently would not be. Generally, the Supreme Court has had a somewhat more lenient attitude towards federal aid to religious colleges and universities. *Tilton v. Richardson*, 403 U.S. 672 (1971).

Free Exercise. The Free Exercise Clause is incorporated into the Due Process Clause of the Fourteenth Amendment and applies to the states as well as the federal government. *Cantwell v. Connecticut*, 310 U.S. 296 (1940). The Supreme Court adheres to a basic dichotomy between belief, which is absolute and beyond the power of government to regulate, and conduct, which the government can regulate for good and important reasons. Someone can believe in polygamy with absolute immunity, but the actual practice of polygamy is punishable under the laws prohibiting bigamy, even if the polygamists are acting based on a sincere and genuine religious belief. *Reynolds v. United States*, 98 U.S. 145 (1878). *But cf. supra* § 9 (Equal Protection—Marriage).

A statute would be invalid if the legislature passed it with the purpose or intent to prohibit a religious practice or to burden a religious practice. That is a kind of "smoking gun" unconstitutional legislative intent. For example, when a city passed an ordinance prohibiting animal slaughter for the sole purpose of ridding the city of a particular religious sect, the

Supreme Court sided with the disfavored sect against the city. That was the kind of *animus* that rendered the regulation invalid. *Church of Lukumi Babalu Aye, Inc. v. City of Hialeah*, 508 U.S. 520 (1993). Likewise, a state administrative agency must remain neutral, fair, and impartial, and cannot exhibit a hostility towards religion in the enforcement of a state public accommodation law. *Masterpiece Cakeshop, Ltd. v. Colo. Civil Rights Comm'n*, 138 S. Ct. 1719 (2018). A state program that disqualified a church *qua* church for a grant to subsidize a parish school playground refurbishment violated the Free Exercise Clause, pure and simple. *Trinity Lutheran Church of Columbia, Inc. v. Connor*, 137 S. Ct. 2012 (2017). It was noteworthy to the dissent that the grant money was paid directly to the church and nonetheless this was approved by the majority. But a state college scholarship program that did not allow a recipient to use the funds to train to be a minister did not violate the Free Exercise Clause, even though the state could have allowed it without violating the Establishment Clause. *Locke v. Davey*, 540 U.S. 712 (2004). It is said in this regard that "there is room for play in the joints," that is, "there are some state actions permitted by the Establishment Clause but not required by the Free Exercise Clause." *Id.* at 719.

The typical fact pattern for a Free Exercise Clause claim is for a religious adherent to go to court to claim a religious exemption from a general law that does not have this kind of unconstitutional legislative intent behind it. For a time, the Supreme Court applied a two-step balancing test that purportedly applied a variety of constitutional strict scrutiny. The

Court first looked to see how the law interfered with the religious observance of the adherent. The Court then considered whether granting a religious exemption would frustrate a compelling government interest balanced against the free exercise burden. Religious observers could not be fired and then denied unemployment compensation for refusing to work on their Saturday Sabbath. *Sherbert v. Verner*, 374 U.S. 398 (1963). Old Order Amish parents and their children were afforded a constitutional exemption from a state compulsory school attendance policy past the eighth grade that, the Court was persuaded, would compromise the parents' and their children's separatist religious life in their community. *Wisconsin v. Yoder*, 406 U.S. 205 (1972).

The balancing test came out in favor of the government and against the claim of religious exemption more times than not, certainly more often than would be expected from a variety of strict scrutiny. The Court upheld Sunday closing laws against a challenge by business owners who observed their Sabbath on Saturday without affording them the option of closing on Saturday and staying open on Sunday. *Braunfeld v. Brown*, 366 U.S. 599 (1961). A military doctor who was an observant Jew was not allowed to wear a yarmulke while on duty per uniform regulations. *Goldman v. Weinberger*, 475 U.S. 503 (1986). Native Americans lost their claim to stop timber harvesting and road building by the government through their most sacred places. *Lyng v. Nw. Indian Cemetery Protective Ass'n*, 485 U.S. 439 (1988).

In 1990, the Court revised the free exercise analysis by generalizing from the run of cases that had rejected claims for a religious exemption. *Emp't Div. v. Smith*, 494 U.S. 872 (1990). Adhering to the age-old belief-versus-conduct dichotomy, the majority held that the right of free exercise of religion does not relieve a religious practitioner from complying with a valid and neutral law of general applicability that prescribes (or proscribes) conduct that the person's religion proscribes (or prescribes). The previous strict scrutiny balancing approach was specifically rejected. This newly formatted analysis promised to minimize the likelihood that a religious adherent would succeed in a court claim of a free exercise exemption to most neutral laws of general applicability. Religious exemptions could be enacted into these laws by the legislature, of course, in its discretion.

Congress enacted the Religious Freedom Restoration Act of 1993, specifically to negate this holding. The statute sought to restore the strict scrutiny balancing test that requires a compelling state interest to refuse a religious exemption for laws that burdened the free exercise of individuals. While Congress depended on its power under Section 5 of the Fourteenth Amendment, the Supreme Court was not sufficiently impressed. The Court struck down the 1993 Act for being beyond the power of Congress: the statute was neither narrowly tailored nor proportionate and congruent. Congress thus was not "enforcing" the free exercise rights protected in the Due Process Clause; Congress was creating new rights or expanding existing rights in a way the

Constitution would not allow—by invading the province of the Supreme Court. *City of Boerne v. Flores*, 521 U.S. 507 (1997). This holding returned the state of the law of the Free Exercise Clause to where it was before the 1993 Act, where *Employ't Div. v. Smith* had left it, insofar as state laws were concerned. RFRA is still on the books, however, when it comes to federal laws. *E.g.*, *Burwell v. Hobby Lobby Stores, Inc.*, 134 S. Ct. 2751 (2014) (striking down HHS regulations that required closely held corporation to provide contraceptive under their employee group health plans in violation of their religious beliefs); *Gonzales v. O Centro Espirita Beneficente União do Vegetal*, 546 U.S. 418 (2006) (recognizing an exemption from the federal Controlled Substances Act for a sect that used a Schedule I hallucinogen it its rites). What RFRA does for federal laws, the Religious Land Use and Institutionalized Persons Act (RLUIPA), 42 U.S.C. § 2000cc does for land use regulations and the treatment of institutionalized persons. *E.g.*, *Holt v. Hobbs*, 135 S. Ct. 853 (2015) (ruling in favor of a prisoner who sought a religious exemption from a state prison regulation prohibiting beards); *Cutter v. Wilkinson*, 544 U.S. 709 (2005) (upholding RLUIPA against a facial challenge). Finally, for the sake of completeness, it should be mentioned that Title VII of the Civil Rights Act of 1964 makes it an unlawful employment practice to discriminate against someone on the basis of race, color, religion, national origin, or sex. The Equal Employment Opportunity Commission has jurisdiction over religious discrimination in the workplace. Title VII also requires that employers reasonably accommodate applicants' and employees' sincerely held religious practices, unless doing so would impose an undue hardship on the operation of the employer's business.

The eternal tension between the Establishment Clause and the Free Exercise Clause is captured in the juxtaposition of two quotations from two noted jurists who were both devout civil libertarians. First, Justice Black borrowed a metaphor from Thomas Jefferson to proclaim, "The First Amendment has erected a wall between church and state. That wall must be kept high and impregnable. We could not approve the slightest breach." *Everson v. Bd. of Educ.*, 330 U.S. 1, 18 (1947). Second, Justice Douglas reverently observed, "We are a religious people whose institutions presuppose a Supreme Being." *Zorach v. Clauson*, 343 U.S. 306, 313 (1952). Jefferson did not originate that metaphor of the wall, however. In 1644, a Puritan clergyman and the founder of the Rhode Island colony named Roger Williams delivered a famous sermon about "the hedge or wall of separation between the garden of the church and the wilderness of the world" that would protect the church from worldly corruption and untoward government influence. For Thomas Jefferson, the wall was a matter of political faith; for Roger Williams, the wall was a matter of religious faith. The popular slogan "separation of church and state," which is not explicitly in the text of the First Amendment, might be equally rendered as the "separation of state and church from each other."

12. BLESSINGS OF LIBERTY

This *Leading Case Outline of Constitutional Liberty* is, at once, inspiring and sobering. Our Blessings of Liberty are great. But the Constitution is a mere parchment barrier. The Supreme Court acts as a bulwark of our civil rights and civil liberties, exercising its awesome power of judicial review. But the Court is not always true to the Constitution; the Justices do not always perform with judicial heroism. *See Korematsu v. United States*, 323 U.S. 214 (1944) and *Hirabayashi v. United States*, 320 U.S. 81 (1943) (Japanese-American internment); *Buck v. Bell*, 274 U.S. 200 (1927) (eugenic sterilization); *Plessy v. Ferguson*, 163 U.S. 537 (1896) (*de jure* segregation); *Dred Scott v. Sandford*, 60 U.S. (19 How.) 393 (1856) (slavery).

Judge Learned Hand, who was the Nestor of his day, understood the constitutional truth that individual freedom is yoked with individual responsibility. He delivered an inspired speech, in the critical World War II year 1944, on what it means to be an American. His timeless words challenge us:

I often wonder whether we do not rest our hopes too much upon constitutions, upon laws and upon courts. These are false hopes; believe me, these are false hopes. Liberty lies in the hearts of men and women; when it dies there, no constitution, no law, no court can save it; no constitution, no law, no court can even do much to help it. While it lies there it needs no constitution, no law, no court to save it.

Learned Hand, *The Spirit of Liberty*, *in* THE SPIRIT OF LIBERTY—PAPERS AND ADDRESSES OF LEARNED HAND 189–90 (Irving Dilliard ed., 3d ed. 1974). This is how we keep the pledge in the Constitution to "secure the Blessings of Liberty to ourselves and our Posterity." U.S. Const., pmbl.

APPENDIX B

CONSTITUTION OF THE UNITED STATES OF AMERICA

WE THE PEOPLE of the United States, in Order to form a more perfect Union, establish Justice, insure domestic Tranquility, provide for the common defence, promote the general Welfare, and secure the Blessings of Liberty to ourselves and our Posterity, do ordain and establish this Constitution for the United States of America.

ARTICLE I.

SECTION 1. All legislative Powers herein granted shall be vested in a Congress of the United States, which shall consist of a Senate and House of Representatives.

SECTION 2. The House of Representatives shall be composed of Members chosen every second Year by the People of the several States, and the Electors in each State shall have the Qualifications requisite for Electors of the most numerous Branch of the State Legislature.

No Person shall be a Representative who shall not have attained to the Age of twenty five Years, and been seven Years a Citizen of the United States, and who shall not, when elected, be an Inhabitant of that State in which he shall be chosen.

Representatives and direct Taxes shall be apportioned among the several States which may be included within this Union, according to their respective Numbers, which shall be determined by adding to the whole Number of free Persons, including those bound to Service for a Term of Years, and excluding Indians not taxed, three fifths of all other Persons. The actual Enumeration shall be made within three Years after the first Meeting of the Congress of the United States, and within every subsequent Term of ten Years, in such Manner as they shall by Law direct.

The Number of Representatives shall not exceed one for every thirty Thousand, but each State shall have at Least one Representative; and until such enumeration shall be made, the State of New Hampshire shall be entitled to chuse three, Massachusetts eight, Rhode-Island and Providence Plantations one, Connecticut five, New-York six, New Jersey four, Pennsylvania eight, Delaware one, Maryland six, Virginia ten, North Carolina five, South Carolina five, and Georgia three.

When vacancies happen in the Representation from any State, the Executive Authority thereof shall issue Writs of Election to fill such Vacancies.

The House of Representatives shall chuse their Speaker and other Officers; and shall have the sole Power of Impeachment.

SECTION 3. The Senate of the United States shall be composed of two Senators from each State, chosen by the Legislature thereof, for six Years; and each Senator shall have one Vote.

Immediately after they shall be assembled in Consequence of the first Election, they shall be divided as equally as may be into three Classes. The Seats of the Senators of the first Class shall be vacated at the Expiration of the second Year, of the second Class at the Expiration of the fourth Year, and of the third Class at the Expiration of the sixth Year, so that one third may be chosen every second Year; and if Vacancies happen by Resignation, or otherwise, during the Recess of the Legislature of any State, the Executive thereof may make temporary Appointments until the next Meeting of the Legislature, which shall then fill such Vacancies.

No Person shall be a Senator who shall not have attained to the Age of thirty Years, and been nine Years a Citizen of the United States, and who shall not, when elected, be an Inhabitant of that State for which he shall be chosen.

The Vice President of the United States shall be President of the Senate, but shall have no Vote, unless they be equally divided.

The Senate shall chuse their other Officers, and also a President pro tempore, in the Absence of the Vice President, or when he shall exercise the Office of President of the United States.

The Senate shall have the sole Power to try all Impeachments. When sitting for that Purpose, they shall be on Oath or Affirmation. When the President of the United States is tried, the Chief Justice shall preside: And no Person shall be convicted without the Concurrence of two thirds of the Members present.

Judgment in Cases of Impeachment shall not extend further than to removal from Office, and disqualification to hold and enjoy any Office of honor, Trust or Profit under the United States: but the Party convicted shall nevertheless be liable and subject to Indictment, Trial, Judgment and Punishment, according to Law.

SECTION 4. The Times, Places and Manner of holding Elections for Senators and Representatives, shall be prescribed in each State by the Legislature thereof; but the Congress may at any time by Law make or alter such Regulations, except as to the Places of chusing Senators.

The Congress shall assemble at least once in every Year, and such Meeting shall be on the first Monday in December, unless they shall by Law appoint a different Day.

SECTION 5. Each House shall be the Judge of the Elections, Returns and Qualifications of its own Members, and a Majority of each shall constitute a Quorum to do Business; but a smaller Number may adjourn from day to day, and may be authorized to compel the Attendance of absent Members, in such Manner, and under such Penalties as each House may provide.

Each House may determine the Rules of its Proceedings, punish its Members for disorderly Behaviour, and, with the Concurrence of two thirds, expel a Member.

Each House shall keep a Journal of its Proceedings, and from time to time publish the same, excepting such Parts as may in their Judgment require Secrecy; and the Yeas and Nays of the Members of either House on any question shall, at the Desire of one fifth of those present, be entered on the Journal.

Neither House, during the Session of Congress, shall, without the Consent of the other, adjourn for more than three days, nor to any other Place than that in which the two Houses shall be sitting.

SECTION 6. The Senators and Representatives shall receive a Compensation for their Services, to be ascertained by Law, and paid out of the Treasury of the United States. They shall in all Cases, except Treason, Felony and Breach of the Peace, be privileged from Arrest during their Attendance at the Session of their respective Houses, and in going to and returning from the same; and for any Speech or Debate in either House, they shall not be questioned in any other Place.

No Senator or Representative shall, during the Time for which he was elected, be appointed to any civil Office under the Authority of the United States, which shall have been created, or the Emoluments whereof shall have been encreased during such time; and no Person holding any Office under the United States, shall be a Member of either House during his Continuance in Office.

SECTION 7. All Bills for raising Revenue shall originate in the House of Representatives; but the Senate may propose or concur with Amendments as on other Bills.

Every Bill which shall have passed the House of Representatives and the Senate, shall, before it become a Law, be presented to the President of the United States; If he approves he shall sign it, but if not he shall return it, with his Objections to that House in which it shall have originated, who shall enter the Objections at large on their Journal, and proceed to reconsider it. If after such Reconsideration two thirds of that House shall agree to pass the Bill, it shall be sent, together with the Objections, to the other House, by which it shall likewise be reconsidered, and if approved by two thirds of that House, it shall become a Law. But in all such Cases the Votes of both Houses shall be determined by Yeas and Nays, and the Names of the Persons voting for and against the Bill shall be entered on the Journal of each House respectively. If any Bill shall not be returned by the President within ten Days (Sundays excepted) after it shall have been presented to him, the Same shall be a Law, in like Manner as if he had signed it, unless the Congress by their Adjournment prevent its Return, in which Case it shall not be a Law.

Every Order, Resolution, or Vote to which the Concurrence of the Senate and House of Representatives may be necessary (except on a question of Adjournment) shall be presented to the President of the United States; and before the Same shall take Effect, shall be approved by him, or being disapproved by him, shall be repassed by two thirds of the Senate and House of Representatives, according to the Rules and Limitations prescribed in the Case of a Bill.

SECTION 8. The Congress shall have Power To lay and collect Taxes, Duties, Imposts and Excises, to pay the Debts and provide for the common Defence and general Welfare of the United States; but all Duties, Imposts and Excises shall be uniform throughout the United States;

To borrow Money on the credit of the United States;

To regulate Commerce with foreign Nations, and among the several States, and with the Indian Tribes;

To establish an uniform Rule of Naturalization, and uniform Laws on the subject of Bankruptcies throughout the United States;

To coin Money, regulate the Value thereof, and of foreign Coin, and fix the Standard of Weights and Measures;

To provide for the Punishment of counterfeiting the Securities and current Coin of the United States;

To establish Post Offices and post Roads;

To promote the Progress of Science and useful Arts, by securing for limited Times to Authors and Inventors the exclusive Right to their respective Writings and Discoveries;

To constitute Tribunals inferior to the supreme Court;

To define and punish Piracies and Felonies committed on the high Seas, and Offences against the Law of Nations;

To declare War, grant Letters of Marque and Reprisal, and make Rules concerning Captures on Land and Water;

To raise and support Armies, but no Appropriation of Money to that Use shall be for a longer Term than two Years;

To provide and maintain a Navy;

To make Rules for the Government and Regulation of the land and naval Forces;

To provide for calling forth the Militia to execute the Laws of the Union, suppress Insurrections and repel Invasions;

To provide for organizing, arming, and disciplining, the Militia, and for governing such Part of them as may be employed in the Service of the United States, reserving to the States respectively, the Appointment of the Officers, and the Authority of training the Militia according to the discipline prescribed by Congress;

To exercise exclusive Legislation in all Cases whatsoever, over such District (not exceeding ten Miles square) as may, by Cession of particular States, and the Acceptance of Congress, become the Seat of the Government of the United States, and to exercise like Authority over all Places purchased by the Consent of the Legislature of the State in which the Same shall be, for the Erection of Forts, Magazines, Arsenals, dock-Yards, and other needful Buildings;— And

To make all Laws which shall be necessary and proper for carrying into Execution the foregoing Powers, and all other Powers vested by this Constitution in the Government of the United States, or in any Department or Officer thereof.

SECTION 9. The Migration or Importation of such Persons as any of the States now existing shall think proper to admit, shall not be prohibited by the Congress prior to the Year one thousand eight hundred and eight, but a Tax or duty may be imposed on such Importation, not exceeding ten dollars for each Person.

The Privilege of the Writ of Habeas Corpus shall not be suspended, unless when in Cases of Rebellion or Invasion the public Safety may require it.

No Bill of Attainder or ex post facto Law shall be passed.

No Capitation, or other direct, Tax shall be laid, unless in Proportion to the Census or Enumeration herein before directed to be taken.

No Tax or Duty shall be laid on Articles exported from any State.

No Preference shall be given by any Regulation of Commerce or Revenue to the Ports of one State over those of another: nor shall Vessels bound to, or from, one State, be obliged to enter, clear, or pay Duties in another.

No Money shall be drawn from the Treasury, but in Consequence of Appropriations made by Law; and a regular Statement and Account of the Receipts and

Expenditures of all public Money shall be published from time to time.

No Title of Nobility shall be granted by the United States: And no Person holding any Office of Profit or Trust under them, shall, without the Consent of the Congress, accept of any present, Emolument, Office, or Title, of any kind whatever, from any King, Prince, or foreign State.

SECTION 10. No State shall enter into any Treaty, Alliance, or Confederation; grant Letters of Marque and Reprisal; coin Money; emit Bills of Credit; make any Thing but gold and silver Coin a Tender in Payment of Debts; pass any Bill of Attainder, ex post facto Law, or Law impairing the Obligation of Contracts, or grant any Title of Nobility.

No State shall, without the Consent of the Congress, lay any Imposts or Duties on Imports or Exports, except what may be absolutely necessary for executing it's inspection Laws: and the net Produce of all Duties and Imposts, laid by any State on Imports or Exports, shall be for the Use of the Treasury of the United States; and all such Laws shall be subject to the Revision and Controul of the Congress.

No State shall, without the Consent of Congress, lay any Duty of Tonnage, keep Troops, or Ships of War in time of Peace, enter into any Agreement or Compact with another State, or with a foreign Power, or engage in War, unless actually invaded, or in such imminent Danger as will not admit of delay.

ARTICLE II.

SECTION 1. The executive Power shall be vested in a President of the United States of America. He shall hold his Office during the Term of four Years, and, together with the Vice President, chosen for the same Term, be elected, as follows

Each State shall appoint, in such Manner as the Legislature thereof may direct, a Number of Electors, equal to the whole Number of Senators and Representatives to which the State may be entitled in the Congress: but no Senator or Representative, or Person holding an Office of Trust or Profit under the United States, shall be appointed an Elector.

The Electors shall meet in their respective States, and vote by Ballot for two Persons, of whom one at least shall not be an Inhabitant of the same State with themselves. And they shall make a List of all the Persons voted for, and of the Number of Votes for each; which List they shall sign and certify, and transmit sealed to the Seat of the Government of the United States, directed to the President of the Senate. The President of the Senate shall, in the Presence of the Senate and House of Representatives, open all the Certificates, and the Votes shall then be counted. The Person having the greatest Number of Votes shall be the President, if such Number be a Majority of the whole Number of Electors appointed; and if there be more than one who have such Majority, and have an equal Number of Votes, then the House of Representatives shall immediately chuse by Ballot one of them for President; and if no Person have a Majority, then from the five highest on the List the said House shall in like Manner chuse the President. But in chusing the President, the Votes shall be taken by States, the Representation from each State having one Vote; A quorum for this Purpose shall consist of a Member or Members from two thirds of the States, and a Majority of all the States shall be necessary to a Choice. In every Case, after the Choice of the President, the Person having the greatest Number of Votes of the Electors shall be the Vice President. But if there should remain two or more who have equal Votes, the Senate shall chuse from them by Ballot the Vice President.

The Congress may determine the Time of chusing the Electors, and the Day on which they shall give their Votes; which Day shall be the same throughout the United States.

No Person except a natural born Citizen, or a Citizen of the United States, at the time of the Adoption of this Constitution, shall be eligible to the Office of President; neither shall any Person be eligible to that Office who shall not have attained to the Age of thirty five Years, and been fourteen Years a Resident within the United States.

In Case of the Removal of the President from Office, or of his Death, Resignation, or Inability to discharge the Powers and Duties of the said Office, the same shall devolve on the Vice President, and the Congress may by Law provide for the Case of Removal, Death, Resignation or Inability, both of the President and Vice President, declaring what Officer shall then act as President, and such Officer shall act accordingly, until the Disability be removed, or a President shall be elected.

The President shall, at stated Times, receive for his Services, a Compensation, which shall neither be encreased nor diminished during the Period for which he shall have been elected, and he shall not receive within that Period any other Emolument from the United States, or any of them.

Before he enter on the Execution of his Office, he shall take the following Oath or Affirmation:—"I do solemnly swear (or affirm) that I will faithfully execute the Office of President of the United States, and will to the best of my Ability, preserve, protect and defend the Constitution of the United States."

SECTION 2. The President shall be Commander in Chief of the Army and Navy of the United States, and of the Militia of the several States, when called into the actual Service of the United States; he may require the Opinion, in writing, of the principal Officer in each of the executive Departments, upon any Subject relating to the Duties of their respective Offices, and he shall have Power to grant Reprieves and Pardons for Offences against the United States, except in Cases of Impeachment.

He shall have Power, by and with the Advice and Consent of the Senate, to make Treaties, provided two thirds of the Senators present concur; and he shall nominate, and by and with the Advice and Consent of the Senate, shall appoint Ambassadors, other public Ministers and Consuls, Judges of the supreme Court, and all other Officers of the United

States, whose Appointments are not herein otherwise provided for, and which shall be established by Law: but the Congress may by Law vest the Appointment of such inferior Officers, as they think proper, in the President alone, in the Courts of Law, or in the Heads of Departments.

The President shall have Power to fill up all Vacancies that may happen during the Recess of the Senate, by granting Commissions which shall expire at the End of their next Session.

SECTION 3. He shall from time to time give to the Congress Information of the State of the Union, and recommend to their Consideration such Measures as he shall judge necessary and expedient; he may, on extraordinary Occasions, convene both Houses, or either of them, and in Case of Disagreement between them, with Respect to the Time of Adjournment, he may adjourn them to such Time as he shall think proper; he shall receive Ambassadors and other public Ministers; he shall take Care that the Laws be faithfully executed, and shall Commission all the Officers of the United States.

SECTION 4. The President, Vice President and all civil Officers of the United States, shall be removed from Office on Impeachment for, and Conviction of, Treason, Bribery, or other high Crimes and Misdemeanors.

ARTICLE III.

SECTION 1. The judicial Power of the United States, shall be vested in one supreme Court, and in such inferior Courts as the Congress may from time to time ordain and establish. The Judges, both of the supreme and inferior Courts, shall hold their Offices during good Behaviour, and shall, at stated Times, receive for their Services, a Compensation, which shall not be diminished during their Continuance in Office.

SECTION 2. The judicial Power shall extend to all Cases, in Law and Equity, arising under this Constitution, the Laws of the United States, and Treaties made, or which shall be made, under their Authority;—to all Cases affecting Ambassadors, other public Ministers and Consuls;—to all Cases of admiralty and maritime Jurisdiction;—to Controversies to which the United States shall be a Party;—to Controversies between two or more States;—between a State and Citizens of another State;—between Citizens of different States,—between Citizens of the same State claiming Lands under Grants of different States, and between a State, or the Citizens thereof, and foreign States, Citizens or Subjects.

In all Cases affecting Ambassadors, other public Ministers and Consuls, and those in which a State shall be Party, the supreme Court shall have original Jurisdiction. In all the other Cases before mentioned, the supreme Court shall have appellate Jurisdiction, both as to Law and Fact, with such Exceptions, and under such Regulations as the Congress shall make.

The Trial of all Crimes, except in Cases of Impeachment, shall be by Jury; and such Trial shall be held in the State where the said Crimes shall have been committed; but when not committed within any

State, the Trial shall be at such Place or Places as the Congress may by Law have directed.

SECTION 3. Treason against the United States, shall consist only in levying War against them, or in adhering to their Enemies, giving them Aid and Comfort. No Person shall be convicted of Treason unless on the Testimony of two Witnesses to the same overt Act, or on Confession in open Court.

The Congress shall have Power to declare the Punishment of Treason, but no Attainder of Treason shall work Corruption of Blood, or Forfeiture except during the Life of the Person attainted.

ARTICLE IV.

SECTION 1. Full Faith and Credit shall be given in each State to the public Acts, Records, and judicial Proceedings of every other State. And the Congress may by general Laws prescribe the Manner in which such Acts, Records and Proceedings shall be proved, and the Effect thereof.

SECTION 2. The Citizens of each State shall be entitled to all Privileges and Immunities of Citizens in the several States.

A Person charged in any State with Treason, Felony, or other Crime, who shall flee from Justice, and be found in another State, shall on Demand of the executive Authority of the State from which he fled, be delivered up, to be removed to the State having Jurisdiction of the Crime.

No Person held to Service or Labour in one State, under the Laws thereof, escaping into another, shall, in Consequence of any Law or Regulation therein, be discharged from such Service or Labour, but shall be delivered up on Claim of the Party to whom such Service or Labour may be due.

SECTION 3. New States may be admitted by the Congress into this Union; but no new State shall be formed or erected within the Jurisdiction of any other State; nor any State be formed by the Junction of two or more States, or Parts of States, without the Consent of the Legislatures of the States concerned as well as of the Congress.

The Congress shall have Power to dispose of and make all needful Rules and Regulations respecting the Territory or other Property belonging to the United States; and nothing in this Constitution shall be so construed as to Prejudice any Claims of the United States, or of any particular State.

SECTION 4. The United States shall guarantee to every State in this Union a Republican Form of Government, and shall protect each of them against Invasion; and on Application of the Legislature, or of the Executive (when the Legislature cannot be convened) against domestic Violence.

ARTICLE V.

The Congress, whenever two thirds of both Houses shall deem it necessary, shall propose Amendments to this Constitution, or on the Application of the Legislatures of two thirds of the several States, shall call a Convention for proposing Amendments, which, in either Case, shall be valid to all Intents and Purposes, as Part of this Constitution, when ratified by the Legislatures of three fourths of the several States, or by Conventions in three fourths thereof, as the one or the other Mode of Ratification may be proposed by the Congress; Provided that no Amendment which may be made prior to the Year One thousand eight hundred and eight shall in any Manner affect the first and fourth Clauses in the Ninth Section of the first Article; and that no State, without its Consent, shall be deprived of its equal Suffrage in the Senate.

ARTICLE VI.

All Debts contracted and Engagements entered into, before the Adoption of this Constitution, shall be as valid against the United States under this Constitution, as under the Confederation.

This Constitution, and the laws of the United States which shall be made in Pursuance thereof; and all Treaties made, or which shall be made, under the Authority of the United States, shall be the supreme Law of the Land; and the Judges in every State shall be bound thereby, any Thing in the Constitution or Laws of any State to the Contrary notwithstanding.

The Senators and Representatives before mentioned, and the Members of the several State Legislatures, and all executive and judicial Officers, both of the United States and of the several States, shall be bound by Oath or Affirmation, to support this Constitution; but no religious Test shall ever be required as a Qualification to any Office or public Trust under the United States.

ARTICLE VII.

The Ratification of the Conventions of nine States, shall be sufficient for the Establishment of this Constitution between the States so ratifying the Same.

DONE in Convention by the Unanimous Consent of the States present the Seventeenth Day of September in the Year of our Lord one thousand seven hundred and Eighty seven and of the Independence of the United States of America the Twelfth.

IN WITNESS whereof We have hereunto subscribed our Names,

Geo. Washington, President and deputy from Virginia

[Signed also by the deputies of twelve States.]

ARTICLES IN ADDITION TO, AND AMENDMENT OF, THE CONSTITUTION OF THE UNITED STATES OF AMERICA, PROPOSED BY CONGRESS, AND RATIFIED BY THE LEGISLATURES OF THE SEVERAL STATES, PURSUANT TO THE FIFTH ARTICLE OF THE ORIGINAL CONSTITUTION.

AMENDMENT I

[1791]

Congress shall make no law respecting an establishment of religion, or prohibiting the free exercise thereof; or abridging the freedom of speech, or of the press; or the right of the people peaceably to assemble, and to petition the Government for a redress of grievances.

AMENDMENT II

[1791]

A well regulated Militia, being necessary to the security of a free State, the right of the people to keep and bear Arms, shall not be infringed.

AMENDMENT III

[1791]

No Soldier shall, in time of peace be quartered in any house, without the consent of the Owner, nor in time of war, but in a manner to be prescribed by law.

AMENDMENT IV

[1791]

The right of the people to be secure in their persons, houses, papers, and effects, against unreasonable searches and seizures, shall not be violated, and no Warrants shall issue, but upon probable cause, supported by Oath or affirmation, and particularly describing the place to be searched, and the persons or things to be seized.

AMENDMENT V

[1791]

No person shall be held to answer for a capital, or otherwise infamous crime, unless on a presentment or indictment of a Grand Jury, except in cases arising in the land or naval forces, or in the Militia, when in actual service in time of War or public danger; nor shall any person be subject for the same offence to be twice put in jeopardy of life or limb; nor shall be compelled in any criminal case to be a witness against himself, nor be deprived of life, liberty, or property, without due process of law; nor shall private property be taken for public use, without just compensation.

AMENDMENT VI

[1791]

In all criminal prosecutions, the accused shall enjoy the right to a speedy and public trial, by an impartial jury of the State and district wherein the crime shall have been committed, which district shall have been previously ascertained by law, and to be informed of the nature and cause of the accusation; to be confronted with the witnesses against him; to have compulsory process for obtaining witnesses in his favor, and to have the Assistance of Counsel for his defence.

AMENDMENT VII

[1791]

In Suits at common law, where the value in controversy shall exceed twenty dollars, the right of trial by jury shall be preserved, and no fact tried by a jury, shall be otherwise reexamined in any Court of the United States, than according to the rules of the common law.

AMENDMENT VIII

[1791]

Excessive bail shall not be required, nor excessive fines imposed, nor cruel and unusual punishments inflicted.

AMENDMENT IX

[1791]

The enumeration in the Constitution, of certain rights, shall not be construed to deny or disparage others retained by the people.

AMENDMENT X

[1791]

The powers not delegated to the United States by the Constitution, nor prohibited by it to the States, are reserved to the States respectively, or to the people.

AMENDMENT XI

[1798]

The Judicial power of the United States shall not be construed to extend to any suit in law or equity, commenced or prosecuted against one of the United States by Citizens of another State, or by Citizens or Subjects of any Foreign State.

AMENDMENT XII

[1804]

The Electors shall meet in their respective states, and vote by ballot for President and Vice-President, one of whom, at least, shall not be an inhabitant of the same state with themselves; they shall name in their ballots the person voted for as President, and in distinct ballots the person voted for as Vice-President, and they shall make distinct lists of all persons voted for as President, and of all persons voted for as Vice-President, and of the number of votes for each, which lists they shall sign and certify, and transmit sealed to the seat of the government of the United States, directed to the President of the Senate;—The President of the Senate shall, in the presence of the Senate and House of Representatives, open all the certificates and the votes shall then be counted;—The person having the greatest number of votes for President, shall be the President, if such number be a majority of the whole number of Electors appointed; and if no person have such majority, then from the persons having the highest numbers not exceeding three on the list of those voted for as President, the House of Representatives shall choose immediately, by ballot, the President. But in choosing the President, the votes shall be taken by states, the representation from each state having one vote; a quorum for this purpose shall consist of a member or members from two-thirds of the states, and a majority of all the states shall be necessary to a choice. And if the House of Representatives shall not choose a President whenever the right of choice shall devolve upon them, before the fourth day of March next following, then the Vice-President shall act as President, as in the case of the death or other constitutional disability of the President.—The person having the greatest number of votes as Vice-President, shall be the Vice-President, if such number be a majority of the whole number of Electors appointed, and if no person have a majority, then from the two highest numbers on the list, the Senate shall choose the Vice-President; a quorum for the purpose shall consist of two-thirds of the whole number of Senators, and a majority of the whole number shall be necessary to a choice. But no person constitutionally ineligible to the office of President shall be eligible to that of Vice-President of the United States.

AMENDMENT XIII

[1865]

SECTION 1. Neither slavery nor involuntary servitude, except as a punishment for crime whereof the party shall have been duly convicted, shall exist within the United States, or any place subject to their jurisdiction.

SECTION 2. Congress shall have power to enforce this article by appropriate legislation.

AMENDMENT XIV

[1868]

SECTION 1. All persons born or naturalized in the United States, and subject to the jurisdiction thereof, are citizens of the United States and of the State wherein they reside. No State shall make or enforce any law which shall abridge the privileges or immunities of citizens of the United States; nor shall any State deprive any person of life, liberty, or property, without due process of law; nor deny to any person within its jurisdiction the equal protection of the laws.

SECTION 2. Representatives shall be apportioned among the several States according to their respective numbers, counting the whole number of persons in each State, excluding Indians not taxed. But when the right to vote at any election for the choice of electors for President and Vice President of the United States, Representatives in Congress, the Executive and Judicial officers of a State, or the members of the Legislature thereof, is denied to any of the male inhabitants of such State, being twenty-one years of age, and citizens of the United States, or in any way abridged, except for participation in rebellion, or other crime, the basis of representation therein shall be reduced in the proportion which the number of such male citizens shall bear to the whole number of male citizens twenty-one years of age in such State.

SECTION 3. No person shall be a Senator or Representative in Congress, or elector of President and Vice President, or hold any office, civil or military, under the United States, or under any State, who, having previously taken an oath, as a member of Congress, or as an officer of the United States, or as a member of any State legislature, or as an executive or judicial officer of any State, to support the Constitution of the United States, shall have engaged in insurrection or rebellion against the same, or given aid or comfort to the enemies thereof. But Congress may by a vote of two-thirds of each House, remove such disability.

SECTION 4. The validity of the public debt of the United States, authorized by law, including debts incurred for payment of pensions and bounties for services in suppressing insurrection or rebellion, shall not be questioned. But neither the United States nor any State shall assume or pay any debt or obligation incurred in aid of insurrection or rebellion against the United States, or any claim for the loss or emancipation of any slave; but all such debts, obligations and claims shall be held illegal and void.

SECTION 5. The Congress shall have power to enforce, by appropriate legislation, the provisions of this article.

AMENDMENT XV

[1870]

SECTION 1. The right of citizens of the United States to vote shall not be denied or abridged by the United States or by any State on account of race, color, or previous condition of servitude.

SECTION 2. The Congress shall have power to enforce this article by appropriate legislation.

AMENDMENT XVI

[1913]

The Congress shall have power to lay and collect taxes on incomes, from whatever source derived, without apportionment among the several States, and without regard to any census or enumeration.

AMENDMENT XVII

[1913]

The Senate of the United States shall be composed of two Senators from each State, elected by the people thereof, for six years; and each Senator shall have one vote. The electors in each State shall have the qualifications requisite for electors of the most numerous branch of the State legislatures.

When vacancies happen in the representation of any State in the Senate, the executive authority of such State shall issue writs of election to fill such vacancies: *Provided*, That the legislature of any State may empower the executive thereof to make temporary appointments until the people fill the vacancies by election as the legislature may direct.

This amendment shall not be so construed as to affect the election or term of any Senator chosen before it becomes valid as part of the Constitution.

AMENDMENT XVIII

[1919]

SECTION 1. After one year from the ratification of this article the manufacture, sale, or transportation of intoxicating liquors within, the importation thereof into, or the exportation thereof from the United States and all territory subject to the jurisdiction thereof for beverage purposes is hereby prohibited.

SECTION 2. The Congress and the several States shall have concurrent power to enforce this article by appropriate legislation.

SECTION 3. This article shall be inoperative unless it shall have been ratified as an amendment to the Constitution by the legislatures of the several States, as provided in the Constitution, within seven years from the date of the submission hereof to the States by the Congress.

AMENDMENT XIX

[1920]

The right of citizens of the United States to vote shall not be denied or abridged by the United States or by any State on account of sex.

Congress shall have power to enforce this article by appropriate legislation.

AMENDMENT XX

[1933]

SECTION 1. The terms of the President and Vice President shall end at noon on the 20th day of January, and the terms of Senators and Representatives at noon on the 3d day of January, of the years in which such terms would have ended if this article had not been ratified; and the terms of their successors shall then begin.

SECTION 2. The Congress shall assemble at least once in every year, and such meeting shall begin at noon on the 3d day of January, unless they shall by law appoint a different day.

SECTION 3. If, at the time fixed for the beginning of the term of the President, the President elect shall have died, the Vice President elect shall become President. If a President shall not have been chosen before the time fixed for the beginning of his term, or if the President elect shall have failed to qualify, then the Vice President elect shall act as President until a President shall have qualified; and the Congress may by law provide for the case wherein neither a President elect nor a Vice President elect shall have qualified, declaring who shall then act as President, or the manner in which one who is to act shall be selected, and such person shall act accordingly until a President or Vice President shall have qualified.

SECTION 4. The Congress may by law provide for the case of the death of any of the persons from whom the House of Representatives may choose a President whenever the rights of choice shall have devolved upon them, and for the case of the death of any of the persons from whom the Senate may choose a Vice President whenever the right of choice shall have devolved upon them.

SECTION 5. Sections 1 and 2 shall take effect on the 15th day of October following the ratification of this article.

SECTION 6. This article shall be inoperative unless it shall have been ratified as an amendment to the Constitution by the legislatures of three-fourths of the several States within seven years from the date of its submission.

AMENDMENT XXI

[1933]

SECTION 1. The eighteenth article of amendment to the Constitution of the United States is hereby repealed.

SECTION 2. The transportation or importation into any State, Territory, or possession of the United States for delivery or use therein of intoxicating liquors, in violation of the laws thereof, is hereby prohibited.

SECTION 3. This article shall be inoperative unless it shall have been ratified as an amendment to the Constitution by conventions in the several States, as provided in the Constitution, within seven years from the date of the submission hereof to the States by the Congress.

AMENDMENT XXII

[1951]

SECTION 1. No person shall be elected to the office of the President more than twice, and no person who has held the office of President, or acted as President, for more than two years of a term to which some other person was elected President shall be elected to the office of the President more than once. But this

Article shall not apply to any person holding the office of President when this Article was proposed by the Congress, and shall not prevent any person who may be holding the office of President, or acting as President, during the term within which this Article becomes operative from holding the office of President or acting as President during the remainder of such term.

SECTION 2. This article shall be inoperative unless it shall have been ratified as an amendment to the Constitution by the legislatures of three-fourths of the several States within seven years from the date of its submission to the States by the Congress.

AMENDMENT XXIII

[1961]

SECTION 1. The District constituting the seat of Government of the United States shall appoint in such manner as the Congress may direct:

A number of electors of President and Vice President equal to the whole number of Senators and Representatives in Congress to which the District would be entitled if it were a State, but in no event more than the least populous State; they shall be in addition to those appointed by the States, but they shall be considered, for the purposes of the election of President and Vice President, to be electors appointed by a State; and they shall meet in the District and perform such duties as provided by the twelfth article of amendment.

SECTION 2. The Congress shall have power to enforce this article by appropriate legislation.

AMENDMENT XXIV

[1964]

SECTION 1. The right of citizens of the United States to vote in any primary or other election for President or Vice President, for electors for President or Vice President, or for Senator or Representative in Congress, shall not be denied or abridged by the United States or any State by reason of failure to pay any poll tax or other tax.

SECTION 2. The Congress shall have power to enforce this article by appropriate legislation.

AMENDMENT XXV

[1967]

SECTION 1. In case of the removal of the President from office or of his death or resignation, the Vice President shall become President.

SECTION 2. Whenever there is a vacancy in the office of the Vice President, the President shall nominate a Vice President who shall take office upon confirmation by a majority vote of both Houses of Congress.

SECTION 3. Whenever the President transmits to the President pro tempore of the Senate and the Speaker of the House of Representatives his written declaration that he is unable to discharge the powers and duties of his office, and until he transmits to them a written declaration to the contrary, such powers and duties shall be discharged by the Vice President as Acting President.

SECTION 4. Whenever the Vice President and a majority of either the principal officers of the executive departments or of such other body as Congress may by law provide, transmit to the President pro tempore of the Senate and the Speaker of the House of Representatives their written declaration that the President is unable to discharge the powers and duties of his office, the Vice President shall immediately assume the powers and duties of the office as Acting President.

Thereafter, when the President transmits to the President pro tempore of the Senate and the Speaker of the House of Representatives his written declaration that no inability exists, he shall resume the powers and duties of his office unless the Vice President and a majority of either the principal officers of the executive department or of such other body as Congress may by law provide, transmit within four days to the President pro tempore of the Senate and the Speaker of the House of Representatives their written declaration that the President is unable to discharge the powers and duties of his office. Thereupon Congress shall decide the issue, assembling within forty-eight hours for that purpose if not in session. If the Congress, within twenty-one days after receipt of the latter written declaration, or, if Congress is not in session, within twenty-one days after Congress is required to assemble, determines by two-thirds vote of both Houses that the President is unable to discharge the powers and duties of his office, the Vice President shall continue to discharge the same as Acting President; otherwise, the President shall resume the powers and duties of his office.

AMENDMENT XXVI

[1971]

SECTION 1. The right of citizens of the United States, who are eighteen years of age or older, to vote shall not be denied or abridged by the United States or by any State on account of age.

SECTION 2. The Congress shall have power to enforce this article by appropriate legislation.

AMENDMENT XXVII

[1992]

No law varying the compensation for the services of the Senators and Representatives, shall take effect, until an election of Representatives shall have intervened.

INDEX

References are to Pages

THEORY